Travaux
d'Humanisme et Renaissance

N° CDXXXI

PHILIP BENEDICT

GRAPHIC HISTORY

The *Wars, Massacres and Troubles* of Tortorel and Perrissin

LIBRAIRIE DROZ S.A.
11, rue Massot
GENÈVE
2007

Ouvrage publié avec le soutien
du Fond national de la Recherche scientifique

www.droz.org

ISBN: 978-2-600-00440-4
ISSN: 0082-6081

To the memory of my mother Ruth B. Benedict,
who introduced me to the world of prints

CONTENTS

LIST OF TABLES

ILLUSTRATIONS

FOLD OUT ILLUSTRATIONS IN PART 2

ABBREVIATIONS

AD	Archives Departementales
AEG	Archives d'Etat (Geneva)
AM	Archives Municipales
AN	Archives Nationales (Paris)
Arsenal	Bibliothèque de l'Arsenal (Paris)
Audin and Vial	Marius Audin and Eugène Vial. *Dictionnaire des artistes et ouvriers d'art du Lyonnais.* 2 vols., Paris, 1919.
Baudrier	Henri Baudrier. *Bibliographie lyonnaise.* 13 vols., Lyon, 1895.
BHR	*Bibliothèque d'Humanisme et Renaissance*
BL	British Library (London)
BM	Bibliothèque Municipale
BN	Bibliothèque Nationale de France (Paris)
C & P	Département de Cartes et Plans
Estampes	Cabinet des Estampes
BPF	Bibliothèque de la Société de l'Histoire du Protestantisme Français (Paris)
BPU	Bibliothèque Publique et Universitaire (Geneva)
Brit. Mus.	British Museum (London)
BSHAG	*Bulletin de la Société d'Histoire et d'Archéologie de Genève*
BSHPF	*Bulletin de la Société de l'Histoire du Protestantisme Français*
Chantilly	Musée Condé (Chantilly)
CIG	Centre d'Iconographie Genevoise
Corr. Bèze	*Correspondance de Théodore de Bèze.* Ed. Henri Meylan et al., 28 vols., Geneva, 1960-.
HE	*Histoire ecclesiastique des Eglises réformées au royaume de France.* Ed. E. Baum and G. Cunitz, 3 vols., Paris, 1883-9.
Hollstein Dutch and Flemish	F.W.H. Hollstein et al. *Dutch and Flemish Etchings, Engravings and Woodcuts, ca. 1450-1700.* 57 vols., Amsterdam, 1949-.

Hollstein German	F.W.H. Hollstein et al. *German, Engravings, Etchings and Woodcuts, ca. 1450-1700.* 55 vols., Amsterdam, 1954-.
JWCI	*Journal of the Warburg and Courtauld Institutes*
LC	Library of Congress (Washington)
Maz.	Bibliothèque Mazarine (Paris)
MC	*Mémoires de Condé.* 6 vols., London, 1743.
NKJ	*Nederlands Kunsthistorisch Jaarboek*
PQ	*Print Quarterly*
Préaud et al.	Maxime Préaud, Pierre Cassselle, Marianne Grivel and Corinne Le Bitouzé. *Dictionnaire des éditeurs d'estampes à Paris sous l'Ancien Régime.* Paris, 1987.
Robert-Dumesnil	A.P.F. Robert-Dumesnil. *Le peintre-graveur français.* 11 vols., Paris, 1835-71.
Thieme-Becker	*Allgemeines Lexikon der bildenden Künstler von der Antike bis zur Gegenwart begründet von Ulrich Thieme und Felix Becker.* Ed. Hans Vollmen, 37 vols., Leipzig, 1907-50.
UB	Universitätsbibliothek or Universiteitsbibliotheek

ACKNOWLEDGEMENTS

Two wonderful institutions and the people associated with them were particularly important in the preparation of this book. A Frese Senior Fellowship at the Center for the Advanced Study in the Visual Arts gave me access to the collections and library of the National Gallery of Art in Washington, D.C., facilitated my foray into art history by integrating me into a congenial and generous group of fellows, and afforded me the exceptional privilege of an office just down the hall from Peter Parshall and Andrew Robison. They graciously put up with numerous interruptions to respond to my ill-informed questions about prints and printmaking. My subsequent appointment to the Institut d'histoire de la Réformation in Geneva gave me access to that institution's exceptional bibliographic and human resources concerning all things Genevan and French Reformed. Much of the research that I did for this book could have been done as efficiently nowhere else. The unfailing erudition and kindness of Irena Backus, Alain Dufour, Nicolas Fornerod, Hervé Genton, and Béatrice Nicollier provided key leads and clarified points of detail. At Brown University, the William Prescott and Annie McClelland Smith Chair in History and Religion generously supported my research on this project.

In Geneva, I also owe a special debt of gratitude to Christian Grosse, who made a preliminary survey for me of archival holdings relevant to the lives of those involved in the production of the *Wars, Massacres and Troubles*, and Liliane Mottu-Weber, the leading expert on the Genevan economy in this period, who brought to my attention a particularly important, previously unknown document about the entrepreneurs behind the project and clarified many technical matters about it. Many other colleagues also helped me see details of the prints or suggested fruitful research leads: Jim Amelang, Reinhard Bodenmann, Fernando Bouza, Karen Bowen, Larry Bryant, Sylvie Deswarte-Rosa, Alain Dubois, Max Engammare, Dario Gamboni, Jean-François Gilmont, Amy Graves, Godehard Janzing, Guido Marnef, Margaret Meserve, Kristen Neuschel, Kendall Tarte, and Ilja Veldman. To all of them my thanks.

Many librarians and curators went beyond the call of duty in providing me with information. I recall with particular gratitude invaluable assistance provided by Marie-Françoise Bois-Delatte (Grenoble), Peter Bonfitto (Los Angeles), Vendulka Cejchan (Berlin), Susan Danforth (Providence), Françoise Dubourg (Toulouse), Françoise de Forbin (Avignon), Alexandra Franklin (Oxford), Michelle Gait (Aberdeen), Paul Gehl (Chicago), Conny Hödt

(Halle), Christian Hogrefe (Wolfenbüttel), Huigen Leeflang (Amsterdam), Hanno Lietz (Rostock), Valentín Moreno (Madrid), Nadine Orenstein (New York), Maxime Préaud (Paris), Dorothe Schneider (Zurich), Barbara Sibille (Noyon), Martin Steinmann (Basel), Pierre Surchat (Bern). The usual expressions of gratitude to all of the personnel of the libraries, archives, and collections visited apply with particular force in this instance since I ventured into so many previously unfamiliar repositories.

A number of colleagues and friends were kind enough to read preliminary versions of part or all of the manuscript. Karen Bowen, Andrea Carlino, Christophe Chazalon, Alain Dufour, Nicolas Fornerod, Geneviève Gross, Christian Grosse, Jeff Muller, Philip Rieder, Mary Sheriff, and Frédéric Tinguely accepted this chore with good grace, saved me from many errors, and prodded me usefully to reconfigure important parts of the book. A preliminary version of chapter 3 benefited from a stimulating seminar discussion organized at the University of Antwerp. As always, my wife Judy was my severest and hence most useful critic.

Marlène Jaouich, Isabelle Lambert, and Pierre-Olivier Lechot provided valuable editorial assistance in the final stages of preparation of the manuscript. The entire project would never have gotten underway, much less been completed, without Max Engammare's early encouragement and continuing support and advice.

INTRODUCTION

The first centuries after the invention of printing saw a quantum leap in the volume of information available to Europeans about current events and recent history. From the late fifteenth century onward, ever growing quantities of cheap pamphlets, *flugschriften*, and *avvisi* joined oral communication and the copied and recopied letters of merchants and ambassadors as sources of the latest news. Initially pamphlets reported on single happenings as events dictated. As the sixteenth century advanced, German and Italian printers began to cluster brief reports from various destinations into a single publication, then to produce series of reports about major events as they unfolded, and finally to collect the biggest stories of the past six months or five years into larger compendia—all this decades before the appearance just after 1600 of the publications that historians of the press typically categorize as the first newspapers because they were published at regular, brief intervals under fixed titles. Periodical publications of this latter sort then spread outward from Germany across Europe over the course of the seventeenth century. Longer histories of the most noteworthy contemporary affairs in one country or another also proliferated during the first centuries of printing, as did collections of documents and manifestos assembled so that readers could weigh the motives of the various parties to important conflicts on the basis of their own declarations. Far from displacing oral and manuscript communication, this printed information only stimulated more of it. Those avid to be in the know collected, copied, and passed along what they had read. People soon grew so sceptical about the reliability of the printed news accounts that a new profession grew up of specialized intelligencers who made it their business to be better informed about what was really happening than the print publishers. For a hefty price, they dispatched regular handwritten reports to subscribers who did not want to be cut off from the events of the day simply because they lived far from the great nodes for the exchange of information that were Venice, Paris, London, and Rome. Print, manuscript, and speech at once competed with and stimulated one another in a growing echo chamber of rumor and news.

The proliferation of recent studies about the history of information in early modern Europe has made this well known.[1] Less well known is that visual

1 See especially Mario Infelise, *Prima dei giornali. Alle origini della publica informazione* (Rome, 2002); Brendan Dooley and Sabrina A. Brown eds., *The Politics of Information in Early Modern Europe* (London, 2001); Adam Fox, *Oral and Literate Culture in England*

media occupied an important place in the economy of information alongside the channels of communication provided by letterpress printing, manuscript, and speech.[2] Gutenberg's press was not the only new information technology of the late middle ages; the era also saw the appearance and spread of woodcut printing and copper engraving. The first single sheet print depicting a contemporary battle appeared before Gutenberg's Bible. Imitations were slow to follow, but by the end of the fifteenth century graphic depictions of battles, sieges, monstrous births and other important or portentous events were appearing with some regularity in both South Germany and Italy. From there the technology for producing them gradually spread to France and the Low Countries. By the later part of the sixteenth century, pictures and words were recognized to be complementary ways of keeping the public informed about current events. Etchings of battle scenes urged buyers to acquire the printed news reports of the battle so that they could better understand the picture, and vice versa. Depictions of peddlers selling news sheets show them hawking both printed and pictorial accounts of naval engagements, assassinations and sieges. (See figure 1.)

This book is a study of a single print series that I believe occupies an important place within this story of the use of visual media to report on current events and recent history. Insofar as I have been able to establish, it is the first extended print series offering a pictorial account of recent events where the images do not simply illustrate a written history but carry the burden of telling the story themselves, and that was intended not to glorify a ruler's deeds but to show a broad general public the events of their time. Produced in Geneva in 1569-1570 by a group of entrepreneurs and artists, its title page reads:

First Volume,
CONTAINING FORTY TABLEAUS OR
divers memorable histories concerning the wars, massacres and troubles
that have occurred in France in these last years. All gathered
from the testimony of those who were there in person
and saw them, and truly
portrayed.

1500-1700 (Oxford, 2000); Paul Arblaster, "Current-affairs Publishing in the Habsburg Netherlands, 1620-1660, in Comparative European Perspective" (Oxford University D. Phil. thesis, 1999); Richard Cust, "News and Politics in Early Stuart England," *Past and Present* 112 (1986), 60-90; and the still valuable Karl Schottenloher, *Flugblatt und Zeitung: Ein Wegweiser durch das gedruckte Tagesschrifttum* (Berlin, 1922).

2 A few recent studies have begun to explore facets of this issue, notably Michael Schilling, *Bildpublizistik der frühen Neuzeit. Aufgaben und Leistungen des illustrierten Flugblatts in Deutschland bis um 1700* (Tubingen, 1990); Brendan Dooley, "The Wages of War: Battles, Prints and Entrepreneurs in Late Seventeenth-Century Venice," *Word and Image* 17 (2001), 7-24; and now Christi M Klinkert, *Nassau in het Nieuws. Nieuwsprenten van Maurits van Nassaus militaire ondernemingen uit de periode 1590-1600* (Zutphen, 2005).

FIGURE 1. Jacob Kempner publisher, *The Broadsheet Peddler*, 1589, etching, 29.5 × 22 cm, BN, Estampes, Hennin 542, cliché Bibliothèque nationale de France. The events reported in the various publications offered for sale by this itinerant peddler date this print to 1589. In his right hand he holds a view of the January 1589 siege of Orléans. With his left he offers a pamphlet account of the Spanish Armada. In his hat is the "*Neu Zeitung* from France about the shocking murder of the duke of Guise". His box contains accounts of the sieges of Bergen op Zoom (also illustrated in the background behind the peddler) and Wachtendonk. This etching was long attributed to Jost Amman but is now thought to have been made in the Frankfurt workshop of Theodore de Bry.

The "*quarante tableaux*" in question in fact comprise 39 images plus the title page and/or a preliminary note "To the Reader", these last both placed somewhat incongruously within an elaborate decorative border. Each print measures about 32 cm high by 50 cm wide, an impressive size, bigger than two sheets of modern office paper laid side by side. If sixteenth-century Europe had coffee tables, this would have been a coffee table book—although its detail-packed depictions of battles, massacres, and great public occasions demand more than the casual browsing of a bored guest waiting for the host to bring the drinks. A title identifying the event and a lettered key or legend explicating the details frame each image. Early buyers typically bound the prints by folding them in the middle as was commonly done with large maps as well, so that the scenes opened one after another as one leafed through the volume. Versions of the series appeared with the titles and captions in French, German, Italian, and Latin.

The episodes depicted in the volume run from the special meeting of the Parlement of Paris in June 1559 at which Anne Du Bourg spoke out before king Henry II against the harsh repression of Protestantism through a minor skirmish between Huguenot and Catholic forces along the Rhône in March 1570. The first dozen or so plates show the events that led up to the outbreak of open civil war in spring 1562. The remainder of the series is composed of events from the first three French Wars of Religion (1562-1563, 1567-1568, and 1568-1570). Above all it is a compendium of battles (15 pictures), sieges (5 pictures), raids (4 pictures) and massacres (3 pictures—5 if the massacres from prior to the outbreak of the First Civil War are included). The series is most commonly known as "Tortorel and Perrissin" after the names of the artists who signed most of the plates. I shall refer to it interchangeably as Tortorel and Perrissin, the *Quarante Tableaux*, and the *Wars, Massacres and Troubles*.

Virtually everybody with even a passing interest in the history of sixteenth-century France has seen images from Tortorel and Perrissin, even if they may not be aware of it. Its depictions of events such as the fatal wounding of Henry II and the massacre of Vassy have been endlessly recycled to illustrate books about this period. Museum curators and television producers seeking to convey the intolerance and religious violence of the sixteenth century no less frequently display scenes from the series. Print dealers also know it well, for individual sheets are readily available on the market, and bound volumes containing the entire suite come up for sale from time to time.

For all of the familiarity of at least some of the images in the series, and for all of the wide dissemination that they achieved in their day, these prints and the publication project they comprised have not received the attention they deserve. Historians have generally used the prints as they use most images—as illustrations—without considering the artistic conventions shaping them, the aims and strategies of the artists, or the possibility that they might contain information unavailable anywhere else that could make them the visual equivalent of a written primary source. Typical in this regard is the most important work based upon and dedicated to the series, Alfred Franklin's 1886 *Les grands scènes historiques du seizième siècle*, which combines a facsimile reproduction of all of the prints with commissioned essays about each of the events depicted. With the noteworthy exception of Ernest Lavisse's chapter on the massacre of Vassy, all of these essays narrate the event in question on the basis of the standard written sources about it while failing to analyze the prints themselves, as if the prints were an unproblematic snapshot of the events. Recently, Pierre Bonnaure has taken an important step beyond this approach in a long article that identifies many of the sources for the prints and seeks to identify some of the layers of meaning within what he considers "first and foremost a work of propaganda". He suggests that the images encode a great deal of biblical symbolism that would have been second nature to Protestant artists steeped in Scripture.[3] Another recent historical treatment of the prints by David El-Kenz likewise diagnoses a coherent ideological impulse behind the prints by assimilating them to Protestant martyrologies.[4] Valuable as these essays are in pointing the way to a more historical and critical understanding of these prints, they betray a limited understanding of the actual history of the series' production and circulation and apply a single grill of interpretation to a complex set of images that invite multiple forms of appropriation.

Within the domain of the history of art, the generation of late nineteenth century archivists and *érudits* who first put the history of French and Swiss art on a solid documentary basis performed an essential service for all who would seek to understand this print series by exhuming the contracts involved in its production and discovering virtually everything that is known today about the biographies of the artists who worked on it. But most nineteenth- and twentieth-century connoisseurs and art historians saw little interest in looking closely at the prints. As the standard catalogue raisonné of French printmakers tartly observes, while the prints may be of historical value, they "offer scant interest from the point of view of art". Jean Ehrmann considered them briefly in his studies of Antoine Caron's troubling contemporaneous images of ancient Roman massacres.[5] Because they constitute a sequential narrative of current events, they make cameo appearances in David Kunzle's

---

[3] Pierre Bonnaure, "Des images à relire et à réhabiliter. L'œuvre gravé de Tortorel et Perrissin," *BSHPF* 138 (1992), 475-514.

[4] David El Kenz, "La sacralisation par l'image, au temps des guerres de religion. (Etude comparée des massacres d'un livret calviniste et d'un livret catholique)" in Michèle Menard and Annie Duprat eds., *Histoire, images, imaginaires, fin XVe siècle-début XXe siècle* (Le Mans, 1998), pp. 223-33. See also his *Les bûchers du roi. La culture protestante des martyrs (1523-1572)* (Seyssel, 1997), esp. pp. 203-7, 222-9.

[5] Ehrmann, "Massacre and Persecution Pictures in Sixteenth-Century France," *JWCI* 8 (1945), 195-99.

The Early Comic Strip: Narrative Strips and Picture Stories in the European Broadsheet from c. 1450 to 1825 (1973), his subsequent *From Criminal to Courtier: The Soldier in Netherlandish Art* (2002), and Francis Haskell's *History and Its Images: Art and the Interpretation of the Past* (1993). For Kunzle the work is "the true monument to the sufferings of the Huguenots" whose "subjects are selected to reveal the pattern and extent of Huguenot victimization."[6] For Alain Erlande-Brandenburg, formerly director of the Musée de la Renaissance at Ecouen which contains several tapestries made after prints from the series, they were made "to glorify the great deeds (*hauts faits*) of the Protestants."[7] But even these treatments are cursory. The recent move by art historians to widen their focus beyond high art to take in all of "visual culture" has not dramatically altered this situation of neglect. Of course, the history of sixteenth-century French art is in general an understudied corner of European art history.

I first looked closely at these prints when I was asked in 1993 to write a catalogue essay on polemical and propaganda prints of the Wars of Religion for the exhibition *The French Renaissance in Prints from the Bibliothèque Nationale*. What I saw puzzled me. Together with events that any historian of the Wars of Religion knows well like the conspiracy of Amboise or the battle of Dreux were episodes that I could not identify at all. What principles governed the selection of scenes to be included? More perplexing yet—and more pressing, given my assignment—was the question: were these propaganda prints? Some features of the series certainly suggest as much. Many of the strongest and most frequently reproduced images are scenes of Huguenot martyrdom and victimization, while the series is silent about many of the Protestant deeds of these years that particularly outraged contemporary Catholic opinion, such as the numerous incidents of iconoclasm that accompanied the Huguenot takeover of many towns in 1562. But other features of the series complicate too facile an assumption that it served partisan Protestant purposes. Quite unusually for the age, scenes of Protestants massacring Catholics are interspersed among the more numerous scenes where Catholics massacre Protestants. Still more numerous yet are battle scenes that show "two French armies" killing one another. Most captions adopt a descriptive tone that betrays no immediately evident partisanship for one side or the other. The front matter proclaims the creators' intent to depict what happened on the basis of the most reliable, impartial eyewitness testimony that could be assembled. Rather than being an instrument of Protestant propaganda or self-celebration, might the work have been an attempt to transcend the partisan divisions of the time—perhaps even as a cry of protest against the

---

6 Kunzle, *Criminal to Courtier*, pp. 165-6. See also idem, *The Early Comic Strip*, p. 40; Haskell, *History and Its Images*, p. 86.

7 *Musée national de la Renaissance. Chateau d'Ecouen. Guide* (Paris, 1987), p. 77.

violence of both sides in a fratricidal civil war? In the essay I wrote, I sketched out some of these ambiguities, observed that a good critical study of the series was needed, and turned my attention back to the very different topics then occupying my attention.

But anomalous phenomena haunt you. In the past few years, I have started working again on the Wars of Religion, specifically on the critical years of the French Reformation from the foundation of the first Reformed churches modeled on Geneva's in 1555 through the end of the First Civil War in 1563. As I immersed myself in the primary sources of this period, I realized that I was encountering more and more documents that could have been direct sources for Tortorel and Perrissin. Other documents that I examined illuminated the distinctive spin of the prints by offering contrasting accounts of the same events. I decided to attempt myself the critical study of the print series that I had called for and set out to identify all printed or manuscript reports of the events depicted in the series that would have been in circulation by 1570 and thus could have been known to the creators of the prints. I then compared all of the contemporary written accounts that I could find of the events depicted in the series with the visual narratives of the prints in order to lay bare both the sources used by the makers of the series and the distinctive features of their representation of the event.

Valuable as this line of investigation proved for clarifying the channels through which information circulated in the sixteenth century and how the *Wars, Massacres and Troubles* fit within the history of Protestant historical consciousness, it soon became apparent that understanding this work of graphic history required attending not only to its written sources, but also to the generic and representational conventions of sixteenth-century visual culture that shaped the design of the prints. The new graphic media of the fifteenth and sixteenth centuries were not just used to produce visual propaganda. They also were used to convey information about things from the structure of the human body to the appearance of different kinds of plants to the latest happenings of import. For all they claimed to offer a "true portrait", a "*ware contrafactur*". A second goal of my study became to reconstruct how the new technologies of printmaking were used to figure current events during the first centuries of these media, so that I could determine the place of the *Wars, Massacres and Troubles* within this history and understand better the iconographic choices and representational strategies shaping the prints. The result is that this book contains what I believe to be the first synthetic account of the use of printmaking to report on current events in the first centuries after its invention, with special reference to France.

Perhaps the methodological lesson that took the longest time to absorb was one that print curators or art historians will regard as self-evident, namely how much can be learned about a set of prints simply by looking carefully at as many impressions and albums of them as possible. Ever since Théophile Dufour first discovered the contracts pertaining to these prints in the Genevan archives and reported them in Franklin's monumental facsimile reproduction late in the nineteenth century, those few scholars who have considered this series have tended to assume that these contracts offer the surest guide to the series' elaboration. After initially assuming the same thing myself, I gradually came to realize that different impressions and sets of the prints offered additional clues about their fabrication and use. I consequently made it a priority to locate as many sets as possible. Today, these images are amphibians. Some live in the print rooms of art museums. Others survive in libraries. In print rooms, they are usually preserved as loose sheets in large cases or hinged into modern portfolios. In libraries, they are almost always found in bound volumes. The modern portfolios are particularly valuable for allowing the close comparison of different impressions and versions of the same scene, since they often contain multiple states of the same print. The bound volumes shed light on how the prints were acquired, assembled, and used across the centuries. Especially revealing are the older albums: either those in bindings that can be dated to the sixteenth, seventeenth, or eighteenth centuries, or those subsequently rebound by collectors that can nonetheless be identified as intact older sets of the prints from hand-written numbers or other kinds of marginalia that appear consistently throughout the set in an old hand.[8] My search ultimately turned up sets of the prints in 42 different museums and libraries, housing in all 48 bound volumes with some or all of the prints from the series, at least 37 of which are old albums. I was able to compile detailed descriptions of all of these bound volumes, either by consulting them myself or thanks to the aid of cooperative curators. The clues they provided led me to a new understanding of the project's elaboration, as well as allowing me to work out who bought these prints and how they used them in unusual detail.

Studying this series never ceased to fascinate, because the more I learned and looked, the more layers of complexity, hesitation, and contradiction I saw. Like so many works in this century when printing was still new and the Renaissance and Reformation were destabilizing old cultural forms and encouraging new ones, the *Quarante Tableaux* was an experimental work. It was experimental in the sense that it was produced by a group of artists and entrepreneurs with no prior experience in producing such a work. It was experimental in the more profound sense that no exact generic precedents could guide the series. Some earlier graphic works had sought to carry a his-

---

8 For the remainder of this study I will use the term "old album" in a precise, technical sense to designate either a bound volume containing some or all of the prints preserved in a pre-1800 bindings or on album that was evidently rebound in the nineteenth century but that keeps together prints that can be inferred from internal evidence to be an older set of the prints. These may be easily distinguished from other sets of the prints that one encounters that were evidently assembled from diverse sources by nineteenth- or twentieth-century print dealers or curators and bound together after acquisition. The status of several volumes in nineteenth-century bindings is ambiguous. When in doubt, I have not classified the volume in question as an old album.

torical narrative through pictures and accompanying text, but these were typically accounts of the victories of a great ruler containing a strong element of panegyric. In proclaiming their goal to be the presentation of an impartial eyewitness view of the events in question, the makers of the *Quarante Tableaux* took this emerging genre in a new direction, one inspired by both the growing market for single-sheet news prints that claimed to offer true portraits of individual events, and the prevailing rhetoric of written historiography in Geneva. The challenge of conveying contemporary events faithfully in pictures placed the series within what the great literary critic Mikhael Bakhtin writing about the early novel called "the zone of maximal contact with the present", in turn generative of an indeterminacy or open-endedness in storytelling.[9] The manner in which the creators of the series chose to relate printed text to image further heightened this indeterminacy or open-endedness. Reliance on Protestant networks of information recurrently subverted the creators' proclaimed goal of offering an impartial view of events, yet they used multiple informants and made a clear effort to transcend a purely partisan or one-sided view of events. The end result was a complex, even internally contradictory work that invited different forms of appropriation.

Much recent art historical study of history painting has focused on identifying the "political work" done by historical paintings or prints. In a society as saturated by visual media as ours, revealing the manner in which apparently neutral images can be used to mold public opinion is certainly a useful enterprise. My premise here, however, is that this suite of historical prints deserves more than a hermeneutic of suspicion. Its claim to offer information to satisfy the curiosity of those eager to know about the great events of the time deserves to be taken seriously. It merits being read within the multiple frames of analysis that the best historians of historiography bring to the study of written works of history, that is to say with attention to the working methods of the historian and the sources used as well as to the interpretation encoded within the history. The story of its production and reception also deserves attention. This study is consequently organized as follows. The initial chapters examine the production of the print series and the entrepreneurs and artists who made it. Chapter 3 analyzes the visual languages of the prints and attempts to situate the *Quarante Tableaux* within the broader history of the use of images to report on contemporary history. Chapters 4 and 5 look at the sources and spin of the work, placing it within both the circuits of information at the time and the history of Protestant historical consciousness. The final chapter explores the work's reception and influence. To enable readers to acquaint themselves directly with the prints—and since the entire thrust of this book is to suggest that showing and telling about something are alternative

---

9 David R. Smith, "Willem Buytewech as a Journalist: Perspectives on Description and Narration," *Konsthistorisk Tidskrift* 60 (1991), 179.

means of communicating information, each with their own strengths and limitations—all of the scenes from the *Quarante Tableaux* are reproduced in Part 2. Accompanying them are notes with basic technical information about each print; a brief historical introduction to each event depicted; a bibliography and iconography of other early accounts of the event; and an explication of where each image replicates information found in a prior printed source and where it offers an independent view of the event. *Ami lecteur* (as the makers of the volume would have said): you may wish to examine Part 2 before Part 1, or move back and forth between the two as you progress.

PART 1

A GRAPHIC HISTORY

CHAPTER 1

THE PROJECT

The *Quarante Tableaux* began with a contract drawn up in the office of the Genevan notary Aimé Santeur on April 18, 1569. On one side of the table sat two brothers-in-law and textile merchants from the Low Countries, Nicolas Castellin, originally from Tournai, and Pierre Le Vignon, originally from Soignies in Hainault. The two had been "*compagnons en marchandise*" in Antwerp since 1559 or 1560 and had moved together to Geneva in 1568. Across from them sat two artists: Jacques Le Challeux, a "carver of histories (*tailleur d'histoires*)" from Rouen, and Jean Perrissin, a painter from Lyon. Under the terms of the bargain they struck, Perrissin agreed to "portray (*pourtraire*)" and Le Challeux to carve in woodblock "all of a history and its circumstances that will be shown and furnished them by the aforesaid Castellin and Le Vignon." Perrissin was to start work immediately. Le Challeux would begin cutting what Perrissin had drawn in two weeks, on May 1. For their work, both men were to be paid 15 livres per month. They had to swear not to divulge anything about the project until it was finished and printed. They also bound themselves to work exclusively on the project until it was completed.[1]

That refugees from both the Netherlands and France should undertake a project such as this together in Geneva in 1569 should occasion no surprise: the city was crammed at that moment with foreigners trying to survive by putting their skills to use. Three years previously, the "Wonderyear" had intoxicated the Netherlands with its promise of religious transformation. Enthusiastic open air preaching in the spring had given way to widespread iconoclasm by the summer and drawn thousands into the orbit of Reformed Protestantism. By winter, the religious status quo ante had been restored. Soon the iron duke of Alba arrived to administer exemplary punishment. As

---

1 AEG, notaire A. Santeur III, fo. 248. The full text of this contract is provided in Appendix I. This and the other contracts pertaining to this series were discovered in the Genevan archives in the late nineteenth century by Théophile Dufour. They were published in part in E. and E. Haag, *La France protestante* (2nd ed., 6 vols, Paris, 1877-88), s.v. "Castellin", vol. III, cols. 453-60, and more fully in Dufour, "La vie de Tortorel et de Perrissin" in Franklin ed., *Les grandes scènes historiques*, pp. 7-9. I have checked all documents quoted in that work against the originals.

many as 60,000 people fled, most to England or nearby regions of the Germany, some to Geneva. In France, the Peace of Amboise collapsed in 1567. The Second Civil War was brief, but so was the peace that followed it. When the Third Civil War broke out in 1568, king Charles IX accused the Huguenots of seeking to "establish and constitute in this kingdom another sovereign principality in order to undo our own ordained by God."[2] He put an end to the toleration of Reformed worship and barred Protestants from all royal offices. Prominent among the cities secured by the royal and Catholic forces was Geneva's neighbor and rival Lyon, one of France's greatest centers of both commerce and printing and a town that the Huguenots had controlled during the First Civil War of 1562-63. As in previous periods of religious persecution, many French Protestants looked to Geneva for refuge. Lyon furnished a particularly large contingent.[3]

It is also not entirely surprising that a pair of textile entrepreneurs from Antwerp should have taken the lead in assembling and producing a volume of prints. Amid the general flowering of its commerce and luxury trades, Antwerp had emerged over the course of the preceding half century as one of the leading European centers of print production. In the decades around mid-century, a number of specialists had begun to dominate the business of publishing prints there: Hans Liefrinck, Gerard De Jode, and especially Hieronymus Cock, who from his shop at the sign of the four winds sold a wide range of maps, devotional images, moralizing prints, and reports on current events, all made for him under contract by a range of affiliated artists. But these entrepreneurs never monopolized the production of prints. Particularly during the formative years of local printmaking, those who experimented with putting the young technologies of woodblock and intaglio printing to new uses came from a wide variety of backgrounds, ranging from textile printing to the manufacture of playing cards. These entrepreneurs were not necessarily trained artists or people affiliated with the book trades.[4]

Geneva, by contrast, had little in the way of indigenous printmaking traditions. Even the spectacular growth of the book trades that followed the Reformation could not summon a tradition of permanently resident woodcutter-book illustrators to life. Only a tiny fraction (2 per cent) of the books

---

2 A. Stegmann ed., *Edits des guerres de religion* (Paris, 1979), p. 63.

3 For Geneva's swollen population in 1567-1570 and the importance within it of refugees from Lyon, see E. William Monter, "Historical Demography and Religious History in Sixteenth-Century Geneva," *Journal of Interdisciplinary History* 9 (1979), 402-7. Only in 1558-60, another great period of refuge, did sixteenth-century Geneva house more people than in 1568-70.

4 Jan van der Stock, *Printing Images in Antwerp: The Introduction of Printmaking in a City, Fifteenth Century to 1585* (Rotterdam, 1998); David Landau and Peter Parshall, *The Renaissance Print 1470-1550* (New Haven, 1994), pp. 220-23; Timothy A. Riggs, *Hieronymus Cock: Printmaker and Publisher* (New York, 1977).

produced in Geneva between 1536 and 1564 contained illustrations.[5] The few illustrated Geneva Bibles produced in the 1550s and 1560s were far less copiously furnished with maps and pictures than their counterparts produced at the same time in Lyon, where an important school of book illustration had emerged in the 1540s and 1550s. One printmaker of note, Pierre Eskrich, the Paris-born son of a German engraver, settled in the city from 1552 to 1565, but he ultimately left for Lyon after several clashes with employers over matters of pay and productivity. While in town, he executed the two most ambitious printmaking projects made in Geneva prior to the *Wars, Massacres and Troubles*: a reworking of Lucas Cranach's *Passional Christi und Antichristi* into sixteen pairs of woodcuts contrasting the life of Christ and the Pope that went through nine printings between 1557 and 1600; and a vigorous satire of the church of Rome in the form of a gigantic map, the *Mappe-Monde Papistique Nouvelle*, devised in 1561 but not completed and published until 1566.[6] The paucity of permanently resident printmakers explains why such visual material occupied a relatively small place in Genevan Reformation propaganda as compared to German. When the renewed civil wars in France brought refugees like Perrissin and Le Challeux to Geneva, they created new opportunities to launch large printmaking projects.

Since Castellin and Le Vignon had been business partners in Antwerp since 1559 or 1560, they had been in a position to observe the projects of print publishers there. When they arrived in Geneva in late 1568, they also had more than the usual refugee's need to find new ways to put their capital and knowledge to work. The chief focus of their business ventures was the production and exportation of linen thread. A few days after acquiring the status of *bourgeois de Genève* in November 1568 for the hefty reception fee of 25 écus each—only the wealthiest Lucchese merchants paid more in this era—they jointly acquired a house on the rue des Allemans, the main commercial street near the Rhône, where they installed or took over four mills to spin thread. But their economic situation was more precarious than outward

---

5 Christophe Chazalon, "Histoire du livre illustré à Genève (1478-1600)," *Art et Architecture en Suisse*, 57 (2006), 27.

6 Paul Chaix, *Recherches sur l'imprimerie à Genève de 1550 à 1564* (Geneva, 1954), pp. 136-7; idem, "Un pamphlet genevois du XVIe siècle: *l'Antithèse* de S. Du Rosier. Recherche iconographique" in *Mélanges offerts à M. Paul-E. Martin* Mémoires et Documents publiés par la Société d'Histoire et d'Archéologie de Genève 40 (Geneva, 1961), 467-82; Waldemar Deonna, *Les arts à Genève des origines à la fin du XVIIIe siècle* (Geneva, 1942), pp. 483-6; Natalis Rondot, *Graveurs sur bois à Lyon au seizième siècle* (Paris, 1898); idem, "Pierre Eskrich, peintre et tailleur d'histoires à Lyon au XVIe siècle," *Revue du Lyonnais* 5th ser., 31 (1901), 241-61, 321-54; *Schweizerisches Künstler Lexikon* (4 vols., Frauenfeld, 1905-17) s.v. "Cruche, Pierre"; Robert Brun, *Le livre français illustré de la Renaissance* (Paris, 1969), pp. 77-85; Philip Benedict, "Of Marmites and Martyrs: Images and Polemics in the Wars of Religion" in *The French Renaissance in Prints from the Bibliothèque Nationale de France* (exhibition catalogue, Los Angeles, 1994), pp. 118-9, 134; Henri Zerner, *L'art de la Renaissance en France. L'invention du classicisme* (Paris, 2002), pp. 324-5.

appearances might have suggested. They had left behind in Antwerp large debts and angry creditors. Their largest debt was to Le Vignon's late brother-in-law Loys de Behault, to whom they owed numerous promissory notes. His widow assigned some to other merchants, who soon appeared demanding their money. Ultimately, she would have to appoint an agent to renegotiate the still unpaid debt in 1570.[7] Another angry creditor was none other than the great Antwerp printer Christopher Plantin, who, together with an associate Jean Gassen, had made some unwise loans against the revenue of a local nobleman for whom Castellin and Le Vignon acted as an agent. According to a letter of Plantin's pleading with the lord to pay him, Gilles Castellin, the company's factor, had put Plantin off with "various delays, subterfuges and sleights of hand in bad faith", unsuccessfully sued him, and finally paid him only a fraction of what he owed him.[8] Ultimately, Castellin et cie would seek to eradicate what remained of their debt to Plantin by sending him unspecified merchandise in 1571.[9] Within months of purchasing the house on the rue des Allemans, and just three days after signing the contract with Perrissin and Le Challeux to begin work on their history in pictures, the two merchants appeared before the Large Council of Geneva requesting a delay in the payments they owed for their house "in recognition of the great losses they have had."[10]

Several features of the contract drawn up between Castellin, Le Vignon, Perrissin, and Le Challeux deserve particular attention. First, the contract

---

[7] AEG, Bourgeoisie, A 6, Livre de Bourgeois, esp. fo. 108v; notaire A. Santeur III, fo. 64; notaire P. Cusin, II, fos. 126-30; III, fo. 67; Dufour, "Vie de Tortorel et de Perrissin," pp. 7n-8n.

[8] Plantin to Claude de Withem, Sr de Risbourg, November 2, 1569: "Car vous estes, comme j'entends, asses bien informé comme Gilles Chastelain, par diverses prolongations, subterfuges et finesses de mauvaise foy, m'a trainé l'année passé, en proces, qu'il a fait durer jusques apres l'an passé, qu'il eust deu payer les sommes deus, et que finalement, ayant esté condamné, il m'ay payé une partie seulement des sommes escheutes, passé ung an, et quelque autre partie à Jehan Gassen, vers lequel il a esté aussi condamné pour les termes de Pasques et la S. Jehan dernierement passés, sans que jamais il ait voulu liquider les premiers payements, ni despens deus et raisonnables, et que depuis il a juré n'avoir rien à ses maistres et n'avoir le moyen aucun de payer, et autres cavillations, trop longues à réiterer par lectres. De sorte que j'en porte une fascherie, dommage et perte inestimables, tant en mon honneur et biens, que principalement en mon crédict." Max Rooses ed., *Correspondance de Christophe Plantin* (9 vols., Antwerp, 1885-1918; repr. Liechtenstein, 1968), II, 76. See also *Ibid.*, I, 117, 152, 301-2. I owe thanks to Alain Dubois for calling the interest of the Plantin correspondence to my attention.

[9] AEG, Registres des Particuliers, v. 16, act of 23 March 1571. There is no evidence from Plantin's account books that this merchandise took the form of copies of the *Wars, Massacres and Troubles*. Still another lawsuit, this one pitting Castellin against the Zilli brothers, merchants of St Gall, is revealed by AEG, Pièces Historiques 1880, letter of September 8, 1570.

[10] AEG, Registres du Conseil, v. 64, fo. 63r. I owe this information to the kindness of Christian Grosse.

demonstrates that the parties to it envisaged making a series of prints from the start, for it commits the artists to depict and carve "*all* of a history" (italics mine) to be "shown and furnished them" by Castellin and Le Vignon. The *Quarante Tableaux* was not a collection of previously produced individual news prints assembled and issued with a title page, as some later volumes of current event prints would be. The contract did not, however, specify the exact number of scenes that would make up the series.

Second, though detailed in many regards, the contract leaves imprecise just how much influence each of the various participants in the project had over the final form and content of the prints. It is clear that Perrissin was responsible for drawing the images to be produced and that Le Challeux had the task of turning his drawings into woodblocks for printing, a division of responsibility that was common in printmaking and that came in certain moments and milieux to be acknowledged in the way artists signed prints, with the person responsible for the design of the image being identified as its *inventor* and the one who did the actual cutting of the block being said to have *fecit*, *sculpsit*, or *incidit* the work. (Publishers who financed and oversaw the process sometimes got their due as well by being listed with the phrase *excudit* or *formis*.) It also appears that Castellin and Le Vignon were chiefly responsible for the content of the prints and Perrissin for their form. But just how detailed was the "history and its circumstances" that the two merchants were to "show and furnish" the artist? Did they give him a written text? A series of sketches? A simple list of events to be depicted? Did they leave it to Perrissin to find out factual details about the scenes they asked him to represent? Since Antwerp merchants rarely were widely read, did they rely on a man of letters to help write a detailed history, if this is what they furnished Perrissin?[11] Elements of answers to these questions will emerge in the pages to follow, but a full response to most of them is impossible. What can be said is that the *Wars, Massacres and Troubles* was a work designed by a committee. The precise responsibility of each committee member cannot be parsed.

This committee soon changed composition. Within three weeks of signing the contract, one of the merchants, Le Vignon, died. During his final illness, he convinced Castellin to carry on their partnership with his widow. Castellin was true to his word. He continued to ship out thread produced by the firm to towns from Turin to the Netherlands, although the recurring visits of the plague that struck refugee-swollen Geneva each year between 1568 and 1571 often interrupted trade, while the continuing civil war in France

---

[11] For evidence of the limited culture of Antwerp merchants, see H.A. Enno van Gelder, *Gegevens betreffende roerend et onroerend bezit in de Nederlanden in de 16e eeuw* (The Hague, 1972), pp. 380, 510; "L'inventaire de la mortuaire de Gilbert van Schoonbeeke," *Antwerps Archievenblad* 17 (n.d.), 236; Guido Marnef, *Antwerp in the Age of Reformation: Underground Protestantism in a Commercial Metropolis, 1550-1577* (Baltimore, 1996), pp. 160-1.

brought further difficulties when a cartload of his wares was seized in Lorraine, taken to France, and impounded on the pretext that Geneva was an enemy city.[12] At the same time, Castellin moved firmly ahead with the project of the history in pictures. He signed a contract in July to have 400 reams of paper weighing 18-19 pounds per ream "of the size called *papier grand royal*" to be delivered over the course of the next eight months.[13] He struck a deal for printing 100 reams by the first of November with Jean de Laon, a printer who worked on contract for better capitalized merchant-booksellers and would subsequently become as much of a specialist in illustrated books as the Genevan book world permitted.[14] He appeared before the Small Council to request an exclusive privilege for his picture history for three years. The Council promised him it would take this under advisement, then said no more about the subject, suggesting that it decided not to grant a formal privilege to protect the work but was willing to allow its anonymous publication.[15] The title page of the completed series would bear no mention of any privilege, no indication of the identity of any of the producers, and no place or date of publication.

At some point in mid-summer 1569, Castellin also made a bold change of medium. He decided he wanted the prints made as etchings. On July 29, he returned to the *étude* of *maître* Santeur with two artists: Perrissin once again, and another refugee from Lyon, Jacques Tortorel. They contracted to "carve in copper and acid the entire history furnished and put forward by the aforesaid Castellin like that which he began and to pursue the aforesaid task until it was complete and without leaving it off." Instead of a monthly wage, they agreed on a piece rate of 4 écus or 10 livres per plate, to be paid as each one was completed.[16]

---

12 Dufour, "Vie de Tortorel et de Perrissin," p. 8n; AEG, Registres du Conseil, v. 64, fo. 144v; Registres des Particuliers, v. 16, fo. 63; Liliane Mottu-Weber, *Genève au siècle de la Réforme. Economie et Refuge* (Geneva, 1987), p. 12.

13 AEG, notaire A. Santeur, VI, fo. 61v, published in Dufour, "Vie de Tortorel et de Perrissin," p. 9. Castellin agreed to pay 32 sols du roy per ream. Royal paper typically measured 44.5 by 61.5 cm. Bruno Weber ed., *Wunderzeichen und Winkeldrucker 1543-1586: Einblattdrucke aus der Sammlung Wickiana in der Zentralbibliothek Zürich* (Zurich, 1972), p. 30.

14 De Laon had not previously printed any illustrated books, but he would subsequently print Jacques Besson's *Theatrum instrumentorum et machinarum* (1578) and Theodore Beza's portrait gallery of famous reformers and their supporters, the *Icones* (1580). Dufour, "Vie de Tortorel et de Perrissin," p. 9; Chaix, *Recherches sur l'imprimerie à Genève*, pp. 169, 228; Hans Joachim Bremme, *Buchdrucker und Buchhändler zur Zeit der Glaubenskämpfe. Studien zur Genfer Druckgeschichte 1565-1580* (Geneva, 1969), pp. 187-8. For understanding de Laon's career, I have also drawn upon the data base of Genevan imprints currently being prepared by Jean-François Gilmont and of illustrations in Genevan books being prepared by Christophe Chazalon, who is also writing a thesis on Jean de Laon.

15 Dufour, "Vie de Tortorel et de Perrissin," p. 9.

16 AEG, notaire A. Santeur VI, fo. 70; *Ibid.*, p. 9. The text of this contract is reproduced in Appendix 1. Although this contract was signed on July 29, the decision to make etchings

This second contract did not specify the division of labor between the two artists, nor did it make any mention of Le Challeux. Most previous historians of the series have assumed that Le Challeux was let go. It is more likely, as we shall see, that he continued silently carving wood blocks. In any event, none of the prints bear his signature or mark. Tortorel worked alongside Perrissin as a sort of junior partner. Of the 55 different identifiable plates produced for the series, 28 are signed by Perrissin alone, 6 by Tortorel alone, and 20 by both, usually with an interconnected "TP".[17] (See Table 1.) Four woodcuts bear both Perrissin's mark and the phrase "Tortorel fecit". This may indicate that Perrissin designed the image and Tortorel carved it. Twenty additional plates are signed only "Tortorel fecit" or "Perrisin fecit". Most of these are etchings, but four are woodcuts. This might similarly indicate that one artist or the other was responsible for both stages in the production of these, but it appears that the artists only began to utilize the Latin verb "fecit" in their signatures part way through the project, so this may simply have been added to underscore each person's design responsibility more clearly. What the signatures certainly tell us that the contracts do not is that at least one print was given over for carving to still another artist in a manner that was not uncommon for large print series at this time. The monogram of Jean II de Gourmont appears on the woodcut of scene 20 *The Third Charge at Dreux*. Ultimately, then, four artists had a hand in the project: Perrissin, Tortorel, Le Challeux, and Gourmont. The prints are typically identified as being by "Tortorel and Perrissin" because theirs are the signatures that appear most often and most prominently throughout the series.

We can only speculate about why Castellin decided to have the prints made as etchings. Although French artists had less experience making etchings than woodcuts, the medium had begun to be cultivated during the 1540s and 1550s by artists such as Jean Duvet, Etienne Delaune, and the printmakers of the school of Fontainebleau. Internationally, intaglio printing enjoyed greater prestige than woodcutting and was beginning to replace it as the preferred medium in book illustration. Italian mapmakers and news print publishers typically etched their plates, although the majority of German news print publishers continued to prefer woodcutting.[18] The shift may thus have indicated that Castellin wanted to embrace the latest technology and was

was taken somewhat earlier, as the contract with Jean de Laon dated July 8 specifies that de Laon was to "imprimer en taille douce sus cuyvre".

17 One plate is unsigned: scene 5 (a woodcut), *The Execution of Anne Du Bourg*.

18 Harry Oelke, *Die Konfessionsbildung des 16. Jahrhunderts im Spiegel illustrierter Flugblätter* (Berlin, 1992), p. 153; Michel Pastoureau, "L'illustration du livre: comprendre ou rêver?" in Roger Chartier and Henri-Jean Martin eds., *Histoire de l'édition française* (4 vols., Paris, 1982-6), I, 508-9; Leon Voet, *The Golden Compasses: A History and Evaluation of the Printing and Publishing Activities of the Officina Plantiniana at Antwerp* (2 vols., Amsterdam, 1972), II, 197-200.

Table 1. Signatures

Print	Medium	Signature
Title Page and To the Reader	etching	Persinus fecit
Mercuriale	etching 1 etching 2	TP Perrissin fecit 1570
Tournament	woodcut 1 woodcut 2 etching (=2)	IP Perrisim fecit 1570 Perrisim fecit 1570
Death of Henry II	woodcut	IP
Execution of Du Bourg	woodcut	[unsigned]
Conspiracy of Amboise	woodcut etching	I. Tortorel fecit TP
Executions of Amboise	woodcut	IP
Estates of Orleans	etching	I. Tortorel fecit 1570
Colloquy of Poissy	etching 1 etching 2	TP I. Tortorel fecit
Massacre of Cahors	woodcut etching	IP, I. Tortorel fecit IP
Massacre of Vassy	woodcut	IP
Massacre of Sens	etching	Perrisin fecit 1570
Capture of Valence	etching	TP
Massacre of Tours	woodcut etching	IP IP
Capture of Montbrison	woodcut etching	IP, I. Tortorel fecit IP
Battle of St Gilles	etching	IP
Battle Order Dreux	etching	TP
1st Charge Dreux	woodcut etching	IP, I. Tortorel fecit IP
2nd Charge Dreux	etching	TP; I. Tortorel fecit added in later state

Print	Medium	Signature
3rd Charge Dreux	woodcut etching	IP, JDG IP; J. Perrisim fecit added in later state
4th Charge Dreux	etching	IP
Retreat Dreux	etching	TP
Siege of Orléans	etching	TP
Guise Wounded	woodcut etching	Perrisin fecit TP
Peace near Orléans	etching	TP
Execution Poltrot	woodcut etching	IP IP
Michelade	etching	TP
Battle of St Denis	woodcut etching	IP Perrisin fecit
Battle of Cognat	woodcut etching	TP TP
Siege of Chartres	etching	Perrisim fecit 1570
Battle Order Jarnac	etching	Persinus fecit 1569
Battle of Jarnac	woodcut etching	IP, I. Tortoel fecit TP, I. Tortorel fecit
Battle of La Roche	etching	I. Tortorel fecit
Siege of Poitiers	etching	Perrisin fecit
Order Moncontour	etching	I. Tortorel fecit
Rout at Moncontour	etching	Perrisim fecit 1570
Siege St Jean d'Angély	woodcut	Perrisim fecit 1570
Capture of Nîmes	etching	I. Tortorel fecit 1570
Attempt on Bourges	etching	Perrisim fecit 1570
Crossing of Rhône	etching	Perrisim fecit 1570

reaching for a higher end audience. Probably more importantly, etching a copper plate required far less time than carving a wood block and allowed the designer to make the plates directly. While the crude woodcuts characteristic of most German single-sheet news prints could be made in a matter of days, large, complicated and artistically ambitious woodcuts such as those from Dürer's Apocalypse series required up to two months to complete.[19] Given the large size and abundance of detail of the wood blocks that had to be cut for this series—not to mention the artists' penchant for including charming but irrelevant touches such as hares grazing in the wood where the duke of Guise was shot (plate 24) or swans swimming in a pond as the conspiracy of Amboise unfolds (plate 6)—Le Challeux probably needed close to a month to carve each design furnished him. One of the wood blocks from the series survives. (Figure 2) It testifies to the remarkable labor required to make it. Castellin must thus quickly have realized that it would take years to finish his series if he did not change to etchings to hasten the project along. The change in the second contract from a monthly wage to piece rates further supports the hypothesis that he wanted to increase the tempo of production. But there were risks as well as rewards in the shift to a new medium. Most French artists were inexperienced at making etchings, so there was little guarantee they would be made well. Furthermore, copper plates wear out more quickly than woodblocks. Etched plates wear out more quickly than engraved ones.[20]

The Evidence of the Prints

After July 1569, the paper trail in Geneva's notarial archives concerning this project grows thinner, but the prints themselves provide further clues about the gradual elaboration of the series, as do the records of the Frankfurt book fair. Looking closely at this evidence disproves a number of suppositions about the series made by those who have based their ideas about it primarily on the contracts.

Work continued on the project for at least eight more months after Castellin signed the second contract with Tortorel and Perrissin in July 1569. This is evident from the fact that the final print in the series depicts a skirmish that took place on March 28, 1570. Indeed, eight of the prints in the series depict events that took place after the first contract was signed. However coherent or episodic the initial "history and its circumstances" furnished the artists by the entrepreneurs might have been, additions were clearly made to take subsequent events into account.

---

19 Weber ed., *Wunderzeichen und Winkeldrucker*, p. 36; Tilman Falk, "Formschneider, Formschnitt" in *Reallexikon zur deutschen Kunstgeschichte* (Stuttgart-Munich, 1937-), X, 199.

20 Weber ed., *Wunderzeichen und Winkeldrucker*, p. 30.

FIGURE 2. Carved wood block for Tortorel and Perrissin, *The Fatal Wounding of the Duke of Guise*, 1569-70, 31.5 × 50 × 2.5 cm, Musée d'Art et d'Histoire de Genève, Cabinet des Estampes, inv. E/M644.

In addition to extending the series forward in time as new battles and sieges took place, the creators of the series also revisited the earlier portion of the chronological period surveyed, adding certain scenes and redesigning others. This can be deduced from the dates that appear on certain plates. Of the twelve prints in the series that indicate their year of production, ten bear the year 1570. (See Table 1.) Five of these, unsurprisingly, are the last five events in the series, which we would expect to have been composed late in the overall production process. The other five are versions of plates 2, 3, 8, 12, and 30 in the series. The first two images in this list—in fact the first two historical scenes in the series, since plate 1 is the title page and note to the reader with decorative border—are exceptional among the prints in the series in that the artists composed two substantially different depictions of these scenes. One version of each scene bears the date 1570. The other three prints dated 1570 fit chronologically in the middle of the sequence of events recounted in the print series. They depict the 1561 Estates-General of Orléans, the 1562 massacre of Sens, and the March 1568 siege of Chartres by the troops of the prince of Condé. They are the only versions we have of these prints. Eight of the prints bearing the date 1570 were made only as etchings. One was made only as a woodcut. One was made in both media.

Though work on the series continued for some months into 1570, a sure *terminus ante quem* for the completion at least one version of all forty plates is provided by the catalogue that the Augsburg bookseller Georg Willers prepared for the Frankfurt book fair of September 1570. It lists this title in German: "Various noteworthy events as they have taken place in France in these last years set forth in artful figures and forty pictures."[21] This does not exactly match the title of the German edition of the *Quarante Tableaux*, but it is close.[22] The volume could be none other.

Willers' catalogue also shows that Castellin had competition to worry about. Immediately after the entry for Tortorel and Perrissin comes one that reads: "the same, in small format, in 22 pictures."[23] This must be Frans Hogenberg's suite of etchings, *Short idea of what has occurred in France since the death of Henry II 1559 and in the following reigns of Francis II and*

---

[21] "Allerley gedenckwirdiger Sachen/so sich in Franckreich in diesen nechsten jaren her verlauffen haben/ in kunstlichen Figuren und vierzig Tafeln verfasset/auff grosse form". *Die Messkataloge Georg Willers* (5 vols., Hildesheim, 1972-2001), I, 323. Frankfurt's fall fairs typically began on the Monday closest to the feast of Mary's Nativity (September 8). Alexander Dietz, *Frankfurter Handelsgeschichte* (Frankfurt, 1910; repr. Glashütten im Taunus, 1970), I, 39-40.

[22] The German title page reads "Der erste teil Mancher layen gedencwirdiger historien von krieg/ mord und aufrueren/ welche sich dise verloffene nechste jaren hehr in francreich zugetragen/ in viertzig taflen begriffen: alles nach glaublicher kunschaft und becewrung der ienigen so selbsten personlich darbei gewesen seine/ und es mit augen geseen haben/ warhaftig abconterfeitet"

[23] *Messkataloge Willers*, I, 323: "Item auff kleine form/in 22. Tafeln."

Charles IX until the year 1569 in affairs of war and such set out here in figures as previously in French in thirty pieces and now with further information and without the unnecessary ones transferred and published in our German tongue in 23 pieces.[24] Hogenberg was another Calvinist refugee from the Low Countries, a painter's son who had just settled in Cologne in 1570 after stays in England and Antwerp, where he had produced current event prints for Hieronymus Cock and maps for Ortelius's *Theatrum orbis terrarum*. His depictions of events in France through 1570 are all direct copies of Tortorel and Perrissin in a smaller format with the image reversed and with a few additional details inserted into several prints. (See figure 3 for an illustration.) His densely printed title page, which offers a brief narration of the events depicted, calls the battle of Moncontour "the last battle that has taken place in France", suggesting that his initial compilation ended with that event. At the next Frankfurt fair the following spring, Hogenberg or his agent reappeared with his series of French events enlarged by ten further prints, as well as with a series of 19 plates depicting events in the Netherlands from 1566 to 1570 and another of Charles V's 1535 conquest of Tunis made after the cartoons done by Jan Cornelisz Vermeyen for the Emperor's splendid tapestry series depicting this campaign.[25] From these debuts Hogenberg would go on to establish a long-running printmaking and map-publishing business in Cologne, one of whose chief specialties was its "*sehr gekauft*" historical series and illustrations of current events.[26] Castellin's bile surely rose when he

---

24 "Kurtzer begriff/desjenigen was sich in Franckreich seidther dem Todt des Konigs heinrichs der zweite/Anno M. D. Lix. und folgends bey regierung des Francisci der zweite/ und Karle der neundte/ biss an das Jar 1569. in Kriegshandlung unnd sunst zugetragen hat/ allhie mit Figuren/ so zuvorens auff Frantzosisch in 30. stuck/ jetzt mit weiterm bescheid/ dieweil etliche Figuren unnothig und vergeblich/ in 23. stuck in unser Teutsche Sprach verfasset und transferiert." Bibliotheek Arnhem, kl 254; UB Rostock, Rb 4654; Fritz Hellwig, *Franz Hogenberg—Abraham Hogenberg: Geschichtsblätter* (Nördlingen, 1983), catalogue entry18a.

25 *Messkataloge Willers*, I, 366 (in the section of the catalogue devoted to copper engravings and books containing pictures): "Begriff desjenigen/so sich in Franckreich/seither dem tod Konig Heinrichs des Andern/bis: in das 1570. jar in Kriegshandlung un sonst zugetragen/ mit Figuren zuvor in 23. stuck aussgangen/ jetzt aber mit 10. notwendigen stucken gemehret"; "Kurtzer begriff dessen/so sich im Niderland in Religionssachen und sonst/von dem 1566. jar/ biss auff das 1570. jar/ zugetragen hat/ ordenlich mit Figuren und schrifflich an tag geben/ in 19. Tafflen"; "Verzeichnuss wie Keyser Carolus der Funfft in Africa dem Konig von Thunis mit Kriegsrustung zu hulff kompt/ mit schonen Figuren furgebildet." These different series may all be clearly identified within Hellwig, *Hogenberg*, the definitive study and catalogue of Hogenberg's historical series and views of current events. For the source for his Tunis series, see Hendrik J. Horn, *Jan Cornelisz Vermeyen: Painter of Charles V and His Conquest of Tunis* (2 vols., Doornspijk, 1989), pp. 130-1, 164. The Fall 1570 catalogue is the only Frankfurt fair catalogue in which the Tortorel and Perrissin series of 40 plates ever appears.

26 Hermann Weinsberg, cited in Hellwig, *Hogenberg*, p. 14. For further biographical details on Hogenberg, see also Vollmer, *Allgemeines Lexikon der bildenden Künstler*, s.v. "Hogenberg," XVI, 306-8; Ilja M. Veldman, "Keulen als toevluchtsoord voor Nederlandse

FIGURE 3. Frans Hogenberg after Jean Perrissin, *The Massacre of Vassy*, 1570, etching, 20 × 28 cm, Rijksmuseum (Amsterdam), Rijksprentenkabinet, 309 J 4 fo. 24. Like all of Hogenberg's copies after Tortorel and Perrissin, this closely follows the original (plate 11 in Part 2) but reverses the image in printing it. Here, Hogenberg has also introduced a label into the scene not found in the original, incorrectly identifying the figure leaning on the wall in the right of the scene, the Cardinal of Guise in the original, as his brother the Cardinal of Lorraine. The caption is far more explicitly partisan than that accompanying the Tortorel and Perrissin woodcut. It reads: "On March 1 those of the reformed religion of Vassy are attacked and fatally struck down with frenzied rage and ferocity, men, women and children without distinction. This conformed to the heart's desire of the Cardinal of Lorraine. March 1 1562."

learned from his agent in Frankfurt that copies of his project had been brought to market almost as quickly as his own originals.

The assertion in Hogenberg's 1570 title page that his series published in 23 plates "in our German tongue" reproduced views previously set out in French "in thirty pieces" also raises an intriguing and heretofore unsuspected possibility, namely that even before completing all forty prints of the full

kunstenaars (1567-1612), *Oud Holland* 107 (1993), 42-6. Karel Kinds ed., *Kroniek van de opstand in de Lage Landen, 1559-1609* (n.p., 1999) is a modern facsimile edition of all 228 prints Hogenberg would ultimately produce about the Revolt of the Netherlands.

series, Castellin and his associates sold earlier sets of the prints with fewer plates. Further evidence also suggests this. First, a valuation of Castellin's house and most important business assets made on February 6, 1570 shows that at this date prior to the occurrence of the final event narrated in the *Quarante Tableaux* he already had multiple copies of a book of histories in stock in his workshop. Offering us a fascinating peek inside the shop on the rue des Allemans, this document lists a series of assets that Castellin mortgaged as collateral to his sister-in-law Gertrude Le Vignon to obtain a three-year extension of his still outstanding debt to her of 1201 livres.[27] The majority of what is listed pertained to his spinning business and included four "mills equipped with everything needed to spin thread", large quantities of flax and cordage, and other tools. But Castellin also mortgaged:

- 4 "presses for printing etchings . . . with the letters . . . used for that purpose" worth 70 livres tournois;
- 47 copper plates (it is not indicated if they are etched or not) worth 200 livres;
- 200 reams of paper "for printing" worth 30 sous per ream, or 300 livres;
- 70 additional reams of white paper for unspecified use worth 24 sous per ream, or 84 livres;
- and 100 "printed books of histories" worth one livre apiece, or 100 livres.

Since the *Wars, Massacres, and Troubles* is the only publishing project in which Castellin is known to have been involved, these "printed books of histories" must have been sets of this work completed at some point before February 6, 1570, i.e. before the last event shown in the full set of forty prints and probably before most or all of the prints that bear the date 1570 were completed.

Still more support for the hypothesis of early editions with about thirty prints comes from the old albums containing prints from the series. Only 16 of the 37 old albums that I have located contain all 40 prints from the series. Ten contain between 34 and 39 of the prints and are worn volumes that seem simply to have lost one or several sheets over the years, if they were not always slightly incomplete.[28] Two contain small groups of the prints within much larger *receuils factices*. But among the remaining nine incomplete volumes, all of which contain 25 to 31 scenes from the series, a clear pattern of absences emerges. As Table 2 reveals, five of these albums lack the same ten scenes. A sixth, containing 31 scenes, lacks all of the same scenes expect one. The recurrently absent scenes are:

Plates 2 *The Mercuriale Where Anne Du Bourg Was Arrested*
5 *The Execution of Anne Du Bourg*
8 *The Estates-General of Orléans*
12 *The Massacre of Sens*

---

27 AEG, notaire P. Cusin, II, fos. 126-30. See also notaire P. Cusin, III, fos. 65-8, 83, 85-6.

28 Five of these albums have 39 prints, two have 38, and one each 37, 35, and 34.

30 *The Siege of Chartres*
34 *The Siege of Poitiers.*
37 *The Siege of St Jean d'Angély*
38 *The Capture of Nîmes*
39 *The Foiled Attempt on Bourges*
40 *Montbrun's Crossing of the Rhône.*

With the exception of scene 5 *The Execution of Anne Du Bourg*, all of these are plates that bear the date 1570 within the image. The tenth scene dated 1570, and the only one that does not turn up missing very often in these incomplete old albums, is plate 36 *The Rout at Moncontour*. Another striking feature also characterizes all six old albums with 25-31 prints that lack these particular scenes: they begin with the page addressed "To the Reader" ("Au Lecteur", "Al Lettore", "Lectori"), rather than the usual title page. By contrast, the other three albums with 25-31 prints, lacking different prints, begin with the title page but do not contain this note to the reader. This is true as well of the great majority of the more complete old albums. In all, 21 old albums begin with the title page, 10 with the page addressed "To the Reader"; 5 have neither. Bibliographers have previously assumed that full sets of the series were supposed to contain both the title page and the longer preface. In fact, only one old album contains both. This is an unusual volume in an eighteenth-century binding that seems to have been made by a collector interested in obtaining multiple states or versions of the different prints in the series, since it includes 47 prints in all.[29] It would thus appear that the page addressed "To the Reader" and that which begins "First Volume containing Forty Tableaux" were two successive title pages.[30] The producers of the series first made the decorative border and inserted the address "To the Reader" within it as an introductory plate for sets of less than forty prints that they sold. Then, after making additional plates and deciding to wrap up the volume, they placed a new title beginning "First Volume containing Forty Tableaux" inside the border, and began to use this as their title page. They probably did this a little while after finishing the fortieth print, since four old albums with 39-40 prints also begin with the page addressed "To the Reader".[31] Only later collectors eager to acquire variant states from the series purchased both.

---

[29] BN, Rés La 21-7 beta.

[30] It can be observed that the decorative border is consistently more worn in impressions of the latter than of the former, as we would expect if this was the case.

[31] Two of these cases where an old album with a full or nearly full set of the prints opens with the page addressed "To the Reader" also suggest that the series was produced and marketed in two stages. In BM Lyon, Rés 22036, the scenes that follow "To the Reader" are not arranged in the usual sequence. Instead, 28 scenes follow one another in chronological order down to the two views of the battle of Moncontour, then the volume jumps back to the first scene chronologically in the series, *The Mercuriale Where Anne Du Bourg Was Arrested*. Nine more scenes follow, once again arranged in chronological order, to take the

TABLE 2
Scenes Missing from Incomplete Old Albums Containing 25-31 Prints

Volume	Number of Prints in Volume	Missing Prints	Front Matter/ Language
Arsenal 331	30	2, 5, 8, 12, 30, 34, 37-40	Au Lecteur/French
Toulouse Rés A XVI 27	30	2, 5, 8, 12, 30, 34, 37-40	Au Lecteur/Latin
UB Rostock Rb 4654	29	2, 5, 8, 12, 15, 30, 34, 37-40	Au Lecteur/Latin
SUB Bern Kp II 47	28	2, 3, 5, 8, 12, 16, 30, 34, 37-40	Au Lecteur/French
BN Florence	25	2, 5, 8, 10, 11, 12, 14, 27, 30, 34, 36-40	Au Lecteur/Italian
Mazarine 5921E	31	2, 8, 12, 30, 34, 37-40	Au Lecteur/French
Metropolitan Museum NY	28	3, 4, 5, 7, 8, 10, 11, 14, 16, 30	both*/French
Real Biblioteca Madrid	29	29, 30, 32-40	title page/French
BPF André 1154	25	1, 2, 3, 5, 8, 9, 12, 27, 32, 34, 36-40	neither/French

* Au Lecteur apparently inserted subsequent to the original binding.

story down to the final print from the set, *Montbrun's Crossing of the Rhône*. (One scene is missing from this volume: plate 15 *The Capture of Montbrison*.) The ten scenes placed at the back of this volume are again scenes 2, 5, 8, 12, 30, 34, 37, 38, 39, and 40. In Zentralbibliothek Zurich, Graphische Sammlung, R 54, all of the scenes that follow "To the Reader" are arranged in the usual order for full sets of the series, but the numbers inserted in a sixteenth-century hand in the upper right hand corner of the prints do not run from 2 to 40. (The first page was not usually numbered.) Instead, they run from 2 to 30, occasionally being left off some of the prints in the volume. They end with *The Rout at Moncontour* as print 30. A second, later hand has inserted different numbers on most of the prints that lack these numbers. These once again include the same prints that most often turn up missing in the incomplete volumes: scenes 2, 5, 8, 12, 30, 34, 37, 38, 39, and 40.

The early editions of the print series with fewer than forty sheets and the title page addressed "To the Reader" were made with titles and captions in Italian and Latin as well as French. The Italian version may have been one of the very first sets made, for the sole surviving set of the prints in Italian contains just 25 plates.[32] These are the only 25 plates from the series known to exist with titles and captions in Italian.[33] This set lacks all of the massacre scenes from the full series as well as the plates that also show up missing in the other early editions, probably a conscious omission for sets made for the Italian market. It also ends with just the first of the two scenes of the battle of Moncontour, *The Battle Order at Moncontour*. Since the second view of Moncontour, *The Rout at Moncontour*, bears the date 1570, it may be that this set of the prints was completed and sold before the end of 1569.

The surviving old albums with the prints in Latin contain 29 or 30 plates including *The Rout at Moncontour*. This suggests that they were offered for sale a short while later, early in 1570. As with the Italian version, no impression of any of the other scenes with titles and captions in Latin has ever been described, nor has the title page. The only editions of the prints every issued in Latin thus contained at most thirty prints. Some of the French sets of the prints with about thirty plates were probably also made during the first few months of 1570. Over the subsequent months, those responsible for the series then added scenes at the beginning, middle, and end, and decided to make versions of this fuller corpus for sale to a German- as well as French-speaking public. All known sets of the prints in German appear to have been made after the switch to the "First Volume" title page, since they all contain this page. No page addressed "To the Reader" in German has ever been found. The eight surviving old albums of the prints in German also all contain more than 30 plates, nearly always close to 40.[34] The versions addressed to different international publics were made at different times and had different contents.

The set of forty plates that Castellin shipped to the fall 1570 Frankfurt book fair must have struck discerning buyers as a surprising mélange, for—extraordinarily among sixteenth-century print series—it mixed the discernibly dif-

---

[32] These prints are all bound within a larger "raccolta Lafreriana", or composite atlas, in the Biblioteca Nazionale, Florence, described in detail in Fabia Borroni Salvadori, *Carte, piante et stampe storiche delle raccolte lafreriane della Biblioteca Nazionale di Firenze* (Rome, 1980), pp. 52-62.

[33] The only other bound set of the prints with titles and captions in Italian ever known to have surfaced, one sold by a Parisian bookseller in 1863, contained 24 prints, a coincidence that suggests that no more than 25 of the plates were ever published with titles and captions in Italian. For the reference to this set, see Dufour, "Vie de Tortorel et de Perrissin," pp. 2-3, n. 11. No version of any other print from the series other than those found in the volume in Florence has ever been described with a title and caption in Italian.

[34] Five contain all 40, one 39, one 38, and one 34.

ferent media of woodcuts and etchings. The July 1569 contract with Tortorel and Perrissin to produce an etched version of the history clearly did not, as most previous students of the series have tended to assume, end the carving of woodcuts for the series. Six woodcuts bear evidence of Tortorel's participation and must have been made after he was brought on board.[35] Two bear the date 1570. One of these, plate 37 *The Siege of St Jean d'Angély*, exists only as a woodcut. The other, version b of plate 3 *The Tournament at Which Henry II Was Fatally Wounded*, was also made as an etching. Down to the very end of the production process, then, the artists made woodcuts as well as etchings, producing some prints in only one medium and others in both. Yet they never made a complete series of all forty prints in either medium. Five of the scenes exist only in woodcut form. Twenty-three exist only as etchings. Twelve were made in both media. One never encounters an early album of the series that does not contain impressions in both media.

It would also seem that throughout the spring and summer of 1570 woodcut versions continued to be produced of certain prints made initially as etchings. This is suggested by the fact that old albums with the early editions of approximately thirty prints typically contain no more than six woodcuts. Later sets of forty most often contain fifteen or sixteen, with woodcuts having replaced a number of etchings found in the editions of thirty. This argues in favor of the hypothesis that Le Challeux was kept on after the signing of the July 1569 contract and continued working throughout the first eight months of 1570, although he did not add the date "1570" to any woodcut that did not contain this as part of the signature of the original design. As additional wood blocks were completed, they replaced the copper plates.

Since those responsible for the series kept on making woodcuts down to the end of the production process, their surprising failure to complete the series in either medium may derive from a lack of concern about the difference in appearance produced by the two techniques. They certainly came to realize that their etched plates had a limited lifespan. Four copperplates were reworked with an engraver's stylus after a number of impressions in order to extend their useful life. An entirely new plate with tiny changes in the decor of the room was made for scene 9 *The Colloquy of Poissy*.[36] But the clearest implication of the fact that both woodcuts and etchings continued to be made throughout the production process but no full series was ever made in either

---

35 See Table 1.

36 The reworked plates are number 13, *The Capture of Valence*; 19, *The Second Charge at Dreux;* 20, *The Third Charge at Dreux*; and 33, *The Battle of La Roche-L'Abeille*. These variant states are described in Michel Hennin, *Les monuments de l'histoire de France. Catalogue des productions de la sculpture, de la peinture et de la gravure relatives à l'histoire de la France et des Français* (10 vols., Paris, 1856-63), IX, 41, 52, 53, 119. For the differences between the two versions of scene 9, see the note on this plate in Part 2.

FIGURE 4. Jean Perrissin, *The Tournament at Which Henry II Was Fatally Wounded*, 1570, etching, 32 × 50 cm, BPU, Ba 4538 Rés. Comparison of this with the following image shows how closely the artists copied the original when making woodcuts after etchings. In this instance, letters have been introduced into the woodcut (Figure 5) for a key that was never printed. This is the only instance of such a modification among the 12 scenes made as both woodcuts and etchings.

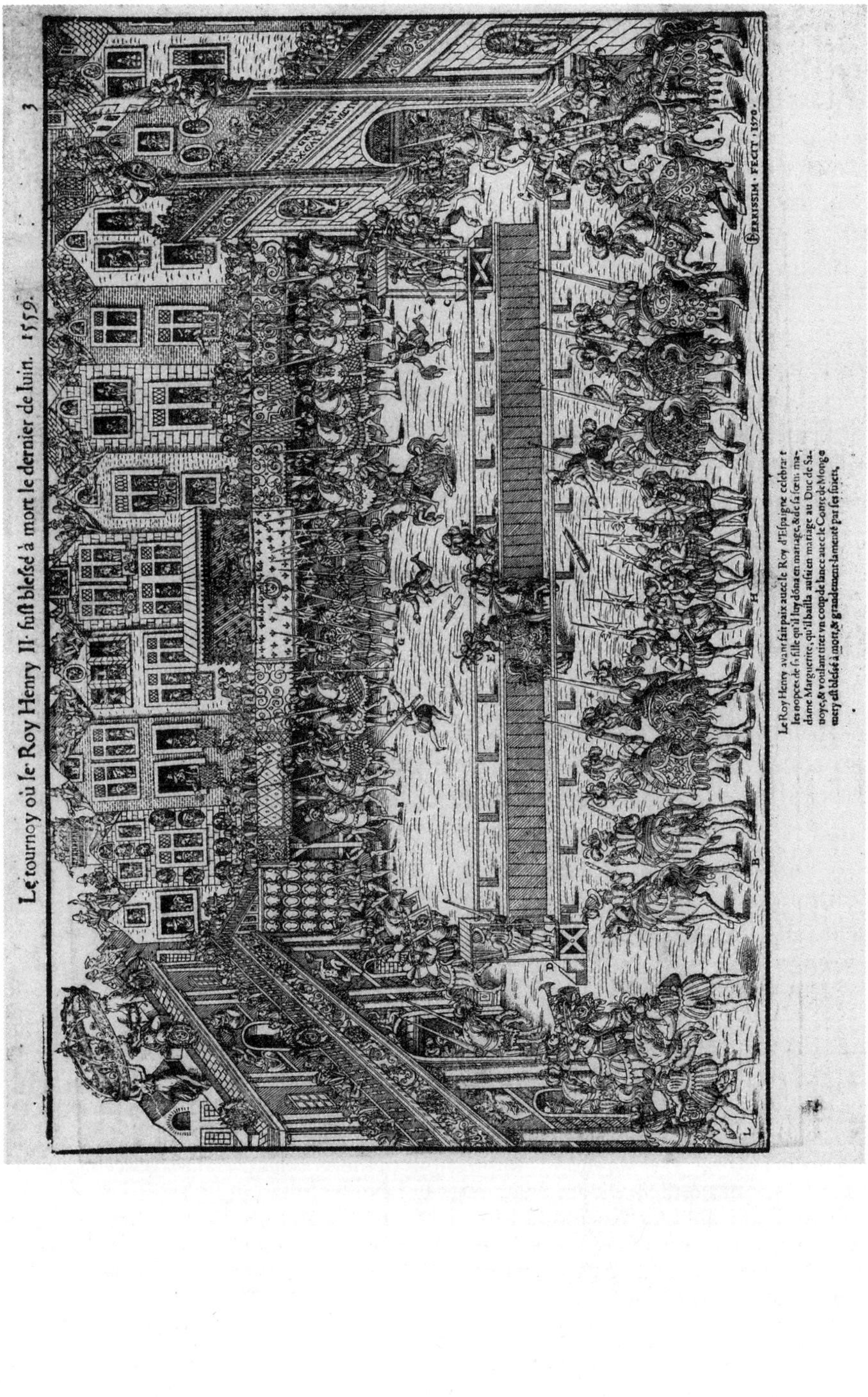

FIGURE 5. Woodcut version of Jean Perrissin, *The Tournament at Which Henry II Was Fatally Wounded*, 1570, woodcut, 32 × 50 cm, BN, Estampes, Ed 9 Rés, Cliché Bibliothèque nationale de France.

medium is that Castellin and his associates had little experience in organizing and completing a major print publishing project. They had to learn and improvise as they went along. Later print publishers faced with the task of making a large number of prints for a series of battle scenes from a just-concluded war learned to spread the work out among large team of artists in order to finish it expeditiously. Castellin did not have the luxury of doing this in artist-poor Geneva, even if he did turn to Jean II de Gourmont to help out with at least one woodblock.

Close attention to the prints shows us that trial and error in fact dominated almost every aspect of the making of this series. Especially eloquent are the surviving impressions of the three different plates made of print 3 *The Tournament at Which Henry II Was Fatally Wounded*. The craftsmen working on the project made a woodcut version of this print that provides a close-up view of the fatal encounter at the tilting barrier between Henry II and Gabriel de Lorges, count of Montgomery (scene 3a in the back of the book), set the type for it, and ran off at least five different printings. They produced, also as a woodcut, a second, different view that depicts the encounter between the two contestants in exactly the same way but sets this within a wider view of the tournament arena. Again they set type and produced some impressions. They also made an etched version of this second scene, which they evidently considered their version of choice, since it is the one that appears in all old albums. Having printed multiple copies of the two woodcut versions of the scene, however, they did not want to waste the paper. They turned over the sheets they had previously printed and printed other scenes on the back of them. When one encounters either of the two woodcut versions of this print today, it is almost always printed back to back with another scene from the series—any one of at least eleven different scenes.[37]

The producers also experimented with the format of the accompanying title and caption. In the large majority of cases, the caption took the form of a key tied to letters within the print. In some, it took the form of a brief descriptive prose legend. The two scenes of individual Protestants being executed (numbers 5 *The Execution of Anne Du Bourg*; and 26 *The Execution of Poltrot de Méré)* have only a descriptive legend in all known impressions. Three scenes (numbers 14 *The Massacre of Tours*; 15 *The Capture of Mont-*

[37] Instances of such back to back printing may be found in the BN, Estampes; Arsenal 212; UB Amsterdam, OF 79-1; BM Lyon, 24601; LC, Rosenwald 1074; and Free Library Philadelphia, Art dept. P769 T63. Scenes that I have seen printed on the back of this print are numbers 11, 14, 17-24, 30, and 40. Impressions of the woodcut versions of scene 3 without another print on the back are much rarer but can be found in BN, Rés La 21-7; the British Museum; and LC, Rosenwald 1074. Dufour, "Vie de Tortorel et de Perrissin", p. 3 n. 11, also records a version of scene 7 *The Execution of Anne Du Bourg* printed back to back with scene 24 *The Fatal Wounding of the Duke of Guise*. I thank Cécile Galinier for calling this detail to my attention.

brison; and 24 *The Fatal Wounding of the Duke of Guise*) have legends in some printings and keys in others. Scene 8 *The Estates-General of Orléans*, has both a letter key and a brief legend. In the woodcut of version b of the *Tournament at Which Henry II Was Fatally Wounded*, letters appear within the image, as if the artist making the plate expected a key to be set beneath it, but the block was printed with a legend instead. The same is true of one printing of *The Massacre at Tours*. A consistent format was never created for all of the prints in the series.

Other than vacillating between using letter keys and prose legends, the producers of the series rarely changed the text accompanying each image when they made new printings or translated the titles and captions from one language to another, but rare states have been described of two scenes that depart markedly from all others in this regard. The prints in question are scene 26 *The Execution of Poltrot de Méré* and version a of scene 2 *The Mercuriale Where Anne Du Bourg Was Arrested*. In both rare states, the caption takes the form of a pair of verse quatrains rather than a letter key or descriptive prose legend. Verse accompaniments are quite common in other print series or books of emblems from this era. Hogenberg would use them for his historical series. These, however, are the only two scenes from this series for which such legends have been described.

These legends depart from the norm for the series in another way too. All of the other French titles and captions accompanying the prints are striking for their sobriety of tone and neutrality of terminology. The sensationalizing adjectives so often found in the titles of news prints from this era—"horrible", "cruel", "wondrous", "glorious", "gruesome"—never appear, even when the scene in question is a massacre. The same sobriety carries over into the translated titles as well with a single exception: the "massacre of Vassy" becomes in German the "horrible slaughter (*grueliche wurgerey*) that occurred in Vassy". The titles and captions likewise strain to avoid partisan party labels, to the point where they often fail to identify at all the religious affiliation of the warring sides or of the victims of an incident of violence. Battles are most often said to involve "two French armies". Twice the Protestant forces are described as the prince of Condé's army. The term of choice for the Protestants, relatively rarely used, is "those of the religion", a label they would have preferred to "Huguenots" or "those of the so-called Reformed religion". Even this is a far cry from the language of many contemporary works, where it is not uncommon to find Protestant authors opposing "Christians" and "Papists" and Catholic authors labeling the Protestants "heretics". This extreme restraint suggests strongly that the makers of the series hoped to transcend confessional divisions and sell their prints to Catholic as well as Protestant buyers.

The two verse legends by contrast position themselves at the far extreme of Huguenot partisanship. Thus, where the prose caption found with most printings of *The Execution of Poltrot de Méré*, simply informs the viewer,

"Seigneur Jean Poltrot called du Meray is drawn by four horses and dismembered in the Place St Jean en Greve in Paris for killing Monsieur de Guise before Orléans," the verses invite the viewer to sympathize with the assassin being executed and laud his deed for hastening the end of the First Civil War:

> "O hideous spectacle! Cruel ingratitude/ Repaying a great deed with such harsh punishment/ Poltrot is imprisoned for being/ The reason why so many people could live in freedom.
> Life is cruelly torn from him/ for saving the lives of so many/ Poltrot is dismembered for reuniting/ all Frenchmen who were enemies."[38]

Earlier Huguenot writings of 1563-1564 had similarly hailed the assassin as a divinely inspired David whose slaying of Goliath brought peace back to France.[39] The verse legend of *The Mercuriale Where Anne Du Bourg Was Arrested* is equally partisan, equating Protestantism with the cause of the Gospel and casting the king's imprisonment of Anne Du Bourg, the outspoken judge who urged the moderation of anti-heresy laws, as a choice of force over reason and divine law:

> The king sat amid his assembled court/ To deliberate in the matter of Religion,/ Hoping that force and persecution/ Might finally cripple the Gospel.

---

[38] O spectacle hideux! Cruelle ingratitude
Payant un grand bien faict d'une peine si rude
Poltrot est prisonnier par ce qu'il a esté
La cause à tant de gens de vivre en liberté.

La vie est à Poltrot cruellement ravie
Parce qu'il a sauvé de tant de gens la vie
Poltrot est desmembré par ce qu'il a remis
En un tous les Francois qui estoyent ennemis.

[39] The *Petit traitté des guerres civiles advenues en France sous les Roys François II et Charles IX* ([Lyon], 1564), pp. 59-60, likens Poltrot to a "petit David encontre Goliad, meu & mené d'un courage du tout voué au bien public, & sentant en soy une vocation speciale à ce faire, jointe avec la volonté de Dieu, & authorité du magistrat, pour la juste defence du pays." The collection of occasional poems made by the Parisian doctor François Rasse de Noeux includes several verses similarly praising Poltrot, as for instance:

"Mon cher enfant, par qui la paix retourne en France,
Qui n'as d'un si haut fait autre bien attendu,
En souffrant ce tourment contre ton esperance,
Les loyer t'en sera ès deux mondes rendu.

Un jour ne sera plus la France opiniastre:
Lors elle te sera mère, et non plus marastre,
Te faisant vivre entier à la posterité.

P. Tarbé, *Receuil de poésies calvinistes (1550-1566)* (2nd ed., Reims, 1866; repr. Geneva, 1968), pp. 143-55, esp. 143.

> Then Du Bourg remonstrated that all human force/ Was vain against God and his Law,/ For having well spoken he was sent to prison:/ Giving rein to force and not to reason.[40]

These verse legends may have been first runs of an alternative, never completed version of the series aimed at committed Protestant buyers. They may have been special versions of these two prints made for sale as single sheets. Whatever the intention behind them, they appear to have been an experiment that the producers of the series did not judge worth continuing. These versions of these prints never appear in the old albums containing the series and are extremely rare in general. Only one printing of each has ever been described. For the series as a whole, the creators strove to preserve as value-neutral and matter-of-fact a tone as possible in the accompanying text to ensure salability to a wide audience.

Not only did the makers of the series fail to create a consistent format for the text accompanying the *Quarante Tableaux*; after running off multiple printings of the different plates, they got the idea of inserting numbers in the titles to help buyers and bookbinders put the prints in the correct order. Since these typeset numbers appear in only one or two printings of every scene from the series, it would appear that this idea came to them relatively late. Many complete sets of the prints are found in old albums without these typeset numbers.

The producers' lack of experience in producing a print series of this sort is also revealed by their poor quality control of the printing process. When woodcuts were printed with letterpress text, the type was set above and below the wood block, and the entire sheet was printed in a single go. In the case of the etchings, text and image were each printed separately on different presses. Those responsible for coordinating the printing of words and images were quite careless about how they aligned the sheets here. The text and the image often overlap slightly or are set askew. In composing the type for the titles, the printers also got different battle scenes confused and mislabeled or misnumbered scenes in several printings. Occasionally, their confusion is understandable. The series contains more than one image of several battles and scenes of two different battles that took place near towns named "Cognac" or "Cognat".[41]

---

40 Le roy fut au milieu de sa cour assemblée
Pour aviser au faict de la Religion,
Esperant que la force et persecution
Rendroient finalement l'Evangile accablee.

Lors du bourg remonstra que toute force humaine
Contre Dieu et sa Loy ne peut estre que vaine,
Mais pour avoir bien dit, on l'envoye en prison:
Donnant lieu à la force et non à la raison.

41 At least two printings of plate 31 *The Battle Order at Jarnac* bear the title that should have been placed above the next image in the series, *The Battle of Jarnac*. One previously

Less pardonable was the mistake made in setting the title for one of the two versions of *The Colloquy of Poissy*, which places Theodore Beza's address to the assembled prelates in December, rather than September, 1561. The technical quality of certain of the etchings also left much to be desired. Most egregious is plate 23 *The Siege of Orléans*, where the acid was allowed to burn the copper for so long that one almost never encounters a good impression of the scene. Despite this, the makers of the series did not see fit to etch another version of the same scene or replace it with a woodcut.

One of the hardest things to determine is when the various printings were made, since the blocks or plates used in printmaking can outlive their creators and be re-utilized decades or even centuries later. Some of the wood blocks from Tortorel and Perrissin certainly survived into the seventeenth century, for Théophile Dufour, the learned librarian who first found most of the archival documents pertaining to the series, reported seeing a late set of ten of the woodcuts that he estimated from the spelling used within their titles to date from around 1650.[42] Among these was an impression of scene 7 *The Executions at Amboise* that re-labels this "*The Escalade*" (figure 6). As print publishers are known occasionally to have done, whoever now owned the block had re-cycled it to show a more recent event, the punishment meted out to the soldiers involved in the duke of Savoy's ill-fated attempt to seize Geneva by night in 1602. As we have already seen, one wood block (illustrated above, p. 25) still survives.[43] The fate of the copperplates is unknown. They do not appear in the record of the sale of the possessions remaining in the estate of Castellin and Le Vignon carried out over a year after Nicolas Castellin's death, which suggests that they may have passed immediately to Le Vignon's sister Gertrude and her heirs, since they were among the objects offered as

undescribed impression of plate 22 *The Retreat from Dreux* that may be found at the British Museum is mislabeled *The Fourth Charge at Dreux*. A large portion of the key was omitted from some printings of the *Battle Order at Jarnac.* Once those in charge of the project got the idea of numbering all 40 prints sequentially, the compositors put the wrong number on scene 32 *The "Battle between Coignac and Chasteauneuf"* (i.e. Jarnac), confusing it with scene 29 *The Battle at "Cognat near Gannat in Auvergne"*. Most of these errors are described in Robert-Dumesnil.

42 Dufour, "Vie de Tortorel et de Perrissin," p. 11. The scenes in question are numbers 3 *The Tournament at Which Henry II Was Mortally Wounded* (both versions), 4 *The Death of Henry II*, 7 *The Executions at Amboise*, 11 *The Massacre of Vassy*, 14 *The Massacre of Tours*, 15 *The Capture of Montbrison*, 24 *The Fatal Wounding of the Duke of Guise* 26 *The Execution of Poltrot de Méré*, and 37 *The Siege of St Jean d'Angély*.

43 It may be found today in Geneva's Musée d'Art et d'Histoire, Cabinet des Estampes, inv. E/M644. For its provenance see Waldemar Deonna, "Un bois gravé de J. Perrissin (XVIe siècle) au Musée de Genève" in *Mélanges Louis Bosset* (Lausanne, 1950), p. 19. Other wood blocks from the series may yet slumber in an attic somewhere. Alain Dufour, a leading historian of sixteenth-century Geneva and the grandson of Théophile, recounts that when his father was a boy, a peddler who claimed to have many blocks from the set for sale came to his house looking to sell them to his grandfather. The elder Dufour was out. The peddler promised to return, but never did.

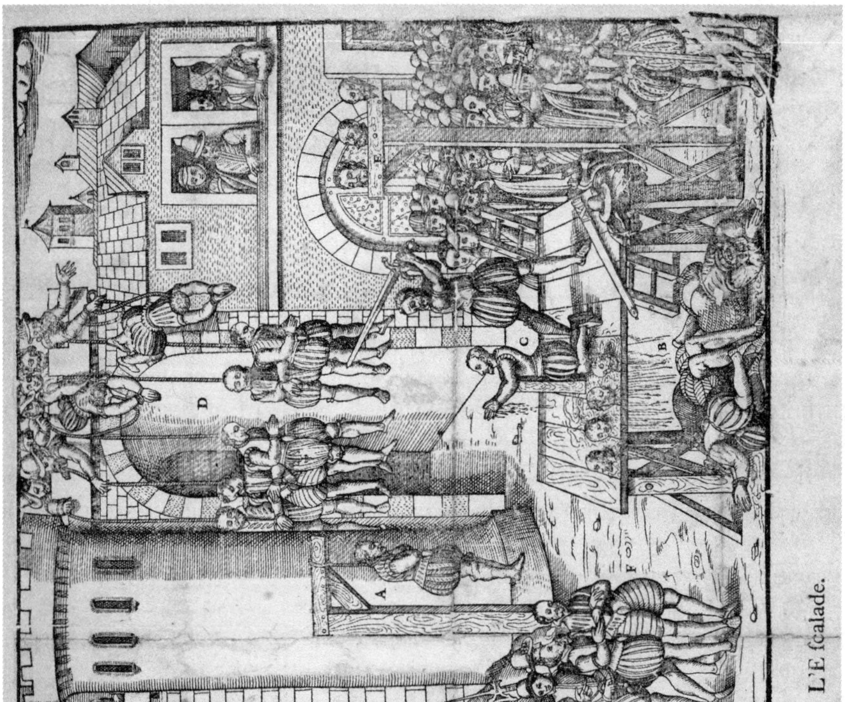

FIGURE 6. Jean Perrissin, *The Executions at Amboise* labelled as *The Escalade*, c. 1650, woodcut, 32 × 50 cm, BPU, Ba 4538 Rés, photo Jean-Marc Meylan. The cracks in the margin and image in the lower right corner betray how worn the wood block was when this impression was made.

collateral in their February 1570 debt renegotiation[44] Or they may simply have been worn past the point of exhaustion in 1569 and 1570.

The blocks and plates for the series certainly got intensive use in those years, for massive quantities of paper can be determined to have moved through Castellin's workshop in 1569-70, enough to produce thousands of copies of the prints. Castellin's first contract with his paper supplier, François Chautemps, dated July 12, 1569, called for the delivery of 400 reams of paper over the next eight months (i.e. through March 12, 1570) at a rate of at least 50 reams per month.[45] As we have seen, he still had 200 reams of paper "for printing" and another 70 reams of less expensive "white paper" in his shop on February 6, 1570, when he offered this as collateral in renegotiating his debt to his sister-in-law. He may still have been expecting one or two more deliveries from Chautemps as well. Despite this ample stock, he felt compelled to buy another 30 reams of paper of higher quality a few weeks later.[46] Three months after this, on May 20, he bought still another 100 reams of the paper of the initial quality ordered from Chautemps.[47] A ream of paper contained from 480 to 500 sheets, enough to produce 12 full sets of the 40-print series, or 16 of the 30-print series. Castellin bought at least 530 reams of paper. Unless he was using much of it for his thread production, reselling it to other printers, or using his presses to produce other prints of which no trace survives today, his consumption of so much paper suggests a total production of more than 6,360 copies of the series.

For a long time, experts in the history of printmaking would have scoffed at the possibility that so many copies could be pulled from etched plates. Some older works on etching, relying on the testimony of modern artists concerned about impression quality, indicate that etchings begin to lose their bite after as few as fifty impressions. The standard recent works on Renaissance printmaking agree that printers could make up to 2,000 copies of an engraving by reworking the plate after a thousand impressions, but that etchings rarely produced half as many good impressions.[48] However, new evidence

---

44 AEG, Juridiction Civil H 1 a, 7, unfoliated register, entries for November 13-15, December 1, 4, and 10, 1572. This document is discussed further below. The credit for discovering it and understanding its importance belongs to Liliane Mottu-Weber, who very kindly brought it to my attention and helped me to make sense of it.

45 Dufour, "Vie de Tortorel et de Perrissin," p. 9.

46 *Ibid.*, p. 9. It might be thought that this costlier paper was intended for a deluxe edition of the prints, but I have not detected an old album that I could confidently say contained a higher quality of paper from most. On the contrary, within certain old albums clear differences can be detected between successive prints in the weight of the paper used.

47 AEG, notaire A. Santeur, VI, fo. 417 v.

48 Landau and Parshall, *The Renaissance Print*, p. 31; David Woodward, *Maps as Prints in the Italian Renaissance: Makers, Distributors and Consumers* (London, 1996), pp. 47-8; Michael Bury, *The Print in Italy 1550-1620* (London, 2001), p. 47. No less an authority than Christopher Plantin warned one associate considering using engraved illustrations,

from the Plantin-Moretus archives reveals that this printing house used one frequently reworked set of engraved plates to produce more than 18,000 copies of the title page of Caesar Baronius's *Annales ecclesiastici*.[49] It drew 3,000 impressions from a set of etched copperplates used to illustrate Justus Lipsius' *De cruce libri tres*.[50] To judge from the poor quality of many of the surviving impressions of the Tortorel and Perrissin etchings, its makers sought to wring as many copies as possible from their plates. The evidence of the paper flows through Castellin's shop may provide additional evidence that etched plates could provide more impressions than experts long believed possible. It also argues for the possibility that the producers of the series worked the plates to the point of exhaustion, which would mean that most or all surviving copies of the prints, or at least of the etchings, were made in 1569-1570 rather than at a later date.

From the minor differences that have been described in the typeface, spelling, and alignment of the titles and captions accompanying each print, it is clear that each scene was printed anywhere from four to eleven different times. Only one printing with accompanying text in Italian is known for the 25 prints from the series for which an Italian version has been described. Two printings have been described for some, but not all, of the scenes in both German and Latin. French versions of the prints were printed anywhere from three to seven times depending upon the specific image. (See Table 3.) Even in the old albums in which the size and type of the titles above each plate is the most consistent, full sets of the prints never display identical typefaces throughout the entire volume. This suggests that the printers made a sizeable number of copies of each image as it was completed, then accumulated these in their shop and assembled them together into sets for sale as demand required, rather than setting the type for and printing all of the scenes from the series at the same time. As they exhausted their supply of one image or another, they set the type needed to accompany it again and printed more copies. If entire sets of the full volume had been run off in coherent editions of fixed size, we would expect to find far less variation between the number of printings of the different individual images than we in fact find, and far more coherence in appearance within early bound sets of the prints than these display.

"one must consider that the plates for such illustrations can yield no more than 1,000 impressions of the illustration before the plate is worn out." Cited in Karen L. Bowen, "Illustrating Books with Engravings: Plantin's Working Practices Revealed," *PQ* 20 (2003), 3.

49 Karen. L. Bowen and Dirk Imhof, "18,257 Impressions from a Plate," *PQ* 22 (2005), 265-78. I would like to thank the authors for kindly providing me a copy prior to publication.

50 Karen. L. Bowen and Dirk Imhof, *Plantin and the European Book Market: Introducing Engraved Illustrations in the Sixteenth Century* (forthcoming Cambridge, 2007). Again my thanks the authors for providing me a copy of the relevant pages of this book prior to publication.

Table 3. Media, Languages, and Printings

Print	Medium		Languages				Number of Printings			
	woodcut	*etching*	*French*	*Italian*	*Latin*	*German*	*French*	*Italian*	*Latin*	*German*
1. Title Page		X	X			X	5			1
1a. *To the Reader*		X	X	X	X		2	1	1	
2a. *Mercuriale* version a		X	X				1			
2b. *Mercuriale* version b		X	X			X	4			1
3a. *Tournament* version a	X		X		X		4		1	
3b. *Tournament* version b	X	X	X	X	X	X	6	1	1	1
4. *Death of Henry II*	X		X	X	X	X	4	1	1	1
5. *Execution of Du Bourg*	X		X			X	3			1
6. *Conspiracy of Amboise*	X	X	X	X	X	X	4	1	2	2
7. *Executions at Amboise*	X		X	X	X	X	3	1	1	2
8. *Estates General of Orléans*		X	X			X	5			2
9. *Colloquy of Poissy*		X(2)	X	X	X	X	7	1	1	2
10. *Massacre of Cahors*	X	X	X		X	X	4		1	2
11. *Massacre of Vassy*	X		X		X	X	4		1	2
12. *Massacre of Sens*		X	X			X	3			1
13. *Capture of Valence*		X	X	X	X	X	4	1	1	2
14. *Massacre of Tours*	X	X	X		X	X	6		1	1
15. *Capture of Montbrison*	X	X	X	X	X	X	7	1	1	1
16. *Battle of St Gilles*		X	X	X	X	X	4	1	1	2
17. *Battle Order Dreux*		X	X	X	X	X	5	1	1	1
18. *1st Charge Dreux*	X	X	X	X	X	X	5	1	1	1
19. *2nd Charge Dreux*		X	X	X	X	X	6	1	1	1
20. *3rd Charge Dreux*	X	X	X	X	X	X	7	1	1	1
21. *4th Charge Dreux*		X	X	X	X	X	4	1	1	1
22. *Retreat Dreux*		X	X	X	X	X	6	1	1	1
23. *Siege of Orléans*		X	X	X	X	X	3	1	1	1
24. *Wounding of Guise*	X	X	X	X	X	X	6	1	1	2

Print	Medium		Languages				Number of Printings			
	woodcut	*etching*	*French*	*Italian*	*Latin*	*German*	*French*	*Italian*	*Latin*	*German*
25. *Peace near Orléans*		X	X	X	X	X	5	1	2	2
26. *Execution of Poltrot*	X	X	X	X	X	X	5	1	1	2
27. *Michelade*		X	X		X	X	4		2	1
28. *Battle of St Denis*	X	X	X	X	X	X	4	1	1	2
29. *Battle of Cognat*	X	X	X	X	X	X	5	1	1	1
30. *Siege of Chartres*		X	X			X	5			1
31. *Battle Order Jarnac*		X	X	X	X	X	4	1	1	1
32. *Battle of Jarnac*	X	X	X	X	X	X	5	1	2	1
33. *Battle of La Roche*		X	X	X	X	X	3	1	1	2
34. *Siege of Poitiers*		X	X			X	3			2
35. *Order Moncontour*		X	X	X	X	X	4	1	1	2
36. *Rout at Moncontour*		X	X		X	X	4		1	2
37. *Siege St Jean d'Angély*	X		X			X	4			1
38. *Capture of Nîmes*		X	X			X	3			1
39. *Attempt on Bourges*		X	X			X	3			1
40. *Crossing of Rhône*		X	X			X	4			1

Sources: Four reference works provide relatively complete lists or catalogues of the prints in the series: Jacques-Charles Brunet, *Manuel du Libraire et de l'amateur des livres* (5th ed., Berlin, 1922), V, 892-4; Michel Hennin, *Les monuments de l'histoire de France. Catalogue des productions de la sculpture, de la peinture et de la gravure relatives à l'histoire de la France et des Français* (10 vols., Paris, 1856-63), VIII, 390-IX, 129; Robert-Dumesnil, X, 258-84; and Haag, *La France protestante* (2nd ed.), III, cols. 463-7. None is entirely complete or trustworthy. The most extensive and reliable are Hennin, whose comments display the most acute scrutiny of the largest number of impressions, and Robert-Dumesnil, the only work to attempt a catalogue raisonné describing each printing or state. This table combines the information from all of these works, corrected and supplemented in light of my own examination of numerous copies of the prints. The data given about the number of printings in different languages generally follows Hennin, which appears more complete than Robert-Dumesnil. Where Robert-Dumesnil describes a larger number of printings than Hennin, his listing has been used. None of the authorities cited records the existence of any of the views from the series with Italian titles other than page addressed "To the Reader". The existence of the scenes listed here in that language is reported in Fabia Borroni Salvadori, *Carte, piante e stampe storiche delle raccolte lafreriane della Biblioteca Nazionale di Firenze* (Rome, 1980).

This raises a further set of questions. If the sheets were printed one by one, were they meant primarily for sale as full sets, or did the producers expect to sell many of them singly? If they were intended for sale as sets, were buyers expected to buy all thirty or forty prints in the series at once, or could they select those subjects from the series of particular interest to them, forming albums of their own composition? This latter practice was how certain graphic publications of the years around 1570 were marketed. The atlases and views of ancient monuments produced by Antonio Lafréry in Rome at this time had no fixed contents. Buyers selected the maps and views that pleased them from Lafréry's ample stock and had them bound with the engraved title page he supplied. Each volume was a *unicum*.[51] Suites of prints with title pages at this time were thus not necessarily fixed entities in the same way that modern books are. Might the buyers of Tortorel and Perrissin similarly have determined which prints they wanted to include in their copies of what might not have been exactly forty *tableaux*?

Two bits of archival evidence suggest that the prints were sold both singly and as sets, but the latter was more common. First, the list of objects that Castellin offered as collateral for the renegotiation of his debt to Gertrude Le Vignon makes no mention of any quantities of individual sheets from the series. It does, however, list 100 "printed books of histories" valued at one livre tournois apiece. This suggests that the prints were seen as having value primarily when assembled into complete books. Second, the record of a posthumous sale of Castellin's possessions shows that individual images from the series were sold in small batches, but in smaller quantities and at lower prices than complete sets.

This melancholy remainder sale took place between November 13 and December 10, 1572, more than a year after Castellin's death, after his creditors had obtained a judgment against his heirs to have the remainder of his and his partner's possessions sold at auction to satisfy their claims.[52] Most of the items sold were household possessions, including an impressive stock of arms, two horses, and furniture and clothing for both adults and children in substantial quantities. A few remaining items from the spinning enterprise also fell to the auctioneer's candle. Only in December did the authorities get around to selling off what remained in the way of books and prints. This included 250 copies of the *Quarante Tableaux* that were sold in small lots for between 9 s 3 d and 12 *sols de Savoye* per volume; nine *mains* of "*papiers figurés*" (a *main* contained 25 sheets of paper) sold for just under 2 *sols* apiece;

---

51 Woodward, *Maps as Prints*, p. 43 For another graphic publication of slightly later date for which buyers chose the pieces they wished to have included, see Ilja Veldman, *Crispijn de Passe and His Progeny (1564-1670): A Century of Print Production* (Rotterdam, 2001), pp. 161-5.

52 AEG, Juridiction Civil H 1 a, 7, unfoliated register, entries for November 13-15, December 1, 4, and 10, 1572.

and 35 "*pourtraictures*" sold for 2 *deniers* each.[53] If we assume, as seems probable, that the *pourtraictures* were individual sheets from the *Wars, Massacres, and Troubles*, substantially more copies of the complete set were sold than individual prints from the series. Furthermore, while the price obtained for the full volumes was less than half the amount at which they had been valued in the 1570 inventory—one Savoyard florin of twelve *sols* was worth just under a half a *livre tournois* in 1572[54] —it was still more on a per print basis than the price obtained for the sheets sold individually. (At two *deniers* a sheet, forty prints would have cost 6 s 8 d.) The record of this sale also appears to confirm that the producers of the series had packets of individual sheets from the series in their shop—not to mention a sizeable stock of unsold copies of full sets of the series two years after it was first completed.

The surviving old albums of the prints also suggest that contemporary buyers more often acquired full sets of the prints than assembled selections of their own. If they had regularly followed the latter course, we would expect that old albums with less forty prints would contain widely varying numbers of prints from the series, and that these would often be organized in a manner that reflected the owner's particular interests or outlook. As we have seen, the number of prints found in most old albums clusters around either 30 or 40, and in many sets with fewer than 40 prints the same plates turn up missing time and again. Only a few albums hint at the prints from the series having been selected to fit a particular interest or point of view. Where this is the case, it seems that their purchasers often did this by discarding a few sheets from the set, rather than by acquiring the sheets one by one according to their preferences.[55]

---

53 The books are variously listed in the inventory as "*livres de portraictz de guerre*", "*livres de portraictures*", or "*livres des portraictures des guerres*", but since they are always estimated prior to sale at the same price per volume, we can be confident that they are the same work, the *Wars, Massacres, and Troubles*. Most of the copies sold were acquired by the solicitor overseeing the sale. The bookseller Reymond Savyon also bought fifty copies for his stock, and a few individual buyers bought one or two copies for prices ranging from 10 s 6 d to 12 s. The only other remnants of Castellin and Le Vignon's foray into the printmaking business disposed of at this sale were a tray of letters, a broken roller press, a *lavoir d'imprimerie* and approximately four reams of paper. No books that might have belonged to either merchant's personal library went under the hammer. Their creditors did receive six sous for two objects that might have been either prints or cheap paintings, one representing the Spanish Inquisition and the other the seven liberal arts.

54 For an explanation of the monetary systems in use in sixteenth-century Geneva and a table of exchange rates, see Mottu-Weber, *Genève au siècle de la Réforme*, appendix 7, pp. 476-7.

55 BM Lyon, Rés 24014 contains just five scenes of sieges and battles from the last part of the print series (plates 34 and 36 through 39) inserted along with a number of older maps and city views from other sources between sheets from Bouguereau's 1594, *Le theatre françois ou sont comprises les chartes generales et particulieres de la France* in order to make a composite atlas of its owner's own assembling. These five prints are all among those produced in 1570 that report the most recent events from the ongoing civil war. Is this a clue that

Conclusion

While the full implications of some of the findings of this chapter will only become clear once we have delved more deeply into the historical narrative provided by the *Quarante Tableaux*, the story of the project revealed here has already moved us closer to a better understanding of the series and its makers' intentions. The prints were clearly conceived of as a series from the start and seem most often to have been sold as a series, but their creation was not guided throughout by a single, experienced hand. Instead, the project was the work of a committee, many of whose members had little or no prior experience with a project of this sort. It grew and changed in the course of production. Throughout, hesitation, experimentation, and reconsideration left their marks on it.

The initial contract makes it clear that the merchants responsible for the series were supposed to provide the artists working on it with a "history and its circumstances" that the artists were to transform into pictures, but it is impossible to know how detailed a preliminary version of the story the merchants in fact furnished the artists, and what form this history took. Since it can be doubted whether two Netherlandish textile merchants were sufficiently well informed about current French events to write or sketch a detailed history of it themselves, one may also suspect that they also turned for help to some of the numerous refugee pastors or men of letters who crowded into Geneva at this time with tales to tell about events back home. They may have expected the artists to assemble some of the information themselves from their eyewitness experience or from others they encountered in Geneva. The precise contribution of each person who worked on these prints to their ultimate content and design cannot be determined with certainty. The preliminary note addressed "To the Reader" may speak in the first person singular, but this was standard piece of rhetoric designed to win the reader/viewer's confidence.

---

these prints were sold separately as current events prints or in smaller sets for those who wanted to add them to those they had already acquired? Maz., Rés 5921F contains fourteen of the plates from the series within a mélange of current event prints and a few depictions of Jerusalem in biblical times. The bound volume in the Metropolitan Museum of Art's Prints and Drawings collection (classified under the artists' names) moves quickly from the Mercuriale scene to the Conspiracy of Amboise to the Colloquy of Poissy and then to the battle scenes of the civil wars, skipping most (though not all) of the massacres suffered by the Protestants. Might this have been a set assembled by an attentive and partisan Catholic? BM Lyon, Rés 24601 omits from an otherwise complete set of the prints with typeset numbers two of the events that certain Protestants might be most ashamed of, the Conspiracy of Amboise, and the capture of Montbrison, where dozens of Catholics were thrown to their death from a tower by the bloody baron des Adrets. Was this a set winnowed by a Protestant owner? These are the only old albums that suggest conscious choice on their owners' part.

Although the first contract implies that the initial "history and its circumstances" existed in some tangible form, verbal or visual, the initial project did not envisage precisely forty plates. Early sets of the series were printed with about thirty plates and sold with a frontispiece "To the Reader" explaining the work's intention. Latin and Italian as well as French versions were prepared of this shorter series. The series was then expanded to forty plates over the course of the winter and spring of 1570. Some of the new plates depicted events that had occurred after the initial contract for the series was signed, serving to keep it current. Others added episodes to the beginning and middle of the series. Only once these changes were made did those responsible for the prints declare the series complete and produce the title page announcing the work as the *First Volume Containing Forty Pictures*. This full set went through multiple French printings and was made with German titles and captions as well.

Not only were additional plates added in the course of production; the entrepreneurs responsible for it changed media in midstream. After starting with woodcuts, they shifted to etchings after a few months, continued to make woodcuts as well, and never completed all forty sheets in either medium, so that complete sets of forty prints always mix woodcuts and etchings. They also struggled to find the best format for their series, tried different experiments, and never settled upon a single definitive structure for the relationship between text and images to be employed throughout the series. Errors marred many printings.

For all these hesitations and alterations, one thing remained constant throughout the roughly sixteen months during which work proceeded on the project: the entrepreneurs backing it had to face serious reverses in their other business dealings. They consequently sought to maximize the commercial potential of this project. They experimented briefly with versions of two of the prints with highly partisan verse captions aimed at the niche market of committed Huguenots, but this experiment does not seem to have lasted long. The full sets of the prints in old albums never include impressions with these captions. Except in these two instances, the accompanying legends carefully avoided partisan party labels and used a sober rhetoric of unembroidered description. This suggests that the producers sought to reach an international, multi-religious audience, as does the fact that the produced versions in four languages. The sets produced for different linguistic markets also appear to have been tailored to appeal to the market in question. Thus, the Italian version of the series omits the massacre scenes, predominantly scenes of Huguenot victimization. In an age when information increasingly was seen to have commercial value, commercial considerations powerfully guided this series.

At the same time, the additions made to the series in the course of production suggest that other considerations and perhaps other voices also contributed to the final selection of scenes composing it. The new scenes added at the beginning and middle of the series transformed the meta-narrative sketched by the series as a whole. The early versions of about thirty scenes would have begun with the sudden, accidental death of Henry II. In putting before this the scene of the Mercuriale at which Anne Du Bourg protested against Henry II's harsh treatment of heresy and suffered imprisonment for speaking out, and in adding as well a representation of Du Bourg's subsequent execution, the additions made in the winter and spring of 1570 created a chronicle that opened with an act of royal injustice against a courageous Protestant man of the law and implied a measure of divine retribution in the king's death that followed so soon thereafter. The initial sequence of the prints would then have shown the tumult of Amboise and the repression that followed it, the Colloquy of Poissy, and a number of massacres of Protestants that precipitated the descent into violence. In inserting scenes of the Estates-General of Orléans and the massacre of Sens into this sequence, the additions reinforced the contrast between a short-lived period of attempted conciliation and consultation with the political nation and a season of Catholic violence that touched off the civil wars. Furthermore, the massacre of Sens was one of the two episodes of anti-Protestant violence from the spring of 1562 that most aggrieved the Reformed at the time. One of the conditions that hard-line Protestant ministers wanted to see inserted in any peace agreement in 1563 was that justice be done for this event as well as for the massacre of Vassy. These changes so clearly re-tailor the narrative of the *Wars, Massacres and Troubles* to conform with what we might call the orthodox Protestant version of the origins of the Wars of Religion that one wonders if prominent advocates of the cause did not urge these changes on Castellin and his team.

While hesitations, changes of direction, and multiple ambitions marked the *Wars, Massacres and Troubles*, they decidedly did not condemn it to failure. The prints in the series were reprinted up to eleven times and appear to have been run off in extraordinarily large quantities. Indeed, the series received the highest possible compliment for a printed work of this era: it was immediately pirated by another etcher-entrepreneur. An experimental work that bears many of the marks of having been made by a group of artists and entrepreneurs with little experience in the production of print series, "Tortorel and Perrissin" was nonetheless a sufficiently original, informative, and intriguing experiment to attract numerous buyers and inspire copyists and imitators.

Did it also offer Nicolas Castellin a lifeline to solvency as he struggled to satisfy his creditors amid the commercial disruptions of the civil wars? The standard monograph on the Genevan book trade in this era by Hans Joachim Bremme suggests that it did. Bremme asserts that the venture earned Castellin and Le Vignon nearly 100 per cent profit on an original investment of about 3,500 livres tournois—enough to pay off their debt to Gertrude Le

Vignon several times over.[56] This is not certain. Bremme's estimates contain a number of mistakes, since he missed several critical documents, misinterpreted others, and did not understand all of the details about the project's elaboration. Appendix 2 spells out his calculations in detail, subjects them to criticism, and attempts to offer a more accurate estimate of just what Castellin and Le Vignon invested in the project. As those who consult this appendix will see, the fixed costs the entrepreneurs incurred in purchasing a set of copper plates and having them designed and etched, in paying for the design and carving of 18 wood blocks, and in purchasing presses and type with which to print the images can be estimated to have amounted to about 865 livres tournois. Paper and printing costs for each 100 reams of paper, enough to produce 1,200 to 1,600 copies of the series, added up to another 460 livres. Their profit from the series would then have depended above all on the price they could get for each of their thousands of volumes. Bremme's optimistic evaluation of their profits derived from his acquaintance with just one of the two pieces of evidence that we have about the cost of a copy: the February 1570 valuation of possessions that Castellin offered Gertrude Le Vignon as collateral, which sets the value of each volume at one livre tournois. At that price, with fixed capital costs of 865 livres and production costs for each 1,200-1,600 copies of 460 livres, the associates would have been able to cover their total costs and perhaps obtain a small profit if they sold out the first 100 reams worth of copies at that price. For every subsequent 1,200-1,600 copies sold, they would have netted three times their production costs, or as much as 1,000 livres. But the 1572 sale of the goods remaining in the family's possession showed us that by this date full sets of the work only brought prices ranging from 9 to 12 sols de Savoie per set, at best the equivalent of half a livre tournois. (There were 20 sous in a livre.) If copies of the book brought no more than this from the start, the volume would only have become profitable once close to 400 reams worth of books, or more than 5,000 copies, were sold—an enormous number for a sixteenth-century book. Everything would have depended upon whether the producers were able to sell most copies of the work for a price close to their original estimate of the book's value, an estimate that may have been generous since it was made to secure a loan, or whether they only obtained prices like those they received in 1572, prices that may have been depressed by a glut of copies already on the market.

Castellin called his final version of forty plates the "First Volume", indicating that further series would follow. This may have been a sign of his confidence that his new venture was paying off. It may have been the bravado of a man eager to assure his creditors that all was well. In any event, the plague ensured that no second volume would ever appear. The disease could be

---

56 Bremme, *Buchdrucker und Buchhändler zur Zeit der Glaubenskämpfe*, p. 31.

pitiless when it took hold in a household, as it did in the big house on the rue des Allemans in the late summer of 1571. It killed three of Pierre Le Vignon's four children between August 7 and 19, then Castellin and three of his children between August 20 and 22, and finally his brother and factor Gilles on September 10.[57] The partnership of Castellin and Le Vignon was shattered. Even if it had not been, there is no guarantee that it would have been able to hire artists to produce more volumes of historical scenes in Geneva after 1571. Most of the Huguenots who had flooded into the city between 1567 and 1570 left once the Peace of Saint-Germain ended the civil war and restored their rights of worship in France. Among those who returned to France were Perrissin, Tortorel, and Le Challeux.

[57] Dufour, "Vie de Tortorel et de Perrissin," p. 8n.

CHAPTER 2

THE ARTISTS

As the preceding chapter has shown, making the *Quarante Tableaux* involved collaboration among the entrepreneurs who launched it, the artists who drew and carved the prints, and perhaps other, unidentified individuals who offered information incorporated into the series. Since the producers of the series may have given the craftsmen considerable leeway in figuring the events and may even have expected them to gather some of the information about them, the lives of the four artists who participated in the project become relevant to understanding the final work. If they had resided in any of the places depicted or lived through any of the events represented, their personal experience could have conferred on the prints the eyewitness authority they claimed. The extent of their prior experience as history painters would have shaped the manner and skill they brought to the project. Finally, even if much recent work in art history has shown that the Romantic vision of art as the truest expression of its creator's convictions and experience applies at best awkwardly to the early modern era, and that, for example, Jörg Breu produced Catholic images in his workshop for more than a decade after embracing Zwinglianism, while Pierre Eskrich carved the ebulliently anti-Catholic *Mappe-Monde Papistique Nouvelle*, then promptly returned to the Roman church, the zealousness of the artists' attachment to the Huguenot cause could also have influenced how they drew the scenes. Personal religious convictions certainly shaped the art of other sixteenth-century artists.[1]

---

1 Andrew Morrall, *Jörg Breu the Elder: Art, Culture and Belief in Reformation Augsburg* (Aldershot, 2001), p. 195; Rondot, "Eskrich," p. 327; Joseph Leo Koerner, *The Reformation of the Image* (Chicago, 2004); Volker Manuth, "Denomination and Iconography: The Choice of Subject Matter in the Biblical Paintings of the Rembrandt Circle," *Simiolus* 22 (1993-4), 235-52; Menna Prestwich, "Patronage and the Protestants in France, 1598-1661: Architects and Painters" in Roland Mousnier and Jean Mesnard eds., *L'Age d'or du mécénat (1598-1661)* (Paris, 1985), pp. 83-4; Christian Tümpel, "Jordaens, a Protestant Artist in a Catholic Stronghold: Notes on Protestant Artists in Catholic Centres" in *Jacob Jordaens (1593-1678)* (exhibition catalogue, 2 vols., Antwerp, 1993), I, 31-7; idem, "Die Reformation und die Kunst der Niederlande" in Werner Hoffmann ed., *Luther und die Folgen für die Kunst* (Munich, 1983), pp. 314-15; and for the efforts of the French Reformed churches to stop the fabrication of objects "tending toward idolatry": Jean Aymon, *Tous les Synodes*

Where had the prior careers of Jean Perrissin, Jacques Tortorel, Jacques Le Challeux, and Jean II de Gourmont taken them? How much experience did they have in print-making? How strong was their attachment to the Protestant cause? Biographical information about all four of these craftsmen is frustratingly thin. For some, it is practically nonexistent. Still, it is copious enough to enable us to follow at least some of their careers and to suggest answers to these important questions. Furthermore, the biographies of these four obscure artists do not merely illuminate the *Quarante Tableaux*. They also shed interesting light on the crafts of painting and printmaking in sixteenth-century France, reveal the kinds of artists who got involved in early printmaking projects such as this, and offer a fresh cut through the art of early Calvinism.

Jean Perrissin

Fortunately, Jean Perrissin, the artist with the largest individual role in the production of the prints, is also one of the best documented of the four.[2] Few artists in this period had the luxury of specializing in a single medium or genre, or even of focusing primarily on the kinds of objects that we today associate with the "fine arts" and that had already emerged by this time in Italy as the cynosure of the painter's craft, i.e. altarpieces, easel paintings, and frescoes. They also painted chimney fronts, shop signs, and bed enclosures, designed patterns for stained glass or tapestries, and painted temporary festival decors.[3] Perrissin was one such jack of all trades.

Perrissin's name first appears in Lyon's archives in 1561 on a list of inhabitants of the city's *pennonages*, or militia districts.[4] By the middle of that decade, if not before, he was connected with the city's Reformed church, as is

---

Nationales des Eglises Réformées de France (The Hague, 1710), I, 27, 73, 75; "Papier et registre du consistoire de l'église du Mans réformée selon l'évangile 1560-1561" in Anjubault and H. Chardon, *Recueil de pièces inédites pour servir à l'histoire de la Réforme et de la Ligue dans le Maine* (Le Mans, 1867), p. 7; Philippe Chareyre, "Le Consistoire de Nîmes 1561-1685" (thèse de doctorat, Université Paul Valéry Montpellier, 1987), pp. 571-2.

2 The documentation is assembled in Dufour, "Vie de Tortorel et de Perrissin" in Franklin ed., *Les grands scènes historiques*, pp. 3-7; Georges Guigue, "Jean Perrissin peintre lyonnais (1564-1608)," *Réunion des Sociétés des Beaux-Arts des départements* (1891), 429-60; and Audin and Vial, II, 108-9.

3 Guy-Michel Lepreux, *La peinture à Paris sous le règne de François 1er* (Paris, 2001), ch. 1; Anatole de Montaiglon ed., "Statuts de la corporation des peintres de Rouen," *Archives de l'Art Français, Documents* 6 (1858-60), 179ff; G. Guigue, A. Kleinclausz and H. Focillon ed., *Les dessins d'élève et notes de comptabilité de Jérome Durand, peintre et verrier lyonnais 1555-1605* (Lyon, 1924); Zerner, *L'art de la Renaissance en France*, pp. 237-46, 267-307; Peter Sharratt, *Bernard Salomon illustrateur lyonnais* (Geneva, 2005), pp. 25-30; *Hans Holbein the Younger: The Basel Years 1515-1532* (exhibition catalog, Basel, 2006), pp. 11-13.

4 AM Lyon, EE 24, fo. 23; Audin and Vial, II, 108-9.

shown by his first surviving drawings: sketches on the front and back of a sheet of paper bearing his signature that depict the oval exterior and beamed interior of the Temple du Paradis, the church that Lyon's Huguenots built for their own use on land purchased in May 1564, and that would be razed in September 1567 at the outbreak of the Second Civil War (figures 7 and 8).[5] Perrissin also is qualified occasionally in the Lyon records as an "*architecte*." It has been suggested that he may have had a hand in the design of this church.[6]

Together with the often reproduced painting that was also made of the interior of this church and that is frequently attributed to Perrissin as well,[7] these sketches offer one of the few surviving depictions of a purpose-built Reformed church from this era. The drawing of the interior shows the amphitheatre-like character of this auditorium for the word, with its tall pulpit pushed out from the circular wall and surrounded on all sides by benches. One of the front benches has a pew-like enclosure and seat back draped with a cloth that appears to have been embroidered with a coat of arms, perhaps indicating that the pew was reserved for civic officials or other dignitaries. With no service in progress, figures sit or stand around the building in pairs talking. From the second story, one gestures toward the tablets behind the pulpit reading "Tu aimeRA LE SEIGNEUR TON DIEU DE TOUT CŒUR", which are flanked by oval windows bearing the royal fleur de lys. The exterior view reveals stone ornamentation around the windows and doorways, as well as a double wooden staircase leading up to what the interior view shows to be a narrow balcony.

We do not know just when Perrissin moved to Geneva as a result of the Second and Third Civil Wars. His name has not been found in any Genevan archival documents from this period other than the two contracts pertaining to the print project. An etching nonetheless survives from this period that

---

5 AM Lyon, GG 86, piece 1 (réserve). This drawing was first discovered by Guigue and is discussed in his "Perrissin," pp. 434-6.

6 Audin and Vial, II, 108; Natalis Rondot, *Les Protestants à Lyon au dix-septième siècle* (Lyon, 1891), pp. 17, 174-6.

7 *Temple De Lyon, Nommé paradis*, oil on canvas, 123 × 125 cm, BPU, collection de portraits, bustes, miniatures et médaillons, inventory no. 179, now on display at the Musée international de la Réforme, Geneva. The attribution of this painting to Perrissin rests solely on his known authorship of the drawings. Close comparison of the drawn and painted interior views reveals numerous small discrepancies in their rendering of the building and in the decoration of the church, quite apart from the fact that the painting shows a service in progress with a newborn about to be presented for baptism. In the painting, a longer quotation from Matthew 2:2 is inscribed above the pulpit; the upper row of gallery windows also contain coats of arms in stained glass; the balcony doors have rectangular rather than arched frames as in the drawing; a second oval window not found in the drawing appears beside each door; the front pews are constructed differently and are draped with cloth bearing the fleur-de-lys rather than a coat of arms; the arrangement of benches in front of the pulpit is different; and the pulpit is covered by a canopy that is not visible in the drawing. These discrepancies call into question the attribution of the painting to Perrissin.

FIGURE 7. Jean Perrissin, *Exterior of the Temple du Paradis*, c. 1565, crayon and brown ink on paper, 17 × 25 cm, AM Lyon, GG 86, piece 1.

was not known by any of his previous biographers and that demonstrates that he did more work in that medium after making the *Quarante Tableaux* (figure 9). This depicts an elaborate fountain and basin that had been made for and sent to duke Casimir of the Palatinate, the German adventurer and ally of the Huguenots during the Second and Third Civil Wars.[8] The goldsmith who made it—and *orfèvres* were one of the trades whose members were drawn to the Reformed church in disproportionately large numbers in France—knew how to design objects that would have been appreciated at a German princely court of the era.[9] Beneath a castle perched on a crag take place many of the activities that made the fortunes and occupied the days of sixteenth-century

---

8 Perrissin, *Pourtraict de la fonteyne et Rochier faicte et envoyee au duc de Casemil*, etching, 32.5 × 23 cm [repositories: Kunstmuseum Basel, Kupferstichkabinett, Inv. Bi.46.75; Staatliche Museen zu Berlin: Preussischer Kulturbesitz, Kupferstichkabinett, no. 406-72].

9 For the world of the German princely courts, see John Adamson ed., *The Princely Courts of Europe 1500-1750* (London, 1999), chs. 6-8, 11; Helen Watanabe-O'Kelly, *Court Culture in Dresden: From Renaissance to Baroque* (Basingstoke, 2002).

FIGURE 8. Jean Perrissin, *Interior of the Temple du Paradis*, c. 1565, crayon, brown ink and gray wash on paper, 30 × 26 cm, AM Lyon, GG 86, piece 1.

German knights. Soldiers assemble and march. Miners extract the earth's riches. Hunters pursue their prey. At the base of the mountain, liquid spouts from the breasts of sirens into a surrounding basin decorated on its inner edges with chiseled waterfowl and mythological figures. Four satyrs and a pedestal hold up the entire vessel. If the object was a gift to Casimir from Geneva or the French Reformed churches, the etching was probably made as

FIGURE 9. Jean Perrissin, *Portrait of the Fountain Made for Duke Casimir*, 1570, etching, 32.5 × 23 cm, Kunstmuseum Basel, Kupferstichkabinett, Inv. Bi.46.75, photo Kunstmuseum Basel, Martin Bühler.

a record of the gift. It is signed with Perrissin's combination monogram-signature familiar from the *Quarante Tableaux* and bears the date May 1570. If Perrissin remained true to his bond and did not work on any other projects so long as he was employed by Castellin on the *Quarante Tableaux*, this would provide a slightly earlier terminal date by which he had finished drawing and etching the plates for the series than that year's fall Frankfurt book fair.

A gap of four years separates Perrissin's etching of this fountain from the next evidence we have about his activities and whereabouts, a payment to him for work on a civic ceremony in Lyon from 1574. He also appears in the 1575 Lyon tax records, assessed at the minimum tax of five livres, which marks him as a settled householder of modest means.[10] Not only did he return to Lyon. Like many Lyon Protestants of the 1560s, he also returned to the Catholic church. In 1577 he and his wife Simonde Meschin had their baby receive Roman baptism in the parish of St Pierre-le-Vieux. Six more of his children would be baptized in the parish of St Nizier after 1581.[11]

So far as we know, Perrissin remained in Lyon for the remainder of his life, even during the years from 1588 to 1594 when the city was under the domination of the Catholic League. He earned sufficient respect from his peers to be named guild master of the painter's guild six times between 1581 and 1611. The city hired him often for municipal projects. In 1580, he received 18 écus for painting the arms of the king and the city on the weathervane atop the Porte du Rhône, as well as for other unspecified painting and gilding work on the gate. In 1583, in preparation for a royal visit by Henry III, he earned 40 écus for work on the Hôtel de Ville and the Porte St George that included painting a submissive lion being received by the king on the wall of the *salle des pas perdus* of the Hôtel de Ville, an obvious allegory for the town's imagined relationship with the crown. Painting the eight-oared royal skiff used by the king as he travelled the Rhône with a new coat of orange paint for the boat and its oars, as well as golden fleurs de lys to decorate its satin canopy, earned him another 32 livres.[12] Three years later, he won a contract for 60 écus to work on the Porte Scize. Here he gilded the royal arms on the gate, stuccoed the archway and facades, painted two lions holding the royal arms on the facade, and finished the archway with a decorative black-and-white pattern.[13] Jobs like these paid well and guaranteed steady work. It took Perrissin seven months to complete this last job, but the payment equalled a

---

[10] AM Lyon, CC 1233; Dufour, "Vie de Tortorel et de Perrissin," p. 3; Guigue, "Perrissin," p. 440; Audin and Vial, II, 108.

[11] Audin and Vial, II, 108-9.

[12] *Ibid.*, II, 108; Guigue, "Perrissin," pp. 442-6. The next year he painted another royal vessel green and decorated its canopy with the royal motto, crowned H's, and fleurs de lys.

[13] Guigue, "Perrissin," pp. 447-9; Dufour, "Vie de Tortorel et de Perrissin," p. 12.

year's pay at the monthly salary he had accepted from Castellin and Le Vignon in Geneva in 1569.[14]

During the period of the League, his tasks changed character. He painted and gilded three crosses that had just been erected around the city, one on the tower of the Rhône bridge, one on the Boullevard d'Ainay, and one above the St Just gate. He painted designs for the standards and trumpets of a company of fifty light horse raised by the city to fight the battle against Henry of Navarre's accession. He surveyed and drew the ground plan of a rural property close to the city.[15] These were difficult times for artists, as for so many others.

Soon after Lyon submitted to Henry IV in 1594, Perrissin returned to the municipal council chambers to execute a portrait of the newly recognized king. He also was repeatedly hired to design and paint elements for civic entry ceremonies, as he had done prior to 1588 as well. He co-designed Henry IV's *joyeuse entrée* of 1595. Three years later he was one of three "master painters and directors of the celebratory fireworks" for the Peace of Vervins, working alongside François Stellaert or Stella, the father of the future *peintre du roi* and favorite of Richelieu, Jacques Stella. The work that went into these projects is revealed by an unsigned etching of the cortège and monuments for the 1595 entry (figure 10), which shows an array of temporary triumphal arches, colonnades, obelisks, statues, and columns made from paper maché that Perrissin would have painted and gilded. Perrissin may also have drawn the design for this etching, since as part of his contract he and his co-designer Jean Maignan agreed to portray the elements of the entry on "plates that would be subsequently cut for printing".[16] It is worth noting that while he or Maignan were asked to provide the drawing, the etching of the copper plate was left to others. The centerpiece of the 1598 peace celebration was a pyramidal "Tower of Confusion" crowned with the hydra of discord and bedecked with statues representing ambition, pillage, and other vices. This was towed to the middle of the Saône, set afire, and consumed (figure 11).[17] For both this and the 1595 royal entry Perrissin received the hefty fee of

---

14 In 1586 the écu was worth three livre tournois. Perrissin had been paid 15 livres per month in Geneva.

15 Antoine Pericaud, *Notes et documents pour servir à l'histoire de Lyon pendant la Ligue* (Lyon, 1844), p. 62; Guigue, "Perrissin," pp. 451-2.

16 The etching illustrates Pierre Matthieu, *Les deux plus grandes plus celebres et memorables resjouissances de la ville de Lyon* (Lyon, 1598). On this entry and its program, see Yann Lignereux, *Lyon et le roi. De la "bonne ville" à l'absolutisme municipal (1594-1654)* (Seyssel, 2003), pp. 57-65; Guigue, "Perrissin," p. 437; Audin and Vial, II, 108.

17 Matthieu, *Les deux plus grandes plus celebres et memorables resjouissances*; Lignereux, *Lyon et le roi*, pp. 66-8. The destruction of a hydra-headed figure symbolizing the discord and destruction of the League was central to other ceremonies of pacification at this time as well. Benedict, "Marmites and Martyrs," p. 163.

FIGURE 10. Anonymous, perhaps Jean Perrissin, *Henry IV's Joyous Entry into Lyon of 1595* from Pierre Matthieu, *Les deux plus grandes plus celebres et memorables resjouissances de la ville de Lyon*, 1598, etching, 25 × 36 cm, BM Lyon, Rés 116181.

one-and-a-half écus per day. The most lucrative of his commissions were not the most enduring.

The etchings of these two ceremonies and another made for the 1600 entry of Marie de Medici are the only known prints on which Perrissin may have collaborated after those of 1569-70. After working on the *Quarante Tableaux*, which he appears to have done when he was fairly young, he never undertook a similar project again. Instead, he went from drawing battle scenes that figure the standards of rival armies to painting actual standards for the Catholic League in Lyon. Even though he left the Reformed church, however, he evidently retained a lingering loyalty to it, for he made a number of small gifts to the church of Lyon during his later years. At least some of his children also absorbed Reformed convictions. Four of them were married as Protestants, either in Lyon or Geneva.[18] Perrissin died at an unknown date between 1611 and 1618.

---

18 Rondot, *Protestants*, p. 17; Dufour, "Vie de Tortorel et de Perrissin," p. 6.

FIGURE 11. Anonymous, perhaps Jean Perrissin, *The Tower of Confusion Consumed* from Pierre Matthieu, *Les deux plus grandes plus celebres et memorables resjouissances de la ville de Lyon*, 1598, etching, 36 × 23.5 cm, BM Lyon, Rés 116181.

Jacques Le Challeux

While Jean Perrissin returned to the Catholic church in the 1570s, the other artist hired in the first contract, the *tailleur d'histoires* Jacques Le Challeux, remained a steadfast, even militant, adherent of the Protestant cause for as long as he can be followed in the historical record. He probably paid with his life for his convictions.

An early convert to the Reformed faith, Le Challeux left his native Rouen to seek refuge in Geneva at an unknown date before 1556, i.e. prior to the great wave of Protestant conversion and migration that occurred during the years 1559-61. On February 10, 1556 he married in Geneva. His wife also hailed from Rouen. The couple had a child baptized in Geneva before the year was out, then evidently returned to France, for they do not reappear in Geneva's baptism records until 1569, during the Third Civil War.[19] Their movements during the intervening twelve years cannot be confidently traced, but they undoubtedly lived in Lyon at some point in the 1560s or early 1570s. This is shown by the only known example of Le Challeux's art other than the blocks he carved for the *Quarante Tableaux*: a polemical anti-Catholic print signed "A Lyon par Jaques Le Chaleux a larbre d'or pres confort" (figure 12).[20] The print is undated, but from its suggestion that the days of the Roman church are numbered, it would seem best to fit the Huguenot mood of the early 1560s.

Those Who Trust Satan Are Always Deceived utilizes the familiar motif of the tree of Jesse or family tree to depict the rotten fruit of the Roman church. Emerging from the bowels of a Pope amid the flames of hell, the tree bears on its branches a range of figures drawn with a parodic verve and a degree of skill in rendering facial features that surpasses anything seen in the *Quarante Tableaux*. Simoniacal cardinals, a begging bishop with a currycomb in his hat, a nun with an infant bishop in swaddling clothes, and friars brandishing meat, drink, and the overturned marmite that was the subject of another piece of French Protestant visual propaganda all blossom from the plant. The accompanying biblical passage is unsparing: "Every tree that does not bear good fruit is cut down and thrown into the fire." Two verses in a cartouche reiterate that the tree depicted does not come from God but must be uprooted and cast into the flames. In a further echo of the tree metaphor, the viewer is referred to Matthew 7, which contains the verse "by their fruits you will know them". The theme was not new in Protestant visual propaganda. A 1532 German woodcut by Erhard Schoen with text by Hans Sachs had already placed beneath the very similar phrase in Matthew 15, "Every plant which

---

19 Dufour, "Vie de Tortorel et de Perrissin," p. 7n.

20 *CELUY QUI EN SATAN SE FIE JAMES NEN A QUE TRONPERIE*, woodcut, 42.6 × 31 cm, Staatliche Museen zu Berlin: Preussischer Kulturbesitz, Kupferstichkabinett, no. 703-59; Audin and Vial, I, 494.

FIGURE 12. Jacques Le Challeux, *Those Who Trust Satan Are Always Deceived*, c. 1563, woodcut, 42.6 × 31 cm, Staatliche Museen zu Berlin: Preussischer Kulturbesitz, Kupferstichkabinett, no. 703-59.

my heavenly father has not planted shall be rooted up" a more complex allegory that includes four dead trees hung with the paraphernalia of Roman devotion about to be uprooted by God the Father and several angels.[21]

But of course the tree of popery did not fall in France. Instead, the confidence many Huguenots felt in the early 1560s that the Pope's days were numbered evaporated amid the renewed violence of the years 1567-72, especially the Saint Bartholomew's Massacre. Le Challeux himself was probably a victim of that 1572 bloodbath. A contemporary account of the massacre written by the Lyon minister Jean Ricaud, the *Brief and true account of the enraged, inhumane felony committed in Lyon by the roman catholics against those of the reformed religion*, lists among the slain "Iacques le Challeu, tailleur d'histoires, natif de Normandie." When this work was subsequently incorporated into Simon Goulart's 1582 revision of Crespin's *Book of Martyrs*, Le Challeux gained an enduring place in the pantheon of Huguenot martyrs.[22] The pamphlet may in fact have erred. The records of the Reformed church of Rouen show a Jacques Le Chaleur, occupation unknown, standing as godfather for a child baptized on April 3, 1579.[23] But the surname Le Challeur or Le Challeux was not uncommon in Normandy; there is no way of knowing if this was the same person as our tailleur d'histoires. In either event, whether martyred on not, Le Challeux remained loyal to the Protestant cause. Having previously carved scenes of massacre, he may have perished in one.

Jacques Tortorel

The life of Jacques Tortorel, the other principal draftsman of the plates, is exceptionally obscure. No other work from his hand is known. The limited biographical facts about him are these. Nine months before signing the contract with Castellin, he was already in Geneva, for he appears for the first time in Genevan documents as a witness to a will dated September 29, 1568. While he was drawing and etching plates for the *Quarante Tableaux*, a Flemish serving girl working for Nicolas Castellin, Anne de La Haye, caught his eye. They courted and were married on June 25, 1570, probably just around the time when work on the project was wrapping up. Perhaps the money Tortorel

---

21 *Christus spricht/ Ein yede pflantz die Gott mein hymelischer vater nicht gepflantzet had/ wide aussgereut und in das fewr geworffen/ Matthei XV*, woodcut, 39.5 × 36.5 cm, reproduced and discussed in Scribner, *For the Sake of Simple Folk*, pp. 190-92; W. A. Coupe, *German Political Satires from the Reformation to the Second World War* (7 vols., White Plains, 1993), part I, no. 58.

22 Jean Crespin, *Histoire des martyrs* ed. D. Benoît and M. Lelièvre (3 vols., Toulouse, 1885-8), III, 716, 712n; Dufour, "Vie de Tortorel et de Perrissin," p. 7n. I thank Pierre-Olivier Lechot for calling my attention to Le Challeux's inclusion in the *Book of Martyrs*.

23 AD Seine-Maritime, E, Protestants de Rouen et de Quévilly, 1574-85.

earned working on it was what enabled him to marry. After the Third Civil War ended, Tortorel returned to Lyon. His name appears on Lyon tax rolls in both 1572 and 1575. Since it was illegal to worship as a Protestant in Lyon in the latter year, he had almost certainly returned to the Catholic church.[24]

Jean II de Gourmont

Jean II de Gourmont, like Perrissin, is somewhat better documented. His career was different from Perrissin's, however, in that throughout his life he specialized in a single activity, printmaking and book illustration. Indeed, his expertise in this area was probably what led Castellin to call on him to lend a hand in the carving of the wood blocks for the series. De Gourmont was also different from all three of the other artists who worked on the project in a surprising way: no solid evidence ties him either to Geneva or to the Protestant cause. Either he was a very discreet Huguenot, or the makers of the series called in a Catholic colleague to help them complete their project.

Our Jean de Gourmont was the nephew or great-nephew of another, more famous artist of the same name, Jean I de Gourmont (1506-1551), a painter talented enough to merit several pages in Henri Zerner's standard work on French Renaissance art.[25] Jean II's father, Gilles de Gourmont, was a Paris bookseller. Jean himself, already identified as a "tailleur d'histoires", first appears in a document dated January 19, 1559, a partnership agreement with two Parisian book illuminators, Geoffroy Ballain and Jean Pignot, to share jointly in the costs and profits of whatever they might produce "in the form of portraiture and carving for printing and public sale" for as long as all parties cared to continue the association.[26] This must have been de Gourmont's first step in setting out on his own. Four years later, in December 1562, he married, as we know from a reference to the marriage contract in his inventory after death.[27] The document unfortunately does not tell us where the marriage was celebrated. Since the First Civil War was underway at that time and all Protestants had been ordered out of Paris, knowing this would have shed light on his religious preferences.

---

24 Audin and Vial, II, 266; Dufour, "Vie de Tortorel et de Perrissin", p. 7; Carl Brun ed., *Schweizerisches Künstler-Lexikon* III, 323-4. The detail that Anne de La Haye was a servant in the Castellin household escaped these previous authorities but is shown by AEG, Registres du consistoire 27, fos. 102, 103. Because de La Haye's parents were both dead and her guardian lived in Flanders "en la papaulté", de la Haye was called before the consistory prior to her marriage so that the body could be sure that she had consented to the match and that it met with the approval of those closest to her. The case record identifies Nicolas Castellin and Marie Le Vignon as her employers.

25 Zerner, *Art de la Renaissance en France*, pp. 326-8.

26 Catherine Grodecki ed., *Documents du minutier central des notaires de Paris: Histoire de l'art au XVIe siècle (1540-1600)* (2 vols., Paris, 1986), II, 218.

27 AN, Minutier Central XVIII/209; Préaud et al., s.v. "Jean II de Gourmont".

For most of the 1560s, de Gourmont certainly lived in Paris in the heart of the Latin Quarter, where he sold single sheet prints about current or recent events in addition to illustrating books. Two surviving prints show his activity in this domain and reveal his movements. The first, *The true portrait and account of the assembly of the three Estates held in Orléans by the magnanimous and most Christian king Charles IX in January 1561* (figure 13), advertises itself as being offered for sale in Paris by "Jehan de Gourmont, in front of the Collège Sainte Barbe et des Cholletz, and Jehan Pignot at the Silver Lion, rue Saint Jacques."[28] Although it depicts an event of January 1561, it may not have been made until 1564, since only in that year did a royal decree fix the convention of dating each new year from January 1 rather than Easter. At the time the Estates-General actually met, most contemporaries recorded the date as "January 1560".[29] By 1565 de Gourmont had moved. *The True Portrait of the Chateau of Tokay* [figure 14], showing the February 1565 capture of that Hungarian fortress from the Turks by Imperial troops under Lazarus Schwendi, bears the date 1565 and the address "Jehan de Gourmont, Rue S. Jehan de Latran, near the Collège de Cambrai."[30] It was copied from a Venetian news print about the same event by Domenico Zenoi.[31] De Gourmont would subsequently remain on the rue St Jean de Latran at the sign of the dry tree for the rest of the time that he lived in Paris. Several of his later prints bear this address, and his inventory after death shows that he was residing there when he died.

De Gourmont and his associate Ballain also took on jobs on contract for Christopher Plantin, the Antwerp publisher who himself had lived on the rue St Jean de Latran during his youth in Paris. Plantin's accounts show that in 1565 he paid de Gourmont 14 sous a block to carve a set of 55 drawings

---

28 *LE VRAY POURTRAICT ET DISCOURS DE l'assemblée des trois Estatz, tenuz en la ville d'Orléans, par le magnanime Roy de France Treschrestien, Charles neuviesme de ce nom, au mois de Janvier, mil cinq cens soixante & un*, woodcut, 50 × 35 cm, BN, MS Fr 10193, fo 17 bis. Two other versions of this print also survive (repositories: BN, Estampes, Ea.17.Rés; Brit. Mus., Foreign History, 1560), but they are trimmed so close to the margins of the image that it cannot be determined if they also bore Gourmont's name and address. The print could also have been sold not as an individual item but as a fold-out illustration to accompany a pamphlet such as *La description du plant du theatre faict à Orleans, pour l'assemblée des trois Estatz, avec un brief discours de la seance des tenans et representans lesdictz Estatz* (Paris: Vincent Sertenas, Gilles Corrozet, et Guillaume Niverd, 1560). The same observation applies to a second woodcut that Gourmont almost certainly carved as well about this event, a schematic diagram of the seating plan of the Estates, *Pourtraict du plant de la salle des estatz et de l'ordre et seance tenu en iceulx*, woodcut, 38 × 26.5 cm, BN, Estampes, Qb. 1 1560. Gourmont's authorship of this latter work is suggested by the fact that the type face used within it matches that of *LE VRAY POURTRAICT*. It too is trimmed tightly to the margins.

29 As do the makers of the print of the same event illustrated below, figure 27, p. 0.

30 *Le vray pourtraict du Chasteau de Thokay*, hand-colored woodcut, 35 × 24.6 cm, Royal Geographical Society, London, shelfmark 262.H.5.

31 Information kindly furnished via e-mail by Dr. Bela Szalai, Budapest, who is currently preparing a catalogue of early views of Hungary.

FIGURE 13. Jean II de Gourmont and Jean Pignot publishers, *The True Portrait of the Assembly of the Three Estates Held in Orléans*, c. 1564, woodcut, 50 × 35 cm, BN, MS Fr 10193, fo 17 bis, Cliché Bibliothèque nationale de France.

FIGURE 14. Jean II de Gourmont after Domenico Zenoi, *The True Portrait of the Chateau of Tokay*, 1565, hand-colored woodcut, 35 × 24.6 cm, Royal Geographical Society, London, shelfmark 262.H.5.

made by Ballain to illustrate the medical works of Jacques Grevin and 18 sous apiece to cut 72 illustrations by the same artist for *Reynier the Fox*. Although the document is not absolutely clear about this, it appears that de Gourmont and Ballain remained in Paris while they did this work.[32] If that was the arrangement that de Gourmont had with Plantin, it is possible that he made similar arrangements with Castellin for the work he did on the *Quarante Tableaux*. Such an agreement would reveal a surprising degree of commercial interaction between Paris and Geneva amid the disruptions of the Third Civil War. Alternatively, he could have been a Protestant who sought refuge in Geneva. However, his name has never been found in the Genevan records from the period 1567-70. Nor does any firm evidence tie him to Paris between his 1565 news print and his appearance on the capital's 1571 tax roll.

From 1571 until his death in 1598, de Gourmont remained in Paris except for a few years after 1589, when he left the capital amid the troubles of the League.[33] He served as a godparent at several Catholic baptisms from 1577 through April 1589, indicating his attachment to the Roman church. No further news prints like those of the 1560s are known to have issued from his shop, but he got intermittent work illustrating books,[34] and he built up a substantial print publishing business, making both woodcuts and copperplate engravings. His inventory after death, which identifies him as a "*maitre paintre tailleur d'histoires*", shows that he owned both roller and letter presses, a supply of type, 60 engraved copper plates, and more than 260 carved wood blocks. Much of his production involved devotional images, including many figures of saints, crucifixes, and other Catholic images. "One large Moses with the commandments the whole printed in six sheets" is the only such work that might have appealed primarily to Protestant buyers. De Gourmont also made ornamental borders, games ("le jeu de l'oye", "ung tarot de l'evangille"), a few portraits, and *drôleries* like the admonition to foolish mankind *Know Thyself* (figure 15). The inventory makes no mention of any books that he might have owned for his own use.[35]

---

32 A.J.J. Delen, *Histoire de la gravure dans les anciens Pays-Bas et dans les provinces belges des origines à la fin du XVIIIe siècle* Part 2 *Le XVIe siècle – les graveurs illustrateurs* (Paris, 1934), p. 131; Max Rooses, *Christophe Plantin, imprimeur anversois* (Antwerp, 1882), p. 280.

33 Préaud et al., s.v. "Jean II de Gourmont" (reference to the efforts of his landlord to collect unpaid rent from him because of his absence from Paris in the early 1590s).

34 Known illustrations by de Gourmont are the title border of Jean de La Taille, *La Géomancie abrégee* (Paris: L. Breyer, 1574); 2 plates in Jean Thevet, *Cosmographie universelle* (Paris: G. Chaudiere and P. L'Huillier, 1575); title border of Isaac Habert, *Les Œuvres poetiques* (Paris: Abel L'Angelier, 1582); title border of René Bretonnayau, *La Génération de l'homme et le temple de l'âme* (Paris: Abel L'Angelier, 1583); and multiple illustrations in Christophe de Savigny, *Tableaux accomplis de tous les arts libéraux*, one of which is reproduced in *The French Renaissance in Prints* cat. no. 149; Courboin, *Histoire illustrée de la gravure en France*, cat. no. 202. BM Lyon, catalogue des illustrations; Brun, *Livre français illustré de la Renaissance*, pp. 145, 233, 290, 301, 304.

35 AN, Minutier Central XVIII/209.

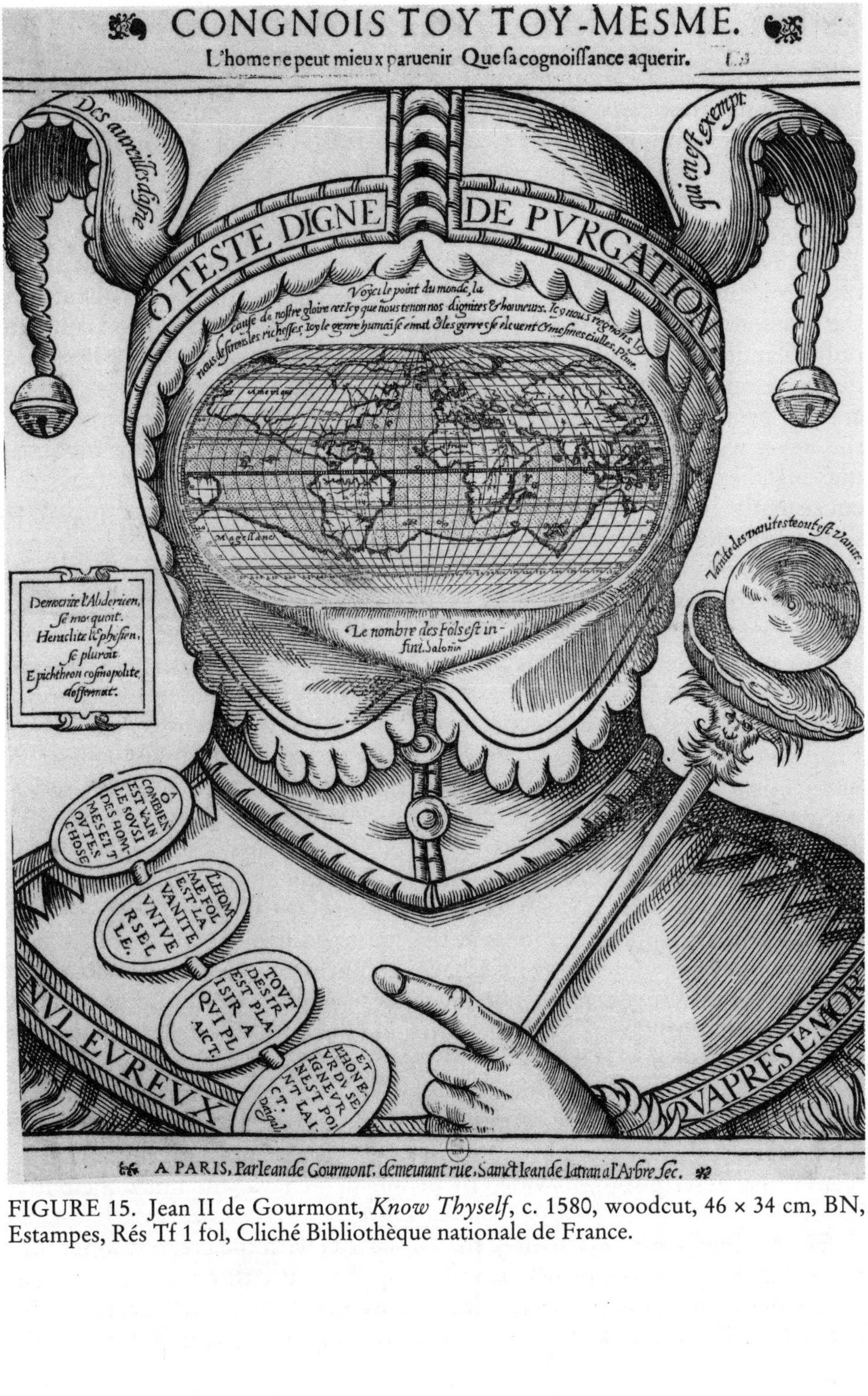

FIGURE 15. Jean II de Gourmont, *Know Thyself*, c. 1580, woodcut, 46 × 34 cm, BN, Estampes, Rés Tf 1 fol, Cliché Bibliothèque nationale de France.

Conclusion

The sparse biographical information about the four artists who worked on the *Quarante Tableaux* yields several conclusions of significance for understanding the work. First, only two of the artists specialized in print-making for an extended portion of their career: Jean II de Gourmont, most obviously, and Jean Le Challeux, whose identification in the first Geneva contract as a *tailleur d'histoires* marks him as a specialist in carving wood blocks, and whose *Those Who Trust Satan Are Always Deceived* reveals him to be a vigorous practitioner of the art. Both were involved in making the woodcuts for the series, not the etchings. Perrissin and Tortorel, by contrast, can be tied to only a handful of etchings other than the *Quarante Tableaux*. When Perrissin designed one late in his career, the actual etching of the plate was left to another person. This difference in print-making skill and experience between the artists who worked on the woodcuts and those responsible for the etchings matches what we can observe from the prints themselves, notably the consistently greater vigor of the woodcuts, and the poor technical quality of some of the copper-plates.

Second, everything that can be learned about Perrissin's and Tortorel's geographic origins and known places of residence ties both of them firmly to Lyon. Le Challeux was originally from Rouen, but he also lived in Lyon for at least part of the 1560s. This means that insofar as the artists who did the majority of the work on the series might have drawn upon their own knowledge of the places or events represented in it as they worked on the plates, Lyon and its surroundings would have been the region they knew best. A modest degree of concentration on this region is indeed evident in the series, for three plates depict minor episodes that took place in this area: number 13 *The Capture of Valence*; number 15 *The Capture of Montbrison*; and number 40 *Montbrun's Crossing of the Rhône*. More than one information network could have brought knowledge of these events to Geneva in 1569-70, of course. Still, their inclusion hints at the artists' influence on the contents of the series. At the same time, Le Challeux's ancestral ties to Normandy did not translate into any scenes concerning that province, even though it was one of the most important theaters of fighting in 1562-1563. Furthermore, unless the artists had traveled far more extensively than the known biographical facts about them indicate, they would not have had the opportunity to visit and sketch most of the widely scattered places depicted in the series. To delineate them accurately, they would have had to work from published city views or from verbal descriptions provided by people in Geneva who knew them first hand.

Finally, Perrissin and Tortorel, the two artists with the greatest input into the actual design of the prints, were among the many thousands of Frenchmen who found themselves drawn into the Reformed cause in the early 1560s, but who ultimately lacked the stomach or conviction to remain loyal to the faith as setbacks and danger multiplied, and who returned to the Catholic fold in the 1570s. As has already been said, the specific religious convictions of sixteenth-century artists did not necessarily determine the character or subject matter of their art. Still, it remains the case that the artist among the four responsible for the most aggressively anti-Catholic image, Jacques Le Challeux, was the one who remained truest to the cause and probably died in the Saint Bartholomew's Massacre. To the extent that Perrissin's and Tortorel's religious and political commitments influenced their designs, these commitments were those not of the Huguenot movement's most die-hard advocates. And just as the audience envisaged by the makers of the series seems clearly to have been an international one of Protestants and Catholics alike, so too its making may even have involved collaboration between Protestant and Catholic printmakers, for de Gourmont seems not to have been a Huguenot at all. Unless he came discreetly to Geneva in 1569 or 1570, making the project involved sending at least one drawing from Geneva to Paris to be carved, then shipping the completing wood block back to Geneva to be printed there.

CHAPTER 3

THE VISUAL REPORTING OF CURRENT EVENTS IN EUROPE BEFORE 1570 AND THE PICTORIAL LANGUAGE OF THE PRINTS

No evidence suggests that either Perrissin or Tortorel had any prior experience as a narrative history painter or draftsman when they set to work drawing the "history and its circumstances" furnished them by Castellin and Le Vignon. Neither appears to have lived in any of the places depicted in the *Quarante Tableaux* or to have been present at any of the events shown. Although the gaps in their biographies make this uncertain, both were probably young when they worked on the project, since Perrissin lived for more than forty more years after completing it, while Tortorel got married as it was being wrapped up. And not only did the project require young artists with little experience in narrative representation to depict events and places unseen by them; the volume they were asked to create had no exact precedents. The artists working on it, like the entrepreneurs who launched it, were trying to make something new when they had very little experience making anything similar.

Even the most creative of artists never create the languages of their art *ex nihilo*. Faced with the task of depicting a wide range of events and unfamiliar places, young artists of modest skill like Perrissin and Tortorel are likely to have drawn particularly heavily on prior representations of similar scenes. Earlier print publishing projects are also likely to have suggested the very idea for the series to the entrepreneurs who launched it, for it is hard to imagine two thread-makers like Castellin and Le Vignon devising the concept of a series of prints "truly portraying" the wars, massacres and troubles of their times and investing in such a project unless they had seen things that suggested the idea to them and led them to believe it might be profitable. Where did those responsible for the project get the idea for the series ? What models did the artists follow as they carried out their commission ? In what ways did they depart from prior traditions as they grappled with the unfamiliar problem of turning "all of a history and its circumstances" into a succession of pictures ? Those are the questions that this chapter will investigate. Answering them requires that we explore the prior history of the visual representation of current events and the still largely unwritten story of the development and spread of the single sheet news print in Europe.

History Cycles, Battle Scenes and Print Series

Cycles of images recounting an important history, whether ancient or recent, sacred or profane, stretch back to antiquity in the history of Western art. Most from the early and high middle ages depict scenes from Christian history, although *The Bayeux Tapestry* is a noteworthy exception. By the fourteenth and fifteenth centuries cycles dedicated to relatively recent events of profane history had begun to proliferate in many forms, including tapestries, frescoes, tomb relief sculptures, *cassone*, and manuscript illuminations. Cities decorated the council rooms of their town halls with painted accounts of their greatest victories. Rulers awed visitors with costly tapestries displaying their and their ancestors' *faits et gestes.*[1]

The most common subject within narrative history cycles devoted to recent events of profane history was the battle scene—the same subject that also recurs most frequently in the *Quarante Tableaux*. As J.R. Hale's classic overview of *Artists and Warfare in the Renaissance* amply demonstrates, sixteenth-century artists, Italian and Northern, depicted battles and warfare in a bewildering variety of manners, from Urs Graf's rapidly drawn sketches of strutting soldiers or plundered corpses laid out on a field as battle rages, to Leonardo da Vinci's close-up focus on the shock of engagement in his *Battle of Anghiari*, to the more panoramic overviews of a city besieged or two armies engaged typical of large Northern European battle paintings. To impose a degree of order on this variety, art historians have proposed a range of typologies that usefully highlight different kinds of scenes and their salient characteristics. Matthias Pfaffenbichler divides battle scenes into four types: (1.) works of glorification; (2.) illustrations of moral or technical lessons about proper military behavior; (3.) narrative scenes focused a specific moment within a battle; and (4.) topographical-analytical paintings that attempt to

---

1 Olle Cederlöf, "The Battle Painting as a Historical Source: An Inquiry into the Principles," *Revue Internationale d'Histoire Militaire* 26 (1967), 119-44; J.R. Hale, *Artists and Warfare in the Renaissance* (New Haven, 1990); Wolfgang Brassart, *Das Historienbild im Zeitalter der Eloquenz von Raffael bis Le Brun* (Berlin, 2003); Peter Schmidt, *Die Grosse Schlacht. Ein Historienbild aus der Frühzeit der Kupferstichs* (Wiesbaden, 1992), pp. 12-13; *Gli Arazzi della Battaglia di Pavia* (exhibiton catalog, Naples, 1999); Hendrik J. Horn, *Jan Cornelisz Vermeyen: Painter of Charles V and His Conquest of Tunis* (2 vols., Doornspijk, 1989); Merlose Huiskamp, "'For the Honour and Reputation of this City and the Glory of Its Scions': War and Peace in the Town and City Halls of the Low Countries" in K. Bussmann and H. Schilling eds., *1648: War and Peace in Europe* Essay Vol. II, *Art and Culture* (exhibition catalog, Munster-Osnabruck, 1998), pp. 547-54.

present an overview of the event and its unfolding.[2] Julie Anne Plax proposes a tripartite division between (1.) genre scenes of war and military life; (2.) scenes of "tumultuous combat" marked by a focus on groups of warriors grappling with one another; and (3.) topographical-analytical paintings characterized by scrupulous attention to the cartography of the battlefield and the details of the engagement.[3] A simpler contrast juxtaposes the heroic figuration against the documentary scene. The former tends to focus on a single figure or moment in the battle and to incorporate elements of allegory or typology into the scene—for instance, depicting sixteenth-century rulers in ancient Roman costume, or assimilating contemporary events to the struggles of the ancient Israelites. Works in the latter mode eschew anachronistic or allegorical elements and are more attentive to the accurate rendering of the setting and details of the specific event depicted.[4] Other art historians have highlighted the different narrative strategies governing the composition of the scene. Some paintings employ "simultaneous narration", compressing several different episodes or more than one day's events into an "*Uberschaubild*". Others focus on a single decisive or exemplary moment within the battle. The former kind of composition is by its very nature less dramatic and even anti-heroic, since the inclusion of several different scenes within the same picture space tends to create multiple points of focus rather than concentrating the viewer's attention on the action of a single figure.[5]

The traditions of tumultuous combat and heroic figuration were both very powerful in sixteenth century history cycles. Historical veracity was often sacrificed to the demands of *laudatio*, so much so that rulers were occasionally even painted into scenes of battles in which they did not take part. Yet some of the era's costliest and most spectacular tapestry series were documentary scenes of a topographical-analytical character, not heroic figurations. A particularly noteworthy example is the set of tapestries of Charles V's 1535 conquest of Tunis that became one of the jewels of the Alcazar in Madrid, woven after cartoons made by Jan Cornelisz Vermeyen, who had accompanied the troops on the campaign. The tapestries abound in vignettes of camp life set within a topographically precise depiction of Tunis and its environs. Comparison of their contents with surviving written accounts of the event

---

2 Matthias Pfaffenbichler, "The Early Baroque Battle Scene: From the Depiction of Historical Events to Military Genre Painting" in Bussmann and Schilling eds., *1648: War and Peace in Europe*, II, 493-500.

3 Julie Anne Plax, "Seventeenth Century French Images of Warfare" in Pia Cuneo ed., *Artful Armies, Beautiful Battles: Art and Warfare in Early Modern Europe* (Leiden, 2002), p. 134.

4 Cederlöf, "Battle Painting as Historical Source"; Jean-Claude Boyer, "Les représentations guerrières et l'évolution des arts plastiques en France au XVIIe siècle," *XVIIe Siècle* 148 (1985), 291-307.

5 Horn, *Vermeyen*, I, 259-61 usefully summarizes a copious older literature here.

shows them to be rich and generally reliable depictions of what happened, despite the occasional insertion of historically inaccurate details for reasons of formal or dramatic effect.[6] The lavish tapestry cycle of the battle of Pavia designed by Bernard van Orley and offered by the States-General of the Netherlands to Charles V likewise compresses a vast amount of carefully rendered detail about the setting, participants, and unfolding of this great Habsburg triumph into seven tightly packed simultaneous narratives whose abundance of detail and absence of a single focal point adds to their reality effect while working against the glorification of the participants.[7] (See figure 16.) The intense concern with topographic and reportorial accuracy displayed in these works can be related to the tendency for Renaissance rulers to assemble increasingly accurate maps and topographical views and to use them in palace decoration to figure their far-flung possessions. Vermeyen's series opens with a map of the Mediterranean whose cartouche promises that the entire sequence was been made "in strict accordance with cartography."[8] It also arose from the increasingly close connection between military command, mathematical cartography, and drawing skills in this period. As well as patronizing such leading cartographers as Mercator, Charles V was himself a student of mathematics and a competent draftsman, "knowing that these arts were most necessary for war in leading armies into distant lands, preparing encampments, and attacking cities."[9]

In the seventeenth century, it would become common for the same drawing of a battle or other history scene to be worked up into tapestries, paintings and prints. Scenes of Louis XIV's conquests by his great Flemish "peintre des batailles et conquêtes du roi" Adam Frans van der Meulen were not only woven as tapestries for the Gobelins *Histoire du Roy*, incorporated as paintings into the decor of the grand ceremonial staircase used by visiting ambassadors at Versailles, and made as smaller paintings to decorate the lodges and chateaux at Marly, Choisy, and Sceaux. They were also reproduced as engravings that were advertised in the *Mercure Galant*, sold singly to the general public, and assembled into larger series that the crown bought and distributed to visiting dignitaries and members of the royal entourage.[10] In the fifteenth and sixteenth centuries, however, rulers were slow to see the propaganda value of the new graphic media. Entrepreneurs likewise needed time to discover

---

6 Horn, *Vermeyen*, passim, esp. pp.178, 288.

7 Brassart, *Historienbild*, pp. 311-13.

8 Molly Bourne, "Francesco II Gonzaga and Maps as Palace Decorations in Renaissance Mantua," *Imago Mundi* 51 (1999), 51-82; Horn, pp. 181, 261.

9 William Eisler, "The 'Wunderkammer' of Charles V: The Emperor, Science, Technology and the Expanding World," *Annali dell'Istituto storico italo-germanico in Trento* 19 (1993), 11-20.

10 *A la gloire du Roi. Van der Meulen, peintre des conquêtes de Louis XIV* (exhibition catalog, Dijon, 1998), esp. pp. 110-17, 203-9, 220-31, 290-6, 322-6.

FIGURE 16. Bernard van Orley, *The Capture of Francis I at Pavia*, 1528-31, tapestry, 435 × 880 cm, Museo Nazionale di Capodimonte, Naples, photo Soprintendenza per i Beni Artistici et Storici e Demoetnoantropologico di Napoli. Francis I may be identified in the tangle of figures around the fallen horse to the left of center. That the central event narrated in this tapestry is not placed at the visual focus of the composition is typical of this series and a number of other tapestry cycles of the period.

that a general public might respond favorably to series of prints showing their sovereign's triumphs. Even the one ruler of this period who turned with alacrity to graphic artists to trumpet his fame, Maximilian I, Holy Roman Emperor from 1493 to 1519, did not widely disseminate the images he commissioned. This glory-hungry emperor hired such artists as Albrecht Dürer, Albrecht Altdorfer, and Hans Burgkmair to carve woodcuts for three of his most important works of self-promotion: the *Theuerdank*, an epic poem limning his youthful adventures and marriage; the *Weisskunig*, a longer commissioned biography left incomplete at his death; and an immense triumphal procession and arch displaying his conquests assembled from numerous individual wood blocks, also unfinished during his lifetime. But while personally supervising the design of these prints, he restricted the number of copies produced during his lifetime to a single limited edition of the *Theuerdank* printed on vellum with hand-colored woodcuts, that he gave as a gift to those he particularly wanted to impress. Only well after his death would less lavish commercial editions of the *Theuerdank* and *Triumphal Procession* appear, carrying the prints to a wider audience. The first such work to be composed exclusively of pictures did not appear until 1559, when Raphael Hofhalter in Vienna assembled and published the 24 historical scenes from the triumphal arch as *The Battles and Knightly Deeds of the Most Illustrious and Most Powerful Prince and Lord Maximilian*.[11]

Hofhalter's production of this volume was almost certainly inspired by the appearance three years previously of an extremely successful volume from the presses of the Antwerp print publisher Hieronymus Cock, *The Victories of Charles V*.[12] Cock's suite cannot be called the first print series depicting a recent event or events. Beginning with an account of Charles V's entry into Bruges in 1515, festival books describing royal entries or other court cere-

---

11 *Des aller Durchleuchtigisten Grossmechtigsten fursten und herrn herrn Maximilans Romischen Kaysers . . . Schlachten und Ritterliche Thaten* (Vienna: Raphael Hofhalter, n.d. [1559]); *Die Geuerlicheiten und eins Teils der Geschichten des loblichen Streitbaren und hochberumbten Helds und Ritters Tewrdannckhs* (Nuremberg, 1517; repr. Stuttgart, 1968, Cologne, 2003, the latter with an excellent historical introduction by Stephen Füsell); Ludwig Baldass, *Der Kunstlerkreis Kaiser Maximilians* (Vienna, 1923); *Hans Burgkmair, das graphische Werk* (exhibition catalog, Stuttgart, 1973); Hermann Weisflecker, *Kaiser Maximilian I. Das Reich, Osterreich und Europa an der Wende zur Neuzeit* (5 vols., Munich, 1971-86), V, ch. 5.

12 Bart Rosier, "The Victories of Charles V: A Series of Prints by Maarten van Heemskerck, 1555-56," *Simiolus* 20 (1990-91), 24-38. Cock was not the first to envisage a cycle of prints showing the Emperor's military triumphs. In 1549, the Italian artist Enea Vico received a pledge of patronage from duke Cosimo I of Tuscany to make such a series. But after traveling to the imperial court at Augsburg with a letter of introduction from Cosimo, he abandoned the project, probably because of the Emperor's lack of interest and support. Rosemary Mulcahy, "Enea Vico's Proposed Triumphs of Charles V," *PQ* 19 (2002), 331-40; Fernando Checa Cremades, *Carlos V. La Imagen del poder en el Renacimento* (Madrid, 1999), p. 258 and passim.

monies began to be illustrated with woodcuts.[13] Self-standing print series reporting these events had appeared by 1530, when the Emperor's peregrinations around Europe gave rise to two large strip-like depictions of imperial processions, one for Charles's coronation by the Pope in Bologna, made by Robert Peril and Nicolaus Hogenberg (Frans' father), the other for his entry into Augsburg for the Imperial Diet, made by Jörg Breu.[14] But Cock's volume was the first self-standing suite of prints to show a succession of important recent historical events rather than a single royal ceremony. After the Emperor began to hand over his lands and titles to his son Philip II, the enterprising print publisher saw the potential of a work that was nominally dedicated to Philip to show him "images of paternal triumph", but was in fact intended for general purchase. On his own initiative, he prepared a title page and commissioned twelve numbered prints to be designed by Maarten van Heemskerck and engraved by Dirck Volckertsz Coornhert showing events from the 1525 battle of Pavia (figure 17) to the 1546 capitulation of the Protestant princes after the battle of Mühlberg. Latin titles beneath each print announce the subject. Quatrains in French as well as Latin further elucidate the image. Completed and first published in 1556, the work was successful enough for new editions to follow in 1558 and 1563. As merchants in Antwerp in the late 1550s and early 1560s, Castellin and Le Vignon are likely to have seen the *Victories of Charles V* and to have observed its success. It more than any other work probably gave them the idea of producing a graphic history of recent events.

---

13 Helen Watanabe-O'Kelly, "Festival Books in Europe from Renaissance to Rococo," *The Seventeenth Century* 3 (1988), 181-201, esp. p. 182.

14 Bernhard Schimmelpfennig, "The Two Coronations of Charles V at Bologna, 1530" in J.R. Mulryne and Elizabeth Goldring eds., *Court Festivals of the European Renaissance: Art, Politics and Performance* (Aldershot, 2002), pp. 142-7; W. Stirling Maxwell, *The Procession of Pope Clement VII and the Emperor Charles V after the Coronation of Bologan* (Edinburgh, 1875); John T. Spike ed., *L'incisione del corteo trionfale di Carlo V di Nicolaus Hogenberg* (Urbania, 1999); Geisberg, *German Single-Leaf Woodcut*, I, 327-37; Pia F. Cuneo, *Art and Politics in Early Modern Germany: Jörg Breu the Elder and the Fashioning of Political Identity ca. 1475-1536* (Leiden, 1998), plates 2-11 and ch. 4. In these suites of prints, the various participants in the processions are shown marching one after another, sometimes with brief identifying labels above or below them. A similar series showing the funeral ceremonies that Philip II staged in his father's honor in Brussels in 1558, *La Magnifique et sumptueuse pompe funèbre faite aux obsèques et funerailles du tres grand et très victorieux empereur Charles celebrées par Philippes, roy catholique d'Espagne, son fils*, was published by Christopher Plantin in Antwerp in 1559 with plates designed by Hieronymus Cock and engraved by the van Duetecum brothers. Both this series and the Hogenberg suite of the Bologna coronation procession were reprinted in the early seventeenth century in The Hague by Hendrik Hondius. For a copy of both bound together in book form: British Library 114.g.3. For a hand colored version of the 1558 funeral procession assembled as a continuous band: Charles Terlinden, *Kaiser Karl V. Vorläufer der europäischen Idee* (Zurich, 1978), fold-out reproduction at the back of the volume. On the latter ceremony and the prints about it: Stephanie Schrader, "'Greater than Ever He Was': Ritual and Power in Charles V's Funeral Procession," *NKJ* 49 (1998), 68-93.

FIGURE 17. Maarten van Heemskerck, *The Battle of Pavia* from the *Victories of Charles V*, 1556, engraving, 15.5 × 23 cm, BN, Estampes, QB1-1525, Cliché Bibliothèque nationale de France.

Inspiration for their project also came from a broader publishing trend that gathered steam in the 1550s and 1560s and crested in the early 1570s, namely a tendency for publishers and printmakers to produce new kinds of print series and picture books of many sorts. During the 1550s, the vigorous group of printers and book illustrators active in Lyon produced not just many illustrated Bibles, but also what can be called picture Bibles: octavo volumes of woodcut biblical scenes accompanied by brief verse captions—*Carved figures from the New Testament*, to translate the Dutch title of one such book.[15] At

[15] Guillaume Borluyt, *Ghesneden Figueren wyten nieuwen testamente* (Lyon: Jean de Tournes, 1557). The copy of this work in the LC, Rosenwald 1062, is bound together with two other volumes of Bible stories in pictures, Guillaume Paradin, *Historiarum memorabilium ex Genesio descriptio* (Lyon: Jean de Tournes, 1558); and Guillaume Borluyt,

around the same time, the Paris woodcutters clustered on the rue de Montorgueil started making shorter series of Biblical scenes, six or eight to a set, depicting episodes from different books of the Old and New Testaments. (Figure 18 is one such scene.) These used a standard large, horizontal format (typically 38.5 × 50 cm), set the image within an elaborate decorative border, and placed a type-set title above the top border and a brief legend inside the bottom one. These series proved hugely successful; massive numbers were exported to England and Spain.[16] The plates of the *Quarante Tableaux* are 32 × 50 cm. They too have a type-set title above the image. Their similarities with the rue de Montorgueil prints in these regards are so great that it seems probable that the latter provided the model followed by the makers of the *Wars, Massacres and Troubles* with regard to the size and format of their prints, although Perrissin and Tortorel did not wrap a decorative border around their scenes like the woodcutters of the rue de Montorgueil.

Other new kinds of picture books or suites of prints that appeared in this period drew on profane history, cartography and chorography. The first French compilation of city views, Guillaume Gueroult's *First Book of Figures and Portraits of the Most Famous and Illustrious Cities of Europe*, appeared in Lyon in 1552, to be followed a year later by his expanded *Epitome of the Chorography of Europe, Illustrated with the Portraits of Its Most Famous Cities*, then in 1564 by the *Plans, Portraits and Descriptions of Several Cities and Fortresses of Europe, Asia, Africa, the Indies and the New Lands*, printed by Jean d'Ogerolles with text by the Protestant Antoine Du Pinet.[17] The Roman publishers Giovanni Battista de' Cavalieri and Antonio Lafréry brought out their first compilations of antiquities, ancient statuary, and portraits of contemporary men of note in the 1560s. In 1569 a group of artists in the same city began work on what ultimately became a set of 130 engravings showing the Dacian wars as depicted on Trajan's column.[18] The prolific

Historiarum memorabilium ex Exodo, sequentibusque libris descriptio (Lyon: Jean de Tournes, 1558). The genre of such picture cycles was not invented at midcentury. The tradition that can be traced back to 1529, and beyond that to Durer's *Passion* series and to illustrated manuscripts of the twelfth century. On this genre and its proliferation in graphic forms in the second half of the sixteenth century, see Max Engammare, "Les figures de la Bible. Le destin oublié d'un genre littéraire en image (XVIe-XVIIe s.)," *Mélanges de l'Ecole française de Rome: Italie et Méditeranée* 106 (1994), 549-91, esp. 552-3, 561-5. For more on Lyon picture Bibles: Sharratt, *Salomon*, pp. 129-50.

16 For important collections of these scenes: BN, Estampes, Ed.5g.rés; *Images parisiennes du XVIe siècle rue de Montorgueil* (auction catalog, Galerie de Chartres, 2004). On their production and distribution: Jean Adhémar, "La rue Montorgueil et la formation d'un groupe d'imagiers parisiens au XVIe siècle," *Le Vieux Papier* 21 (1954), 25-34; Tessa Watt, *Cheap Print and Popular Piety, 1550-1640* (Cambridge, 1991), pp. 179-89; Préaud et al., s.v. "Germain Hoyau".

17 Mireille Pastoureau, "Les atlas imprimés en France avant 1700," *Imago Mundi* 32 (1980), 49-54.

18 Bury, *Print in Italy*, pp. 50-65; van der Sman, *Siècle de Titien*, pp. 177-9.

FIGURE 18. Nicolas Prévost (active 1571-1599), *The Flood*, woodcut, 37 × 45 cm, BN, Estampes, Rés Ed 5 g, p. 108, Cliché Bibliothèque nationale de France. This Biblical scene is typical in presentation and format of those made on the rue Montorgueil. By the last three decades of the sixteenth century when it was made, it had become common for Catholic as well as heterodox printers and artists to use the Tetragrammaton to represent God the Father, as is done here. Nicolas Prévost is not known to have had any connection with the Reformed cause. He illustrated several broadsheets for the Catholic League.

Zurich-born woodcutter Jost Amman completed in 1572 a set of 108 numbered images with titles and brief accompanying verse texts illustrating Livy's Roman history, the *Icones Livianae* or *Neuwe livische Figuren*.[19] Significantly, a new category of books appeared for the first time in Willers' Frankfurt fair catalogue for the spring of 1571, the fair immediately following that

19 *Neuwe livische Figuren* (Frankfurt: Georg Raben, 1573); Gero Seelig and Giulia Bartrum eds., *Jost Amman*, (New Hollstein German 4, 2 vols., Rotterdam, 2001), II, esp. pp. 37, 40; Andreas Andresen, *Jost Amman, 1539-1591, Graphiker und Buchillustator der Renaissance* (Amsterdam, 1973), esp. pp. 327-8; C. Becker, *Jobst Amman, Zeichner und Formschneider, Kupferätzer und Stecker* (Nieuwkerk, 1961), pp. 60-61.

at which the *Quarante Tableaux* was sold: "copper pictures and little books containing only pictures." This category recurs for the next four years, then gradually fades away.[20] The *Wars, Massacres and Troubles* appeared at a moment when experimentation with new kinds of picture books was cresting. As Frans Hogenberg's rapid reworking of it shows, it also contributed to furthering this trend.

While Cock's *Victories of Charles V* was the most direct precedent for the *Wars, Massacres, and Troubles* as a graphic history of recent events, the two works differ radically in style and stated purpose. The former is dedicated to Philip II in honor of his father; the latter promises the general reader a truthful portrayal of the events depicted. The former contains printed text that lauds the Emperor; the latter contains printed text that scrupulously avoids the language of praise and blame. As figure 17 (above, p. 82) makes evident, Heemskerk's boldly composed mannerist plates for *The Victories* are heroic figurations. The compositions focus on a moment of dramatic action or the submission of the Emperor's enemies. Charles V himself usually occupies center stage, at times garbed in full armor, at others dressed anachronistically but evocatively as a Roman emperor. The specific event represented is quickly evoked by a few details in the scene. Historical veracity is not the prime concern. Indeed, one print in the series shows Charles driving the Turks from the walls of Vienna in 1529, when he was in fact in Italy.[21] By contrast, Tortorel and Perrissin's woodcuts and etchings multiply specific details, frequently employ simultaneous narration, and eschew allegorical elements. Figures in the background of the picture space are often drawn nearly as large as those in the foreground, as in maps, in order to capture the details of yet another episode within the event represented. Most of the prints lack a single point of focus. The accompanying key often adds further particulars about the episodes illustrated within the picture frame.

If the *Victories of Charles V* may have suggested to Castellin and Le Vignon the feasibility and sales potential of a graphic account of contemporary history, the chief stylistic and compositional influences for the prints of Tortorel and Perrissin must be sought in another direction, that of the single-sheet news prints produced in growing quantities over the course of the sixteenth century. These offered the artists a range of schematic languages for figuring multiple details of a battle or siege in a manner more topographical-analytical than heroic.

---

20 *Messkataloge Willers*, passim.

21 Rosier, "The Victories of Charles V," esp. p. 29.

The Graphic Reporting of Contemporary Events to 1570

The first copperplate engraving to depict a contemporary event appeared almost as soon after the medium itself in the early fifteenth century; in fact, it is the very first metal engraving to which any sort of approximate date of manufacture can be attached. Illustrated in figure 19 and long known simply as *A Battle* or *The Large Battle*, it seems at first glance a generic combat scene rather than an account of a specific battle. Soldiers grapple with one another in clusters arranged almost randomly across a space defined as a landscape only by a few hills and fortified places at the top and by a tree near the lower left edge. But on the basis of both stylistic and iconographic evidence, notably the kinds of weapons used and the images on the banners carried by the troops, Michael Schmidt has convincingly shown that the scene depicts the victory of John, count Palatine of the Rhine, over the Hussites at Hilfersreid in 1433.[22] This was the first major defeat suffered by the Hussites in their wars against their German opponents. The count considered his victory sufficiently important to have it celebrated annually with a procession in his *Residenzstadt* of Neunberg.

Both in size (29 × 41 cm) and subject matter, *The Large Battle* was very unusual for an early metal engraving. It inspired few immediate imitators. Survival rates for early printed ephemera are low. They are especially low for larger prints that would have been hung or pinned up on walls rather than being pasted into books or bound into albums. The earliest important inventory of a major print collection, that of the would-be encyclopedic collection assembled by Ferdinand Columbus between 1510 and 1539, lists four big multi-sheet depictions of important events from the first decades of the sixteenth century, only one of which survives today.[23] Still, even taking this loss rate into account, it does not appear to have been until after the medium of the printed news report began to spread widely in Europe in the late fifteenth century that visual reports of specific recent events began to be made with any regularity in the new graphic media. *Zeitungen*—short printed pamphlets passing along news of a recent event of note—first appeared in significant numbers in Germany in the 1470s. By the end of the century similar news pamphlets were also being produced with some regularity in Italy and France as well.[24] From early on, a fraction of these news pamphlets attempted to

---

[22] Louvre, Rothschild 78 LR, metal engraving, 29 × 41 cm; Schmidt, *Grosse Schlacht*, passim. I owe thanks to Peter Parshall for this important reference.

[23] Mark McDonald ed., *The Print Collection of Ferdinand Columbus (1488-1539): A Renaissance Collector in Seville* (3 vols., London, 2004), I, 191.

[24] Schottenloher, *Flugblatt und Zeitung*; Jean-Pierre Seguin, *L'information en France de Louis XII à Henri II* (Geneva, 1961); Tullio Bulgarelli, *Gli Avvisi a stampa in Roma nel Cinquecento* (Rome, 1967); Infelise, *Prima dei giornali*. I also rely here upon my perusal of the catalogs and collections of the Biblioteca Marciana and Trizulviana in Venice and the Oesterreichesche Nationalbibliothek in Vienna.

FIGURE 19. Anonymous, *The Large Battle*, c. 1433, metal engraving, 29 × 41 cm, Louvre, Collection Rothschild 78 LR, photo RMN.

attract buyers with woodcut title pages offering a crude depiction of the kind of event reported. The wood blocks used for this purpose were often recycled from pamphlet to pamphlet.[25] These illustrations should not be confounded with current event prints properly speaking, which attempt to figure specific events. After the *Large Battle* of c. 1433, the first known print of this latter sort is a depiction and account of a dramatic celestial phenomenon seen over Constantinople in 1491 that the Nuremberg humanist Hartmann Schedel purchased and pasted into a bound album.[26] At least six other graphic depictions of current events are known from the second half of the 1490s, several of them large woodcuts assembled from more than one sheet that are quite astonishing in their verve and density of detail, such as the 85-centimeter wide colored woodcut of the 1499 battle of Dorneck now in Basel made by an unknown Swiss or South German artist (color plate 3).[27] From this period forward, an ample check-list of surviving copies of such prints can be compiled.[28]

For the first half of the sixteenth century, the production of prints depicting recent events remained confined primarily to South Germany and Italy, the two great poles of early European printmaking. Wondrous births and strange meteorological phenomena garnered as much attention as battles and ceremonies. In Germany, woodcuts were the dominant medium until 1570. They ranged from technically accomplished scenes made by some of the leading printmakers of the era—most prominent early German printmakers made a few views of contemporary events, although none specialized in this area—to crude woodcuts with extensive accompanying text, such as that illustrated in figure 20. Nuremberg and Augsburg were the leading early centers for the production of such current events prints, but single-sheet *flugblätter* are known to have been made in upward of 32 different towns.[29] In Italy, the production

---

[25] Jean-Pierre Seguin, "L'illustration des feuilles d'actualité non périodiques en France aux XVe et XVIe siècles," *Gazette des Beaux-Arts* 6th ser., 52 (1958), 35-50.

[26] *Die Graphiksammlung des Humanisten Hartmann Schedel* (exhibition catalog, Munich, 1990), pp. 272-3. Ecker, *Einblattdrucke*, p. 309 lists a woodcut of a monster from 1490 that may be a slightly earlier example of this genre if the illustration attempts to describe the specific features of the beast.

[27] *Einblattholzschnitte des XV. Jahrhunderts aus dem Kupferstichkabinett Basel* (exhibition catalog, Basel, 1994), 34; *Collection of Ferdinand Columbus*, I, 335; *Graphiksammlung Schedel*, pp. 272-3; Hale, *Artists and Warfare*, pp. 48-51, 260; Ecker, *Einblattdrucke*, p. 269. The single-sheet strip report of a case of Jewish host desecration in Passau in 1477 that can be determined from stylistic considerations to have been published in Nuremberg in the 1490s can also be assimilated to this group of early news prints and depictions of current or recent events. Kunzle, *Early Comic Strip*, pp. 21, 26.

[28] I have made such a checklist for all European prints depicting recent events prior to 1570 and all French prints of this sort from the entire sixteenth century, based upon my reading and visits to a range of print rooms, map collections, and libraries. This list, which now contains 300 entries but cannot claim to be exhaustive, is the basis for much of what follows in the subsequent paragraphs.

[29] A good impression of the place of news and battle prints in the production of the more artistically accomplished German woodcutters can be formed from Max Geisberg, *The*

FIGURE 20. Anonymous, *The Capture of Modon*, c. 1502, woodcut, 23 × 39.5 cm, Bayerische Staatsbibliothek Munich, Xyl 54.

FIGURE 21. Anonymous, *The Siege of Boulogne*, 1549, etching, 30 × 45 cm, BN, Estampes, Hennin 321, Cliché Bibliothèque nationale de France.

of such images concentrated more heavily in Rome and Venice, where map-maker-print publishers such as Antoine Lafréry and Tommaso Barlacchi in the former and Niccolo Nelli and Domenico Zenoi in the latter competed to be the first in the streets and *piazze* with pictures of recent events. Etching quickly emerged as the dominant medium here. The view of Boulogne under siege by Henry II (figure 21) is a typical Italian current events print of this era. The production of similar images was only part of the trade of the leading Italian producers of current events prints. They also made devotional images, portraits, maps, and views of Roman antiquities.[30]

From Germany and Italy, the regular production of current events prints spread to the Low Countries and France in the middle of the sixteenth century.[31] In Antwerp, Hans Liefrinck received a privilege to produce a print of an imperial victory in 1543.[32] Hieronymus Cock published the first of his many prints of this sort in 1549.[33] In France, such works seem first to have emerged from the innovative soil of Lyon's publishing and book illustration world, although it is hard to identify with confidence the oldest self-standing current events print among several candidates for the honor that can be found standing alone within old albums of city views and historical scenes. One is a highly schematic depiction of Metz under siege by Charles V's forces made by the Lyon master printer Philibert Rollet in 1553 (figure 22)—if this print, which is known to have accompanied a pamphlet account of the siege, was also sold by itself.[34] Another is a woodcut of the 1551 siege of Parma that

---

German Single-Leaf Woodcut 1500-1550 (rev. ed., 4 vols., New York, 1974) and Hale, *Artists and Warfare*, pp. 13-22. For cruder *flugblätter*, see Ecker, *Einblattdrucke*, vol. 2; Wolfgang Harms ed., *Deutsche Illustrierte Flugblätter des 16. und 17. Jahrhunderts* (5 vols. to date, Munich and Tübingen, 1980-); Weber ed., *Wunderzeichen und Winkeldrucker*. Illuminating general remarks in Landau and Parshall, *Renaissance Print*, pp. 226-31.

30 Leo Bagrow, *Giovanni Andreas di Vavassore: A Venetian Cartographer of the Sixteenth Century: A Descriptive List of His Maps* (Jenkintown, Pa., 1939); Hale, *Artists and Warfare*, p. 143; Francesco Ehrle, *Roma prima di Sisto V* (Rome, 1908); van der Sman, *Siècle de Titien*, pp. 174-6.

31 Isolated precursors of such prints had already appeared in both areas around 1500. An unsigned, uncaptioned engraving of a battle thought to depict Fornovo (1495) and to be of French origin survives in the National Gallery, Washington. A large woodcut view of Aden besieged in 1513 with Dutch text survives in the British Museum. See Hale, *Artists and Warfare*, pp. 260-61; McDonald ed., *Print Collection of Ferdinand Columbus*, inventory numbers 3131 and 3177 and figure 443.

32 Arblaster, "Current-affairs Publishing,", pp. 26-7.

33 Not 1550, as suggested by Riggs, *Cock*, p. 280; Nina Eugenia Serebrennikov, "Plotting Imperial Campaigns: Hieronymus Cock's Abortive Foray into Chorography," *NKJ* 52 (2001), pp. 189-93. *Boloniae*, intaglio print, 38 × 43 cm, "Hieronymus Cock factor Antwerpi anus F. et excudebat 1549", Chantilly, estampe H.21.

34 The woodcut appears without accompanying pamphlet in BM Lyon, Rés 24014. For a copy of it with the pamphlet: *Bref Discours du siege de Metz en Lorraine avec la figure de l'assiette de la Ville, et partie de la campagne, du cours des rivieres, et des lieux auxquelz camperent les imperialistes* (Lyon, 1553) [BN, Lb31 42 Réserve].

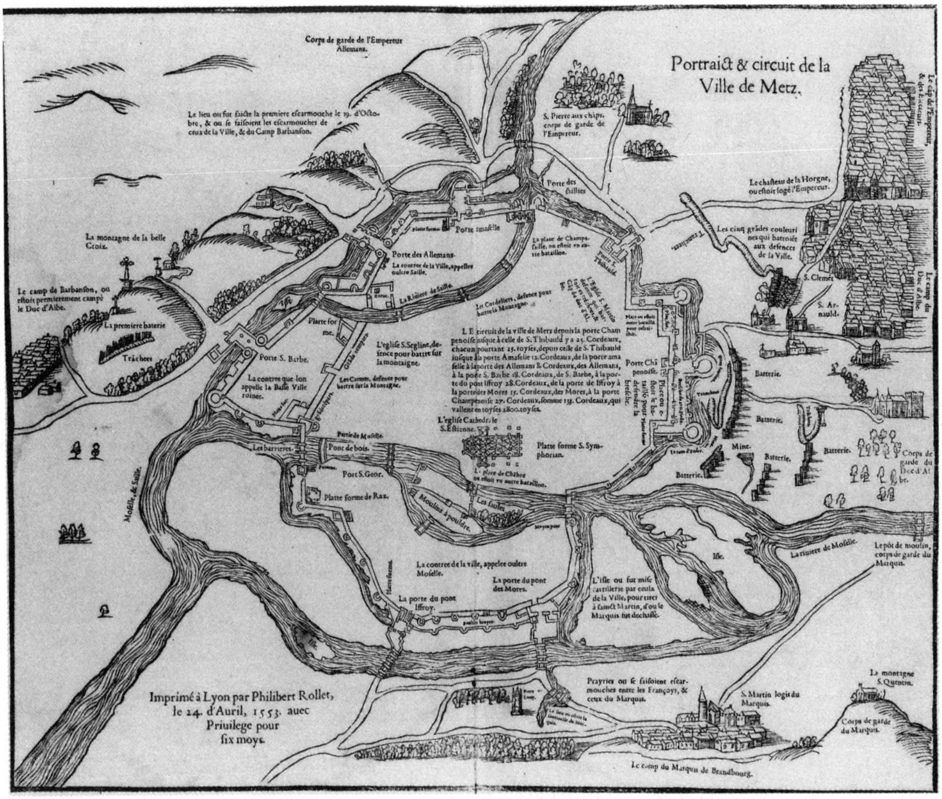

FIGURE 22. Philibert Rollet publisher, *The Siege of Metz*, 1553, woodcut, 37 × 44.5 cm, BM Lyon, MS Rés 24014 fo. 95.

bears the indication that it was printed by Bartholomy Bonhomme in Lyon in 1557 (figure 23)—if this has not been removed from a rare edition of the same year of Guillaume Gueroult's *Epitome de la corographie d'Europe*.[35] It is certain at any event that by the end of the 1550s visual reports of current events were being produced and offered for sale as single items in Paris, for a colored woodcut of the French siege of Calais in 1558 (color plate 4) bears the indication that it could be purchased on the rue de Montorgueil at the sign of the broken heart.[36]

---

35 *La Ville de Parme, representant par vraye figure sa situation avec l'ordonnance de l'armee, Papistique et Imperiale, mise devant la ville, deffendue par les Francoys*, described in Paolo Arrigoni and Achille Bertarelli, *Le stampe storiche conservate nella Raccolta del Castello Sforzesco* (Milan, 1932), p. 15. The evidence for a now lost edition of Gueroult's work may be found in Baudrier, X, 184-5.

36 *Le pourtraict de la ville de Calais, faict au naturel*, colored woodcut, 34 × 44 cm, "on les vend a Paris, rue de Montorgueil, au cueur navré", Maz., 5921F.

FIGURE 23. Bartholomy Bonhomme publisher, *The Siege of Parma*, 1557, woodcut, 24.5 × 32 cm, Civica Raccolta Stampe Bertarelli Milan, AS m 1-8.

French current event prints multiplied in the subsequent decade. Table 4 lists all known prints of this sort made in France in the first three decades of their production. As can be seen, at least 17 such prints were made between 1560 and 1570. A few may have accompanied pamphlets as fold-outs. Most were clearly intended for sale on their own. Woodcuts were by far the most common medium. Paris was the leading center for their production. The most popular subjects were battles or sieges involving French armies. Monstrous births, important national assemblies, and episodes from Christendom's wars against the Turks followed well behind. The scenes of distant events were often copied from prints made by artists and publishers closer to the events in question, as Jean II de Gourmont had copied Domenico Zenoi in making his *Siege of Tokay*. Occasionally, the time lag was considerable; the Lyon printer Benoit Rigaud issued a broadsheet view of the execution of Egmont and Hoorn in 1570, two years after the event took place in Brussels.[37]

[37] *L'esecution & supplice faict par sentence Iudiciaire, à l'encontre des nobles & illustres Chevaliers de la Toison, les Contes d'Aiguemont, & de Horne*, single sheet of five woodcuts

Most of the prints listed in Table 4 survive in only a single copy, suggesting that the list reveals just a fraction of the images actually made.

Craftsmen of various backgrounds tried their hands at this new corner of print publishing. Some of those who appear in Table 4 were artists and printmakers, such as Pierre Woeriot, perhaps the greatest and most prolific goldsmith and engraver of his generation;[38] Jean Le Maistre, a *tailleur d'histoires* with a modest specialty in practical picture books for other artists;[39] and Olivier Truschet, an *imagier en papier* best known for his collaboration with Germain Hoyau on the 1553 map of Paris.[40] More were master printers or *marchands-libraires* ranging in scale from Benoist Rigaud, one of Lyon's most important publishers and probably the largest producer of *occasionnels* anywhere in France, to figures like Rollet and Jean Dallier known to have published only a few dozen books or pamphlets.[41] Adepts of both faiths got

---

with accompanying text, Lyon, Benoist Rigaud, 1570, a copy of *Execution, Oder Enthaubtung der Edlen und Wolgebornen beider Graffen/ Graffen von Egmondt/ und Graffen von Horn*, engraving, Wolfgang Meyerpeck, 1568, illustrated and described in Daniel Horst, *De Opstand in zwart-wit: Propaganda-prenten uit de Nederlandse Opstand (1566-1584)* (Zutphen, 2003), pp. 83, 318-19. Still another example of one print being copied after another is *Le vray plant et pourtraict de l'assiette des villes de Modon & Navarrin*, woodcut, 41.5 × 28 cm, Paris, Nicolas Chesneau, 1573, BN, C & P, Rés Ge D 17227, copied from *Disegno dove al presento ci Ritrova l'armata della santa legha contro la Tuchescsa nel promontorio della Morea dirincontro a Modon*, etching, 48.5 × 35 cm, Rome, Antonio Lafréry, October 1572, BN, C & P, Rés Ge DD 626 (70).

38 *The Dictionary of Art* (34 vols., New York, 1996), s.v. "Woeiriot"; Robert-Dumesnil, VII, 43-140, XI, 324-52. Woeiriot is known to have made 431 engravings, of which the view of the 1565 siege of Malta is the only depiction of a current or recent event.

39 Le Maistre also published *Les cinq ordres des colomnes d'architecture . . . nouvellement pourtraictes et mises en lumiere, au service et proufit des paintres, massons, tailleurs de pierres, orfevres . . .* (Lyon: Jean Le Maistre, 1562), listed in Baudrier, I, 244; and *Recueil de plusieurs pieces de pourtraitture, tres-utiles et necessaires generalement à tous Orfevres, Tailleurs, Graveurs, Damasquineurs, Sculpteurs, Paintres, Brodeurs, Tapissiers, Tissotiers, Couturiers, Lingieres et autres* (Lyon: Jean Le Maistre and Anthoine Voulant, 1565), BN, Estampes, Lh 95 Rés. On the title page of this latter work Le Maistre is identified as a "tailleur d'Histoires demeurant en rue merciere".

40 Préaud et al., s.v. "Truschet".

41 For Rigaud, see Baudrier, III, 175-471; Nathalie Blanc, "Imprimeurs et imprimés à Lyon pendant le consulat protestant 1562-1563" (mémoire de maitrise, Université de Lyon II, 1999), pp. 111-15; Jean-Pierre Seguin, *L'information en France avant la périodique: 517 canards imprimés entre 1529 et 1631* (Paris, 1964), p. 18; *Histoire de l'édition française*, I, 277, 329, 334, 346, 401, 597. Rigaud published 1057 titles between 1557 and 1596, 88 of them pamphlets about current events or wondrous happenings. His news reports could have been widely distributed, since he is known to have had dealings with business associates in Toul, Le Puy, St Flour, Pau, Montpellier, and Aix-en-Provence. Rollet was a master printer who did most of his work for larger merchant-booksellers but also published 33 titles under his own imprint between 1547 and 1561. Baudrier, X, 432-47. The title page of *Coustumes du comté et bailliage d'Auxerre* (Paris: Jean Dallier, 1563) lists Dallier as a "marchand libraire demeurant sur le pont St Michel à l'enseigne de la rose blanche". The on-line catalog of the BN reveals that he published 25 *occasionels* between 1559 and 1572. On him, see also *Histoire de l'édition française*, I, 243, 346.

TABLE 4. French News Prints and Their Publishers: The First Three Decades (1553-1582)

This list records all known prints depicting recent or current events found as or reported to be single sheet items (i.e. not book illustrations). Some may have originally been illustrations of pamphlets or pages from compilations of city views removed from these works by an owner.

Publisher	City and Date of Publication When Given	Subject	Medium (W=woodcut; I=intaglio)	Location(s)
Philibert Rollet	Lyon, 1553	Siege of Metz (1552)	W	BM Lyon, MS 24014, fo. 95
Bartolomy Bonhomme	Lyon, 1557	Parma Defended by the French (1551)	W	Castello Sforzesco, Milan
Unknown	"a Paris, rue de Montorgeuil, au cueur navré"	Siege of Calais (1558)	W	Mazarine 5921F
Olivier Truchet and Richard Breton	Paris, 1560	"La Vraye Figure d'un Monstre né au pais de Berry"	W	SUB Zurich, Wickiana
Unknown	Unknown	Estates-General of Orléans (1560)	W	Arsenal, Est 213 (37); Chantilly, Est H 22; Dresden, Sächsischen Hauptstaatsarchiv, Geh Rat 9083/1; BN, Estampes, Hennin 466, 467
Jean de Gourmont and Jehan Pignot	Paris	Estates-General of Orléans (1560)	W	BN, MS Français 10193, fo. 17 bis; Estampes, Ea.17.Rés
De Gourmont	Paris, 1565	Siege of Tokay (1565)	W	London, Royal Geographical Society, 262.H.5
Mathurin Bréville	Paris	Colloquy of Poissy (1561)	W	Listed in Hennin, *Monuments*, IX, 32; perhaps BN, Estampes, Hennin 474
	Paris, 1562	Siege of Bourges (1562)	W	BN, MS Français 10193, fo. 188 bis
	Paris, 1562	Siege and Capture of Rouen (1562)	W	BN, MS Français 10193, fo. 223 bis; B.M. Rouen, Estampes topo plan II
	Paris, 1562	Battle of Dreux (1562)	W	BN, MS Français 10193, fo. 278 bis; Bodleian Gough 43 f. 167
	Paris, 1566	Siege of Szeget (1566 ?)	W	London, Royal Geographical Society, 262.H.5

Publisher	City and Date of Publication When Given	Subject	Medium (W=woodcut; I=intaglio)	Location(s)
	Paris	Battle of St. Denis (1567)	W	BM St Denis, MS E 1
Unknown	"a Paris au clos Bruneau à l'enseigne saincte Catherine"	Battle of Dreux (1562)	I	BN, MS Français 10193, fo. 259 bis
Unknown	Unknown	Siege of Le Havre (1563)	W	Dresden, Loc 9083, LM, 1
André Thevet	Paris, 1565	Siege of Malta (1565)	W	BN, Estampes, Vb 133 (II)
Pierre Woeiriot	Lyon, 1565	Siege of Malta (1565)	I	UB Basel, AA79; BN, C & P, Ge DD 2987(5744)
Jean Dallier	Paris, 1569	"Pourtraict d'un monstre nay d'une vache ... 1569 ... pres d'Abeville"	W	Location(s) unknown; listed in Hennin, *Monuments*, IX, 116-7
Jean Le Maistre	Lyon, 1570	Battle of St Denis (1567)	W	BN, C & P, Res Ge D 23410
Benoist Rigaud	Lyon, 1570	Execution of the counts of Egmont and Hoorn (1568)	W	BN, Estampes, Hennin 598
Nicolas Chesneau	Paris, 1573	Siege of Modon (1572)	W	BN, C & P, Res Ge D 17227
	Paris, 1578	Exorcisms of Laon (1566)	W	BN, Estampes, Hennin 570
E. Desprez	Paris	Siege of La Rochelle (1573)	W	UB Amsterdam OF 79-1
Jean Le Fevre	Lyon	Siege and Conquest of Sommières (1573)	I	BN, Estampes, Hennin 687
Robert Le Mangnier	Paris, 1577	Estates-General of Blois (1576)	W	Blois, Chateau Musée, inv. 927.41; BN, Estampes, Hennin 704
Denis Villerval	Troyes, 1577	Monster born in Winzelburg, Bohemia	W	No surviving copy known—purchased 1608 by Pierre de l'Estoile
	Troyes, 1577	Monster born in Cher, Piedmont	W	No surviving copy known—purchased 1608 by Pierre de l'Estoile
Unknown	Unknown	"Admirable discours d'un brigand nomme Christeman"	W	Wolfenbüttel
Jean Savine	Sens, 1582	"Pourtrait d'un prodige et enfant Petrefié"	W	Wolfenbüttel

involved. Richard Breton was one of the leading purveyors of Calvinist books in Paris in the periods when the sale of such works was permitted there; Nicolas Chesneau, who was briefly his landlord, embraced the Catholic cause and specialized in works of anti-Protestant controversy.[42] Of all these men, the only one known to have made the production of news prints a regular activity was the Parisian Mathurin Bréville, who produced six current events prints between 1561 and 1567. Bréville may have been one of those master printers like Jean de Laon who was something of a specialist in printing images and did much of his work under contract to larger publishers. Aside from his current events prints, he is known only as the printer of a few short books and pamphlets between 1558 and 1564 and again between 1577 and 1583.[43] Our own Jean II de Gourmont is the only other Frenchman beside Bréville to appear prior to 1570 as the producer of more than one of these kinds of images.

The remarkable catalogue of views of the 1565 siege of Malta compiled by two scholars who made it their mission to track down every surviving depiction of this event in over a hundred repositories demonstrates just how widespread the visual reporting of current events had become across western

42 Georges Wildenstein, "L'imprimeur-libraire Richard Breton et son inventaire après décès, 1571," *BHR* 21 (1959), 364-79, esp. 368; Annie Parent, *Les métiers du livre à Paris au XVIe siècle (1535-1560)* (Geneva, 1974), p. 161; Préaud et al., s.v. "Chesneau". Books published by Chesneau include René Benoist, *Remonstrance chrestienne aux religieuses professes qui ont este séduites et desbauchées par les serviteurs et ministres de leur ventre soubs prétexte d'une liberté évangélique et licite mariage* (1565) and Jean Le Masle, *Chant d'allegresse sur la mort de Gaspar de Colligny* (1572). Breton was also bookbinder to the court and the university of Paris. He published both books and print series, including the Huguenot psalter, *Les songes drolatiques de Pantagruel* (1565), and *Receuil de la diversité des habitz qui sont de present en usage tans es pays d'Europe, Asie, Affrique et iles sauvages* (1564). Woeiriot and Rigaud were also drawn into the Reformed church for a period. See on the latter Natalie Zemon Davis, "On the Protestantism of Benoît Rigaud," *BHR* 17 (1955), 246-51.

43 The on-line catalog of the BN lists the following works published by Bréville: *Ordonnances du roy Charles neufiesme à présent régnant, faictes en son Conseil, sur les plainctes, doléances et remonstrances des députez des troys Estats tenus en la ville d'Orléans* (with J. Dallier and V. Sertenas, 1561); Antoine Mizauld, *Singuliers secrets et secours contre la peste* (1562); *Discours de l'Entree de Tresillustre, Trespuissant, Treschrestien, et Tresvictorieux Prince Charles de Valois neuvième de ce nom Roy de France en sa tres renommée et fameuse ville de Lyon . . . Avec la declaration des arcz triomphans, et autres magnifiques figures et portraicts* (1564); Claude de Bauffremont, *Proposition de la noblesse de France* (1577); and *Discours tres veritable du passage et arrivee de messeigneurs les duc de Montpensier et mareschal de Biron et de leur armée dans le Païs Bas* (1583). On the basis of the manuscript notes of the historian of Parisian printing Philippe Renouard, Frank Lestringant, "Quatre 'canards' topographiques d'André Thevet au début des guerres de religion, 1562-1563," *Le Livre et l'Estampe*, 32 (1986), 161, adds *Discours de la guerre et descente que les Anglois et Flamens se sont efforcez faire en Bretaigne* (1558). See also Etienne Vitelli, *Commentaires sur la guerre civile de France 1567* ed. Anne Lombard-Jourdan (Paris, 2005), pp. 21-2.

Europe by the 1560s.[44] No less than 29 different prints of this event were made during the year of the siege itself. Some publishers, in their zeal to provide an up-to-the-minute depiction of the situation of the attacking and defending forces, reworked the same prints up to four times at brief intervals to add new information arriving from the front. These multiple states increase the total number of different images of the siege made in 1565 to 55. Production was most intense in Rome and Venice, the two great centers for news gathering in the Christian Mediterranean, where at least ten printers produced maps or views of the event. Their prints were in turn copied by other print publishers in Augsburg, Nuremberg, Antwerp (Cock), Lyon, and Paris, spreading images of the event across the continent.

As such depictions spread, they whetted the desire of those who read about distant events to visualize them as well. No testimony to this is more eloquent than the notebooks of the Zurich pastor and news gatherer Johann Jakob Wick. Amid the recopied letters, songs, poems, news sheets, and excerpts from assembly minutes with which he filled two dozen notebooks, he not only pasted many illustrated *flugblätter*, but also made 1028 pen drawings of his own, the better to form a visual record of the events that he read or heard about. Some of the drawings appear to have been copied from prints he saw. Others, such as his drawing of the 1562 execution of Augustin Marlorat that incongruously makes Rouen look like a Swiss lakeside town (figure 24), clearly represent his own efforts to imagine the scene in question.[45] Wick's contemporary Marcus zum Lamm, a Heidelberg jurist and professor, similarly assembled a "Thesaurus Picturarum" that mixed printed news sheets with drawings of current events made by artists hired by zum Lamm.[46] Later in the century, the Le Puy tanner Jean Burel drew into the margins of his memoirs portraits of noteworthy figures he mentioned the text, views of historical events of note in the region, and pictures of unusual celestial or natural phenomena.[47]

---

44 Albert Ganado and Maurice Agius-Vadalà, *A Study in Depth of 143 Maps Representing the Great Siege of Malta of 1565* (2 vols., Valetta, 1994). The rich material provided in this volume is also discussed by Woodward, *Maps as Prints*, pp. 94-7.

45 Wick's collection is now in the Zentralbibliothek Zurich, MSS F 12-19, 21-35. See also Weber ed., *Wunderzeichen und Winkeldrucker*; Matthias Senn, *Johann Jakob Wick (1522-1588) und seine Sammlung von Nachrichten zur Zeitgeschichte* (Zurich, 1974); idem, *Die Wickiana. Johann Jakob Wicks Nachrichtensammlung aus dem 16. Jahrhundert. Texte und Bilder zu den Jahren 1560 bis 1571* (Zurich, 1975). While these works provide an excellent introduction to the man and his collection, one must examine the original collection to obtain a precise sense of his news gathering and collecting practices.

46 Wolfgang Harms and Cornelia Kemp eds., *Die Sammlung der hessischen Landes- und Hochschulbibliothek in Darmstadt* Deutsche Illustrierte Flugblätter des 16. und 17. Jahrhunderts Vol. 4 (Tübingen, 1987), pp. viii-xi; Frieder Hepp, *Religion und Herrschaft in der Kurpfalz um 1600 Aus der Sicht des Heidelberger Kirchenrats Dr. Marcus zum Lamm (1544-1606)* (Heidelberg, 1993), esp. pp. 16-30.

47 *Memoires de Jean Burel* (Saint-Vidal, 1983). I owe this reference to Jim Amelang.

FIGURE 24. Johann Jakob Wick, *The Execution of Augustin Marlorat*, 1562, ink and watercolor on paper, 11 × 14.5 cm, Zentralbibliothek Zurich, MS F 15, fo. 228 recto.

Like the history paintings examined in the previous section, graphic depictions of current events must be situated within a field of tension between the goals of accuracy and *laudatio*, information and commemoration. They served a variety of purposes and responded to a variety of desires. First, they offered a useful complement to written accounts of the same events. Geographers and mapmakers considered their craft to be an auxiliary science of history. Cosmography, Josse Hondius's preface to Mercator's 1609 atlas declared, offered readers of history an "artificial memory without which their reading would be barren."[48] In similar fashion, maps of distant places where important events were taking place could serve as an artificial memory to fertilize the reading of accounts of these events. Recognizing the complementary nature of word and image, printmakers and pamphlet publishers often worked in tandem and advertised one another's products. News of the 1565 siege of Malta was not only conveyed to France by pictures; six French publishers, including Benoît Rigaud and Jean Dallier, two men who also appear in Table 4

[48] Quoted in Frank Lestringant, *André Thevet. Cosmographe des derniers Valois* (Geneva, 1991), p. 11.

as publishers of current events prints, produced written accounts of the event.[49] Dallier's pamphlet recommends Thevet's "beautiful and ample portrait" of the island for readers who want to understand the siege better.[50]

More profoundly, contemporary epistemology accorded sight a powerful role in transmitting knowledge of material things and in fixing them in the mind. As Fernando Bouza has written, "during the sixteenth and seventeenth centuries hearing, seeing, and reading and writing were viewed as three perfectly valid ways to obtain and disseminate knowledge."[51] Petitions to the crown seeking redress for crimes sometimes included drawings so that the king could see and grasp just what happened. Exactly repeatable images were used in a range of fields such as botany or anatomy to convey knowledge of these subjects. The eye, Leonardo da Vinci wrote at the beginning of the century, "is the master of astronomy, it makes cosmography, it advises and corrects all human arts, it carries me to different parts of the world, it is the prince of mathematics, its sciences are most certain."[52] Even when historical events were communicated in words, authors urged their readers to form mental images of them, the better to remember and be inspired by them. Thus, Jean Crespin told the readers of the first edition of his martyrology that they should "commit to memory and *have in view before their eyes* [*se proposer devant les yeux*; italics mine] the examples of those who upheld the truth of the teachings of the Son of God."[53] For such purposes pictures could be even more effective than words, Jean Le Clerc, a fin-de-siècle Paris print publisher, assured prospective buyers of his view of the 1606 baptism of the future Louis XIII:

> The accounts made of this event will not persuade you as well as this *peinture*; men are more often moved and persuaded by what they see than by

---

49 Ganado and Agius-Valadà, *Study in Depth*, I, 175.

50 Ganado and Agius-Valadà, *Study in Depth* I, 182. For the same kind of collaboration between printmakers and pamphlet publishers in the Low Countries, see Arblaster, "Current-affairs Publishing," p. 27.

51 Fernando Bouza, *Communication, Knowledge and Memory in Early Modern Spain* (Philadelphia, 1999), p. 15.

52 Quoted in Svetlana Alpers, *The Art of Describing: Dutch Art in the Seventeenth* Century (Chicago, 1983), p. 46, a pioneering study of the place of visuality and the "art of describing" in the transmission and accumulation of knowledge in the sixteenth and seventeenth centuries, only slightly marred by its overly schematic division between Italian and "Northern" theories of art and of knowledge. Important subsequent examinations of this theme include Bouza, *Communication, Knowledge and Memory*, pp. 23-6; Peter Parshall, "Imago Contrafacta: Images and Facts in the Northern Renaissance," *Art History* 16 (1993), 544-79; Barbara J. Shapiro, *A Culture of Fact: England, 1550-1720* (Ithaca, 2000), esp. ch. 4; Andrea Carlino, "Fatti contraffatti tra curiosità e scienza. Note su Konrad Gesner e la collezione di fogli volanti di Johann Jacob Wick," *Art + Architecture en Suisse* 17 (2006), 37-44. See also Marie-Madeleine Fragonard, *La poésie religieuse d'Agrippa d'Aubigné et son expression* (Paris, 2004), pp. 668-74.

53 Crespin, *Histoire des martyrs* ed. Benoit, I, xxxxiii.

> what they hear, and as the Philosopher said, What is received by the ear does not move the heart as much as what passes through the eye. This present [sheet] will confirm this maxim.... I hope you enjoy the perfection of the portrayal and the truth of the history.[54]

Despite the famous argument of Lucien Febvre and Robert Mandrou that sight was less important relative to the other senses in the sixteenth century than it is today, contemporary theories of the mind accorded it a powerful role.[55] But if pictures were to substitute adequately for direct eyewitnessing in conveying knowledge of a thing or event, they had to be accurate simulacra. Hence, the most insistent refrain of the texts accompanying current events prints was that they offered a "*vray pourtraict*", "*wahrhafftige Contrafactur*" or "*vero ritratto*" of the events they claimed to depict. "Here most beloved readers is the real site of the battle given July 13 1558 near Gravelines," promises one Italian print.[56] "This is the true portrait of Boulogne in France occupied by the king of England and now besieged by the most Christian king of France," states another.[57]

Commemoration and celebration also entered into the making of current events prints. While especially true of large, multi-block woodcuts that required months to produce, this also applied to many more rapidly produced woodcuts or etchings, as the text accompanying them frequently suggests. Thus, Thevet's text for Mathurin Bréville's broadsheet of the battle of Dreux explains that this "rough portrait" of the event displays the great deeds of the "most virtuous" duke of Guise and the "brave captains" who served with him. To immortalize them, some 31 are listed by name.[58] An Italian view of the 1569 siege of Poitiers likewise recounts how the city resisted the "terrible" siege of the admiral Coligny through the "vigilance, prudence, valor, *virtù*, and daring" of the Catholic commanders, its governor the count of Lude, and its inhabitants. Since it is directed at an Italian audience, it takes particular care to list the efforts of "lords Paulo Sforza, Giovanni Orsino and Agnolo Cesi, deputies of His Holiness, and Adriano Baglioni, Palavicino

---

54 *Representation des ceremonies de l'ordre gardé au Baptesme de Monseigneur le Daulphin... le 14 de Septembre 1606*, engraving, 26.5 × 35 cm, "L. Gaultier sculp, Jean Le Clerc exc", "A Paris, Jean Le Clerc, 1606", Louvre, Rothschild 5820LR.

55 Febvre, *Le problème de l'incroyance au 16e siècle. La religion de Rabelais* (Paris, 1968), pp. 402-3; Mandrou, *Introduction à la France moderne (1500-1640). Essai de psychologie historique* (Paris, 1974), pp. 79-82.

56 *Eccoui amantsmi lectori il vero sito della battaglia data nal anno 1558 a di 13 di luglio intorno a Graveline*, engraving, 43 × 29.5 cm [repositories: BN, C & P, Rés GeDD 1140(81); Arsenal, Est. 212 (83); BL, Maps c 7.e.2].

57 *BOLOGNA IN FRANCIA*, engraving, 45 × 30 cm [repositories: BN, Estampes, Hennin 321; BN, C & P, GeDD (II, 80); BM Lyon, 24014, fo. 80; BL, Maps, c 7.e.2].

58 *LE VRAY POVRTRACIT DE LA BATAILLE DONNEE PAR M. DE GVYSE VEVANT DREVX*, woodcut, 46 × 39 cm, BN, MS Français 10193, fo. 278 bis.

Rangone, and other Italian lord adventurers."[59] A student of printed Italian *avvisi* has detected that these were far more likely to report Christian or Catholic victories over infidels or heretics than the reverse.[60] Visual reports of recent events likewise seem most often to report events in which the cause or country with which the printer or patron was associated emerged triumphant. The circulation of images of a cause or a country's triumphs allowed those who acquired these images to celebrate these victories and to demonstrate and reinforce their attachment to the winning cause.

Some prints sounded multiple chords. The schematic depiction of the battle of Dreux entitled *The True Portrait and Plan of the Battle Given to the Huguenots by Monsieur de Guise, Sent to the King by the Aforesaid Lord*[61] (figure 25) employs one of the earliest examples of a symbolic language that military engineers and commanders trained in drawing, geometry and the art of fortifications would increasingly use over the subsequent century to delineate battlefield maneuvers. Different kinds of troop units are denoted with different clusters of dots. Crosses locate the points on the battlefield where these units clashed. Text below the print explains the day's maneuvers. Such close attention to the details of the engagement suggests that military men formed one of the intended audiences for this print, just as a contemporary Italian pamphlet about the same event advertises itself as offering "matters pleasing to historians and useful for professionals of war."[62] At the same time, a sonnet addressed to the viewer found beneath the key and legend suggests other audiences for the print and other reasons to acquire it as well. This both hails the Catholic victory as a divine deliverance and promises a vicarious yet danger-free experience of the clash:

See here depicted as in nature	Voy-cy la place au naturel despeinte
The place where the Lord of hosts	Ou le Seigneur des puissantes armees
Consumed the mutinous's forces	Vit des mutins les forces consommées
Striking fear and terror in their hearts.	Frappant leur coeur de frayeur et de crainte
Here is where the earth was stained	Voycy la place où la terre fut teinte
With blood and sown with heads,	Du sang des corps et des testes semées
Where Frenchmen with inspired arms	Ou des Francais les dextres animées
Fought the holy fight.	Ont combatu pour la querelle sainte

[59] *Vero disegno della nobilissima Citta di Poitiers . . . Con il tremendo assedio di essa*, etching, 40 × 33 cm, BN, C & P, Rés Ge DD 1140 (78).

[60] Bulgarelli, *Avvisi a stampa in Roma*, p. 17. See also Arblaster, "Current-affairs Publishing," p. 27.

[61] *LE VRAY POURTRAICT ET PLANTE DE LA BATAILLE DONNEE PAR MONSIEUR DE GUISE CONTRE LES HUGUENOTZ, ENVOYE AU ROY PAR LEDICT SEIGNEUR*, intaglio, 38.5 × 33 cm, BN, MS Français 10193, fo. 259bis.

[62] *Avvisi novamente venuti de le cose di Francia* (Padua: Griffo, 1563), unpaginated.

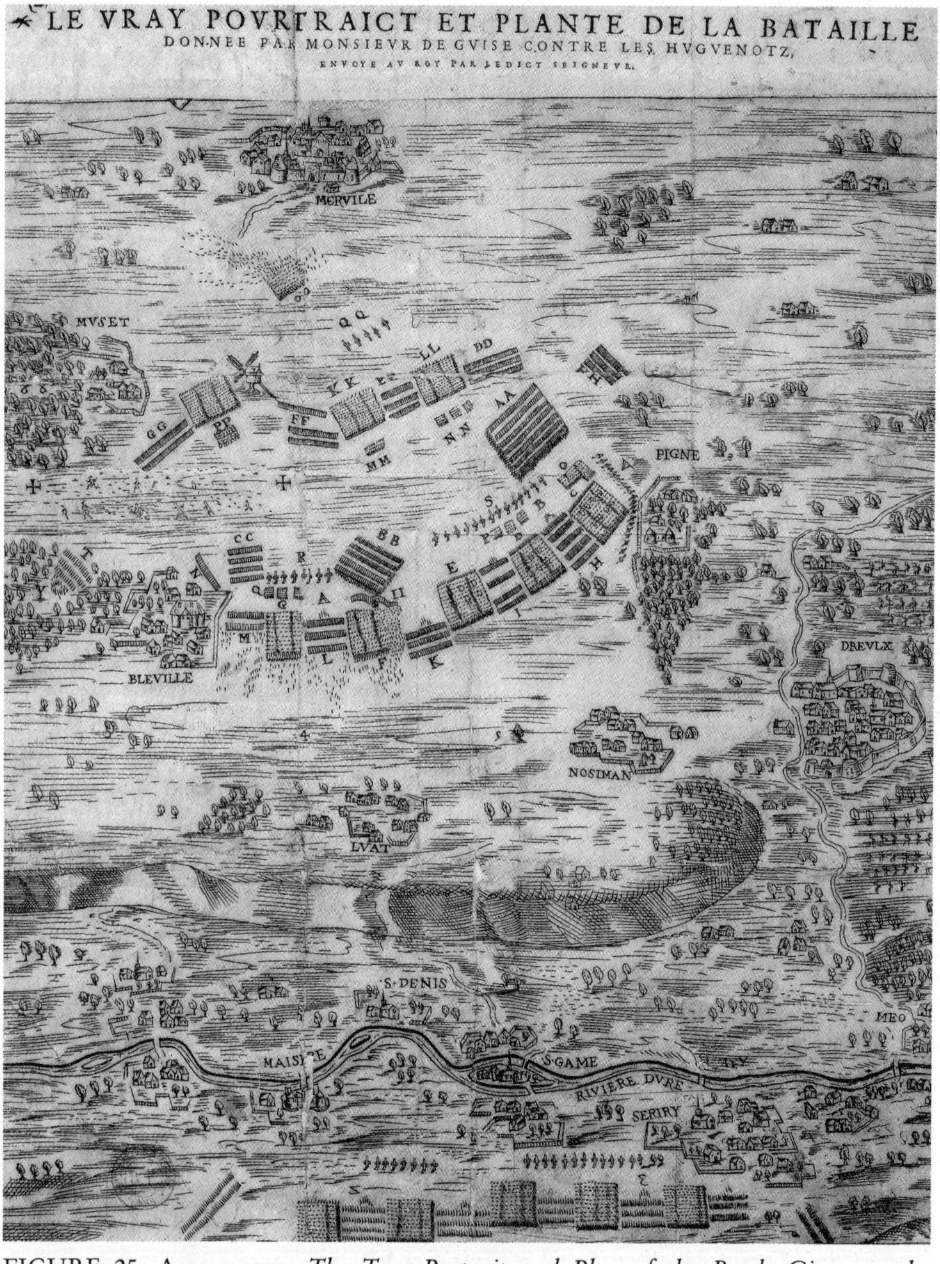

FIGURE 25. Anonymous, *The True Portrait and Plan of the Battle Given to the Huguenots by Monsieur de Guise, Sent to the King by the Aforesaid Lord (The Battle of Dreux)*, 1562, intaglio, 38.5 × 33 cm, BN, MS Français 10193, fo. 259 bis, Cliché Bibliothèque nationale de France. Printed beneath the image are explications of the letter keys identifying the units of the royal and Huguenot armies, a description of their movements on the battlefield, and two poems: a sonnet and a longer poem "Au peuple François".

Here, reader, in safety you may see Lances shatter and harnesses break, For this paper is a true account	Icy, lecteur, sans nul danger tu vois Lances briser et rompre les harnois Car ce papier t'est une vraye histoire
Further you can see in this place The power of God's miracles That gave victory to the vanquished.	Et si tu vois d'avantage en ce lieu Le grand pouvoir des miracles de Dieu Qui des vaincus fist naistre la victoire.

A second, longer poem laments that Frenchmen are fighting Frenchmen and that the scepter has slipped from the king's hands. He nonetheless is trying to pick it up. We should obey him rather than quarreling, and should not attribute our own shortcomings to the church. This "true account" offers vicarious adventure, military knowledge, a political lesson, a display of God's power, and a commemoration of a Catholic triumph, all at the same time.

Despite the omnipresent assurance that these prints offered a true picture of what they showed, relatively few were actually drawn from life or copied from drawings by eyewitnesses in this era. *The True Portrait and Plan of the Battle Given to the Huguenots by Monsieur de Guise, Sent to the King by the Aforesaid Lord* was the only one of the 30 French current events prints listed in Table 4 to claim to reproduce an eyewitness sketch. Five of the 29 views of Malta under siege in 1565 claim to be based on sketches brought from the scene, a claim that often seems plausible.[63] Earlier in the century, Nicolaus Meldemann published a remarkable circular depiction of Vienna under siege in 1529 based on 360 degrees worth of sketches made from the tower of St Stephen's church by a "famous painter" often thought to be Hans Sebald Beham.[64] Two Augsburg woodcuts of the duke of Parma's later siege of Antwerp are known to have been produced after a drawing of the operations circulated through the Fugger news network.[65] At the opposite extreme from these rare cases of prints based on eyewitness drawings were equally rare instances where the makers of current event prints simply recycled or reworked scenes of other events that they already had in their shop, as the subsequent owner of the wood blocks from Tortorel and Perrissin who turned *The Executions at Amboise* into "*The Escalade*" would do.[66]

The great majority of current events prints from this period seem to have been made by turning written reports of an event into an image. Take, for instance, the unsigned Italian depiction of the 1569 battle of Moncontour, *Victory of the Catholics Against the Huguenots*, where numbered clusters of

---

63 Ganado and Agius-Vadalà, *A Study in Depth*, I, 104, 223.

64 *The Siege of Vienna*, woodcut, 81 × 85.5 cm, Hollstein German, III, 226; Hale, *Artists and Warfare*, pp. 17-19.

65 Schilling, *Bildpublizistik*, pp. 98-101, 448-9.

66 *Abraham Bosse savant graveur* (exhibition catalog, Paris, 2004), no. 61; Eckhard Leuschner and Philippe Rouillard, "Metamorphoses of a Plate: *The Battle of Las Navas de Tolosa* by Villamena after Tempesta," *PQ* 19 (2002), 235-53.

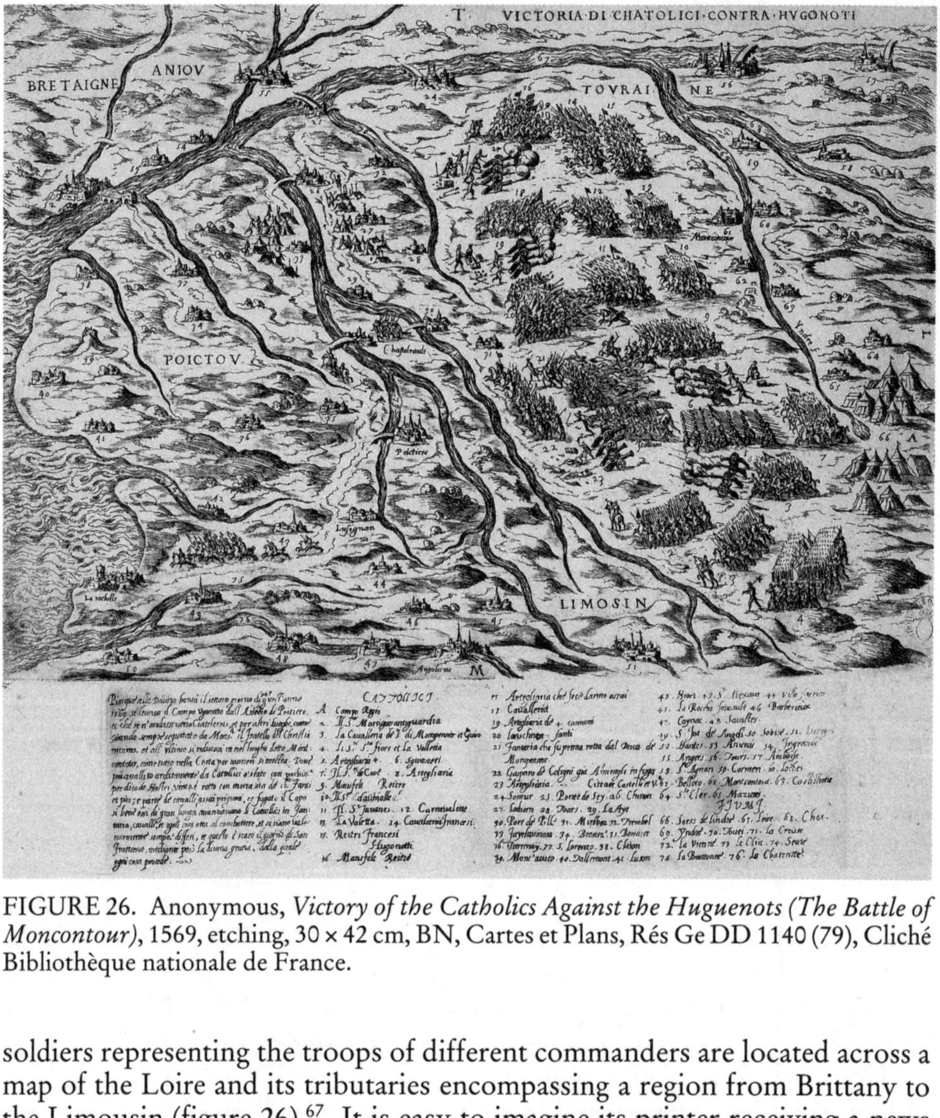

FIGURE 26. Anonymous, *Victory of the Catholics Against the Huguenots (The Battle of Moncontour)*, 1569, etching, 30 × 42 cm, BN, Cartes et Plans, Rés Ge DD 1140 (79), Cliché Bibliothèque nationale de France.

soldiers representing the troops of different commanders are located across a map of the Loire and its tributaries encompassing a region from Brittany to the Limousin (figure 26).[67] It is easy to imagine its printer receiving a news account from France and inserting the details into a map of the region that he already had in his shop or was able to find in circulation. Another Italian engraving of the same battle dramatically arranges the troops of the rival sides in two long facing lines of massed units on a wide plain, with merely a river and a few named villages in the upper left of image to localize where the battle

[67] *VICTORIA DI CHATOLICI CONTRA HVGONOTI*, etching, 42 × 30 cm, BN, C & P, Rés Ge DD 1140 (79); Borroni Salvadori, *Carte, piante e stampe storiche delle raccolte lafreriane della Biblioteca Nazionale di Firenze*, no. 294.

FIGURE 27. Anonymous, *The Battle of Moncontour*, 1569, etching, 33.5 × 44.5 cm, BN, Estampes, Hennin 631, Cliché Bibliothèque nationale de France.

took place.[68] The number of men in each unit and their commanders are carefully noted within the image itself. (See figure 27.) This could easily have been constructed from a written account of the battle that spelled out how the troops arrayed themselves from right to left, as many such accounts did. Some current events prints explicitly claim to be based on letters received from the site of the event, or even offer excepts from these letters in the accompanying text to augment their credibility. In this they echo the printed *zeitungen* or *avvisi* of the time, that commonly took the form of reprinted letters. The fact that so many current events prints were made by turning written or oral reports into pictures clarifies why those who produced the largest number of such prints included men such as Cock or Lafréry who also produced many maps and city views. They had a stock of images at their disposal that

[68] *Il ORDENE DEL FATTO DARME fatto tra catollici et Ugonoti alle 3. di Ottobre 1569 nella gran campagna di Marcounet vicina a Moncontur*, etching, 33.5 × 44.5 cm, BN, Hennin 631; Borroni Salvadori, *Carte, piante e stampe storiche delle raccolte lafreriane della Biblioteca Nazionale di Firenze*, no. 148

they could adapt to make such prints by situating within them details gleaned from the news reaching them.

To suggest that the largest number of current events prints were made in this manner is not to dismiss as groundless their claim to offer an accurate view of what they show. That Italian printmakers altered their views of the siege of Malta to incorporate new details arriving from the war zone shows that they were impelled by a concern to provide timely, precise information. But the process of making their images as accurate as possible involved a particularly clear illustration of one of the fundamental points of E.H. Gombrich's classic *Art and Illusion*, namely that the art of creating realistic depictions of specific places or events involves adapting stereotyped schemes of representation to the particulars of the thing represented.[69] The degree to which the makers of current events prints were able to move the different images they made away from the state of pure stereotypes and toward the ideal of perfect accuracy depended upon the detail and precision of the information they received, the accuracy of the maps or views of the place in question to which they had access, and the skill and exactitude with which they were able to introduce the information about the event into the topographic setting.

As the illustrations to this chapter have already made clear, early current events prints experimented with many different schemes of representation to figure the events and places they sought to show. As the century advanced, the visual conventions of the genre nonetheless converged around certain regular features. By mid-century, few prints were as densely packed with charging groups of soldiers as early sixteenth-century German battle woodcuts had been. Philibert Rollet's view of the siege of Metz (figure 22 above, p. 91) utilized an unusually high level of schematization in its delineation of the city's defenses, but the growing influence of cartography and city views can be seen in many current event prints. Typically, these prints now sketched the position of different groups of troops from a fairly high angle of imagined observation, disposing them around a besieged city or across a landscape that either filled up the entire picture space as in a map or ended at a very high horizon set just below the top margin of the print. Rather than focusing the reader's eye on a single point, the composition invited the viewer to peruse the many details shown in different parts of the picture space. The besieged town or fort and its defenses were often carefully rendered according to the conventions of city views. Letter keys or labels within the image frequently identified key geographic landmarks and participants, while accompanying text explained features of the view that were not be immediately legible from the picture itself.

---

[69] E. H. Gombrich, *Art and Illusion: A Study in the Psychology of Pictorial Representation* (New York, 1961), esp. pp. 66-90.

FIGURE 28. Anonymous, *Portrait of the Assembly of the Estates held in the city of Orléans in January 1560*, c. 1561, woodcut, 30 × 21 cm, Sächsischen Hauptstaatsarchiv Dresden, Geh Rat, 9083/1.

Given the production of single-sheet current events prints in both Antwerp and Lyon during the 1560s, both the entrepreneurs and the artists who worked on the *Quarante Tableaux* can be presumed to have seen such prints. Indeed, it seems that they directly copied at least one and probably two. Scene 8 from the series, *The Estates-General of Orléans*, drawn by Tortorel, reproduces scrupulously the composition, seating pattern, and even many of the individual gestures found in the anonymous *Portrait of the Assembly of the Estates held in the city of Orléans in January 1560*, as the comparison of plate 8 at the back of the book with the reproduction of this print in figure 28 makes clear.[70] Tortorel introduced a number of minor decorative changes, placing fleurs de lys on the hangings around the room and adding a more elaborate floor and carpet pattern, to give the hall a greater aura

70 *Pourtraict de l'assemblée des Estatz, tenuz en la ville d'Orléans, au mois de Ianvier, mil cinq cens soixante*, woodcut, 30 × 21 cm [repositories: Sächsischen Hauptstaatsarchiv Dresden, Geh Rat, 9083/1; Arsenal, Est. 213 (37); Chantilly, Est. H. 22; BN, Estampes, Qb. 1 1560]. Cf also figure 13 Jean II de Gourmont and Jean Pignot publishers, *The True Portrait of the Assembly of the Three Estates Held in Orléans*, above p. 68, which differs slightly in composition from these two image.

FIGURE 29. Anonymous, perhaps Mathurin Bréville publisher, *The Colloquy of Poissy*, c. 1561, woodcut, 12.5 × 15.5 cm, BN, Estampes, Hennin 474, Cliché Bibliothèque nationale de France.

of magnificence than is conveyed by the bare setting of the news print. He also made one potentially important change whose significance I have not been able to determine. Where the original print shows an unidentified figure in a short robe, presumably the spokesman of the nobility Jacques de Silly, sieur de Rochefort, standing to address the assembly, Tortorel gave the speaker a long robe and identified him as the spokesman for the clergy Jean Quintin. Despite these changes, the inspiration of the prior news print is undeniable. Scene 9 *The Colloquy of Poissy* likewise may be copied from an earlier print. According to Georges Duplessis, the late nineteenth-century continuator of Hennin's catalogue of scenes from French history, Mathurin Bréville made an "extremely rare" view of this event "that agrees, except in a few details, with the plate from the Tortorel and Perrissin series."[71] This may be the same as the woodcut in the Bibliothèque Nationale (figure 29) that

[71] Hennin, *Monuments*, IX, 32.

indeed matches the image from the print series almost exactly. Unfortunately, this woodcut has been trimmed to the margins of the image, eliminating the text that (to judge by the letter key within the image) must once have accompanied it.[72] If this is indeed the view published at the time by Bréville, the only changes introduced by Tortorel and Perrissin involved modifying the dimensions of the image to fit the format of their series and identifying more of the participants shown in the scene.

Direct copying of the sort that is certain for *The Estates-General of Orléans* and probable for *The Colloquy of Poissy* hardly exhausts Tortorel and Perrissin's debt to the tradition of single-sheet news prints. The front matter of *Quarante Tableaux* echoes the text accompanying many of these prints in addressing the reader directly in the first person singular and claiming that the volume offers a true and useful depiction of the events shown. "Aware the desire of many to know accurately [*savoir au vray*] the remarkable things that have occurred in France," says the note To the Reader, "I have been impelled, dear reader [*ami lecteur*], to present to you these little pictures in order that such great affairs may always be before your eyes". The events are "truly portrayed", assures the title page.

Most importantly of all, many of the compositional features found in the single sheet news prints recur in the battle and siege scenes of the *Wars, Massacres, and Troubles*. Here too we find an elevated angle of observation, a high horizon, a concern to plot the location and actions of different units across the landscape, the absence of a single focal point, and the extensive use of identifying letter keys or captions. Like the news prints, most of Tortorel and Perrissin's scenes provide an *überschaubild* of the events they show. The attentive looker must scan the entire picture frame and refer back and forth often to the key to comprehend the full story being told. If Tortorel and Perrissin took the emerging genre of the graphic history cycle away from the heroic figurations of the *Victories of Charles V* in the direction of topographical-analytical scenes that figured more of the particulars of the events in a manner that was at once schematic and detailed, the single sheet current events prints showed the way.

At the same time, close observation reveals some significant differences between the battle and siege scenes in the *Quarante Tableaux* and most contemporary current events prints of such subjects. Tortorel and Perrissin's siege scenes bring the viewer closer to the action and adopt a lower angle of observation than do most news prints. The view rarely takes in the entire circuit of the besieged town's walls. Instead, the viewer is placed behind the attacking forces and is able to observe specific incidents or actions from the siege at various points around the walls. This at once involves the viewer more immediately in the action and allows the artists to narrate more specific

[72] *The Colloquy of Poissy*, woodcut, 12.5 × 15.5 cm, BN, Estampes, Hennin 474.

episodes from the event. Many of these scenes also employ simultaneous narration, where most contemporary siege views show either the moment at which the attacking forces were able to enter the besieged city or the placement of their batteries and quarters around it. Curiously, although Perrissin and Tortorel pack more episodes about the unfolding of the event into their views, they often fail to show its denouement, or to report it in the accompanying text. The otherwise uninformed viewer/reader of the series would never know that the sieges of Chartres and Poitiers ended with the withdrawal of the attacking Protestants, while that of St Jean d'Angély saw the royal forces capture the city, but only after the small band of Huguenot defenders put up a long, glorious defense and surrendered under terms that spared their lives and those of their co-religionists.

Other distinctive features of Tortorel and Perrissin's siege scenes become apparent when they are compared with a second kind of siege picture from this era: paintings of sieges commissioned after the event by cities that had experienced attack, usually in celebration and thanksgiving for their deliverance. At least two French cities that repelled Protestant assaults in the early civil wars, Poitiers and Chartres, commissioned such paintings, Poitiers to mark the fiftieth anniversary of its siege in 1619, Chartres at an unknown date late in the sixteenth or early in the seventeenth century.[73] Since both of these sieges also appear in the *Wars, Massacres, and Troubles* (scenes 30 and 34), the comparison with these paintings, reproduced in color plates 5 and 6, becomes particularly fruitful. Where the prints are packed with details of attacking maneuvers, breaches in the walls, and sorties by the defenders, the two municipal siege views appear tranquil by comparison, so distant and broadly encompassing is their higher angle panorama of the city under siege, and so small do the figures of the attacking forces consequently become. Even the foregrounded cannon aimed menacingly at the *faubourgs* of Chartres and the smoke coming from Poitiers' citadel do not significantly disrupt the sense of tranquility. At the same time, the civic siege paintings are far more attentive to rendering precisely the town's monuments and appearance. Each painting

---

[73] *The Siege of Chartres in 1568*, oil on canvas, 112 × 166 cm, Musée des Beaux-Arts de Chartres; François Nautré, *The Siege of Poitiers by the Admiral Coligny*, oil on canvas, 194 × 365 cm, Musée Sainte-Croix, Poitiers. The inscription on the latter painting reads "la dite figure levee par commandement de Sire Jan Pidoux maire et messieurs les pairs et eschevins, l'an 1619". For brief notes on it see *Bulletin de la Société des Antiquaires de l'Ouest*, 3rd ser., 4 (1916-18), 337, 341, 418-21. Between 1587 and 1630, many cities in the Low Countries that had experienced sieges during the Eighty Years War commissioned tapestries or paintings of these events to adorn their town halls with a record of their resistance and God's assistance. Marloes Huiskamp, "'For the Honour and Reputation of this City and the Glory of Its Scions': War and Peace in the Town and City Halls of the Low Countries" in Bussmann and Schilling eds., *1648: War and Peace in Europe*, II, 547-54; Frans Verbiest, "De Lierse Furie, Anno 1595 in Beeld, Boek en Blad," *Noordgouw*, I (1961), 119-43, II, 13-42.

minutely traces the distinctive street pattern of the city depicted. The major buildings are painted with close attention to detail. By contrast, Perrissin's view of the siege of Chartres depicts what could be any town—more a notional urban agglomeration than an actual city view, a solid mass of generic buildings behind crenellated walls. His view of Poitiers depicts that city's situation on the river Clain and the bridges that led to it with considerably more fidelity, but it renders as densely packed with houses and churches a city that in fact had exceptional amounts of open space within its extensive walls. Curiously—but characteristically for the series—it also gives many of the buildings circular domes of a sort almost never found in the still essentially gothic cities of sixteenth-century France.

City Views and the Topographic Fidelity of the Prints

This brings us to another aspect of the artists' working methods and debt to prior representational traditions: the question of how they went about drawing cities that they had never seen. As we have already learned, neither Perrissin nor Tortorel are likely to have seen most of they places they were asked to represent. While contemporary mapmakers could construct siege views by figuring details from the event around views of the besieged city drawn from those already in their stock, Geneva was not a center of mapmaking in this period, and the makers of the *Quarante Tableaux* were not prior specialists in this domain of print publishing. They could, however, have relied on published views to form an idea of about half of the cities they needed to depict, since the 1550s and 1560s had seen Lyon publishers begin to multiply and compile city views. Did the makers of the series search out and use any such city views? How faithfully did they reproduce them? How do they seem to have worked when they lacked a good picture of the place they had to represent? And what can the examination of topographic setting of the prints tell us about their claim to have truthfully portrayed the wars, massacres, and troubles of their time?

Ten different cities appear prominently in one or more prints in the series. These ranged in size from important provincial capitals such as Orléans, Tours, Bourges, and Poitiers, through the mid-sized provincial towns of Nîmes, St Jean d'Angély, Chartres, and Amboise, to the little burgs of Le Pouzin and Montbrison. Three scenes were also set within Parisian streetscapes, two of them in the Place de Grève, the traditional site for executions in the city.

When Perrissin and Tortorel set to work drawing their scenes, published views of four of the places that they had to depict certainly existed, all of them produced in their home town of Lyon over the preceding decade. These four cities were Tours, a view of which appeared in both Gueroult's 1553 *Epitome of the Chorography of Europe* and Du Pinet's 1564 *Plans, Portraits and Descriptions of Several Cities and Fortresses of Europe, Asia, Africa, the Indies*

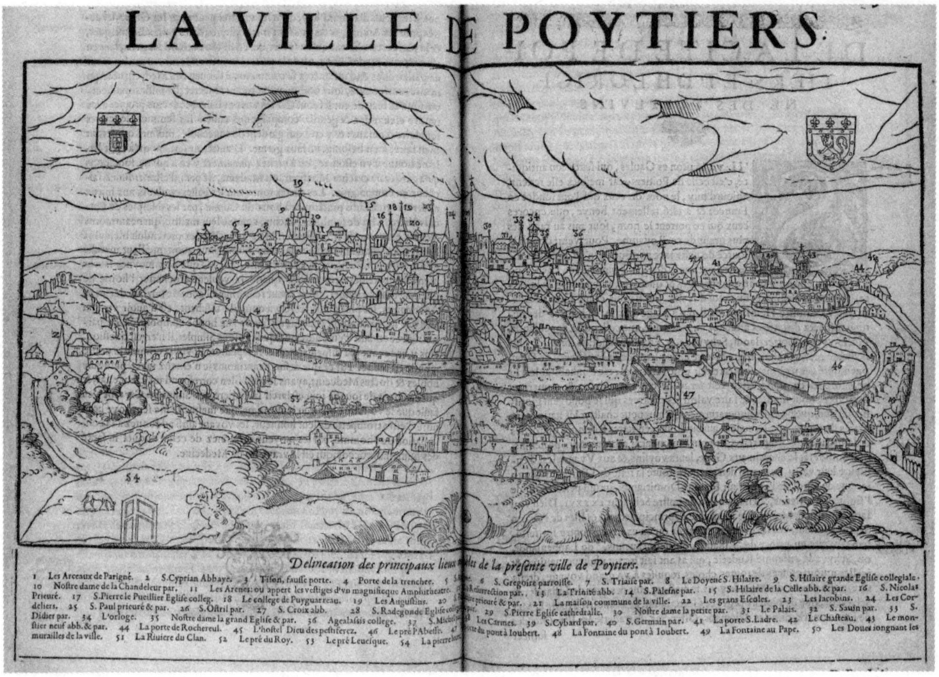

FIGURE 30. Anonymous, *Poitiers* from Antoine Du Pinet, *Plans, Portraits and Descriptions of Several Cities and Fortresses of Europe, Asia, Africa, the Indies and the New Lands*, 1564, woodcut, 20 × 39.5 cm, The John Carter Brown Library at Brown University, 2-size E 564.D934p.

and the New Lands; Poitiers, also included in the latter work; Bourges, a view of which accompanied Jean Chaumeau's 1566 *History of Berry*; and Nîmes, whose general aspect and leading monuments were illustrated in Jean Poldo d'Albenas's *Historical Discourse on the Ancient and Illustrious City of Nîmes*.[74] Since city views were regularly made and sold as single sheet items before being assembled into volumes, views might also have been available of Orléans and Chartres, for François de Belleforest's 1575 *Universal Cosmography* includes depictions of both of them.[75]

---

[74] *Epitome de la corographie d'Europe, illustré de pourtraitz des villes plus renommées d'icelle* (Lyon: Balthazar Arnoullet, 1553); Antoine Du Pinet, *Plantz, pourtraitz et descriptions de plusieurs villes et forteresses tant de l'Europe, Asie et Afrique, que des Indes, et terres neuves* (Lyon: Jean d'Ogerolles, 1564); Chaumeau, *Histoire de Berry* (Lyon: Antoine Gryphius, 1566); Poldo d'Albenas, *Discours historial de l'antique et illustre cité de Nismes* (Lyon: Guillaume Rouillé, 1560). For a guide to early atlases and collections of city views, see Mireille Pastoureau, *Les Atlas français XVI*[e]*-XVII*[e] *siècles. Répertoire bibliographique et étude* (Paris, 1984).

[75] Belleforest, *La cosmographie universelle de tout le monde* (Paris: Nicolas Chesneau, 1575).

Perrissin and Tortorel appear to have used only the view of Poitiers. Perrissin's depiction of this city in plate 34 shows the city from exactly the same perspective as the earlier city view, which is reproduced in figure 30. So many details, such as the location and appearance of the bridges, the houses and hill in the foreground, and the rhythm of the city's steeples and towers, match precisely that there can be little doubt that Perrissin worked with the view in front of him. But he also made a number of noticeable changes. Not only, as already suggested, did he fill in virtually all of the open space within the city walls with large buildings, some of a circular sort atypical for the era. He made the walls larger than in the earlier city view, and he failed to capture the steep slope leading down to the river from the southwest (left) side of the city. Instead, he made that side of the town, which was located on a promontory, appear to nestle inside a valley. Atop the new hill that he placed beyond the city, he figured the sortie made by Poitiers' defenders on August 12, 1569. Altering the topography in this way gave him more room to show details of the engagement and the breaches made in the city's walls.

With this one exception, the makers of the series do not appear to have been very assiduous in seeking out printed information that could provide them with sketches of the places or buildings they had to represent, but this does not mean that they made no effort to inform themselves about and to evoke characteristic features of these localities. In drawing Tours (scene 14) and Orléans (scenes 23 and 24), the artists knew enough about the cities to make them both sizeable riverside agglomerations. The two views of Orléans are also consistent with one another and depict to the right of the bridge into the city the windows of the Châtelet, which may also be observed in contemporary painted views of the town from across the Loire.[76] To evoke Nîmes in plate 38, Tortorel included depictions of its ancient Roman Coliseum and Maison Carré, labeling these in the accompanying key with the names they were usually given at the time ("Amphitheatre", letter G; "Capitolle", letter M). Alas, the buildings so labeled scarcely resemble their Roman originals, as any one who has ever visited the town can testify, and as Tortorel could have learned from a copy of Poldo d'Albenas. (See Figures 31 and 32.) Perrissin may have done a better job of informing himself about the appearance of the Grosse Tour of Bourges, which figures prominently in scene 39. As Cécile

---

[76] Close comparison of these views of Tours and Orléans with other period depictions also reveals numerous discrepancies: *faubourgs* shown as little more than open ground when they were in fact densely built; gates and towers placed incorrectly along each city's walls, an improbable skyline, and so forth. Most helpful for this comparison are the city views collected in Claude Petitfrère, "Une ville mise en scène: Tours d'après l'iconographie générale des XVIe-XVIIIe siècle" in Petitfrère ed., *Images et imaginaires de la ville à l'époque moderne* (Tours, 1998), pp. 175-210; Jacques Debal, "Les plans et perspectives d'Orléans de Gilles Hotot à Charles Pensée," "Les plans et perspectives d'Orléans de Gilles Hotot à Charles Pensée," *Bulletin de la Société d'Archéologie et d'histoire de l'Orléanais* 13 (1994), 102-27; and idem, *Orléans, une ville, une histoire* (Orléans, 1998), esp. p. 136.

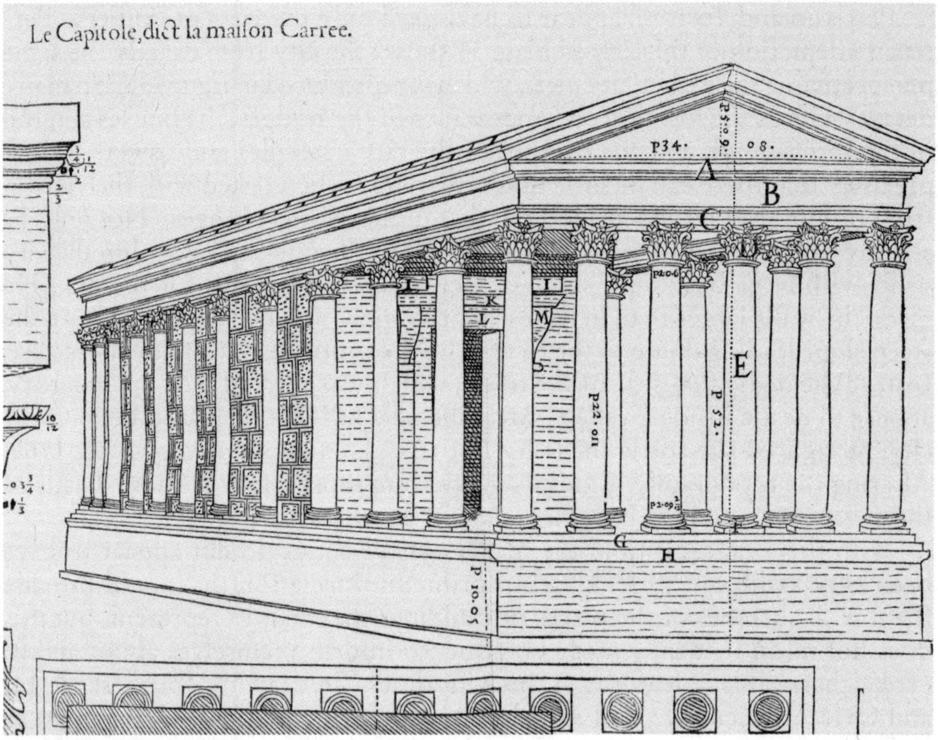

FIGURE 31. Anonymous, *The Capitol, also called the Maison Carré* from Jean Poldo d'Albenas, *Historical Discourse on the Ancient and Illustrious City of Nîmes*, 1560, woodcut, 32 × 45 cm, Library of Congress, Rosenwald Collection DC801.N72 P56 1559.

Galinier first discovered, Belleforest's 1575 description of Bourges accords considerable space to this "superb edifice" and highlights the rustic "diamond point" treatment of its circular exterior, which Perrissin may be seen to have tried to evoke in the print.[77] The depiction of the chateau of Amboise in plate 7 also seems fairly faithful to the actual appearance of that building as shown by the view of it in Jacques Androuet de Cerceau's 1576 *Les plus excellents bastiments de France*. Finally, it is known that a large cross stood in the Place de Grève in Paris within sight of the spot where executions usually took place. A cross also appears in both of Tortorel and Perrissin's Place de Grève execution scenes, but the actual cross was made of metal and stood atop a tall stone stele on the right side of the square as one faced the Hôtel de Ville, while Tortorel and Perrissin made a lower cross and set it on the left side. The actual Hôtel de Ville had a far more elaborate Renaissance facade than the sober Italian palazzo from which spectators watch Anne Du Bourg and Poltrot de

[77] Cécile Galinier, "Le receuil de Tortorel et Perrissin" (mémoire de maitrise, Université de Paris IV-Sorbonne, 1996), p. 36.

FIGURE 32. Jacques Tortorel, *The Capture of Nîmes,* "M. Le Capitolle", 1570, etching, 32 × 50 cm, detail, BPU, Ba 4538 Rés.

Méré meet their fate in the Tortorel and Perrissin prints.[78] The smallest localities, such as Montbrison (plate 15), St Jean d'Angély (plate 37), or Le Pouzin (plate 40), are never shown as anything other than generic cityscapes.

In conclusion, the artists made an effort to evoke the more celebrated places and monuments that they included in their scenes, but their prints were not accurate representations of most of them, although they did show the bridges, watercourses, and fortifications around Poitiers, the chateau of Amboise, and the Grosse Tour of Bourges with some precision.[79] Rather than

78 *Ibid.*, pp. 39-40; David Thomson, *Renaissance Paris: Architecture and Growth, 1475-1600* (Berkeley, 1984), pp.75-6.

79 The absence of topographical precision seems greater yet in the battle scenes from the series—hardly surprisingly, since most of the battle sites only gained notoriety as a result of the engagement that took place there. One enthusiastic military historian claimed that the artists' depiction of the site of the battle of Dreux is so faithful that they must have visited it. Indeed, he asserted, old timers had even been able to show him where the windmill that figures prominently within the six prints of the battle had stood. They had found slates from it while digging in the fields. Raymond de Coynart, *L'année 1562 et la bataille de Dreux* (Paris, 1894), p. vi. Far more plausible, however, is the careful assessment of the print of the battle of La Roche-l'Abeille in Franck Delage, *La troisième guerre de religion en Limousin, combat de La Roche-l'Abeille 1569* (Limoges, 1950), appendix 1, which concludes (p. 120) "Il ne faut donc pas chercher dans l'estampe de Tortorel une figuration exacte du site où se livra la bataille. . . . Ces vagues indications n'ont pas de valeur topographique."

interrogating informants closely about the appearance of the cities they were asked to depict or seeking views of them in the libraries of Geneva's learned, they were usually content to evoke the places in question in a fairly general manner. They also did not hesitate to modify topographic details as necessary to provide space for the stories being narrated in the image. For those familiar with the places in question, of course, the way in which they were depicted would have subverted the claim to eyewitness authenticity made in the title page and note "To the Reader", especially in this era when published collections of city views were beginning to spread information about the appearance of distant cities.

And then there are those curious circular buildings that recur so often in Tortorel and Perrissin's cityscapes. These point to the influence exercised over the artists by another important visual source for the series identified some time ago by Jean Ehrmann. More broadly, they serve to remind us that as they worked on the series, they were not only influenced by single sheet news prints, battle scenes, and city views. Since they had to make views not just of battles and sieges, but also of tournaments and massacres, deathbeds and peace parleys, echoes of other kinds of paintings and prints also found their way into the work.

As Ehrmann observed, several massacre scenes in the series owe an evident compositional debt to Antoine Caron's paintings of the *Massacre of the Triumvirs*, multiple versions of which were made for leading court figures between 1556 and 1566, and of which a woodcut in the style and format of the rue de Montorgueil (figure 33) was also made.[80] In all of these versions, as in Tortorel and Perrissin's scene 12 *The Massacre of Sens* and scene 14 *The Massacre of Tours*, numerous small, separate episodes of butchery unfold within a large open space framed by the buildings of an imagined city. Like Tortorel and Perrissin's cityscapes, the Caron paintings also include many circular domes and buildings. (Note the structure at the vanishing point of the rue de Montorgueil print.) Such structures likewise appear with improbable frequency in a contemporary painting of the Huguenot occupation of Lyon in 1562 modeled after this print, which suggests that they may have become something of a convention in Lyon paintings of city scenes at this time.[81] The compositional format used in these paintings and prints allowed an artist to narrate numerous different episodes of a single killing spree within a single picture space, just as pamphlet accounts of massacres narrated multiple episodes in a small booklet. At the same time, even while immediately conveying a sense of a swarm of killers let loose through a city, it obliged the artist to diminish the scale of the individual acts of violence shown, thereby reducing

---

80 Ehrmann, "Massacre and Persecution Pictures," 195-9.

81 Illustrated in Denis Crouzet, *Les guerriers de Dieu. La violence au temps des troubles de religion (vers 1525-vers 1610)* (2 vols., Seyssel, 1990), I, plates.

FIGURE 33. Anonymous, *The Massacre of the Triumvirs*, c. 1565, woodcut, 46.5 × 73 cm, BN, Estampes, Rés AA5 Gourmont, Cliché Bibliothèque nationale de France.

FIGURE 34. Augustin Hirschvogel, *The Massacre of the Innocents*, 1545, etching, 28.5 × 52 cm, Graphische Sammlung ETH Zurich, photo Graphische Sammlung ETH Zurich.

as well the immediate emotional impact of the scene, but obliging the viewer to look at the specific details and thus gradually to discover the full horror of the event.

Another of the massacre scenes in the *Quarante Tableaux* echoed a different iconographic tradition. Scene 11 *The Massacre of Vassy* brings the viewer much closer to the violence. The victims are shown packed claustrophobically together inside the barn where they had gathered to worship. Men crouch in terror and cover their heads. Women cradle their infants, trying to shelter them from the drawn weapons of the onrushing soldiers. Such a mass of victims desperately trying to protect themselves or their children also regularly appears in depictions of the Massacre of the Innocents, including those made as prints by Marc-Antonio Raimondi after Raphael (1511), Augustin Hirschvogel (1545), and Giovanni Battista de Cavalieri after Francesco Salviati (1561).[82] (See figure 34.) Needless to say, this visual association would have added to the pathos of the scene for those familiar with paintings or prints of the Massacre of the Innocents.

Still other kinds of scenes required different compositional strategies yet again. In representing scene 3 *The Tournament at Which Henry II Was Fatally*

---

[82] Philippe Rouillard, "Marc-Antoine Raimondi. Les Massacres des Innocents," *Nouvelles de l'Estampe* no.179-180 (2001-2002), 12; Augustin Hirschvogel, *The Massacre of the Innocents*, etching, 28.5 × 52 cm, *Hollstein German*, XIIIA, 147; Suzanne Boorsch, "*The Massacre of the Innocents* after Francesco Salviati by Giovanni Battista Cavalieri," *PQ* 16 (1999), 270-71.

FIGURE 35. Monogrammist HCB, *Tournament in the Belvedere Courtyard*, c. 1565, engraving and etching, 43.5 × 58 cm, British Museum, 1871-8-12-775.

Wounded, Perrissin appears to have been responding to the extensive prior tradition of depicting tournaments in prints for the purposes of recording major aristocratic festivities.[83] Comparison of his two different compositions for this event with earlier German and Italian depictions of similar scenes such as that illustrated in figure 35 offers suggestive hints about why he may have revised his initial composition. Several conventional features recur throughout prior tournament scenes. The competition is shown taking place within an enclosed space filled with onlookers. Serried ranks of horsemen surround the tiltyard and enclose it across the front. Considerable care is devoted to the visual description of the square in which the tournament takes

[83] Some examples: *Lucas Cranach d. Ä. Das gesamte graphische Werk* (Munich, n.d.), pp. 380, 392, 394, 396; Geisberg, *German Single-Sheet Woodcut 1500-1550*, IV, 1561-3; Jost Amman, *Eigentliche verzeichnuss eines gantzen Thurniers*, woodcut, 20.3 × 35.3 cm, *Hollstein German*, II, 28; [Georg Rüxner], *Anfang, ursprung und herkomen des Thurniers inn Teutscher Nation* (Simmern, 1532); [idem], *Thurnier Buch* (Frankfurt, 1566); Bury, *The Print in Italy*, pp. 162-3; Antonio Lafréry, *Designo del torneamento fatto il lunedi Carnouale in Roma nel Theatro Vaticano*, etching, 1565, Anne SK Brown Military Collection, John Hay Library, Brown University.

place. In Perrissin's composition that I have labelled 3a and that would not be retained for full sets of the prints, the artist takes the viewer right into the tiltyard close to the barrier where the king and his accidental assassin break their lances, focusing the viewer's attention on the fragment of Montgomery's lance entering the king's visor and wounding him fatally in the eye. In the upper left hand corner, a second smaller scene shows several attendants rushing to the aid of the wounded king as he gamely clings to his mount in the aftermath of the accident. The second composition stands much closer to other representations of tournament scenes, showing the entire tiltyard and surrounding ranks of watching knights, as well as many details of the decoration of the *place* including the Latin inscription "Henry II by grace of God unconquered king of France", which assumes a heavy weight of irony in view of the event taking place in the yard. The depiction of the fatal collision of the two combatants is taken over from the previous composition and remains the focal point of the scene, but by framing the combat in the square, whoever was responsible for suggesting this alteration created a version that conformed more closely to the prevailing conventions for representing tournament scenes. The view would consequently have been more immediately legible to contemporaries.

Conclusion

Those responsible for designing the forty plates of the *Wars, Massacres, and Troubles* thus drew upon a broad range of visual sources, from tournament views to scenes of ancient massacres. Two prior traditions of visual representation nonetheless appear to have been especially important in inspiring both the idea for the series and the composition of the greatest number of its scenes. The first is that of the large scale history cycles that had long been a staple of artistic production and that began to be produced in graphic form in the middle decades of the sixteenth century in Antwerp, Lyon, and Paris. In particular, Hieronymus Cock's *Victories of Charles V* adapted the tradition of narrative history cycles to the format of the picture book or suite of prints and showed that a graphic history of recent events could be a commercial success. The second is that of single-sheet images depicting current events, whose production also spread into both France and the Low Countries in the decades immediately prior to 1570. Like the *Wars, Massacres, and Troubles*, these latter prints promised to provide a "true portrait" of the events they showed. They also disseminated a range of visual languages for representing battles and sieges characterized by attention to the specifics of the engagement set within a landscape drawn in a manner inspired by cartography and city views. The creators of the *Wars, Massacres, and Troubles*, working at a moment when experiments with new kinds of picture books of many sorts were multiplying, applied elements of these languages, a general avoidance of anachronism and typology, and the frequent use of simultaneous narration to the new form of the graphic narrative history cycle. One or two contemporary current events prints were copied directly to make scenes for the series. The result was a suite of prints that were generally, although not always (as we shall see), anti-heroic in character and closely engaged with the specifics of the events shown.

These two traditions do not exhaust the artists' debts. Since the series included many different kinds of scenes, the artists drew upon a range of figurative traditions. At the same time, they made only limited efforts to palliate their lack of direct knowledge about the architectural details and layout of the cities they showed by searching out published views of the cities in question. Instead, when they did not draw purely stereotypical images of walled cities, they were most often content to evoke a specific place through a rough approximation of its geographic situation or prominent landmarks. This may reflect the haste with which they had to work to complete so large a project. It partially subverted their claim to present a true picture of the events shown. Yet it also suggests that they considered it less important to render exactly the physical appearance of the places where the events took place than to convey the narrative details of what happened. Indeed, within the limits provided by their modest artistic skill, Perrissin and Tortorel did more than simply copy prior models. They also devised compositional elements of their own that further intensified the "you are there" effect by bringing the spectator closer to the action of sieges and allowing more incidents to be packed into a single scene—even at the cost of modifying the topography of the one city that they drew on the basis of a published city view.

Conveying narrative detail, then, was clearly a high priority. But how accurate were the details provided in the scenes or their accompanying keys? From what sources, and with what care, were they gathered? What was included and what was omitted? Having analyzed the visual language of the prints and the accuracy of their settings, we must next attend to their narrative content.

CHAPTER 4

THE PRINTS AS HISTORY AND INFORMATION: THE SOURCES

The note "To the Reader" that prefaced the early versions of the *Wars, Massacres and Troubles* tells the "*ami lecteur*" that "these little *tableaux*" were made to satisfy the wish of many people to "truly know (*savoir au vray*)" the remarkable things that have occurred in France in the past years and to inform posterity faithfully about them. Since the truth is often obscured by partisan affections, the text continues, those responsible for it "have with great effort and labor sought to represent these varied events according to the reports of those who were eyewitnesses and who have faithfully and dispassionately recounted all of the circumstances." The title page that subsequently replaced the note "To the Reader" similarly announces a suite of forty pictures "all gathered from the testimony of those who were there in person and saw [the events], and truly portrayed."

These promises of eyewitness authority and impartiality cannot be accepted at face value. As the preceding chapter has shown, the claim to offer a "true portrait" was an absolutely conventional element of contemporary *flugblätter*, whether they were in fact based on eyewitness testimony or not. The manner in which the cities in the series are represented shows that the prints' creators had little direct knowledge of these places and made only a moderate effort to find out their actual appearance. At best, the *Quarante Tableaux* represent the efforts of a group of people working in Geneva to imagine what events at which they were not present might have looked like and to develop effective strategies of visual representation to narrate what they were able to learn about them. But at the same time, as the preceding chapter also showed, the compositions often strove to maximize the amount of narrative detail that could be squeezed into the picture space. Many of the legends accompanying the prints report exceptionally precise bits of information. Purchasers who examined scene 15 attentively could learn, for instance, that the Protestants who took Montbrison used three artillery pieces to open the breach in the wall through which the attackers entered and two other cannon to lob shots at an angle into the city near the breach, and that as the attacking soldiers advanced through the breach, a piece of the wall collapsed, killing four or five. Key letter L to scene 37 indicates that, during the siege of St Jean d'Angély a sortie from the Niort gate led by the captain La Motte resulted in the capture of an enemy standard, the spiking of an unspecified number of coulevrines, the destruction of five to six barrels of gunpowder, and the killing of thirty to forty enemy soldiers.

From their situation in Geneva, the makers of the series would have been well located to learn such details of the actions they had to represent, for few causes have been as concerned to record their early history as the French Reformed churches. Within the first generation, adherents produced a remarkable range of histories, many of them published in Geneva, dealing with different aspects of the recent past, from Jean Crespin's enormously influential martyrologies to the massive *Ecclesiastical History of the Reformed Churches in the Kingdom of France*, from short pamphlet accounts of specific events to longer document collections and narrative histories of the turbulent affairs of "religion and the republic" since the reign of Henry II. The publication of so many histories dealing with events in France between 1559 and 1570 would have provided ample grist for the mill of the *Wars, Massacres and Troubles*. Furthermore, the refugee-swollen Geneva of 1569-1570 held many people who had personally witnessed events depicted in the series. Even as the artists worked on the project, potential new informants arrived, such as Andrew Melville, the future tribune of Scottish presbyterianism, who reached Geneva in November 1569 after walking across France from Poitiers, which he fled in the wake of the siege that is the subject of plate 34.[1] Rumor and letters offered the printmakers still other possible sources of information. The correspondence of Geneva's leading pastors shows that they developed a substantial network of informants to stay abreast of events in France and communicated what they learned to their colleagues in Switzerland and Germany. Details could have reached the larger Geneva public through their sermons or passing remarks. Of course, the fact that virtually all of these channels of information would have been Protestant ones would have molded what passed through them.

This chapter explores how the makers of the print series gathered their information. It also begins to examine the historical vision expressed in the series through a close look at its representation of a number of events. For these purposes, the abundance of early Huguenot historical works is a godsend, for the ample corpus of such texts provides a range of works that can be examined to see if and when the makers of the *Quarante Tableaux* turned into pictures details found in prior publications. At the same time, comparison of the prints with other available accounts of the same events also brings into focus the distinctive characteristics of the way the prints relate the story. The debt of the printmakers to oral or manuscript sources is harder to establish

---

1 Charles Borgeaud, *Histoire de l'Université de Genève. L'Académie de Calvin 1559-1798* (Geneva, 1900), p. 109.

with precision than their reliance on published histories, but such sources can be presumed to have been used where no prior published source for the information found in the prints can be located. As indicated in the Introduction, a major component of my research has been to compare the scenes of the *Quarante Tableaux* with all other early printed accounts of the same events that I could locate. The notes in Part 2 of this book spell out just where the details of each image and its accompanying caption either follow or depart from prior printed accounts of the same event. Here the chief lessons of this investigation will be summarized; the prints will be located in relation to other channels through which information circulated in Geneva; a number of scenes will be examined to show their debt to prior printed accounts and what was particular about their rendering of the scene in question; and the accuracy of the views in the series will be assessed through comparison with other documents of the period.

French Protestant Historical Writing and Its Relation to the Print Series

Early Huguenot histories dealing with events of the recent French past can be roughly classified into five genres. First to take shape was the martyrology. Jean Crespin's initial compilation of the lives, trials, and deaths of those who professed the true gospel and died for their beliefs appeared in 1554. It was such a success that Crespin produced additional compilations or new editions of martyr's tales virtually every year until 1563, then reorganized and expanded his work into two hugely successful in-folio editions in 1564 and 1570. After his death in 1572, Simon Goulart oversaw three more expansions.[2] Each reorganization added more historical narration of events from church history and especially from the story of the Reformation in France and the Low Countries to the initial tales of martyrdom. The *Book of Martyrs* rapidly became a powerful instrument for shaping the identity and beliefs of the faithful.

The controversial public events in which the cause soon found itself embroiled also led its partisans to turn quickly to the medium of the pamphlet to justify its actions and disseminate its version of events. A short history of the conspiracy of Amboise, probably written by François Hotman, appeared within months of the failed effort of March 1560 to remove the young king

---

[2] Jean François Gilmont, *Jean Crespin, un éditeur réformé du XVIe siècle* (Geneva, 1981), ch. 8; idem, *Bibliographie des éditions de Jean Crespin, 1550-1572* (2 vols., Verviers, 1981), I, 46-8, 56-9, 66-8, 71, 74, 80-81, 128-31, 139-41, 162-3, 168-9, 225-6; Arthur Piaget and Gabrielle Berthoud, *Notes sur le livre des martyrs de Jean Crespin* (Neuchâtel, 1930), ch. 1; Jean Crespin, *Actes des martyrs deduits en sept livres* (Geneva: Crespin, 1564); idem, *Histoire des vrays tesmoins de la verité de l'Evangile* (Geneva: Crespin, 1570); idem, *Histoire des martyrs* ed. Benoit.

Francis II from the control of his Guise relatives.[3] The arrest and trial of Anne Du Bourg was recounted in a pamphlet history first published in 1561.[4] As incidents of violence against the Huguenots multiplied in early 1562, the Protestants multiplied accounts of these to demonstrate their victimization to both domestic and foreign readers.[5]

The French Reformed churches also soon initiated a collaborative project to assemble an ecclesiastical history of their initial formation and early travails. As the First Civil War drew to a close, the numerous ministers who had taken refuge in Orléans instructed those returning to their churches "to put into articles the memorable things that have happened to the churches and bring them to the next general synod." Five months later, the fourth national synod that met in Lyon instructed each congregation to make a "faithful compilation of everything most remarkable that has happened by Divine Providence in the places of their jurisdiction and to send these Relations to our reverend Brothers in Geneva." By 1565 Theodore Beza could report that he had received more relations than a mule could carry and hoped soon to start assembling these into an ecclesiastical history of the churches' origins and growth. The task required another fifteen years to complete, but when the resulting work was finally published in 1580, readers could understand why. It stretched to 1,735 pages.[6]

Also at the end of the First Civil War, Eloi Gibier, the prince of Condé's semi-official printer in Orléans, found himself saddled with excess copies of the many memoranda produced by the Huguenot leaders during the war to justify their actions, and began to sell them in sets. They sold well enough to inspire another, unknown printer to issue many of the same manifestos in

---

3 *L'histoire du tumulte d'Amboyse advenu au moys de Mars MDLX* ([Strasbourg], 1560); Donald R. Kelley, *François Hotman: A Revolutionary's Ordeal* (Princeton, 1973), pp. 110-19, esp. 118-19.

4 *La Vraye Histoire, Contenant l'inique Jugement et fausse procedure faite contre le fidele serviteur de Dieu Anne du Bourg* (n.p., 1561 and Lyon: J. Marceau, 1562).

5 *Histoire de la cruautee exercee par Francoys de Lorraine, Duc de Guyse, et les siens en la ville de Vassy, le premier jour de Mars 1562* (n.p., 1562, also Caen, 1562 as *Destruction du saccagement, exerce cruellement par le Duc de Guise et sa cohorte*); *Discours entier de la persecution et cruauté exercée en la ville de Vaissy, par le Duc de Guyse, le 1 de Mars 1562* (n.p., 1563); *Historia wie Jemerlich und erbarmlich die armen Christen des Reformierten Evangelischen Kirchen zu Sens aus haimlichen Practicken des Cardinals und Ezbischoften daselbst umbbracht geschmecht und verhergt worden sind* (n.p., 1562).

6 *Histoire ecclesiastique des Eglises réformées au royaume de France* [*HE*](original ed. Antwerp [Geneva], 1580; modern ed. by E. Baum and G. Cunitz, 3 vols., Paris, 1883-9); "Conseil et advis donné en la Congregation general faite le 15. Jour de Mars, devant Pasques à Orleans, par les Ministres assemblez de divers parts et Provinces de ce Royaume pour raison des persecutions et troubles, et à l'occasion de la paix qui s'en est ensuyvie", Gemeente Bibliotheek Rotterdam, MS Remonstrant 404, fo. 44; Jean Aymon, *Tous les synodes nationaux des Eglises reformées de France* (The Hague, 1710), I, 47; *Corr. Bèze*, VI, 73; Alain Dufour, *Théodore de Bèze* (Paris, 2002), pp. 432-7, esp. 432-3.

1564 under the title *Summary collection of the memorable things the Prince of Condé proclaimed and did for the glory of God and peace and good of the kingdom of France, against the authors of the troubles that have occurred since 1560 until the present.* This collection added the pamphlets recounting the conspiracy of Amboise and massacre of Vassy to Gibier's *receuil*, thus casting the troubles as an extended struggle on Condé's part against a succession of Guise attempts to disturb the proper order of the kingdom, while implying that the First Civil War began in reaction to the massacre of Vassy rather than with Condé's seizure of Orléans. In the following year, still another unknown printer brought out a yet more extensive set of documents covering the same period.[7] A genre was born, that of the document collection, that would flourish throughout the subsequent decades. These initial compilations formed the documentary kernel from which grew the great eighteenth-century compilation of sources about the period known as the *Mémoires de Condé*. Subsequent document collections of note would include the *Mémoires de l'Estat de France sous Charles IX*, with its rich documentation about the St Bartholomew's massacres, and the *Mémoires de la Ligue*, an invaluable source for that period.[8]

Finally, alongside these document collections Protestant printers also began to multiply volumes of "instant history" that traced the course of events almost as they unfolded. The first great success of this type was the 1565 *Commentaries on the State of Religion and the Commonweal under the kings Henry and Francis the Second and Charles Ninth*, an account of public affairs concerning religion and politics from 1556 to 1561 written by a member of the Paris Cour des Aides and intendant to the prince of Condé, Pierre de La Place. No less than five different printers saw fit to print it—in Orléans, Rouen, Caen, Paris and La Rochelle—in its first year of appearance.[9] The Third Civil War of 1568-70 gave rise to one of these instant histories, the

---

7 *Receuil des choses memorables passees et publiees pour le faict de la religion, & estat de la France. Le Tout Depuis la publication de l'Edit du xvii de Janvier 1560. jusques à l'Edit de la pacification des troubles de ce Royaume 1562* (Strasbourg: Pierre Estiard, 1565); Jean-François Gilmont, "La première diffusion des 'Mémoires de Condé' par Eloi Gibier en 1562-1563," in P. Aquilon and H.-J. Martin eds., *Le livre dans l'Europe de la Renaissance* (Tours, 1985), pp. 58-70; Amy Graves, "La méthode pragmatique: la pratique de l'histoire dans les *Mémoires de Condé* et leurs prolongations," in D. Bohler and C. Maignien Simonin eds., *Ecritures de l'histoire (XIVe-XVIe siècles)* (Geneva, 2005), pp. 455-69.

8 [Simon Goulart], *Mémoires de l'estat de France sous Charles neufiesme* ([Geneva: Vignon], 1576); Robert M. Kingdon, *Myths about the St. Bartholomew's Day Massacres 1572-1576* (Cambridge, Ma., 1988); *Mémoires de la Ligue* ([Geneva], 1590; 2nd enlarged edition in 4 vols., [Geneva], 1602-1604).

9 [Pierre de La Place], *Commentaires de l'Estat de la Religion et Republique soubs les Rois Henry & Francois seconds & Charles neufieme* (n.p., 1565); Jean-François Gilmont, "Les premières éditions des ouvrages historiques de La Place et de La Popelinière" in R. Peter and B. Roussel eds., *Le Livre et la Réforme*, special issue of the *Revue Française de l'Histoire du Livre* (1987), pp. 120-26, 136-44.

Memoires de la III guerre civile et des derniers troubles de France sous Charles IX, so quickly that a first edition appeared even before the end of the war. Jean de Serres, the author of other works of this sort, explained that his goal in compiling them was not so much to offer a true history of the events recounted—it was still too early for this—as to provide materials for such a history and an explanation of recent events for Christians in other countries who love the truth.[10] But it did not take long for other historians to turn the material offered by these "*mémoires*", "*receuils*", and "*commentaires*" into "perfect histories" that sought to view the events of the era with greater dispassion, lay bare the motivations of the various parties, and draw out the lessons of military history and statecraft that could be revealed by judicious comparison with events of the more distant past. This was the ambition of Lancelot Voisin, sieur de La Popelinière's *True and Entire History of These Recent Troubles both in France and Flanders and Surrounding Lands*, first published in 1571 and regularly enlarged and reworked until the folio edition of 1581 entitled simply *History of France* incurred the censure of a national synod for presenting the motives and actions of the members of the Reformed cause in too unflattering a light.[11]

These works of Huguenot history had various purposes and points of view. Crespin's accounts of the edifying lives and still more edifying deaths of those who made the ultimate sacrifice for the faith were meant to inspire. Many of the pamphlets gathered into the early *receuils* offered highly tendentious versions of recent Huguenot actions that sought to deny accusations that the cause was seditious. Some of the histories included prodigious tales of persecutors who met agonizing death or meaning-laden coincidences that were meant to underscore God's providential direction of affairs. La Popelinière strove to illustrate what he called "this new means of showing the aims and actions of both sides as if one were neutral and equally unattached to both, as the historiographer should be."[12] Yet for all their differences of aim and outlook, these works also shared many common characteristics, not least because they copied extensively from one another. All of their authors or

---

[10] B.A. Vermaseren, "La première édition des *Commentaires* de Jean de Serres," *BHR* 23 (1961), 118.

[11] [La Popelinière], *La vraye et entière histoire des ces derniers troubles, advenus tant en France qu'en Flandres et pays circonvoisins* (1st ed. [Caen], 1571; I consulted the 2nd ed. of 1572); idem, *Histoire de France* ([La Rochelle: Pierre Haultin], 1581); *Les Trois Mondes de La Popelinière* ed. Anne-Marie Beaulieu (Geneva, 1997), pp. 16-23; Gilmont, "Les premières éditions de La Place et La Popelinière"; George Wylie Sypher, "La Popelinière's *Histoire de France*: A Case of Historical Objectivity and Religious Censorship," *Journal of the History of Ideas* 24 (1963), 41-54; Kevin C. Robbins, "Rewriting Protestant History: Printing, Censorship by Pastors, and the Dimensions of Dissent among the Huguenots—the La Popelinière Case at La Rochelle, 1581-85" in Andrew Pettegree et al. eds., *The Sixteenth-Century French Religious Book* (Aldershot, 2001), pp. 239-55.

[12] *Corr. Bèze*, XXII, 19.

compilers sought to make their accounts plausible by accumulating as much circumstantial detail as possible. All quoted extensively from relevant documents or printed them in their entirety. All strove to ensure that their enemies could not catch them out in errors. Even when they copied accounts from earlier works or prior editions, they introduced small changes, many of which modified incidental details in an apparent concern to get them right. The same accumulation of circumstantial detail would also characterize the prints of Tortorel and Perrissin.

A few Catholic historians also wrote accounts of these years, but their accounts were at once less numerous, less well documented, and more violently partisan. As Henri Hauser wrote in his classic guide to the sources for the history of sixteenth-century France, "It is striking that on the 'papist' side one scarcely encounters anything other than mediocre annalists . . . or complete fanatics. . . . The talent and sense of history lie on the other side."[13] The amplitude and precision of early Huguenot historical writing arose from several sources. First, the movement took shape at a time of noteworthy changes in historical consciousness that were especially strong in the circles from French Protestantism drew its opinion leaders. The spread of legal humanism in France's law faculties, one of the cause's chief recruiting grounds, bred heightened respect for the evidentiary value of original documents and a more contextual and critical approach to that evidence.[14] Second, just as the first enduring Reformed churches began to take shape, the 1555 publication of Johann Sleidan's *Commentaries on Religion and the Commonweal in the reign of Emperor Charles V* provided an influential model of how extensive research, careful citation, and a professed concern for truth and candor could be combined with engagement in the Protestant cause to produce a history of contemporary religious developments that advanced the interests of the cause while providing a well documented account of its origins and rise to legal recognition. Sleidan, a graduate of Orléans' law faculty and a resident of Strasbourg, was the official historiographer of the Schmalkaldic League, a position that he used to gain access to the archives of several Protestant territories. His history was translated into French within a year of its appearance and printed by the publisher-historian Crespin, also a former law student. Even before this, the project had been known to Geneva's pastors, for Sleidan had written to Calvin in 1553 hunting documents.[15] More broadly, across

---

13 Hauser, *Les sources de l'histoire de France. XVIe siècle (1494-1610)* (4 vols., Paris, 1906-15), III, 14.

14 See especially Donald R. Kelley, *Foundations of Modern Historical Scholarship: Language, Law and History in the French Renaissance* (New York, 1970).

15 Jean Sleidan, *Histoire de l'estat de la religion et republique sous Charles V* ([Geneva]: Jean Crespin, 1556); Gilmont, *Crespin*, p. 149; Donald R. Kelley, "Johann Sleidan and the Origins of History as a Profession," *Journal of Modern History* 52 (1980), 573-98; A.G. Dickens and John M. Tonkin, *The Reformation in Historical Thought* (Oxford, 1985), pp. 10-19.

Europe prudent politicians increasingly appreciated history as a valuable form of knowledge, founded university chairs in the subject, and hired learned scholars to read history to and with them. Authors of treatises on historical method made increasingly strong claims for the importance and utility of historical knowledge as a mirror of life and politics and devoted increasing attention to the problem of how to assure its veracity.[16] The spokesmen of the French Reformed movement were astute political animals aware of these trends. They knew that to advance their cause's interests, they had to control perceptions of its development and goals in the most persuasive way possible.

These printed Huguenot histories were important for the *Quarante Tableaux* in two ways. First, they employed a rhetoric of historical exposition that eschewed coarse polemic or vituperation and sought to convince the reader of the veracity of the exposition through the accumulation of precise circumstantial information about the people and events being narrated. In many ways, Tortorel and Perrissin's compositions were the visual equivalent of this rhetoric. Second, they provided the direct source for an important minority of the Tortorel and Perrissin prints. Close comparison of the details in the *Quarante Tableaux* with the histories published prior to the end of 1570 reveals fourteen images for which specific features of the action shown and the phrasing of the accompanying key match the contents of an earlier book or pamphlet so exactly that this must have been used in making the plate in question. Two books were particularly important sources for the print series. Jean Crespin's 1564 *Acts of the Martyrs in Seven Books* seems to have been used in making prints 2, 5, 6, 7, and 11, the scenes concerning Anne Du Bourg, the conspiracy of Amboise, and the massacre of Vassy. The 1570 *Memoires de la III. guerre civile* was a key source for scenes 32 through 39, those running from the battle of Jarnac to the thwarted Protestant attempt to surprise Bourges. One other print, plate 12 *The Massacre of Sens*, derived from a pamphlet account of that event subsequently incorporated into the 1570 edition of Crespin. It must be added at once that all of the events for which Tortorel and Perrissin appear to have followed the 1564 edition of Crespin were also narrated very similarly in pre-1564 Protestant pamphlets or histories. Some of these that were subsequently incorporated into Crespin match the prints exactly in the details they provide, notably the 1563 *Full account of the persecution and cruelty exercised in the city of Vassy by the Duke of Guyse*, and, for the conspiracy of Amboise, Antoine de La Roche

---

16 Kelley, "Sleidan and the Origins of History as a Profession," pp. 579-85; idem, *Faces of History from Herodotus to Herder* (New Haven, 1998), ch. 5; Anthony Grafton and Lisa Jardine, "'Studied for Action': How Gabriel Harvey Read His Livy," *Past & Present* 129 (1990), 30-78; John L. Brown, *The Methodus ad Facilem Historiarum Cognitionem of Jean Bodin: A Critical Study* (Washington, 1939); Claude-Gilbert Dubois, *La conception de l'histoire en France au XVIe siècle (1560-1610)* (Paris, 1977), pp. 71-158.

Chandieu's *History of the Persecutions and Martyrs of the Church of Paris.*[17] Two considerations argue for the hypothesis that the makers of the prints relied upon Crespin rather than the *Full account* and La Roche Chandieu. First, a few precise details of both versions of scene 2 *The Mercuriale Where Anne Du Bourg Was Arrested* match ones found in the 1564 edition of Crespin but nowhere else.[18] Second, it seems more economical to attribute their borrowings to a single source that contains all of the details that reappear in the prints rather than to presume that they used two or three.[19]

Crespin's martyrology and the 1570 *Memoires de la III. guerre civile* were works of quite different sorts. In drawing heavily upon Crespin for scenes 2, 5, 6, 7, and 11, the makers of the *Wars, Massacres and Troubles* would have ensured, consciously or unconsciously, that these prints were heavily tinted by the elements of self-justification and edification so powerful within certain strands of Huguenot historical writing. Scene 11 *The Massacre of Vassy* illustrates this well. Ernest Lavisse first noted long ago that the *Full account of the persecution and cruelty exercised in the city of Vassy by the Duke of Guyse* is the original source for this print.[20] This was just one of three accounts of the massacre published in its wake, two by Protestant authors who accuse the duke of Guise of instigating the violence, and one by a Catholic author who declares that the duke had simply gone to the barn where the Protestants had gathered to worship to remonstrate with them, and that the violence began after he was pelted with stones by those inside the barn and bloodied, which prompted his men to intervene.[21] The *Full account* was first

---

17 *Discours entier de la persecution et cruauté exercée en la ville de Vaissy*, reprinted in *MC*, III, 124-49, integrated definitively into Crespin, *Histoire des martyrs* in 1564; [Antoine de La Roche Chandieu], *Histoire des persecutions et martyrs de l'Eglise de Paris depuis l'An 1557. jusques au tepms du Roy Charles neufviesme* (Lyon, 1563), pp. 431-41, integrated into Crespin, *Actes des martyrs* (1564) but subsequently removed in favor of the account of the same event in La Place, *Commentaires de l'Estat de la Religion et Republique*, fos. 49v-58.

18 See the notes accompanying prints 2a and 2b in Part 2.

19 Only the 1564 edition of Crespin and Antoine de La Roche Chandieu's 1563 *History of the Persecutions and Martyrs of the church of Paris*, assert, as does the key to this print number 2b, that Henry II on arriving at the Mercuriale ordered the judges to continue their discussions as before. Only these two works recount the final minutes of Anne Du Bourg in terms virtually identical to the wording of the key of scene 5 *The Execution of Anne Du Bourg*, and contain details of the enterprise of Amboise that once again are echoed verbatim in the key to scene 6 devoted to this event (see for further evidence the notes accompanying the relevant plates in Part 2.) Only Crespin and the *Full Account* of Vassy contain many of the details figured in scene 11. It seems more probable that the makers of the series used Crespin alone than that they took some details from Crespin, some from the *Full Account* of Vassy, and some from La Roche Chandieu.

20 Ernest Lavisse, "Le massacre fait à Vassy le premier jour de Mars 1562" in Franklin ed., *Grandes scènes historiques*, p. 3ff.

21 *Discours entier de la persecution et cruauté exercée en la ville de Vaissy*; *Histoire de la cruautee exercee par Francoys de Lorraine en la ville de Vassy*; Guillaume Morel, *Discours au*

published a year after the massacre and appears from internal evidence to have been written by the minister of the congregation. In that regard, it fits the claim of the *Quarante Tableaux*'s front matter that the series was based on eyewitness testimony. But the author hardly qualifies as dispassionate. Of the two Protestant accounts of the massacre of Vassy, the *Full account* is the more strongly partisan. It offers the highest estimate of the number of Protestant dead and wounded. It accuses the duke of Guise in the most unequivocal terms of inciting the attack on the congregation of Vassy. It accuses his men of robbing the congregation's poor box as they charged into the assembly. It recounts the minister's own survival in quasi-miraculous terms: as an enraged soldier raised his sword to dispatch him, the sword broke at the hilt. All of these last details and many other incidental circumstances recounted in this pamphlet also may be found in Perrissin's print: the duke of Guise's men tearing the poor box from the wall as they invade the barn where the Protestants were worshipping (highlighted in the key, letter I); the congregation's minister being miraculously spared when his assailant's sword breaks (key letter D); Guise's trumpeters blowing their horns twice (key letter K); the cardinal of Guise watching the massacre from outside leaning on the cemetery wall (key letter E), etc. In relying on a work like the *Full account* for information about this event, the makers of the print series incorporated a very distinctive, partisan account of the massacre of Vassy into their larger history.

They likewise offered a highly tendentious version of the conspiracy of Amboise by following earlier Protestant accounts of that event. To this day, the precise goal of what contemporary sources variously label the "conspiracy", "enterprise", or "tumult" of Amboise remains uncertain. A number of armed conspirators undoubtedly gathered in the woods around the chateau of Amboise with an eye to removing king Francis II from the control of his Guise councillors and perhaps doing harm to the leading members of the house of Lorraine. At the same time, unarmed groups of Reformed faithful appear to have assembled hoping to present a copy of their recently adopted confession of faith to the king. Foreign ambassadors present with the court at Amboise as the event unfolded report that the royal entourage was gripped with fear that the king's life was in danger. An account sent by the king to the Parlement of Paris two weeks after the event and subsequently published as a pamphlet asserts that the plot "aimed at the full subversion of our state".[22]

---

vray et en abbregé, de ce qui est dernierement advenu a Vassi, y passant Monseigneur le Duc de Guise (Paris, 1562), all reprinted in *MC*, III, 111-49.

22 *MC*, I, 347; *Calendar of State Papers and Manuscripts, Relating to English Affairs, Existing in the Archives and Collections of Venice* ed. R. Brown et al. (38 vols., London, 1864-1940), VII, 153-63; Henri Naef, *La Conjuration d'Amboise et Genève* (Geneva, 1922); idem, "Justice pour La Renaudie," *BSHPF* 117 (1971), 296-316; Lucien Romier, *La conjuration d'Amboise* (Paris, 1923); Jacques Poujol, "De la confession de foi de 1559 à la

Soon after its collapse, several Huguenot pamphlets, eager to establish that the Reformed cause was not seditious, asserted that the nobles who had sworn mutual aid to one another and who constituted a purely "civil and political cause" merely wanted a private audience with the king so that they could remonstrate to him about the harm the Guises were doing to the kingdom with their repressive laws and secret machinations. A group of leading participants in the enterprise had assembled in the chateau of Noizay awaiting the arrival of their chief, La Renaudie, when the duke of Guise sent his boon companion the duke of Nemours from Amboise to investigate suspicious activity in the area. Discovering the men, Nemours asked them what they were about. They explained their desire for an interview with the king. He replied that they had no business bearing arms for such a mission, but that if they laid down their arms, he would guarantee them on his honor that they could have their interview. Trusting him, they followed him unarmed to the castle of Amboise, but on arrival they were immediately imprisoned, tortured, and executed. Soon thereafter La Renaudie was discovered by the seigneur de Pardaillan in a nearby wood and shot. His body was taken to Amboise and hung from the city's fortifications along with those of the other victims of the repression.[23] This version of events subsequently became the accepted Huguenot vulgate. La Roche Chandieu's *History of the Persecutions and Martyrs of the Church of Paris*, Crespin, and La Place all recount the enterprise in nearly identical terms. The first two briefly indicate as well that one group of conspirators attempted an armed raid against Amboise, unaware of what had become of their co-conspirators.[24] Scenes 6 and 7 also incorporate this view of the event and the repression that followed it. The accompanying keys match portions of La Roche Chandieu and the 1564 edition of Crespin word for word.[25] This exercise in spin doctoring that depicted a

---

Conjuration d'Amboise," *BSHPF* 119 (1973), 158-76; Elisabeth A. R. Brown, "La Renaudie se venge: l'autre face de la conjuration d'Amboise" in Yves-Marie Bercé and Elena Fasano Guarini eds., *Complots et conjurations dans l'Europe moderne* (Rome, 1996), pp. 451-74.

23 *L'histoire du tumulte d'Amboyse*; *Avertissement et complainte au peuple Francoys; Ensemble l'Histoire du tumulte d'Amboise* (n.p., 1560); *MC*, I, 320-30.

24 La Roche Chandieu, *Histoire des persecutions et martyrs de l'Eglise de Paris*, pp. 431-41, subsequently copied in Crespin, *Actes des martyrs* (1564), pp. 991-5; *Petit traitté des guerres civiles advenues en France sous les Roys François II et Charles IX* (n.p., 1564), pp. 7-9; La Place, *Commentaires de l'Estat de la Religion et Republique*, fos. 49v-58, subsequently copied in Crespin, *Histoire des vrais temoins* (1570), pp. 557-8; [Jean de Serres], *Rerum gallia ob religionem gestarum, libri tres* ([Geneva: Crespin], 1570), fos. 29-32. When, probably in 1569, those responsible for the scenes of the *Quarante Tableaux* made plate 7 *The Executions at Amboise*, they also either drew on Pierre de La Place's *Commentaires de l'Estat de la Religion et Republique* or had access to the 1570 revision of Crespin's martyrology in advance of its publication, since certain minute details recounted in the key to this print repeat information found only here.

25 See the notes to these two prints in Part 2.

failed aristocratic plot as a peaceful attempt to petition the king eventuating in repression because of a breach of aristocratic honor thus found its way from a series of Protestant historical texts into the prints.

The pamphlet account that is the ur-source of scene 12 *The Massacre of Sens*, the *History of how the poor Christians of the Evangelical Reformed church of Sens were pitifully and miserably struck down by the secret designs of the Cardinal-Archbishop himself*, was also written for evident propagandistic ends. The pamphlet survives today only in a German version published in 1562, undoubtedly as part of the Huguenot campaign of propaganda and diplomacy during the troubled months after the massacre of Vassy to convince Germany's Protestant princes to send aid.[26] It probably circulated as well in a now lost French version, since a letter of Condé's from April 19, 1562 makes reference to such an account, and the 1570 edition of Crespin includes a "Histoire lamentable du massacre des fideles de l'Eglise reformee en la ville de Sens en Bourgogne" with contents identical to the German pamphlet.[27] All of the very precisely described episodes of violence against named individuals found in Perrissin's view of this event also appear in the pamphlet, as does the episode figured in its upper right corner, where the barn in which the Protestants had gathered for worship is demolished and the grapevines around it uprooted. Chapter One showed that this scene, which bears the date 1570, was one of those added late in the production process. This suggests that the pamphlet only came to the attention of those responsible for the work as they made the final scenes for the full series of forty plates. They might have learned about it as a result of its publication in the 1570 edition of Crespin. It may have been brought to their attention in either pamphlet or manuscript form prior to the publication of this work by the same person who urged them to add other scenes such as the Mercuriale and execution of Anne Du Bourg. That person might even have been Crespin or one of the employees in his printing shop who had access to it as the new edition of the martyrology was being prepared. It bears noting in this context that Crespin's printing establishment was located on the rue St Leger near the city walls on the other side of the Rive Gauche from Castellin's house and workshop. Whatever communication of materials might have occurred between Crespin's print shop and the *atelier* of Castellin et cie would not have been a matter of casual neighborly exchange.[28]

---

26 *Historia wie Jemerlich und erbarmlich die armen Christen des Reformierten Evangelischen Kirchen zu Sens umbbracht geschmecht und verhergt worden sind*. BPF, Rés 1776 (7) is the sole known copy of this pamphlet.

27 *Receuil des choses memorables passees et publiees pour le faict de la religion*, sig. t i; Crespin, *Histoire des vrays tesmoins* (1570), fos. 597-8.

28 Crespin's shop was located on the rue St Leger just inside the southern wall of the city beyond the place du Bourg-de-Four, whereas the rue des Allemans was located in the northeastern corner of the Rive Gauche. Distances, of course, were not great within the

The second printed work followed closely by a substantial number of the scenes from Tortorel and Perrissin, the *Memoires de la III. guerre civile*, was also published in Geneva by Crespin, but it was a far less partial, tendentious work of history than the récits historiques subsequently integrated into the *Book of Martyrs*. A close kinship can be observed between the prints and this book for all of the events from the Third Civil War figured in the series except the final scene of *Montbrun's Crossing of the Rhône*. In the case of the four views depicting sieges and raids from this war (scene 34 *The Siege of Poitiers*, scene 37 *The Siege of St Jean d'Angély*, scene 38 *The Capture of Nîmes*, and scene 39 *The Foiled Attempt on Bourges*), the agreement is total. The detailed narratives of these military operations provided by the prints match information in the *Memoires* right down to the specific quantities of cannonballs fired in the sieges.[29] In the case of the plates depicting the battles of Jarnac, La Roche-L'Abeille, and Moncontour, the scenes or portions of the scenes that narrate the principal actions during the battles again closely match the information found in the *Memoires*. Differences emerge, however, in the prints' depiction of the deployment of the troops on both sides prior to the battles, and the keys to the prints identify participants in the battles not named in the *Memoires*. For these aspects of these prints, the makers of the series gathered additional information from other sources.

Crespin published the first edition of the *Memoires de la III. guerre civile* at an unknown point in the year 1570. Its authorship has often been attributed to Jean de Serres, but Gilmont argues convincingly against this and concludes that the work must be deemed anonymous.[30] The last event that it recounts is the thwarted Huguenot plot to seize Bourges in December 1569—the subject of scene 39 of Tortorel and Perrissin. If the work was published just after that event at the beginning of the year 1570, the makers of the print series could have acquired it and used it to make prints 32 to 39 if and only if we assume that all of these scenes were made in that year as well. But scenes 32, 33, 35, and 36 were among the initial thirty scenes made, and of these only scene 36 bears the date 1570. This makes one suspect that the makers of the print series had access to this work or the information it contained even before it was published. Perhaps its anonymous author had a hand in advising the makers of the *Quarante Tableaux*. Or perhaps, once again, the makers of the print series had access to the work as it was being composed in Crespin's shop.

---

little city. Gilmont, *Crespin*, p. 232; E. William Monter, *Calvin's Geneva* (New York, 1967), map p. 116.

29 Numerous illustrations of this may be found in the notes to these scenes in Part 2.

30 Gilmont, *Bibliographie des éditions de Crespin*, I, 230; Gilmont, *Crespin*, p. 154. A second, expanded edition with similar chronological parameters followed in 1571: *Memoires de la troisieme guerre civile et des derniers troubles de France composées en quatre livres* ([Geneva: Jean Crespin], 1571).

The *Memoires de la III. guerre civile* chronicles events from the peace ending the Second Civil War in March 1568 to the dispersal of both sides to their winter quarters at the turn of the year 1569-1570, during the Third Civil War. The preface to the first edition asserts that its author did not originally intend to publish it, but simply noted events from day to day to preserve a record of them. Two considerations moved him to put them before the public. He wanted other nations to know the causes and course of the war so that they would not believe false reports circulated by truth's enemies, and he wanted the French nation to know what happened so that those responsible for the wars might be held in proper detestation. The preface ends with an appeal to the same value of eyewitness authority invoked in the front matter to the *Quarante Tableaux* urging "the reader devoid of passion" to believe "one who has been an eye witness to the greater part of these events."[31] The reasons cited for publishing the work betray an apologetic purpose that also emerges clearly from its opening pages, which present the initial Protestant mobilization as a justifiable act of self defense sparked by acts of violence against the Huguenots and a Catholic plot to seize their leading noblemen, in keeping with the duke of Alba's advice that the head of one salmon was worth more than fifty frogs.[32] Notwithstanding these elements of parti pris, the central core of the history is a narrative that traces in copious detail the changing fortunes of the two parties with only modest hints of favoritism to the Huguenot side, such as some brief words added after the sober account of the death of Artus de Mouy recalling him as a "valiant and brave lord, experienced in war and renowned for his exploits", or the attention given to the feat of two Protestant commanders, the count of Mansfeld and Louis of Nassau, in coordinating an organized retreat of 14 *cornettes* of reiters amid the rout at Moncontour, "a remarkable thing in such a rout".[33] Semi-miraculous elements and providentialist rhetoric of the sort found in many other Huguenot histories are noticeably absent. The work is attentive to Protestant defeats and even embarrassments as well as to victories and feats of daring. While certainly a partisan work, the *Memoires de la III. guerre civile* is a far more balanced chronicle of the changing fortunes of "two french armies" than the historical narratives found in Crespin's martyrology. The Tortorel and Perrissin prints based on this work likewise offer detail-packed views of a sequence of events in which Huguenot defeats outnumber Huguenot victories.

---

31 *Mémoires de la III. guerre civil*, "Au lecteur".

32 *Ibid*., p. 6.

33 *Ibid*., pp. 218, 208.

Information Gathered from Manuscripts or Oral Informants

Twenty-three scenes lack an evident printed or graphic source that I have been able to locate and thus seem to be based on oral or manuscript sources. The events they figure are:

The tournament at which Henry II was fatally wounded (scene 3)
The death of Henry II (scene 4)
The massacre of Cahors (scene 10)
The Huguenot capture of Valence (scene 13)
The massacre of Tours (scene 14)
The Huguenot capture of Montbrison (scene 15)
The battle of St Gilles (scene 16)
The battle of Dreux (scenes 17-22)
The siege of Orléans (scene 23)
The assassination of the duke of Guise (scene 24)
The peace negotiations outside Orléans (scene 25)
The execution of Poltrot de Méré (scene 26)
The Michelade (scene 27)
The battle of St Denis (scene 28)
The battle of Cognat (scene 29)
The siege of Chartres (scene 30)
Montbrun's crossing of the Rhône (scene 40)

As has just been mentioned, the printmakers also gathered some of their information about the forces present at the battles of Jarnac, La Roche-L'Abeille, and Moncontour from sources other than the *Memoires de la III. guerre civile*.

Some of the events just listed were reported in contemporary pamphlets or illustrated news sheets, but either the *feuilles volantes* recounting them did not reach Geneva and come to the attention of the makers of the prints series, or the production team did not trust them enough to follow them. For other events no prior printed account is known. In these instances, the print from the *Quarante Tableaux* becomes the earliest known published historical account of the event. Most of these latter episodes were subsequently narrated in later works of Huguenot historiography, most notably in either La Popelinière's *True and Entire History of These Recent Troubles* or the *Ecclesiastical History of the Reformed Churches of France*. Archival and published document collections also offer abundant independent source material for most of these events. But for one or two episodes, notably scene 14 *The Massacre of Tours* and scene 40 *Montbrun's Crossing of the Rhone*, alternative forms of early documentation about the event are rare. Here the Tortorel and Perrissin print represents one of the fullest and most informative early sources about the event available in either print or manuscript.

The episodes subsequently recounted in the *Ecclesiastical History of the Reformed Churches of France* reveal with particular clarity how the printmakers' information gathering related to other Genevan networks of information. The makers of the *Quarante Tableaux* do not appear to have had direct access to the many memoranda sent to Geneva for compilation into the *Histoire ecclesiastique*. Instead, they used their own sources or informants. Occasionally, however, their informants seem to have been the same people who wrote *mémoires* for the ecclesiastical history, as is suggested by the story behind the story told in scene 10 *The Massacre of Cahors*.

Although most of the manuscript material gathered for the *Histoire ecclesiastique* has disappeared, its apparent source for this massacre of November 19, 1561 survives among the papers of the early seventeenth-century Geneva minister Theodore Tronchin.[34] (No printed account of the event published before 1570 is known.) Both internal clues and the handwriting of this two-page account of the event indicate that it was penned by Corneille Bertram, a pastor and professor in Geneva from 1562 to 1589 who had been in Cahors when the massacre occurred.[35] His narrative attributes the massacre to a plot arranged by the canons of the cathedral, who on the appointed day sounded the tocsin and sent their servants with arms to the house of a certain Cabrerez, where the Protestants had gathered for worship. The servants set fire to the lodging, forced their way through the gate, and massacred many of those who had gathered to pray either within the courtyard of the house or in the surrounding streets. Those inside one portion of the house resisted so stoutly in a spiral staircase that the attackers had to fall back, hoping to seize them when they left the house. Instead, they escaped via the roof once night fell. Among them was the officiating minister Gaspard de La Faverge, who subsequently was sheltered by a student in one of the colleges attached to the university before slipping out of town and making his way to Cabrières, where he was able to recount the piteous news. A rich silk merchant named La Gacherie was caught as he fled, killed, then dragged to his house, where his wife and children were also killed and the house pillaged. When the massacre

---

34 BPU, MS Tronchin 8, fos. 47-8.

35 Bertram (1531-1594) was named pastor of Chancy outside Geneva in December 1562, professor of Hebrew at the academy of Geneva in 1566, and professor of theology in 1572. Related to Beza through marriage with his niece, he authored several works on Hebrew grammar and a study of the relationship between church and state in ancient Israel, *De politia judaica tam civili quam ecclesiastica* (1574), that supported the view advocated by Beza that ecclesiastical and civil jurisdiction were separate for most of the history of ancient Judaism. Borgeaud, *Histoire de l'université de Genève*, pp. 102-4, 195-9. For an instance of his handwriting that can be seen to resemble that of the manuscript, see AEG, Finances P, mandats, July 3, 1578. The attribution of the manuscript to Bertram is also supported by the ample detail within it about the actions of "a certain Corneille", deacon of the church and governor of the children of the sénéchal of Quercy. I owe thanks to Nicolas Fornerod for locating and providing me a photocopy of the document signed by Bertram.

was over, the killers laid out 25 to 30 corpses on the pavement in front of Cabrerez's house "the better to display their fury and cruelty".

The *Ecclesiastical History*'s narration of this event is identical in both structure and substance to this manuscript account except for two small changes that illuminate the work done by its Genevan editor or editors: the narrative has been slightly rewritten and rearranged to make it clearer and more concise; and La Faverge, identified in the Tronchin manuscript as the minister of Montauban temporarily detached from that church to serve Cahors, is now said to have been passing through Cahors on his way back to Geneva, and to have fled from Cahors to Montauban, not Cabrières.[36] Tortorel and Perrissin's scene 10 *The Massacre of Cahors* also agrees in many ways with the Tronchin manuscript, but more telling differences also appear. The caption to the print specifies that fires were set at three corners of "Cabreyret's" house, a detail found in none of the other accounts that suggests that the printmakers had access to independent information about the event. It also specifies, as none of the other accounts do, that people were taken to be killed to the main gateway of house; confines the scenes of killing inside the courtyard; does not identify La Faverge among those who fled via the roof or recount his and others' nocturnal getaway; makes no mention of the pillaging of La Gacherie's house and the killing of his family; and reports the arranging of the corpses on the street without reference to the "fury and cruelty" of the attackers, even while providing the same estimate of the number of bodies laid out. The overlap between the image and the manuscript is so considerable that one suspects that Bertram was also the printmakers' informant about this event, but it does not seem that they used his written memorandum that served as the basis for the *Histoire ecclesiastique*.

In the case of detail-packed scene 14 *The Massacre of Tours*, another event reported in no published works from before 1570 but subsequently recounted in the *Histoire ecclesiastique*, more substantial discrepancies may be observed between Perrissin's rendering of the event and the account in the *Ecclesiastical History*.[37] Among eight specific tales of cruelty incorporated into the print are some of the most memorable vignettes of the entire series, including prodigious tales of a sort rarely found in other prints in the series. Amid the killing, a terrified Huguenot woman gives birth, only to have the newborn snatched away and thrown into the Loire; before the infant dies, it raises its hand to the sky. A soldier holds up another Huguenot baby and offers one of his fellows an écu if he can hit it with a shot from his harquebuse. A prominent Protestant judge rumored to have swallowed some of his

---

36 *HE*, I, 939-41, integrated in 1582 into Crespin, *Histoire des Martyrs* (ed. Benoit), III, 211-2. La Faverge ended his days as a minister in Geneva. The person responsible for the corrections may have fact-checked the original story with him.

37 *HE*, II, 682-700. This account was integrated in 1582 into Crespin, *Histoire des Martyrs* (ed. Benoit), III, 313-9.

riches is strung up from a tree and disemboweled by members of the crowd hoping to find the coins in his stomach. The account in the *Histoire ecclesiastique* likewise abounds in specific instances of cruelty whose victims are often identified by name, but in only two instances are the episodes the same, and even here minor details of the episode differ. Thus, the *Histoire ecclesiastique* also recounts the disemboweling of the judge Bourgeau, but it asserts that he was hung from his feet and lowered into the river before his entrails were cut open, where in the print he is hung upright with a rope placed beneath his armpits. Here the *Quarante Tableaux* and the *Histoire ecclesiastique* would appear to have drawn their information from different traumatized survivors of the violence that followed the Catholic re-taking of Tours during the First Civil War.

The three scenes set around Orléans in early 1563—the siege of the city (scene 23), the assassination of the duke of Guise (scene 24), and the conclusion of the peace that brought the First Civil War to an end (scene 25)—offer further revealing comparisons with the *Histoire ecclesiastique*, since Theodore Beza, the chief and perhaps sole author and compiler of this work, had been in Orléans at the time and devoted considerable space to these events. For the siege of Orléans, again no printed account is known. According to the *Histoire ecclesiastique*, the duke of Guise approached the city with his troops on February 5 and quickly seized the faubourg de Portereau on the north side of the Loire due to the carelessness of the German troops assigned to guard it. The two towers that guarded the north entrance to the bridge across the river fell three days later after one of the attackers scaled a forty-foot ladder to reconnoiter one of the towers, found that its guards were all below warming themselves around a fire, quickly re-descended to notify his fellow soldiers, and led them back up the ladder. But the Protestant captain d'Andelot hastily threw up a set of ramparts in the middle of the bridge. From behind this wall and the islands in the river, the defenders of the city were able to check the advance of the attacking troops and force them to begin a long bombardment of the city.[38] The details of the capture of the tower are precisely the sort that the makers of the print series figured with precision in scenes drawn after the *Memoires de la III. guerre civile* such as plate 39 *The Foiled Attempt on Bourges*, but scene 23 *The Siege of Orléans* simply shows the city, islands and bridge from a distance, identifies with a letter "the towers taken by M. de Guise", depicts the defending troops blocking the way across the bridge, and indicates the general position of the different groups of troops and cannon attacking and defending the city. The title misdates the siege to the month of January. The key adds the details not found in the *Histoire ecclesiastique* that the attackers had 32 pieces of artillery and that the defenders destroyed an arch of the bridge to stop the attackers from crossing

[38] *HE*, II, 340-5.

it. In the sole instance of a detail typical of genre scenes of warfare found in any of the siege views, the lower left corner shows a woman peddling chickens to the soldiers lodged in the faubourg de Portereau. The printmakers may have composed the scene as they did, omitting the details of the capture of the towers even though they knew them, because they wanted to foreground the story of how Orléans' resistance forced the duke of Guise to undertake a prolonged siege. Still, the information in the print that does not appear in Beza's account and its inaccuracy in dating the siege suggest that here too the makers of the series relied on their own network of informants—informants who in this case were not entirely reliable about the date of the event and may not have known the story told by Beza about how the towers were captured.

The next event in the series, the assassination of the duke of Guise, was the subject of two accounts published shortly after the event. The most important of these reproduces the deposition made by the assassin Poltrot de Méré after he was captured, in which he accused the admiral Coligny of putting him up to the attack and stated that Beza had promised him that he would go to heaven if he succeeded in the enterprise. To counter this damaging accusation, Coligny and Beza hastened to publish a *Reply to the interrogation previously made of a certain Jehan de Poltrot, who claims to be Seigneur de Merey, concerning the death of the late Duke of Guise* that reprints and rebuts Poltrot's statements. It was printed at least five times in three languages in pamphlet form before being incorporated into the 1565 *Collection of memorable affairs concerning religion and the state in France*.[39] Poltrot's deposition states that he followed the duke, who was on foot at the time, accompanied by one gentleman walking ahead of him and another mounted on a mule alongside him. As he approached a crossroads near his lodgings, Poltrot shot him from behind three times from a distance of six or seven paces. The *Histoire ecclesiastique* reports the shooting in identical terms.[40] Another account of the duke's last days written by the bishop of Riez simply places the shooting at a crossroads between two large walnut trees, also stating that Poltrot shot Guise three times from behind but saying nothing about any men accompanying him. His wife met him when he reached his lodgings.[41]

---

[39] *L'interrogatoire et deposition faicte a un nommé Jehan de Poltrot* (Paris, 1563); *Response a l'interrogatoire nagueres faict a un nommé Jehan de Poltrot, soy disant Seigneur de Merey, touchant la mort du feu Duc de Guise* (Caen, 1562; Orléans: Eloi Gibier, 1563; n.p. 1563; also German translation n.p., 1563; Latin translation n.p., 1563); *Receuil des choses memorables passees et publiees pour le faict de la religion, & estat de la France*; *Corr. Bèze*, IV, 275-92.

[40] *HE*, II, 350-1.

[41] *Lettre de l'Evesque de Riez, au Roy, contenant les actions et propos de Monsieur de Guyse depuis sa blessure jusques a son trepas* (Paris: Jacques Kerver, 1563), as reprinted in *MC*, IV, 246.

Perrissin's figuration of this event differs from the prior printed accounts in three interesting and revealing ways. First, it shows the duke on horseback accompanied by two other mounted men, one of whom is identified as the captain Rostain. This suggests that the makers of the print series did not have access to the pamphlet account of Poltrot's interrogation or the 1565 *Recueil des choses memorables* that reprinted this, since if they did it is hard to believe that they would not, like Beza, have followed its description of just how Guise and his party were travelling.[42] Yet whatever other source of information they used was not entirely ill informed, for a letter written by Catherine de Medici immediately after the duke's shooting identifies Tristan de Rostaing, a royal financial officer and messenger, as the only person with Guise when he was shot.[43] Second, the key specifies that the duke was returning to his lodgings in the chateau de Vaslins. Several contemporary sources confirm that this is where he was staying.[44] Finally, the upper left hand corner of the print and the portion of the key that explicates it informs the viewer/reader that before carrying out his enterprise, Poltrot tied his horse to a tree and prayed. Here, the makers of the prints incorporate a part of the story of Guise's assassination that appears to have circulated in Geneva and perhaps elsewhere in Protestant circles. The *Histoire ecclesiastique* offers a more expansive version. According to it, Poltrot had already conceived of the idea of shooting Guise and revealed his intentions to the duke of Soubise well prior to the siege of Orléans, only to be told, as Agrippa d'Aubigné would later formulate it, "that it was important not to deceive oneself when it came to extraordinary vocations".[45] As he approached the chateau of Vaslins where he was to lie in ambush and await Guise, he knelt and prayed, entreating God to change his mind if He disapproved of the plan, but to give him the strength to carry it out if He approved it.[46] If this story was widely known among Protestants at the time, we can see in the printmakers' inclusion of the detail of Poltrot praying without specifying the content of his prayer a strategy for reminding potential Huguenot buyers of a tale suggesting God's approval of the assassination without telling the story so explicitly as to offend Catholic purchasers.

Following Guise's assassination, Catherine de Medici, who had recurrently tried to negotiate a settlement throughout the First Civil War, redou-

---

42 Further evidence that the makers of the series did not use the 1565 *Receuil des choses memorables* is provided by the fact that this compilation also includes an account of the battle of St Gilles that overlaps only partially with scene 16's depiction of this event.

43 *MC*, IV, 271.

44 See Alphonse de Ruble, *L'assassinat de François de Lorraine duc de Guise 18 février 1563* (Paris, 1897), pp. 42-3 and the sources cited there.

45 Agrippa d'Aubigné, *Histoire universelle* ed. André Thierry (11 vols., Geneva, 1981-2001), II, 137; *HE*, II, 347-8.

46 *HE*, II, 349.

bled her efforts and had the prince of Condé conveyed from his prison at Amboise, where he had been held since he was captured at Dreux (see scene 20), to the camp outside Orléans. The *Histoire ecclesiastique* simply says of the subsequent parleys that led to peace that Condé met with the Constable Montmorency, whom the Protestants had taken prisoner at Dreux, on March 7 on the Ile aux Boeufs near Orléans in the presence of the Queen Mother. It recounts in greater detail the opposition that arose within the city among the Reformed ministers when they learned that Condé had agreed to preliminary terms that reduced the freedom of worship accorded the Reformed by the Edict of January and ordered no punishment for those responsible for the massacres of Vassy and Sens.[47] No pre-1570 history or pamphlet says anything about the the meeting on the Ile aux Boeufs, but contemporary ambassadors' reports describe it with more precision, specifying that a tent was set up to offer the two interlocutors shelter and privacy on a boat moored alongside the island, but that they preferred to stroll together around the island, while Catherine waited on the river's edge rather than joining the discussions. Further meetings took place on the following days, with Catherine participating. Preliminary terms were worked out by the 12th, and final terms by the 19th, when the edict of Amboise was signed.[48]

Tortorel and Perrissin's rendering of this meeting lacks the abundance and specificity of detail found in most other scenes and turns out to be inaccurate about the physical setting of the meeting and the date of the event. It shows two tents on the island itself. The title to the print misdates Condé's meeting with Montmorency to March 13. Catherine is depicted as taking part in the discussions, an error also found in the *Histoire ecclesiastique*. No allusion is made to the subsequent controversy touched off within the city by the peace terms, nor is there any depiction of the kinds of incidents reported in the shocked letters of the Spanish ambassador on the scene, who recorded that diehards among the Protestants in Orléans taunted the attackers by desecrating holy objects and mocking an effigy of the Pope from atop the city walls in an effort to subvert the peace.[49] Those responsible for the series appear to have been content here with a view that showed that peace was negotiated soon after the duke of Guise was shot, without wishing to evoke or enter into the controversies that the peace terms sparked within the Protestant camp. They confined their information gathering to obtaining a general idea of

---

47 *Ibid.*, II, 364-78.

48 *MC*, II, 138-9 (letter of the Spanish ambassador Chantonnay); Hector de La Ferrière ed., *Lettres de Cathérine de Médicis* (11 vols., Paris, 1880-1943), I, 151ff; Francis Decrue, *Anne duc de Montmorency connétable et pair de France sous les rois Henri II, François II et Charles IX* (Paris, 1889), p. 358; Alphonse de Ruble, *Jeanne d'Albret et la guerre civile* (2 vols., Paris, 1897), I, 401ff.

49 *MC*, II, 140; Bernard de Lacombe, *Les débuts des guerres de religion (Orléans, 1559-1564): Cathérine de Médicis entre Guise et Condé* (Paris, 1899), pp. 322-34.

setting where the negotiations took place and the key interlocutors, and evidently relied on a source or sources with an imperfect knowledge of dates and details. To the extent that they relied on different oral informants for different events, of course, we would expect to find greater precision in some scenes than others.

Instances such as the ambush of the duke of Guise or the negotiations on the Ile aux Boeufs where the Tortorel and Perrissin prints can be compared with independent accounts of the same event are interesting for what they reveal both about the choices made by artists and about the accuracy of the information they gathered. Another case where the accuracy of a scene can be gauged by comparison with other sources close in time to the event itself—and one that is extremely revealing of the printmakers' information gathering efforts—is scene 27 *The Michelade*. No other Protestant historian of this era, not even the independently-minded La Popelinière, so much as mentions this cold-blooded slaying of perhaps fifty of Nîmes' leading Catholics after the Huguenots seized control of the city at the outbreak of the Second Civil War. That the makers of the print series sought information about it and included it among their views reveals their willingness to widen the scope of their history beyond the established canon of events recounted by other Huguenot historians and to recognize the responsibility of both sides in the massacres of the era. An exceptionally rich documentary record survives about this event to which the makers of the series could not have had access in the form of depositions made during a judicial investigation of the crime by two Catholic judges in Beaucaire in 1568.[50] From these depositions, it emerges that the Michelade began with a round-up of the city's leading Catholics, who were placed in custody in several locations around the city. On the night of September 30 to October 1, Saint Michael's night, they were marched by torchlight into the courtyard of the bishop's palace in small groups, where, out of the sight of most of the city's population, they were slain with swords and daggers. Many of the bodies, including that of the Augustinian prior Jean Quatrebras, were thrown down the courtyard well. In Perrissin and Tortorel's rendering of this event, the scene is set at night and dated October 1. The killers use swords and daggers. "Quatrebarres" is thrown into the well. The key identifies six victims by name, five of whom can be confirmed by the depositions to have been among those killed. The key also estimates the number of those thrown down the well at 30 to 40. One deposition puts the figure as high as 72. The makers of the print seem to have been well, if not perfectly, informed about this act of Protestant violence against defenseless Catholics.

[50] Extensive excerpts in Léon Ménard, *Histoire civile, ecclésiastique et littéraire de la ville de Nismes* (7 vols., Paris, 1750-58), V, Preuves, 24-60. For more on this event, see also *Ibid.*, V, 9-21; Joshua Millet, "A City Converted: The Protestant Reformation at Nîmes, 1532-1567," (Ph.D. diss., Harvard University, 2000), ch. 4; Allan A. Tulchin, "The Michelade in Nîmes, 1567," *French Historical Studies* 29 (2006), 1-35.

PLATE 1. Hand colored impression, Jacques Tortorel, *The Conspiracy of Amboise*, 1569-70, woodcut, 32 × 50 cm, Bibliothèque Mazarine, Rés 5921F.

PLATE 2. Hand colored impression, Jean Perrissin, *The Executions at Amboise*, 1569-70, woodcut, 32 × 50 cm, Bibliothèque Mazarine, Rés 5921F.

PLATE 3. Anonymous, *The Battle of Dorneck*, hand colored woodcut, c. 1500, 41 × 85 cm, Kunstmuseum Basel, Kupferstichkabinett, Inv. X. 1876, photo credit: Kunstmuseum Basel.

PLATE 4. Anonymous, *Portrait of the Town of Calais*, c. 1558, hand colored woodcut, 34 × 44 cm, Bibliothèque Mazarine, 5921F.

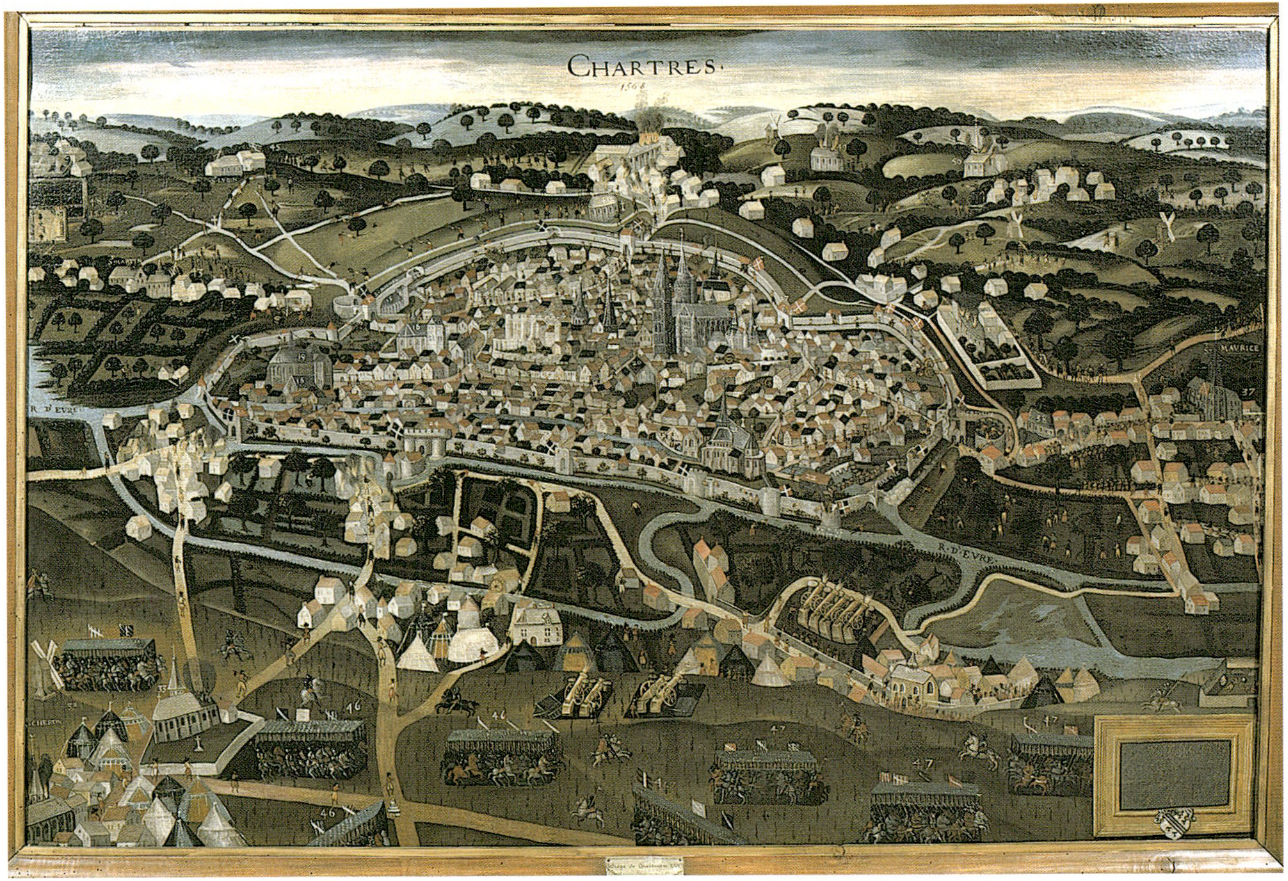

PLATE 5. Anonymous, *The Siege of Chartres*, 1570-1610, oil on canvas, 112 × 166 cm, Musée des Beaux-Arts de Chartres.

PLATE 6. François Nautré, *The Siege of Poitiers by the Admiral Coligny*, 1619, oil on canvas, 194 × 365 cm, Musée Sainte-Croix, Poitiers.

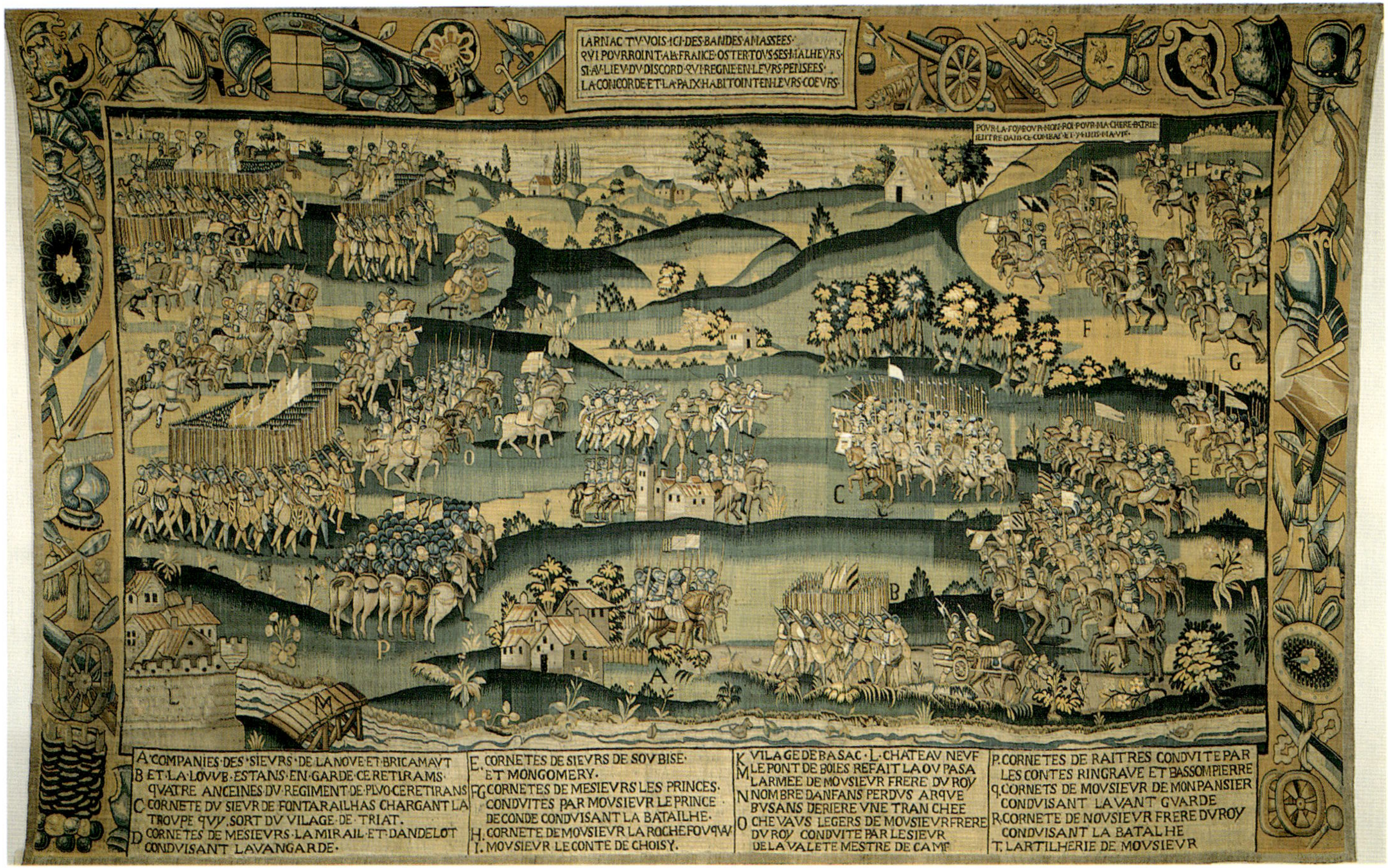

PLATE 7. Tapestry after Tortorel and Perrissin, *The Battle Order at Jarnac*, c. 1600, 325 × 522 cm, Musée national de la Renaissance, château d'Ecouen, E Cl. 2756, photo RMN.

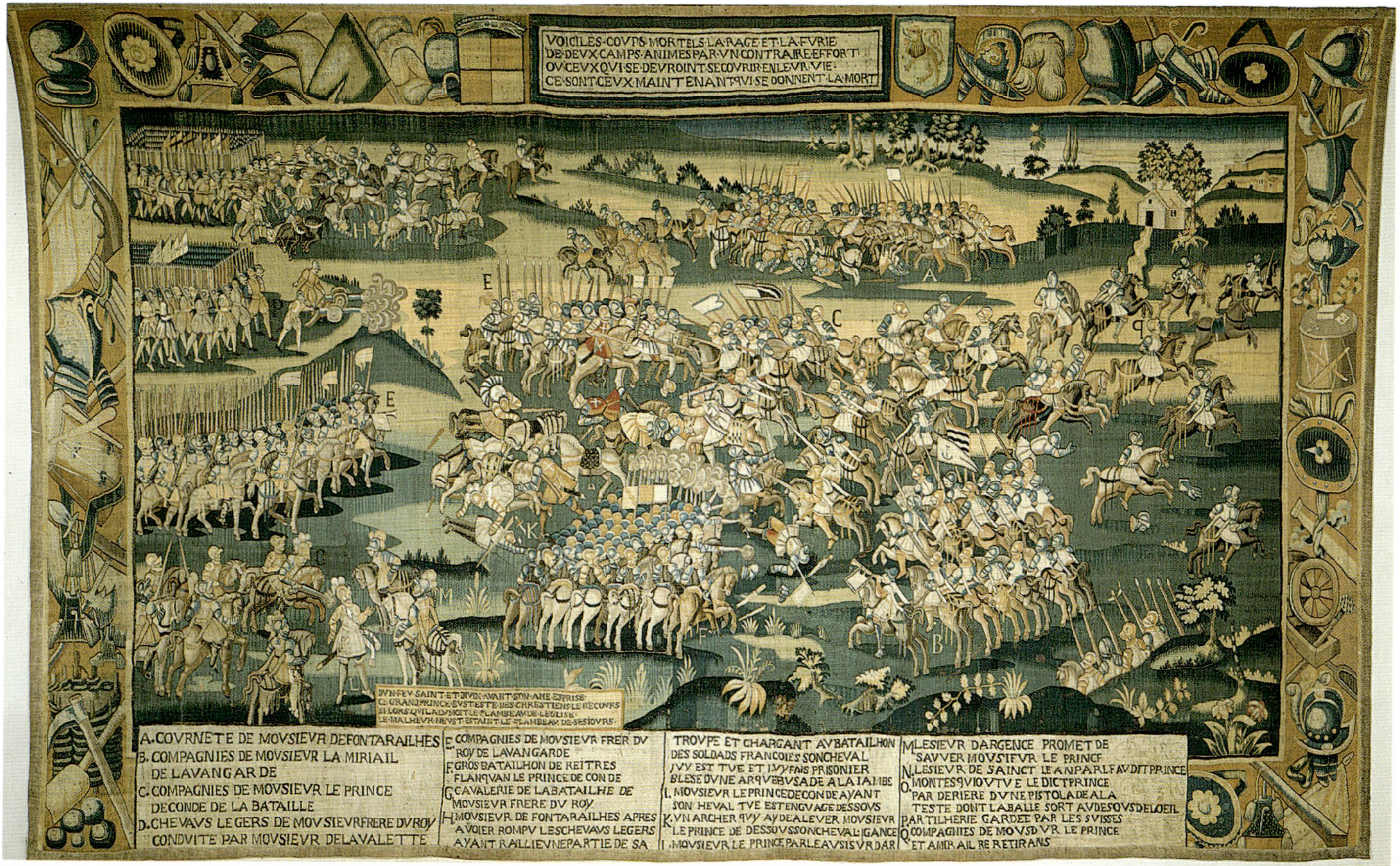

PLATE 8. Tapestry after Tortorel and Perrissin, *The Battle of Jarnac*, c. 1600, 325 × 505 cm, Musée national de la Renaissance, château d'Ecouen, E Cl. 2757, photo RMN.

The many battle scenes in the series offer further evidence that the makers of the prints sought to transcend a purely one-sided or confessional view of events in their information gathering. As the preceding chapter indicated, single sheet current events prints depicting military engagements typically gave the lion's share of attention to the commanders of just one side, as did news pamphlets. The Italian view of the two armies drawn up against one another on the plain of Moncontour (figure 27 above, p. 105) identifies by name eighteen Catholic commanders who took part in this great 1569 engagement but just three Protestants. A widely reprinted news pamphlet about the same event, emanating from a Catholic eyewitness, names seventeen commanders from that side but not a single Huguenot.[51] By contrast, the makers of the *Quarante Tableaux* seem to have pressed their informants about military events to identify the commanders and actions on both sides, albeit with uneven success. Their scene 31 *The Battle Order at Moncontour*— the only print in the series so packed with information that its key exhausts all the letters of the alphabet and has to resort to numbers as well—identifies 28 Catholic and 26 Protestant commanders by name. Scene 28 *The Battle of St Denis* likewise identifies 10 Catholic and 8 Protestant captains. But they were not always so successful in identifying the commanders on both sides. Significantly more Huguenots than Catholics are named in the keys accompanying the views of Dreux (6 Protestants to 4 Catholics), Cognat (5 Protetants to 2 Catholics), Jarnac (10 Protestants to 3 Catholics), and La Roche-L'Abeille (10 Protestants to 2 Catholics).

Details in the battle scenes also testify to the concern of the makers of the series to collect accurate information, even when this did not reflect favorably on the Huguenot cause. The episode shown at the bottom center of plate 21 *The Fourth Charge at Dreux*, identified by key letter N simply as "the death of the Marshal St André", illustrates this. During the final phase of the long encounter at Dreux, St André had his horse shot from beneath him and was quickly surrounded by Protestant soldiers. Forced to surrender, he initially yielded himself up to an ancient rival, Jean Perdriel de Bobigny, but then, fearing harm, gave himself over to the prince of Porcien, who happened upon the scene. Bobigny, angered at losing so rich a ransom, shot him in the head as he

---

51 *Il ordene del fattodarme fano ira Catolici et Ugonotti alle 3 di ottobre 1569*; [Nicolas de Neufville de Villeroy], *Discours de la bataille et cruelz assaultz Donnez entre Mont-contourt et Hervaulx* (Paris: G. de Nyverd, n.d.; Rouen: Martin Le Megissier, n.d.; also under the title *Discours de la bataille du lundy troisieme jour d'octobre 1569*, Paris: Jean Dallier, n.d.; n.p., n.d.; also with modifications under the title *Discours de la bataille et victoire obtenue par le Roy sur ses ennemys et rebelles*, Tours: R. Sifleau, 1569; Orléans: E. Gibier, 1569; also with additional material under the title *Discours de la bataille gaignée par Mgr le duc d'Anjou ... Avec la missive envoyée par S.M. à M. de Mandelot*, Lyon: M. Jove, 1569). Another Italian current events print concerning the battle of Moncontour, *Victoria di Chatolici contra Hugonoti* (figure 26, p. 104), identifies 11 Catholic and 1 Protestant commander.

was mounted behind Porcien.[52] None of the pamphlet news account of the battle of Dreux published in the immediate wake of the event say more about this episode than that St André was killed after being taken prisoner.[53] Poltrot de Méré's published deposition offers a few more details that Poltrot presumably learned while in Protestant-controlled Orléans prior to leaving on his mission to kill the duke of Guise, notably that St André surrendered first to an unidentified nobleman, then to Porcien, which provoked the first nobleman to shoot him.[54] A much later account of the same event, that by the celebrity biographer Brantôme, identifies Bobigny as the first nobleman and asserts that he shot St André through the head as he rode behind Porcien.[55] The vignette in Perrissin's view of the scene also shows St André being shot in the head from close range while mounted behind another knight. The print thus contains details about the circumstances of St André's death found in no previous printed work but concordant with those supplied by the gossipy Catholic courtier-soldier Brantôme. Significantly, the key does not identify the various participants and spell out the details of the killing. One must look closely at the scene to appreciate the work of information gathering that went into it.

While impressive in the amount and accuracy of the information they contain, the battle scenes in the series also simplify the chaos of battle for the purposes of narrative clarity and occasionally employ artistic license. The most careful examination of a battle scene from the series was made by the military historian Franck Delage, who devoted an entire book to the battle of La Roche-L'Abeille that includes a six-page appendix analyzing Tortorel's rendering of it. Delage concludes that the print's depiction of the battle site offers no more than the "vague indication . . . devoid of topographic value" of a place that the artist clearly did not know first hand. However, the ample details about the participating army units found in the print prove to be considerably more accurate, especially on the Protestant side of the conflict. Certain units are placed closer to one another or to features of each side's camp and defenses than they actually were during the battle, but their general deployment is shown with reasonable accuracy with one notable exception: Coligny is given a far more central place in front of the attacking Protestant forces than he would actually have had, the better to emphasize his role as commander of the Huguenot forces. The print also exaggerates the good order and success of the Protestant troops, for in collapsing several different

---

52 Lucien Romier, *La carrière d'un favori. Jacques d'Albon de Saint-André maréchal de France (1512-1562)* (Paris, 1909), pp. 380-81, offers the most authoritative account of St André's last hours.

53 For the list of these works, see the notes accompanying scene 21 in Part 2.

54 *Corr. Bèze*, IV, 287.

55 Pierre de Bourdeille, seigneur de Brantôme, "Les grands capitaines françois" in *Œuvres complètes* ed. Ludovic Lalanne (11 vols, Paris, 1864-82), V, 38-9.

moments of the battle into a single image, it shows the Huguenots advancing in a far tighter battle order than they would have been able to maintain over the repeated assaults that were actually necessary to overrun the Catholic position and to drive their enemies to flight. In all, the print is "a mélange of exactitude and error". Its "synthetic figuring" of the battle conveys clearly the broad outlines and ultimate outcome of the event even while offering only an imprecise idea of the phases and dynamics of the combat. It also possesses considerable documentary value both for its identification of so many units and commanders involved and for its depiction of the costumes and arms of the time.[56]

Conclusion

Around 1570, Geneva was a hub of an exceptional effort to collect and disseminate information about events in France affecting the Reformed cause. The histories produced there displayed an intense concern with precise detail, even while often offering a partial, self-justificatory account of what happened. Effort went into checking the accuracy of the smallest assertions. The *Quarante Tableaux* partook of the same concern to accumulate precise narrative details, but its makers relied on their own network of informants, which only partially overlapped with those used by others in the city. In consequence, although some of the partial and self-justificatory features of other Huguenot histories made their way into scenes within the *Wars, Massacres and Troubles*, the series as a whole offered information unavailable elsewhere in print when it appeared and its own vision of the period 1559-1570.

Roughly a third of the scenes drew much or all of what they depicted from books that were either previously published or in course of publication as the print series was being made. As the preceding chapter showed, one or (most probably) two scenes were drawn after earlier graphic depictions. The majority of the plates thus incorporated information gathered from oral or manuscript sources. These sources cannot generally be identified, but it appears that a survivor of the massacre of Cahors, Corneille Bertram, was the key informant about that event. Except in this instance, the makers of the series did not rely on the same circuits of information as those used to prepare the

---

56 Delage, *La troisième guerre de religion en Limousin. Combat de La Roche-l'Abeille*, pp. 119-24. Anne Lombard-Jourdan, "La bataille de Saint-Denis (10 novembre 1567). Tradition, propagande et iconographie," *Memoires de la Fédération des Sociétés Historiques et Archéologiques de Paris et de l'Ile de France* 29 (1978), pp. 7-54, offers a still more positive evaluation of the accuracy of another battle scene, but her study seems less careful and must be read in connection with the dismissive comments of a contemporary eyewitness about a second image of the battle to which she also accords high marks for accuracy: Etienne Vitelli, *Commentaires sur la guerre civile de France 1567* ed. Anne Lombard-Jourdan (Paris, 2005), pp. 105-7.

Histoire ecclesiastique. Even where they had written sources at their disposal, they often supplemented this with information from other sources, as for the battles of the Third Civil War.

The volume of detail contained in the scenes drawn on the basis of the printmakers' own information gathering varies considerably. Certain plates such as *The Peace Made outside Orléans* or *The Death of Henry II* provide little more than a general reconstruction of the event depicted. In the majority of cases, the number of details and episodes contained in the scenes drawn after manuscript or oral information approaches or exceeds that in the prints made after published accounts. Scenes 14 *The Massacre of Tours* and 40 *Montbrun's Crossing of the Rhone* are among the most important surviving descriptions of these relatively minor events, since few other sources exist about them. It seems quite clear that the makers of the series made more of an effort to inform themselves about the narrative details of most of the events they depicted than they did to learn about the appearance and topography of most of the places where these occurred.

Given the makers' location in Geneva, the sources on which they replied were necessarily overwhelmingly Protestant, but they tried to transcend a purely one-sided or confessional view of events. They researched carefully a massacre where Catholics, not Protestants, were the victims. They sought, with uneven success, to assemble information about the military commanders of both sides, not merely Protestant paladins. They drew with great precision the circumstances of St André's death. Occasionally, as is suggested by the inclusion of a view of Poltrot praying in scene 24 *The Fatal Wounding of the Duke of Guise*, they chose to allude to a story that some of their Protestant buyers might have known without narrating it in full detail in the accompanying key lest the view seem too partisan to Catholic purchasers.

The written histories that provided the basis for one third of the prints differed in identity and character, with the result that the views based on them differ as well. Here is yet another reason for the complex and even contradictory nature of the *Wars, Massacres and Troubles*. The two most important books on which the printmakers drew were Crespin's *History of the Martyrs* and the *Memoires de la III. guerre civile*. Where the former work incorporated prior Huguenot accounts of controversial events that were often highly tendentious and frequently tinged with the pathetic and the miraculous, the latter was a matter-of-fact chronicle of the ups and downs of two rival armies. Where the former work sought to edify and inspire, the latter sought above all to inform. Just like the books, the scenes that follow each of these works contrast with those based on the other in their degree of dispassion and in the presence or absence within them of pathetic or quasi-miraculous details. The diverse oral informants used by the team responsible for the prints are also likely to have recalled the events about which they were interrogated differently, since the degree and nature of their personal involvement in these events is likely to have varied, and since they were being asked to furnish details about events that had happened anywhere from a few weeks to nearly a decade previously. Certain scenes based on oral or manuscript information, notably scene 14 *The Massacre of Tours*, as are heavily packed with episodes of pathos as any of the massacre scenes that follow printed pamphlets written to generate support for the Huguenot cause. Others are devoid of such features.

Insofar as the reliability of the information gathered by the printmakers can be gauged against other sources, inconsistencies once again emerge from scene to scene. Some prints, especially those concerning more distant events, contain errors of date and detail. Others concerning more recent events turn out to be quite accurate when compared with independent documentation, even when the event in question is a Protestant massacre of Catholics. The prints in the early portion of the series that rely on printed sources within the Protestant apologetic or martyrological tradition may be among the most partial and tendentious of all, since they often figure controversial events in a highly partisan fashion. Understanding how and how accurately the makers of the series gathered their information is important for assessing the reliability of prints such as *The Massacre of Tours* and *Montbrun's Crossing of the Rhone* where the etching offers one of the most important surviving descriptions of the event.

Finally, the discovery that some of the printed sources followed closely were not published until 1570 offers a further clue about the process by which the series was made. It would seem that it was once the makers of the series got wind of the project that would become the *Memoires de la III. guerre civile* that they were moved to add additional scenes to keep the series up to the minute. It is likely that the information used to make the view of the massacre of Sens came from the account of this event added in 1570 to Crespin's *Book of Martyrs*. This suggests that somebody who moved in the orbit of Crespin's printing house, perhaps the anonymous author of the *Memoires de la III. guerre civile*, may have been the guiding light shaping the additions made to the series in 1570.

CHAPTER 5

THE PRINTS AS HISTORY AND INFORMATION: THE STORY

Studies of images with historical content often structure their analysis around a simple dichotomy: is the work in question information or propaganda? This question has also preoccupied the few recent scholars who have commented on Tortorel and Perrissin. Most have judged the series to be "first and foremost an instrument of propaganda", either "the true monument to the sufferings of the Huguenots" or a glorification of the *hauts faits* of the Protestant party. As should by now be evident, the print series, like virtually any complex work of historiography, offered both information and propaganda. Important portions of it stood squarely within the Huguenot martyrological and apologetic tradition, yet its makers sought to transcend the limits of a narrowly partisan view of the period, included a few scenes in which Catholics, not Huguenots, were the victims of a massacre, and generally devoted considerable effort to assembling the information that went into it. On occasion they provided vignettes that illustrate a story that circulated in Protestant circles without spelling out the details of the story, as if they were nodding in the direction of a partisan account of the event without wishing to assert it explicitly. On other occasions the image included details that reflected unfavorably on Protestant honor but the key did not allude to them at all, as if they wished to draw a veil of silence over the episode.

In studying works of history, the devil is in the details. Prefaces or introductions may proclaim a history to be inspired by any of a myriad of worthy moral or methodological purposes. Its actual characteristics, methods, and point of view only emerge from a close reading of the entire text. What is included and what is excluded, the way in which individual people and events are described, the overall emplotment of the story, the sources employed, and the manner in which they are used all require scrutiny. All histories encode a certain interpretation of the subject they recount. At the same time, all documents that purport to set forth something that really happened in the past contain an impulse to accuracy or verisimilitude. Both their reliability and their outlook or bias can both only be assessed by comparing them with other testimonies, by determining their relationship to the events they describe, by assessing the motives of their creators, and by identifying the generic codes and distinctive points of view that shaped their manner of representing what they claimed to be reality.

The preceding chapter's examination of a number of images from the series showed that differences can be discerned in the accuracy, detail, and point of view of its constituent scenes. In some instances this is because they follow sources of different characters and purposes. In some it may result from the narrative demands of the scene or the choices made by the artists in composing it. The question that thus arises is whether any consistent point of view may be discerned throughout the series from plates one through forty, or whether the *Wars, Massacres and Troubles* was simply a *bricolage* of information assembled from various sources and informants and figured according to an eclectic variety of conventions of representation. This chapter will explore this question, seeking to discern the larger narrative constructed through the choice of events included within the work, and offering a brief reading of the series as a whole.

The *Wars, Massacres and Troubles* is certainly more than just a chronicle of Huguenot suffering and victimization. Among the events included are not only the Michelade. Two episodes from the First Civil War where Catholics rather than Protestants suffered are also depicted: the Huguenot takeover of Valence in late April 1562 (plate 13), where the royal lieutenant-general Hector de Pardaillan, seigneur de La Motte-Gondrin, was besieged in his lodgings, killed, and strung up; and the conquest of the little town of Montbrison three months later (plate 15), where the Catholic commander and a number of his soldiers were thrown to their deaths from the top of the citadel after the city had been overrun. Nor were all the military events depicted glorious Huguenot feats of arms. Many of the battles shown in the series were included because of their sheer importance. The battles of Dreux (scenes 17-22), St Denis (scene 28), Jarnac (scenes 31-32), La Roche-L'Abeille (scene 33), and Moncontour (scenes 35-36) were simply the largest battles of the years 1562-1569.[1] All but La Roche-L'Abeille are generally reckoned to be Protestant defeats, although certain Huguenots sought to claim otherwise about some of them at the time. The three smaller battles or skirmishes that found their way into the series, all of which took place away from the main theatre of the fighting—the encounters at St Gilles (scene 16), Cognat (scene 29), and the crossing of the Rhône near Loriol (scene 40)—were indeed all Protestant triumphs, sometimes against great odds. On the other hand, the sieges shown in the series were a decidedly mixed bag. They included failed Huguenot sieges of

---

[1] The most authoritative military history of the early French civil wars, James B. Wood, *The King's Army: Warfare, Soldiers, and Society during the Wars of Religion in France, 1562-1576* (Cambridge, 1996), p. 184, identifies seven major battles during the years 1562-1570 that involved the main bodies of Huguenot and Catholic/royal troops, the five battles just mentioned plus Jazeneuil (1568) and Arnay-le-Duc (1570). This last took place too late to be included in the *Wars, Massacres and Troubles*. Fewer troops were involved at Jazeneuil than the other encounters.

Catholic-controlled cities in the case of both Chartres (scene 30) and Poitiers (scene 34), a failed Catholic siege of a Protestant-controlled city in the case of Orléans (scene 23), and a successful albeit costly Catholic siege of a Protestant-controlled city in the case of St Jean d'Angély (scene 37). The Protestant seizure of Nîmes in 1569 (scene 38) was a remarkable exploit of derring-do, a nocturnal commando operation that successfully retook the city. The Protestant attempt on Bourges (scene 39) was an embarrassing failure in which the attackers walked into a trap laid for them after their plan was betrayed.

If the makers of the series were prepared to acknowledge anti-Catholic as well as anti-Protestant violence, if they included many military events in their narrative because of their intrinsic importance rather to memorialize Huguenot victories, and if they even showed lesser episodes such as the foiled Huguenot raid on Bourges that were embarrassments for the cause, the selection of events for the series nonetheless can be seen to have constructed an overall narrative in line with Protestant rather than with Catholic perceptions of the era. Comparison of its contents with the illustrations of its closest Catholic equivalent from the time, the manuscript history *De Tristibus Galliae* that was written in Lyon in the later 1570s and illuminated with forty drawings of historical scenes from 1560 to 1577, reveals this especially well.[2] Table 5 sets out the subjects of the illustrations to the *De Tristibus Galliae* alongside the sequence of scenes from the *Quarante Tableaux*.

Enduring conflicts always engender rival narratives of their origins. As a result, where and how a given history begins the story offers an immediate clue about which side it aligns itself with. Here, the Catholic *De Tristibus Galliae* tellingly opens with four scenes of the Huguenot takeover of Lyon and Montbrison that highlight the accompanying iconoclasm and violence. Then follows a view of the (chronologically prior) conspiracy of Amboise that depicts armed and helmeted Huguenots riding toward the city with a petition and forcing Francis II to flee (figure 36). "They attempt to seize him and establish themselves masters of the kingdom," the legend explains. "The clemency of this monarch was so great that he pardoned them this conspiracy after learning about it, but this did not stop them from hatching others."[3] This opening sequence positions the Protestants as the instigators of the civil wars, with their seditious attempt to seize the king in 1560 and their violent takeover of many cities in the spring of 1562. The same sequence of events recurs in other partisan Catholic histories as well.[4]

---

2 BM Lyon, Ms 156. The work was edited and published by L. Cailhava as *De Tristibus Franciae Libri Quatuor* (Lyon, 1840). The illustrations may also be consulted on line at *http://sgedh.si.bm-lyon.fr/dipweb2/phot/enlum.htm*. The exhibition catalogue, *Iconoclasme* (Bern, Strasbourg, and Zurich, 2001), 59, 62, reproduces several.

3 BM Lyon, Ms 156, fo. 5v.

4 Thomas Beauxamis, *La marmite renversee et fondue, de laquelle Nostre Dieu parle par les saints Prophetes* (Paris, 1572); Gabriel de Saconay, *Genealogie et la fin des huguenaux* (Lyon: Benoist Rigaud, 1572).

TABLE 5. The Sequence of Images in Tortorel and Perrissin and the *De Tristibus Galliae*

Tortorel and Perrissin	*De Tristibus Galliae*
The Mercuriale of June 10, 1559	
Henry II is wounded jousting (June 30, 1559)	
The death of Henry II (July 10, 1559)	
The execution of Anne Du Bourg (Dec. 21, 1559)	
The conspiracy of Amboise (March 13-15, 1560) (2 views)	The conspiracy of Amboise
The Estates-General of Orléans (January 1561)	
The Colloquy of Poissy (September 1561)	
The massacre of Cahors (November 19, 1561)	
The massacre of Vassy (March 1, 1562)	
The massacre of Sens (April 12-14, 1562)	
The Protestant capture of Valence (April 25, 1562)	
	Figurative depiction of the Huguenot domination of Lyon (April 30, 1562-March 1563)
	Iconoclasm in Lyon (2 scenes)
The massacre of Tours (July 1562)	
The Protestant capture and sack of Montbrison (July 1562)	The Protestant capture and sack of Montbrison
The battle of St Gilles (September, 1562)	
	The siege of Rouen and fatal wounding of Anthony of Navarre (October, 1562)
The battle of Dreux (December 19, 1562) (6)	The battle of Dreux
The siege of Orléans (February 1563)	
The fatal wounding of the duke of Guise (February 18, 1563)	The fatal wounding of the duke of Guise
The execution of Poltrot de Méré (March 18, 1563)	
The Peace of Amboise (March 13, 1563)	The Peace of Amboise
	A Protestant synod

Tortorel and Perrissin	*De Tristibus Galliae*
	The Surprise of Meaux (September 26-28,1567)
The Michelade (October 1, 1567)	
The battle of St Denis (November 10, 1567)	The battle of St Denis
The battle of Cognat (January 6, 1568)	
The siege of Chartres (March 1568)	
The battle of Jarnac (March 13, 1569) (2)	The battle of Jarnac (2)
	German troops march to the Protestants' aid
The battle of La Roche-L'Abeille (June 25, 1569)	
The siege of Poitiers (July-September 1569)	The siege of Poitiers
The sattle of Moncontour (October 3, 1569) (2)	The battle of Moncontour
The siege of St Jean d'Angély (October-December 1569)	
The Protestant capture of Nîmes (November 15, 1569)	Cruelties against the Catholics of Nîmes
The foiled attempt on Bourges (December 21, 1569)	
Montbrun's crossing of the Rhône (March 28, 1570)	
	The St Bartholomew's massacre (August 1572)
	The siege of La Rochelle (November 1572-July 1573)
	Huguenot cruelties
	Funeral prayers for Charles IX (May 1574)
	Henry III returns to France (September 1574)
	The Estates-General of Blois (December 1576-March 1577) (6)
	Nîmes besieged (event and date uncertain)
	Henry III restores exercise of two religions
	Huguenots promise to accept peace
	Huguenots act to continue war
	Figures depicting the miseries of war (4)
	The siege of La Charité (April 1577)
	The siege of Issoire (June 1577)

FIGURE 36. Anonymous, *The Conspiracy of Amboise* from *De Tristibus Galliae*, c. 1577, ink on paper, 17 × 16.7 cm, BM Lyon, MS 156, fo 5 vo, photo Bibliothèque municipale de Lyon, Didier Nicole. In this scene, as in all the illustrations for this work, the Huguenots are depicted as apes, a visual analogue of the crudely abusive rhetoric found in much Catholic historical writing of period. Note also the lack of specific narrative detail in comparison with scene 6 from Tortorel and Perrissin.

In the *Quarante Tableaux*, on the other hand, the arrest of Anne Du Bourg and the wounding and death of Henry II precede the two scenes of the conspiracy of Amboise, which show disarmed petitioners betrayed and executed for their actions. Two events at which Charles IX consented to consult with the political nation and hear out the Protestant ministers, the Estates-General of Orléans and Colloquy of Poissy, follow. But this moment of consultation is succeeded by the massacres of Cahors, Vassy, and Sens, the Protestant capture of Valence, the massacre of Tours, and the capture of Montbrison, before the series comes to the battles of the first civil war. Protestant as well as Catholic violence is depicted, but the Catholics initiate the descent into violence and civil war. The later Protestant historian Agrippa d'Aubigné similarly opened his account of the First Civil War with a chapter recounting a season of anti-Protestant violence following the edict of toleration of January 1562. The title he chose for it makes explicit what is implied in the *Quarante*

Tableaux's views of the massacres of Cahors, Vassy, and Sens: "The events that caused the Huguenots to rise up".[5]

The rival accounts diverge even more sharply in the manner in which they figure the onset of the Second Civil War in 1567. The illustrations that follow the 1563 Peace of Amboise in the Catholic work display first a Protestant synod and then the Surprise of Meaux, the ill-fated attempt of the Huguenots to take Charles IX under their control that is generally recognized as the spark of the Second Civil War. Renewed battles follow. Once again, a seditious act of Huguenot violence touches off civil war. The placement of a synod prior to the Surprise of Meaux further suggests ecclesiastical support for this initiative of the leading Protestant grandees. The *Wars, Massacres and Troubles* completely omits the Surprise of Meaux, despite its centrality to understanding the course of events between 1562 and 1570. When the makers of the series added numbers to the titles of the prints, suggesting the sequence in which they were supposed to be bound, they also gave the battle of St Denis number 27 and the Michelade number 28, even though the Michelade took place first. These scenes follow immediately the 1563 Peace of Amboise and subsequent execution of Poltrot de Méré. In this presentation of events, the fighting and violence simply resume; they are not initiated by a failed Protestant attempt to seize control of the young king's person, or even by a successful, admittedly bloody Protestant seizure of towns.

Other telling omissions may also be noted from the *Wars, Massacres and Troubles*. None of the prints depict any of the numerous incidents of Huguenot iconoclasm that so shocked Catholic sensibilities at the time and that are figured in several of the illustrations of *De Tristibus Galliae*. The latter work also devotes an illustration to the German *reiters* who came to the aid of the Huguenots in the Second and Third Civil Wars and cut swaths of destruction across eastern France. Neither these incursions nor the English intervention during the First Civil War that the Huguenots obtained by handing over Le Havre to Queen Elizabeth receives a view in Tortorel and Perrissin, although individual battle scenes within the series note the presence of foreign troops fighting on both sides in the conflict.

As has already been indicated, the additions made to the series following the initial publication of the first thirty plates heightened its partisan Protestant meta-structure. The initial suite began with a regnal change, the wounding and death of Henry II. By inserting the scene of the Mercuriale at which Du Bourg was arrested before the view of the tournament at which Henry II was wounded, the expanded series recalled that shortly before his death the king had refused to heed his judges who urged him to moderate the punishment of heresy and had interfered with their freedom to express their opinions

5 "Des occasions de s'esmouvoir, donnees aux Reformez", D'Aubigné, *Histoire universelle*, II, 7.

inside the Palais de Justice. This placed the entire series under the shadow of the question, "what is to be done about the matter of religion?" and also raised the possibility that Henry's subsequent death might be God's punishment for what the partisan caption to the Mercuriale scene calls the king's choice of force over reason. The addition of the scene of Du Bourg's execution (plate 5) further reinforced the theme of the loyal councilor spurned, especially since the artist drew the scene in a manner that casts the Huguenot movement's greatest early martyr in a heroic light. The composition converges forcefully on the figure of Du Bourg being raised above the flames of the pyre, his hands joined in prayer and his head bowed. (He was allowed to die by strangulation before being lowered into the fire.) The caption informs the reader that he had had the composure to strip down to his shirt by himself before the rope was placed around his neck. His clasped hands point to the cross in the Place de Grève that here is positioned directly in front of him. Clinging to the cross is an onlooker who has climbed up to get a better view and who may symbolize that Du Bourg is also figuratively clinging to the cross.

Other scenes added in 1570 were those of the Estates-General of Orléans and the massacre of Sens. The addition of the view of the Estates-General gave greater amplitude to the moment of dialogue that followed the Conspiracy of Amboise. The addition of the massacre of Sens lengthened the sequence of incidents of Catholic violence that undercut this brief period of entente, all the more so since the new print bears one of the few tendentious titles in the entire series, *The Massacre Carried Out by the Populace at Sens in Burgundy in the Month of April 1562 Prior to the Taking Up of Arms* (emphasis mine). The precise date on which the two sides took up arms is in fact open to dispute, since several months of maneuvers and negotiations elapsed between the Massacre of Vassy and the first episodes of direct combat between large Protestant and Catholic armies. Already prior to the massacre in Sens, however, Condé had seized Orléans and issued his first manifestoes calling upon all true Frenchmen to join him in defense of the king and the Edict of January, while letters had circulated among the Reformed churches urging them to mobilize to defend themselves.[6]

A clear pro-Protestant tilt may also be observed in the tendency of certain plates to highlight Huguenot victimization and downplay Huguenot violence through elements of their composition. At the same time, features of the series, notably its restraint in explaining details in the captions and its greater

---

6 Letters began to circulate among the Reformed churches urging mobilization for self-defense as early as March 13, two weeks after the massacre of Vassy. Condé entered Orléans on April 2 and justified his actions in a declaration dated April 8. The massacre of Sens took place April 12-14. Dom Hyacinthe Morice ed., *Memoires pour servir de preuves à l'histoire ecclesiastique et civile de Bretagne* (3 vols., Paris, 1713-46), III, 1302-3; Arlette Jouanna et al., *Histoire et dictionnaire des guerres de religion* (Paris, 1998), p. 1385.

recognition of Protestant violence than most partisan Huguenot histories, moderated this tendency. Tortorel and Perrissin bears the imprint of its Protestant roots, but within the universe of Protestant histories devoted to this time period it offers one of the least tendentious views of the era. Its inconsistencies of point of view, both from scene to scene and, more clearly yet, between successive sections of the suite, must also be recognized. These emerge particularly clearly if the work is divided into three parts, devoted respectively to the period prior to the First Civil War, to the First Civil War, and to the Second and Third Civil Wars treated here as a single conflict.

To push deeper into the work, let us return to the early portion of the series and to the scenes of the conspiracy of Amboise and massacre of Vassy, whose agreement in content with apologetic or partisan Huguenot pamphlet accounts of these events has already been noted. The composition of these scenes further accentuates these apologetic or partisan features, yet also makes room for details suppressed by certain other Huguenot histories and displays the makers' concern with precision of information. Scene 6 *The Conspiracy of Amboise* is a particularly dense example of simultaneous narration that places five episodes that occurred at different times in different portions of the picture space. The arrangement of the scenes foregrounds the killing of La Renaudie and the negotiations between the duke of Nemours and the conspirators gathered at Noizay. The conspirators' armed raid on Amboise is placed far less obtrusively in the upper left hand corner of the print. The structure of the composition thus downplays the element of Protestant aggression in this event, in agreement with all of the partisan written accounts about it from the preceding years. Yet neither the *Histoire du Tumulte d'Amboise* nor La Place even mention the attack on Amboise. The 1570 revision of Crespin would also remove all reference to it. Like Antoine de La Roche Chandieu and the 1564 edition of Crespin, the print at least acknowledges this component of the event.[7] Finally, comparison with *De Tristibus Galliae*'s illustration of the same event (figure 36 above, p. 156) not only shows the difference in the story each image tells, but also how much more information Perrissin and Tortorel compressed into their views, and how they eschewed the crude language of insult found in so many Catholic histories of the period—both features in keeping with the general character of Huguenot historical writing at this time.

Where scene 6 fragments the viewer's attention by dividing the picture space between different episodes, scene 7 *The Executions at Amboise* focuses the composition squarely on the multiple victims of the ensuing repression, and in particular on the figure of Adrien de Beauvais Briquemault, seigneur

---

[7] La Roche Chandieu, *Histoire des persecutions et martyrs de l'Eglise de Paris*, p. 438; Crespin, *Actes des martyrs* (1564), p. 993. Cf. *Histoire du tumulte d'Amboise*, pp. 14-16; La Place, *Commentaires de l'Estat de la Religion et Republique*, fos. 52-3; Crespin, *Histoire des martyrs* (ed. Benoit), III, 68-9; *HE*, I, 304.

de Villemongis, who also occupies the starring role in this scene in nearly all contemporary published Huguenot accounts of it. As these histories tell the story, as Villemongis knelt before the executioner, he dipped his hands in the blood of his previously decapitated associates, raised his hands skywards, and cried "Lord, here is the blood of your children, avenge it."[8] The unhappy fate of those who trusted the duke of Nemours' promises could hardly be more forcefully underscored than it is by the composition. But the accompanying text only tells part of the story. The key identifying the central figure in the scene simply reads, "Villemongis, having dipped his hands in the blood of his decapitated companions." Once again, it is left up to viewers who knew the rest of the story to supply the meaning of his gesture.

In scene 11 *The Massacre of Vassy* composition and action work together to construct one of the most powerful images of Huguenot victimization. The viewer is brought much closer to the violence than in other massacre scenes. The victims of the violence squeeze so tightly together that the walls of their meeting house seem to be pushed outward by the force of their panic. As has already been suggested, the composition echoes scenes of the Massacre of the Innocents. No doubt is left about the duke of Guise's responsibility for the violence, for he is shown front and center with his unsheathed sword to a woman's breast and identified in the key as "Monsieur de Guise who commanded". This print probably stands closer to the outer limits of Protestant partisanship than any other scene in the series except for the two variant printings of the scenes involving Anne Du Bourg with the verse captions. La Popelinière provided a very different view of the massacre and its origins. Rather than rendering the duke of Guise chiefly responsible for it, he attributed the massacre to an escalation of provocations on both sides. Beza roundly criticized him for this, asserting that since this event was "the source of the first war", it was especially important not to leave the responsibility for it in doubt.[9] He would have found nothing to reproach in Perrissin's rendering of the event.

While scene 11 *The Massacre of Vassy* cleaves tightly to a partisan contemporary account of the event and highlights the pathos of the situation through its forceful composition, certain other scenes in the first third of the work are devoid of partisan details found in written Huguenot accounts of the same event. The printmakers especially bypassed opportunities to highlight providential signs of God's direction of events of a kind often found in the written works. The earliest Protestant accounts of the event reported in scene 3, Henry II's fatal wounding at the tournament celebrating the marriage of his

---

8 *Histoire du tumulte d'Amboise*, p. 15; La Roche Chandieu, *Histoire des persecutions et martyrs de l'Eglise de Paris*, p. 439; Crespin, *Actes des martyrs* (1564), p. 993; La Place, *Commentaires de l'Estat de la Religion et Republique*, fo. 53; Crespin, *Histoire des martyrs* (ed. Benoit), III, 69; d'Aubigné, *Histoire universelle*, I, 277.

9 La Popelinière, *Histoire de France*, I, 284; *Corr. Bèze*, XXII, 85.

daughter to Philip II, link his accident to the ongoing affair of Anne Du Bourg in a manner that strongly suggests that divine retribution was involved. Pierre de La Place's telling of the event underscores that the tournament took place in the vicinity of the Bastille, where the imprisoned judges were held. According to La Place, the wrong done them so weighed on the king's conscience that after he was wounded, he expressed his dismay to those who came to his aid, only to be told by the Cardinal of Lorraine that such thoughts were merely the devil speaking to him.[10] In version "a" of scene 3, it would have been a simple matter for the artists to depict prisoners looking out from behind bars over the portion of the scene where the king's attendants rush to his aid, yet they did not. La Place, Crespin, and a pamphlet *Discours de la mort du roy* all underscore that the other party in the fatal accident, the count of Montgomery, had previously escorted Du Bourg to the Bastille and had just been given a commission to hunt down Protestants in Normandy; the very agent of the king's unjust repression now became the instrument of his undoing.[11] Neither version of scene 3 mentions Montgomery's role in arresting the judges who had spoken out at the Mercuriale, nor does scene 2.

The legends accompanying the prints also pass up opportunities to report the words of the cause's martyrs. All of the earliest Protestant accounts of Anne Du Bourg's martyrdom not only highlight his self-possession as he approached the moment of his death, but also report that he sang psalms as he was conveyed to the Place de Grève and cite the words of his final prayer.[12] The caption to scene 5 *The Execution of Anne Du Bourg* omits these details. The caption to scene 2 *The Mercuriale Where Anne Du Bourg Was Arrested* mentions none of the opinions expressed by Du Bourg at that assembly.

Once the series reaches the fighting of the First Civil War, its coverage of events becomes decidedly patchy and is oriented strongly toward episodes that either occurred in the vicinity of Lyon or were trumpeted within the then-Huguenot-dominated city. No mention is made of the initial Huguenot securing of such provincial capitals as Lyon, Orléans, or Rouen, although the series does show the Protestant taking of Valence and Montbrison and the anti-Catholic violence that accompanied it. No mention is made of the subsequent recapture of many Huguenot-held cities by the combined royal and Catholic forces over the course of the summer and fall of 1562, not even the

---

10 La Place, *Commentaires de l'Estat de la Religion et Republique*, fo. 30.

11 *Ibid*, fo. 30; "Discours de la mort du Roy Henry II" in *MC*, I, 216; Crespin, *Actes des martyrs* (1564), p. 927; Crespin, *Histoire des martyrs* (ed. Benoit), II, 665.

12 "La Vraye Histoire, Contenant l'inique Jugement et fausse procedure faite contre le fidele serviteur de Dieu Anne du Bourg" in *MC*, I, 262; La Roche Chandieu, *Histoire des persecutions et martyrs de l'Eglise de Paris*, p. 428; Crespin, *Actes des martyrs* (1564), p. 930; La Place, *Commentaires de l'Estat de la Religion et Republique*, fo. 35v; Crespin, *Histoire des martyrs* (ed. Benoit), II, 702.

siege of Rouen that François de La Noue called "one of the principal acts of our first tragedies", where king Anthony of Navarre was fatally wounded.[13] The massacre of Tours' Protestants followed the recapture of that city, but this context is not evoked. No mention is made of Coligny's march into Normandy and taking of Caen after the battle of Dreux, nor of the campaign to oust the English from Le Havre after the signing of the Peace of Amboise. The broad course of the First Civil War thus remains totally obscure. Treatment of the military aspects of the conflict focuses overwhelmingly on one event—admittedly, by far its most important one—the battle of Dreux. Six scenes narrate the original disposition of the two armies, the capture of the constable Montmorency and the prince of Condé, the killing of the marshal St André, and the sudden swing of momentum when the duke of Guise threw his men into the fray and dramatically turned the tide of what initially seemed to be a Huguenot triumph. One additional view depicts the smaller battle of St Gilles in Languedoc. This was just one of many smaller engagements between Catholic and Protestant units in the peripheral provinces of the kingdom during the late spring and summer of 1562, but it was a rare Protestant victory that turned back an invasion of Languedoc by Catholic troops from Provence and the Comtat Venaissin. Coming after a long series of Huguenot reverses elsewhere in the country, it was loudly trumpeted in several printed Protestant works as evidence, in the words of one, of "how strongly the Lord arms His own, with an assurance never to abandon them, so long as they walk uprightly in His path.".[14] It was probably as a result of this publicity that the makers of the series knew about it and chose to include it.

For all of the events of this conflict, the makers of the series relied upon their own networks of information and offered views situated between the extremes of partisanship expressed in other contemporary accounts of the same events. Protestant sources indicate that the killing in Valence of the royal lieutenant-general in Dauphiné, Hector de Pardaillan, seigneur de La Motte-Gondrin, came in revenge for his strict enforcement of the legislation against heresy and Protestant conventicles.[15] Both Catholic accounts of the events charge that Huguenot treachery was involved: after vainly trying to calm the angry crowd of Protestants who gathered outside his lodgings, then stoutly resisting them after they broke through the door, La Motte Gondrin laid down his arms when the attackers promised that they would not harm him, but they immediately violated this promise, killed him, and hung him up

[13] François de La Noue, *Discours politiques et militaires* (Basel, 1595), p. 582.

[14] "Brief et veritable discours de la deffaite des Provencaux, appellée la Bataille de Sainct Gilles" in *MC*, III, 676. Similar sentiments in *Ode Hystoriale de la bataille de Sainct Gile* (Lyon, 1563).

[15] *Petit traitté des guerres civiles*, p. 17; "Lettre du Seigneur Baron des Adretz a la Royne Mere touchant la Mort de la Motte-Gondrin" in *Receuil des choses memorables* (1565), piece 21.

from the window of the house.[16] Scene 13 *The Capture of Valence* shows the crowd breaking into La Motte Gondrin's lodgings, killing him, and stringing him up, but the caption simply declares that he was "found, disarmed, and killed with dagger blows". Neither the reasons why the mob was so exercised against him nor the breach of faith alleged by the Catholic authors is mentioned, leaving the motivation and meaning of the event unclear to the otherwise uninformed viewer/reader.

The only known pre-1570 account of the capture of Montbrison and its murderous aftermath is a short *Histoire des triomphes de l'egli[se] Lyonnoise* that breathes the intense militancy characteristic of so many Lyon publications of the First Civil War. It asserts that, rather than being thrown from the tower of the citadel, the Catholic commander and eleven of his men jumped to their death trying to escape.[17] Scene 15 *The Capture of Montbrison* will have none of that. It identifies in the key "the big tower from which the baron Des Adrets forced several gentlemen and soldiers to jump."[18]

The two early Protestant accounts of the battle of St Gilles, one certainly and the other probably also of Lyonnais origin, likewise display intense partisanship. For them, the battle was the victory of a relatively small group of pious soldiers, who prayed before and after every engagement, over a much larger force of "idolators" who, as they laid siege to St Gilles, spent their nights carousing and dancing with their whores.[19] Scene 16 *The Battle of St Gilles* says nothing about the relative size of the two armies and does not show the Protestant troops at prayer, but it echoes one element of these Manichean accounts, for in the left foreground Catholic soldiers may be clearly seen gambling and feasting in their tents before being put to rout by the defenders of St Gilles. Lest the viewer overlook this, key letter B identifies "the camp of the aforesaid [Catholic] lords feasting, gaming, and living high (*faisant grand chere*)." This is the only scene in the series where Catholic soldiers are so depicted, suggesting the influence of the Protestant accounts on the image. Rather than a rigorously consistent and narrowly partisan viewpoint, we see in these three scenes both a willingness to acknowledge instances of Protestant violence that its most highly partisan spokesmen denied and the occasional insertion of details that paint Catholic troops as debauched. The acknowledgement of Protestant violence does not extend so far as to credit and display instances of outright treachery on the part of the Huguenots.

---

16 Loys de Perussiis, *Discours des guerres de la Comté de Venayscin et de la Provence* (Avignon, 1563), p. 27; Francois Joubert and Salomon de Mérez, *Mémoires de divers événements en Dauphiné notamment pendant les guerres de religion* (Grenoble, 1886), pp. 48-50.

17 *Histoire des triomphes de l'egli[se] Lyonnoise. Avec la prinse de Montbrison* (Lyon, 1562), unpaginated.

18 *HE*, III, 266, also asserts Des Adrets's responsibility for the killings. It further claims that his lieutenants tried to talk the future turncoat out of his cruel designs.

19 *Ode Hystoriale*, unpaginated; "Brief et veritable discours" in *MC*, III, esp. 657, 659.

The six scenes devoted to the battle of Dreux focus primarily on recounting the successive stages of the battle. As has already been indicated, scene 21 *The Fourth Charge at Dreux* also shows in some detail the circumstances that led to the Marshal St André being shot by a Protestant after having surrendered but fails to spell out the details of this episode in the key. Scene 22 *The Retreat from Dreux* asserts that both sides withdrew at the end of the battle. The question of who gained the victory in this longest and bloodiest battle of the First Civil War was contested in its aftermath, but the Huguenot military commentator François de La Noue wrote that those who thought that the battle was not a defeat because they had withdrawn at nightfall in an orderly fashion were fooling themselves, since the royal and Catholic forces slept on the battlefield.[20] Far more striking than the partisanship of these scenes, however, is their attention to the military ebb and flow of the long encounter. A portion of scene 22 *The Retreat from Dreux* also forcefully highlights the costs of war. In the upper right, the bodies of the dead on both sides are shown being stripped of their clothing and arms and dragged into piles for burial. As the first major engagement of the civil wars and one in which so many great noblemen either died or were captured, this battle long would be recalled for its harsh lessons about the destructiveness of war. Many of the roughly 6,000 casualties were found frozen and naked the next morning, their bodies having been stripped and looted over the course of the bitterly cold night. Ambroise Paré, who was sent to the scene to tend to the wounded, reported that bodies covered the ground for a league around.[21]

In keeping with its focus on "wars, massacres, and troubles," the series passes without mention over the years of peace from 1563 to 1567 and such important events as the proclamation of Charles IX's majority in 1563, the royal tour of the kingdom in 1564-1565, and Catherine de Medici's meeting with the duke of Alva at Bayonne. With the renewal of civil war in 1567, it becomes an uninterrupted suite of battles, massacres, sieges, and raids until the end, not even alluding to the short-lived peace of Longjumeau of March 1568, even though the initiation of the talks that led to this peace incited the prince of Condé to raise the siege of Chartres that is the subject of scene 30. Thanks in good measure to its reliance on the *Memoires de la III. guerre civile*, the portion of the *Quarante Tableaux* devoted to the Second and Third Civil Wars offers better coverage of the major events of these conflicts than does the portion dedicated to the First Civil War. A number of lesser episodes vividly recounted in the *Memoires de la III. guerre civile*, such as the successful Protestant seizure of Nîmes and failed attempt on Bourges, also find their way into series. It is perhaps surprising to find no mention of the heroic resistance of Navarrenx that thwarted the Catholic incursion into Béarn and

---

[20] Cited in Wood, *The King's Army*, p. 198.

[21] *Ibid.*, p. 199.

near-capture of that Albret territory in 1569, an event that would have bolstered Protestant morale amid the still ongoing civil war, but this also goes unmentioned in the *Memoires de la III. guerre civile*. The makers of the series may not have been well enough informed about this distant theater of the fighting to include a scene about it.[22] Despite the omission of this aspect of the war, the makers made sure to end the volume on a positive note for the Protestant cause. The final scene in the series shows in extensive detail a small incident not recounted in the *Memoires de la III. guerre civile* that occurred relatively close to Geneva and that the makers of the series probably learned about from word of mouth or from eyewitness participants who subsequently reached the city: Montbrun's daring crossing of the Rhône in the face of a heavy Catholic patrol along the river in late March 1570. Although the outcome of the Third Civil War remained uncertain as the volume drew to a close, the final scene showed that the Huguenots had lost neither their pluck nor reason to hope that God would sustain them.

Once again, a few details can be observed in these final scenes that tilt in a Protestant direction. Like the marshal St André at Dreux, the prince of Condé met death at Jarnac when shot after he had surrendered, but where scene 21 depicts the particulars of the Catholic Triumvir's death but does not spell out the details or identify the protagonists in the key, the key to scene 32 underscores and amplifies just how Condé was shot from behind as he negotiated his surrender to the seigneur d'Argence, who had promised to spare his life. The tendency to exaggerate the cohesion and order of the Protestant troops observed by Delage in his analysis of the battle of La Roche-L'Abeille recurs in scene 36 *The Rout at Moncontour*. Even though this was the worst defeat suffered by a Protestant army during the decade covered by the series, the scene highlights the orderly retreat of the units of reiters commanded by Mansfeld and Louis of Nassau that saved a modicum of Huguenot honor amid the debacle. Such touches are nonetheless rarer than in the first two thirds of the series. In some ways, the print series is even more matter of fact than the *Memoires de la III. guerre civile*. Where this latter attempts to put a favorable spin on the battle of Moncontour by stating that the Catholics lost cavalry in "large numbers, including great lords," scene 36 describes the battle frankly as a rout and says nothing about Catholic cavalry losses.[23] Above all, the final dozen images situate the viewer amid a war of uncertain course and outcome, in which battles, sieges and raids succeed one another without yielding any clear sense of which way the overall course of the war is tending. The sense of being caught in a cycle of violence whose meaning and direction escapes understanding is heightened by the sheer abundance of details packed

---

[22] Beza's letters testify that he, on the other hand, was characterically well informed about the events in Béarn. *Corr. Bèze*, X, 203, 214.

[23] *Memoires de la III. guerre civile*, p. 210.

into these images and the meticulous avoidance of language in the accompanying text that would suggest affiliation with one side or the other. Often the caption does not even make clear the final outcome of the event shown. Take, for instance, two scenes found within a few plates of one another, numbers 34 *The Siege of Poitiers* and 37 *The Siege of St Jean d'Angély*. Both offer views of the two cities under siege that display the tactics adopted by the attackers and defenders, locate the breaches made in the city walls, and show sorties made by the defenders. The accompanying keys indicate how many men were involved in the sorties and how many cannon shots were required to open the breaches. From looking at the two scenes, however, the otherwise uninformed viewer would never know that thanks to the efforts of the young duke Henry of Guise and over a thousand experienced troops stationed within its walls, Catholic-controlled Poitiers successfully resisted a siege of more than six weeks by the main body of Huguenot troops under Coligny, costing the attackers thousands of men to combat, disease, and desertion, while Huguenot-controlled St Jean d'Angély finally succumbed, but only after dogged resistance organized by Armand de Clermont, seigneur de Piles, that allowed the defenders to occupy the royal army for nearly two months and then to negotiate an honorable surrender and march out of the city flying their standards.[24]

Conclusion

In the final analysis, the *Wars, Massacres and Troubles* bears the marks of a fair measure of bricolage, as one might expect from a work based on varied sources whose makers updated it in the course of production to keep it abreast of current events. A scene like *The Massacre of Tours*, filled with vignettes of violence of an almost mythic nature and resting in all probability on the oral testimony of survivors filtered through seven years of recollection and retelling, differs in character from *The Capture of Nîmes*, which takes the viewer step-by-step through a recent military operation about which a good written account made soon after the event existed, and yet again from *The Peace Made Outside Orléans*, where the makers were content to evoke the

---

[24] *Discours du succes des affaires passez au siege de Poictiers . . . Envoyé à Monseigneur de Mandelot Gouverneur de Lyon* (Paris, H. de Marnef, 1569); and [Martin Liberge], *Ample discours de ce qui c'est faict et passe au siege de Poictiers* (Paris: Nicolas Chesneau, 1569) are contemporary accounts of the former event that paint it as a Catholic triumph. *Discours au vray de ce qui s'est passe au siege de Sainct Jean d'Angely* (Angoulême: Jean de Minieres, 1569) is a Protestant account of the latter event written by survivors that casts it as a remarkable feat of arms and illustration of how God protects His own. It is noteworthy that the extensive details found in these works do not exactly match those in the *Memoires de la III. guerre civile* or Tortorel and Perrissin, which suggests that they did not reach Geneva and that the makers of the latter works used different informants.

general contours of a six-year-old event. Above and beyond these oscillations of character and focus from scene to scene, the emphasis and outlook of the series also seem to mutate over the course of the volume. Certain early scenes offer views of contested events directly in line with the Protestant apologetic and martyrological tradition. The scenes are clearly chosen to suggest a certain explanation of the origins of the religious wars. Many major events of the First Civil War are overlooked. As the series advances, it becomes a sequence of battles, sieges, and raids whose selection of episodes is more strongly determined by the magnitude and importance of the events themselves than by either their place within a certain picture of the violence's origins or their regional notoriety in southeastern France. The individual scenes seem to grow increasingly impartial.

Considering the work as a whole, a fairly consistent broad perspective may still be discerned. The work is moderately partisan. The narrative of the early civil wars constructed by the sequence of scenes accords with Protestant rather than Catholic understandings of the origins of the conflict. One scene shows Catholic soldiers gambling and banqueting in their tents. Another shows them robbing a poor box. The action of Protestant troops is often made to appear more orderly and more decisive than it actually was. In the course of the civil wars, both sides regularly accused the other of reneging on their word and killing enemies after they had surrendered or laid down their arms. Scene 32 not only shows the Huguenot champion Condé being slain in this manner but spells out the details in the key. Scene 21 shows the Catholic Triumvir St André perishing this way but says nothing about it in the caption. Scene 13 does not even acknowledge that this was how Catholics believed that the lieutenant general La Motte-Gondrin perished at Valence. At the same time, the *Wars, Massacres and Troubles* admits to Protestant as well as Catholic massacres with a frankness not found in most other Huguenot histories. Instances may be detected where the makers of the series bypassed opportunities to introduce details found in other Protestant chronicles that pointed to God's providential concern for the cause. The captions avoid partisan party labels. The images in the series may glorify certain Protestant martyrs by their compositions, but they do not do so by citing their words at length, in the manner of Crespin's *Book of Martyrs*. Certain vignettes in the prints allude to details explained at greater length in other Protestant accounts that circulated at the time, but without providing extensive explanations. In sum, the work's Protestant origin may be discerned, but the *Wars, Massacres and Troubles* was ultimately less tendentious than virtually any other Protestant history of this period, with the notable exception of La Popelinière's *History of France*—and even La Popelinière does not mention the Michelade.

The same production team that made the *Quarante Tableaux* also printed scenes involving Anne Du Bourg and Jean Poltrot de Méré with different captions that place them near the far extreme of Huguenot partisanship. That the series as a whole did not consistently express such a vision reminds us again that the project was first and foremost a commercial venture aimed at an international market. Made in a period when information was an increasingly saleable commodity and when the spread of single-sheet news prints incited people's eagerness to visualize the great events they read about, it strove to offer a trans-confessional public a view of the noteworthy episodes of the past decade that conveyed the character and details of these events with the special force and memorability that images were believed at the time to provide. Many histories in this era claimed to offer readers a "mirror" of the times they described, an instrument for contemplating remarkable things. The *Quarante Tableaux* was a special kind of such a mirror, one that could satisfy the "desire of many to truly know the remarkable things that have occurred in France in these past years" especially well because it was composed of pictures. Its contemplation could reveal a range of lessons—not merely that of the purer motives, more remarkable triumphs, and greater degree of victimization of one side than the other in the civil wars, but also that of the unpredictability of warfare, the violence and treachery of which human beings were capable, and the terrible cost of the spiral of violence in which France found itself. For all the detail of its images, however, this early experiment in telling an extended history through pictures also reveals the difficulty of using a succession of images to tell a continuous story. Perhaps the hardest thing for viewer/readers of the series to grasp would have been the relationship between the successive events depicted, given the failure of so many images to make clear the final outcome of the event in question and the fact that most images were accompanied by letter keys tied to specific details within the image rather than a narrative legend capable of quickly explaining the background and consequences of the event shown.

The *Wars, Massacres, and Troubles* was thus ultimately at once moderately partisan yet neutral in tone, original but also derivative, appealing, informative, uneven, and frustratingly episodic. Above all it was multilayered. It encoded a certain interpretation of Wars of Religion and at the same time provided information that in certain instances could have been found nowhere else in print when it first appeared. It broke new ground in offering a graphic history of the recent past in topographical-analytical pictures, yet copied a few of its scenes from prior single-sheet prints and constructed more by turning previously published written histories into pictures. Attentive to the details of the events shown but less so to their physical setting, it was unstable in accuracy and outlook from plate to plate and section to section, yet generally tilted in a Protestant direction. All this is what might be expected of a work that, as the preceding chapters have shown: (1.) had no clear prototypes when it was launched but drew upon a range of prior artistic and iconographic traditions; (2.) was launched by a group of entrepreneurs and artists with little previous experience in print publishing and varying degrees of commitment to the Protestant cause; (3.) was subject to constant revision, experimentation, and expansion in the course of its production; (4.) depicted events in places the artists had never seen on the basis of information gathered from a range of different sources and informants that stood in different relationships to the events in question; (5.) strove to reach an international, trans-confessional audience yet was constructed from materials gathered through overwhelmingly Protestant channels of information; and (6.) was driven largely by commercial considerations yet open to revisions that brought it more closely into line with the orthodox Protestant vision of the origins of the civil wars.

What remains to be seen is how such a work was received and used.

CHAPTER 6

ECHOES

Multilayered, at times ambiguous or even internally inconsistent, the *Wars, Massacres and Troubles* invited a wide range of uses and appropriations. For those interested in learning more about the first decade of the civil wars, close scrutiny of the images and accompanying texts offered a great deal of very specific information about the events depicted. Those strongly attached to the Protestant cause could discover, despite the clipped wording of most captions, enough instances of unjust treatment of the champions of the Gospel and of their admirable fortitude in the face of adversity to nurture both their sense of victimization and their admiration for those who fought the good fight. For those on either side of the partisan divide, the series provided ample matter for reflection about the conduct of war, its human costs, and the wickedness of fallen humankind.

Because of its originality and plasticity, the *Wars, Massacres and Troubles* shaped historical memory about the Wars of Religion for centuries to come. It also occupied a place of significance in the story of early experiments to incorporate the graphic media into current-events publishing. It was bought by Frenchmen and foreigners, Catholics and Protestants, some noble, some learned, some less so. Some users pored over the prints for the historical information they contained. Others doodled on them. The work nourished the bitterness of a vengeful Huguenot warrior-poet, inspired tapestries to adorn the castle of a Huguenot commander, and was used and praised for its accuracy by a scrupulous Catholic historian in the eighteenth century, by which time it had also become a collector's item for print connoisseurs. It did not immediately spark numerous imitations or the growth of news print production in France, but it did in the Rhineland and Low Countries, from where the production of similar kinds of prints spread back to France at the turn of the seventeenth century.

Owners and Uses

Whether priced at the sum of one livre apiece at which Castellin estimated their value in 1570 or the 8 to 10 sols tournois that they fetched at the estate sale of 1572, full sets of the print series were moderately expensive printed works. An in-octavo Bible from the press of Jean de Laon fell in the same price range. A massive in-folio work of history like La Popelinière's *History of France* could cost far more; Emilian Camus paid 13.5 livres for a copy in Paris in 1584.[1] At the same time, the daily wage of a Genevan mason came to about 6 sols.[2] With such wages, a minority of artisans might save enough to buy a Bible, but few are likely to have been willing to lay out in excess of a full day's pay for a volume of Tortorel and Perrissin. Single sheets from the series at two deniers apiece, however, would have been within their budget.

About twenty early modern owners of the *Wars, Massacres, and Troubles* can be identified from the ex librises and bindings of the old albums. Virtually all, as might be predicted from the cost of the work, were men and women of fairly high status. Even in the first generation, they included Catholics as well as Protestants, foreigners as well as Frenchmen.

Early French owners who can be identified included three leading bibliophiles and *érudits* from the milieu of the high robe: Jacques-Auguste de Thou, Nicolas Moreau, sieur d'Auteuil, and an unidentified member of the prominent Budé family.[3] Some branches of the Budé family embraced Protestantism; de Thou and Moreau were moderate Catholics. The other two French signatures from this period are less easily identifiable: a certain "Bienvenu" who inscribed his name in his copy in 1574, perhaps the Genevan poet and notary Jacques Bienvenu; and (in the version today in the Bibliothèque Municipale of Avignon) "Claude Ayme [surname effaced] davinon", probably a resident of the Papal city, although the spelling "davinon" leaves room for doubt.[4]

Internationally, the first generation of owners included prominent figures from many countries. A Latin copy made its way quickly to the library of duke Johann Albrecht of Mecklenburg (r. 1547-1576), where the ducal librarians bound it together with other prints in 1572. (The date is stamped on the binding.) A set of the prints may have been presented to the earl of Essex, for the copy now in the Bodleian Library in Oxford bears the inscription on the title page "pour Monsieur de Hesecques". Still another set was owned by an unidentified sixteenth-century Englishman of apparent prominence in policy

---

1 Jean de Laon's 1570 in-octavo Bible sold for 7 sous wholesale. Retail prices were two to three times as high. Francis M. Higman, "Le domaine français, 1520-1562" in Jean-François Gilmont ed., *La Réforme et le livre. L'Europe de l'imprimé (1517-v. 1570)* (Paris, 1990), p. 129. Emilian Camus's expenditures for his copy of La Popelinère's *Histoire de France* are recorded on the flyleaf of BPU, Gg 229 (1): "Cest a Emilian Camus achapté iiii écus et demy a Paris le xiime Janvier 1584". For the prices of the *Quarante Tableaux*, see above, pp. 29, 46-7.

2 Mottu-Weber, *Genève au siècle de la Réforme*, p. 422.

3 Maz., 5921D; BM Toulouse, Rés A xvi 27; BPF, fonds André 1154.

4 UB Amsterdam, OF 79-1; BM Avignon, Est. Atlas 75. I owe the suggestion concerning Jacques Bienvenu (1537-1579) to Max Engammare. Ample notes on his life and works may be found in AEG, Mss Historiques Dufour 12.

circles around the court, since it contains copious annotations in English in sixteenth-century hands that indicate that one of the people making them had access to a visiting delegation of French diplomats. The Brabant nobleman Jacques d'Enghien, seigneur de Kerstegan also owned a copy. In 1605, he offered it as a gift to Archduke Albert's Spanish secretary Antonio de Tovares. As he did so, he inscribed Biblical and classical quotations praising true friendship on the title page.[5] The dissemination of the work beyond France is also revealed by seventeenth-century albums with spine titles in Dutch and Italian.[6]

Men and women of prominence continued to acquire the prints in the seventeenth and eighteenth centuries, as did individuals of lesser note. The future duke August of Brunswick-Lüneburg procured a German set in 1655 for his library at Wolfenbüttel.[7] Colbert owned a copy.[8] So did Camille de Neufville-Villeroy, archbishop of Lyon from 1653 to 1693.[9] An old album in a seventeenth-century binding bears the arms of the Bourbon-Condé family.[10] At some point in the seventeenth or eighteenth century, a copy made its way into the library of the Jesuit college of Lyon.[11] Still other seventeenth-century signatures come from obscure owners: Jean Postene, Jacques Nenial, and Charles Moreau or Morélly.[12]

Eighteenth century ex librises found within old albums include the names of three more Catholic churchmen: the Vittel curé Louis Vacher; a Benedictine monk named Louis Vincent; and the bishop of Grenoble Jean de Caulet, a great book collector who bought Colbert's copy from his descendant Seignelay.[13] Madame de Pompadour, Marie Antoinette, and the duke of Vence owned sets, as did a small town solicitor (*procureur*) named de Loches, and the *conseiller du roi* Jacques Olivier Vallée.[14] One unknown owner considered

---

5 UB Rostock, Rb 4654; Bodleian Library (Oxford), Antiq.b.U.1; Newberry Library (Chicago), Wing fZP 539 .T63; Real Biblioteca de Palacio (Madrid), IX/7226.

6 See below, Table 6, p. 176.

7 Herzog August Bibliothek (Wolfenbüttel), 8.12 Hist 2o. I owe thanks to Christian Hogrefe, curator, for information about the date of acquisition of this work.

8 BM Grenoble, S 66 Rés.

9 BM Lyon, 22036.

10 BN, Rés fo La 21a 7.

11 BM Lyon, 24601. The Lyon Jesuits also received a large album of historical prints containing a few scenes from Tortorel and Perrisin through the bequest of the city's late seventeenth-century archbishop, Camille de Neufville.

12 Metropolitan Museum (New York), Prints and Drawings, Elisha Whittelsey Collection, accession no. 51.580.4; BN, Rés La 21 7alpha; BM Toulouse, Rés A xvi 27.

13 BM Rouen, Leber 5950; Metropolitan Museum, Prints and Drawings, Elisha Whittelsey Collection, accession no. 51.580.4; BM Grenoble, S 66 Rés.

14 Maz., Rés 5921E; BN, Rés La 21 7 beta; BM Toulouse Rés A xvi 27; Metropolitan Museum, Prints and Drawings, Elisha Whittelsey Collection, accession no. 51.580.4; BM Versailles, Rés in fol A 82m.

his set to have been part of his "museum", for the title page is inscribed "Ex Musao du Jillion [?] Anno 1700".[15]

Sixteenth-century print collections were normally organized by theme, topic, and size. Thus, prints depicting saints would be grouped together according to size in albums of different dimensions, followed by biblical scenes, ancient mythology, ornament prints, and so forth. Only the works of the greatest early printmakers such as Albrecht Dürer or Lucas van Leyden were occasionally singled out and kept together in portfolios dedicated to an individual artist and his art. Over the subsequent centuries, as prints increasingly came to be appreciated as works of arts and objects of connoisseurship, the tendency grew to organize print collections around the work of individual artists and national schools, although many images continued to be grouped in utilitarian subject categories.[16] Of the 37 albums containing prints from the series that I have been able to locate and examine that were assembled between the sixteenth and eighteenth centuries, just one is what might be called a collector's volume. It is bound in fine leather with the arms of Marie

---

[15] BM Rouen, Leber 5950. On the meaning of the term "museum" (often equivalent to curiosity cabinet or study) in this era, see Krzysztof Pomian, "Leçons italiennes. Les musées vus par les voyageurs français au XVIIIe siècle" in Pomian, *Des saintes reliques à l'art moderne: Venise-Chicago XIIIe-XXe siècle* (Paris, 2003), pp. 272ff. One or more portfolios of Tortorel and Perrissin may also appear in the *Catalogue des estampes et desseins du cabinet de feu M. d'Hermand, ancien Colonel d'Infanterie, Ingenieur des Camps et Armées du Roy* (Paris, 1739), "une collection . . . immense et si precieuse" according to this sale catalogue. This lists "un portefeuille remplie d'une suite d'Estampes representant les Guerres des Religionnaires, au nombre de 67 gravées en bois" (p. 13) and "un volume des guerres civiles des religionnaires" (p. 24) without any indication of the artists responsible for them. No sets of the prints appear, however, in the *Catalogue des estampes, cartes geographiques etc. de Monseigneur le Maréchal Duc d'Estrées* (Paris, 1741), although this included many battle prints and "historical pieces", including three portfolios of Hogenbergs.

[16] McDonald ed., *Print Collection of Ferdinand Columbus*; idem, "The Print Collection of Philip II at the Escorial," *PQ* 15 (1998), 15-35; Hans-Jörg Künast, "Die Graphiksammlung des Augsburger Stadtschreibers Konrad Peutinger" in John Roger Paas ed., *Augsburg, die Bilderfabrik Europas. Essays zur Augsburger Druckgraphik der Frühen Neuzeit* (Augsburg, 2001), pp. 11-19; Elizabeth M. Hajós, "The Concept of an Engravings Collection in the Year 1565: Quicchelberg, *Inscriptiones vel Tituli Theatri Amplissimi*," *Art Bulletin* 40 (1958), 151-5; Peter W. Parshall, "The Print Collection of Ferdinand, Archduke of Tyrol," *Jahrbuch der Kunsthistorischen Sammlungen in Wien* 78 (1982), 139-84; William W. Robinson, "'This Passion for Prints': Collecting and Connoisseurship in Northern Europe during the Seventeenth Century" in *Printmaking in the Age of Rembrandt* (exhibition catalog, Boston, 1981), pp. xxvii-xlviii; Bury, *The Print in Italy 1550-1620*, p. 11; idem, "Giulio Mancini and the Organization of a Print Collection in Early Seventeenth-Century Italy" in C. Baker, C. Elam and G. Warwick eds., *Collecting Prints and Drawings in Europe, c. 1500-1750* (Aldershot, 2003), pp. 79-84; Marjorie B. Cohn, *A Noble Collection: The Spencer Albums of Old Master Prints* (exhibition catalog, Cambridge, Ma., 1992), pp. 11-55, 288-92; *Catalogues de la collection d'estampes de Jean V, roi du Portugal par Pierre-Jean Mariette* eds. Marie-Thérèse Mandroux-Franca and Maxime Préaud (3 vols., Lisbon-Paris, 1996-2003); *Catalogue des estampes de feu M. d'Hermand*; *Catalogue des estampes du Maréchal Duc d'Estrées*.

Antoinette and bears the spine title "Tortorel et Perrisin Tableaux ou histoires diverses".[17] No other pre-1800 volume indicates the artists' names in this manner. As might be expected in an album assembled for purposes of collection, the impressions in this volume tend to be exceptionally good, and the volume contains not just the full set of 39 scenes and a title page, but variant versions of seven of the scenes. The organization of this album suggests that by the end of the eighteenth century Tortorel and Perrissin had entered the collector's canon.[18]

The other 36 old albums were evidently compiled more for their information value than because they satisfied a collector's urge to acquire a full Tortorel and Perrissin in a good state. They never contain more than one copy or version of the same image from the series, but they do occasionally bind them together with other contemporary prints. Where they write or emboss a title on the spine or flyleaf, these are functional descriptions, as shown in Table 6.

Four of these old albums are quite large compilations of maps, city views, current-event prints, and/or historical series in which images from Tortorel and Perrissin comprise just a fraction of the whole. That owned by duke Johann Albrecht of Mecklenburg is the best documented of these composite albums. The duke—or, more properly speaking, his court intellectuals—assembled at his palace of Schwerin between the 1540s and the 1570s a library of some six thousand volumes that was especially rich in theology and jurisprudence but can be seen from the surviving catalogue to have encompassed virtually all of the arts and sciences that thinkers of the time considered useful for conscientious rulers.[19] A portion of this collection survives

---

17 BN, Rés La 21-7 beta.

18 That the series was prized even before the eighteenth century as a historical set worth acquiring, if not as an example of the artists' work, is suggested by a particularly interesting early bound volume in the BM Grenoble, S 66 B. This bears a hand lettered title page that reads "Premier Volume contenant quarante tableaux . . ." followed by a set of Hogenberg's prints after the same series. Since Hogenberg's set does not total forty prints, the seventeenth-century owner who had this album bound added a number of other historical prints depicting French events from the later years of the Wars of Religion in order to have a volume of exactly forty prints. Clearly, this individual wanted to acquire a set of the *Quarante Tableaux* but could not find one with the prints by Tortorel and Perrissin and so made a substitute volume using Hogenberg's views. Tortorel and Perrissin is not, however, mentioned in C-F. Menestrier, *Bibliotheque curieuse et instructive de divers Ouvrages Anciens et Modernes, de Litterature et des Arts* (Trevoux, 1704), a work identified as an essential guide to books and collecting for the would-be *honnête homme* in Jean-Marc Chatelain, *La bibliothèque de l'honnête homme. Livres, lecture et collections en France à l'âge classique* (Paris, 2003), p. 38 and passim. Other print series or illustrated books are mentioned by Menestrier as desirable items for the library of a person of taste, notably Bibles illustrated by Bernard Salomon, Valdor's *Triomphes de Louis le Juste*, and Lafréry's antiquities of Rome.

19 "Catalogus Sive index universalis omnium librorum tam manuscriptorum, quam typis editorum, qui in illustrissimi Principis ac Domini, D. Joannis Alberti Ducis Megalburgensis etc: Bibliotheca Swerinensi continentur" (photocopy of the original from Schwerin in UB

TABLE 6. Spine or Flyleaf Titles of Old Albums Containing Tortorel and Perrissin Prints

Bindings known or estimated to date from late sixteenth century
"Guerres et massacres"
"Guerres et massacres en France"
"Variae Diversorum Temporum Historiae"

Bindings known or estimated to date from seventeenth century
"Guerres Massacres de France"
"Cartes"
"Batailles des Huguenots"
"40 tableaux"
"Daaden van Hendrik de Iie Koning van Vrankrijk 1559 houtsneden"
"Recueil de plans"
"Geografica/tavole moderne di geografia"
"Der erste Teil der historien von krieg mord und aufruren so sich in Frankreich begeben im jahre 1559 bis 1570 in vierzig tafel afgebildet"

Bindings known or estimated to date from eighteenth century
"Chose remarquables 1559-1569"
"Tableau des guerres civiles de France"
"Figures de la Ligue"
"Guerre civile XL Tableaux gravés en bois 1570"
"Krieg zugetragen in Francreich"
"Tortorel et Perrissin Tableaux ou histoires diverses"

today in the rare book collection of Rostock University Library. It includes a Latin version of the series bound within a composite volume of prints labeled "Various Histories of Diverse Eras".[20] The date stamped on the pigskin binding with the duke's mark, 1572, tells us that the volume was assembled very soon after the print series first appeared. The duke's agents were assiduously acquiring historical prints and print series at the time, for the volume also includes a genealogy of the counts of Holland published in Haarlem in 1569 by Philip Galle, the *Victories of Charles V*, Hogenberg's *Short idea of what has occurred in France since the death of Henry II*, and several single-sheet scenes concerning the duke of Alba's regime in the Low Countries and the Revolt of the Alpujarras in Spain. The duke also owned four other bound volumes of prints, one displaying "various ingenious inventions", two with scenes from the Old and New Testaments, and an atlas of maps, predominantly Italian, among which can be found several depictions of sieges or battles, including two different views of the great siege of Malta.[21] To judge by their original shelf marks, these volumes of prints were all kept together in a section of the duke's library. Duke August of Brunswick-Lüneburg would organize his great library at Wolfenbüttel differently. He established no separate category for albums of prints, placing them together with printed books that he arranged according to subject matter and size. His copy of Tortorel and Perrissin was consequently shelved among his folio-size printed books of history.[22]

Where those responsible for organizing the ducal library in Mecklenburg made separate albums for historical scenes and maps, other early purchasers bound them together. Two of the three other composite albums that include plates from the *Quarante Tableaux* are geographic atlases containing maps, city views and battle scenes from all parts of the world, arranged by continent and country rather than chronologically. The first of these is a massive two-volume "raccolta Lafreriana" with over 250 maps, city views, and battle scenes now in the Biblioteca Nazionale in Florence that includes the only 25 plates from the series with titles and captions in Italian known to have survived.[23] The second is a composite atlas made by inserting older maps and city views from many sources within the pages of Bouguereau's 1594 atlas of France. It

---

Rostock, uncatalogued at time of consultation); Antje Sander-Berke, "Die erste herzogliche Bibliothek in Schwerin" in *Stadt und Hof: Schwerin als Residenzstadt im 16. Jahrhundert* (exhibition catalog, Schwerin, 1995), pp. 99-117.

20 UB Rostock, Rb 4654.

21 This atlas (UB Rostock, Qk 3) is the only other of the duke's volumes of prints to survive. W. Rüge, "Alteres kartographische Material in deutschen Bibliotheken," *Nachrichten von der Königliche Gesellschaft der Wissenschäftlicher in Göttingen* (1904), pp. 40-64, provides a detailed catalogue of its contents.

22 Oral communication from Christian Hogrefe, curator.

23 See above, p. 32; Borroni Salvadori, *Carte, piante e stampe storiche delle raccolte lafreriane della Biblioteca Nazionale di Firenze*.

contains five scenes of sieges and battles from the last part of the print series (plates 34 and 36 through 39).[24] That early buyers bound Tortorel and Perrissin's prints alongside city views and maps highlights the absence of a clear separation between these at the time. As we have already seen, single-sheet siege or battle views often incorporated elements of maps or were made by map publishers. Once made, these same publishers then often re-used these scenes in chorographies and atlases. Of the 28 city views in Antoine Du Pinet's 1564, *Plans, Portraits and Descriptions of Several Cities and Fortresses of Europe, Asia, Africa, the Indies and the New Lands*, 5 show the city in question under siege[25].

The few marginalia written in these old albums or directly on prints in modern portfolios suggest that at least some owners looked carefully at the historical details reported in the prints, compared them with other sources of information, and ruminated upon them. One owner noted that *The Massacre at Cahors* erred in dating the event to November 19, 1561; it actually took place, he wrote, on the sixteenth of the month.[26] Another rectified what he thought was an error in the legend of the *Execution of Anne Du Bourg*: "this was in the cemetery of St Jean and not in the Place de Grève."[27] Still another added the names of further Catholic and Protestant churchmen who participated in the Colloquy of Poissy to those listed in the key and noted that "the *dictionnaire historiq.* says it opened on September 4."[28] A Dutch owner wrote identifications of the duke of Alba, the count of Hoorn, the duke of Savoy, and the prince of Orange beneath four of the armored knights gathered around the tiltyard in *The Tournament at Which Henry II Was Fatally Wounded.* Here he was following labels that Hogenberg inserted in his reworking of this scene to enhance its appeal to a Netherlandish audience. It would seem that he was looking at the print alongside a copy of the Hogenberg.[29] A more reflective owner, quoting from Silius Italicus on the Punic Wars, wrote on *The*

---

[24] BM Lyon, Rés 24014. The final composite album, Maz., Rés 5921 F, was assembled in the early seventeenth century and is primarily a collection of historical views like that owned by the duke of Mecklenburg. Most of the prints in it are single-sheet news prints of current events. A few depictions of Jerusalem in biblical times are mixed in. This album contains just fourteen of the plates from the *Quarante Tableaux*.

[25] Du Pinet, *Plantz, pourtraitz et descriptions de plusieurs villes et forteresses*. My thanks to Susan Danforth of the John Carter Brown Library for checking this information for me. On the assimilation of battle scenes and siege views to maps, see also Ehrle, *Roma prima di Sisto V*, p. 54; E. Pognon, "Les plus anciens plans de villes gravés et les événements militaires," *Imago Mundi* 22 (1968), 13-19; van der Sman, *Le Siècle de Titien*, p. 176; Peter Barber, "England II: Monarchs, Ministers and Maps, 1550-1625" in David Buisseret ed., *Monarchs, Ministers and Maps: The Emergence of Cartography as a Tool of Government in Early Modern Europe* (Chicago, 1992), p. 74.

[26] BN, Rés La 21a 7. The date of the 19th is in fact correct.

[27] Mediatheque du Mans, SA F* 4405. Again, the original is correct.

[28] Free Library Philadelphia, Art dept., P769 T63.

[29] Rijksmuseum (Amsterdam), 329 A2; cf. Hellwig, *Hogenberg Geschichtsblätter*, cat. 21a.

Capture of Montbrison "so many fortresses are taken with one breach by the soldiers."[30] He was clearly using the print to reflect on the military lessons offered by history.

A few copies bear such detailed notes as to become intriguing historical sources themselves. In the margins on either side of the legend beneath *The Execution of Anne Du Bourg*, one owner added extensive details about Du Bourg's trial and execution. After listing the members of the special commission appointed by Henry II to try Du Bourg, he added that the French word "*mouchard*" (informant or police spy) derived from the name of one of the members of the tribunal, Antoine de Mouchy, an inquisitor for the faith, theologian and rector of the University of Paris.[31] I have found no confirmation of this etymology, but the first known use of the word dates from 1567.[32] The copy now in the Newberry Library, apparently owned by an English statesman watching events in France attentively, bears particularly heavy annotation. Long paragraphs in English beneath a number of the plates provide additional information about the events depicted or note what occurred in the intervals between successive scenes, suggesting the owner's frustration with the limited amount of contextual information found in the captions and their failure to indicate the connections between one event and the next. On the back of one, a hastily scrawled account in French records information supplied by a member of the French diplomatic party sent to England in the summer of 1571 to seek Queen Elizabeth's hand in marriage to the future Henry III. The admiral Coligny, it states, suspected that an attempt had been made to poison him. As a result, he kept a number of his own informants around the king and his brother at all times.[33]

Another English copy of the volume, now in Oxford's Bodleian Library, is heavily marked up in a different way. An early donation to the library, this copy contains a Latin epitaph on the death of William of Orange, practice pen trials, and a drawing of a dog. Arithmetical calculations are written directly on a few scenes. Whether these were the product of generations of student abuse or earlier markings is unclear.[34]

---

30 BM Grenoble, S 66 Rés, "Tot uno introitu capiuntur militis arces".

31 Hamburger Kunsthalle, Kupferstichkabinett, 1983/24.

32 *Tresor de la Langue Française* (http://atilf.atilf.fr), s.v. "mouchard".

33 Newberry Library, Wing fZP 539 .T63. This last note has been cut off at the top and is extremely difficult to decipher. The best I have been able to do is "... ou Chassanoy serviteur de Monsieur frere du roy accompagna Monsieur de Foiz ambassadeur me dict venant de Vantabridge (?) le 30 Aoust 1571 le facon comment monsr l'amiral tenoit estre empoissonné par un sien serviteur Alba lequel un capitaine de Monsieur aura fait a poste pour ce propos. Et comment ledict serviteur fust [blank, then passage crossed out] et comment l'Amiral a pour le moins entour le Roy et Monsieur 40 ou 50 qui lui baillent avertissement de tout ce qui se faict..." For the context of this mission, see N. M. Sutherland, *The Massacre of St Bartholomew and the European Conflict 1559-1572* (London, 1973), pp. 190-2.

34 Bodleian, Antiq.b.U.1.

If a number of early owners wrote upon their prints in a manner that shows that they studied them carefully as a historical resource about the period, relatively few went to the trouble and expense of having their aesthetic appeal and vividness enhanced through hand coloring. Sixteenth-century printmaking centers such as Nuremberg and Antwerp were home to illuminators who specialized in finishing prints in this manner for an additional charge that could triple or even quintuple the total price of the picture. Elsewhere, artists could also often be hired on a casual basis to do such work. In the shops along the Rue Montorgueil in Paris, children often did this work.[35] Hand colored copies of individual Tortorel and Perrissin prints turn up occasionally, but they are extremely rare. I have found just one complete series of the prints in color.[36] Geneva appears to have lacked specialist illuminators.[37] Hand-colored versions of Hogenberg's historical series seem more numerous.

Appropriations

While the evidence of the old albums and marginalia confirms that the prints of the *Wars, Massacres, and Troubles* reached across national and confessional boundaries and were examined carefully for their informational content, the majority of known instances where subsequent works copied, cited, or drew heavily upon the series involved Huguenot authors, publishers, or patrons who evinced particular interest in the scenes that illustrated Protestant valor or victimization. Their recycling of the images and information found in the *Quarante Tableaux* made the work an important building block of Huguenot historical memory about the years 1559-1570. Three quite different clusters of works in different media and genres illustrate this.

The first is a set of three tapestries now in the Musée National de la Renaissance at Ecouen representing the battles of St Denis and Jarnac.[38] Evidently

---

[35] Van der Stock, *Printing Images in Antwerp*, pp. 59-60; Susan Dackerman, "Painted Prints in Germany and the Netherlands" in *Painted Prints: The Revelation of Color* (exhibition catalog, Baltimore, 2002); Watt, *Cheap Print and Popular Piety*, p. 186.

[36] Biblioteca Nacional, Madrid, ER 2843, a complete set of forty prints with titles and captions in French. Thirteen of the fourteen prints from the series found in the large early-seventeenth-century *recueil factice*, Maz., Rés 5921F, are also hand colored, as are many of the other prints in this volume.

[37] Further evidence of this is provided below, p. 203.

[38] *The Battle of St Denis*, tapestry, 330 × 440 cm; *The Battle of Jarnac I*, tapestry, 320 × 550 cm; *The Battle of Jarnac II*, tapestry, 320 × 550 cm (Musée National de la Renaissance, ECL 2755-7); E. du Sommerard, *Musée des thermes et de l'hôtel de Cluny. Catalogue et description des objets d'art de l'Antiquité, du Moyen Age et de la Renaissance exposés au Musée* (Paris, 1883), pp. 503-4; *Coligny: Protestants et catholiques en France au XVIe siècle* (exhibition catalogue, Paris, 1972), p. 129; Erlande-Brandenburg, *Musée National de la Renaissance. Chateau d'Ecouen. Guide*, pp. 77-8; *D'Encre et de sang. Les guerres de religion gravées par Tortorel et Perrissin (1570)* (exhibition catalog, Ecouen-Noyon, 2006), p. 37.

commissioned by a prominent Huguenot nobleman to memorialize his participation in these battles, these tapestries are almost direct copies of scenes 28, 31, and 32 from the *Wars, Massacres and Troubles*. A few important additions to the two scenes devoted to the battle of Jarnac provide essential clues to the identity of the person for whom they first were produced. The most important of these additions place an additional company of soldiers commanded by the sieur de Fontrailles front and center within scene 31 *The Battle Order at Jarnac* (color plate 7). Like the versions of these scenes on paper, these tapestries have letter keys. The key to this scene informs the viewer that these men would charge the troop of soldiers that emerged from the village of Triat. The same troop of soldiers then reappears in the upper left of the tapestry copied after scene 32 *The Battle of Jarnac* (color plate 8). Here the key reports that after breaking the line of the enemy's light horse, Fontrailles rallied a fraction of his troop and charged a battalion of French infantry. His horse was killed beneath him, and he was wounded in the leg and taken prisoner.[39] In light of these modifications, it seems unlikely that the tapestries could have been initially commissioned for any one other than Michel d'Astarac, baron of Fontrailles and Marestang (c. 1537-1606), a loyal servant of the Bourbon and d'Albret families, sénéchal of Armagnac under Jeanne d'Albret, and lieutenant general of Guyenne under Henry of Navarre—who is known to have lost a leg at Jarnac.[40] Among the coats of arms displayed on the tapestries has also been identified that of Jeanne d'Ornezan Saint-Blancard, the wife of the Catholic captain Armand de Gontaut, baron of Biron. Thierry Crépin-Leblond, current director of the Musée National de la Renaissance, hypothesizes that after a first set of the tapestries was woven in Toulouse for the baron of Fontrailles around the turn of the seventeenth century, Jeanne d'Ornezan so liked them that she ordered copies for her chateau of St Blancard in Guyenne.[41]

A few lines of new verse were also woven into each tapestry. These stanzas exalt the deeds of both the constable Montmorency and the prince of Condé while expressing regret at the fratricidal nature of the civil wars:

> Jarnac you see here the troops assembled
> Who might have removed all of France's ills
> If concord and peace lived in their hearts
> Instead of the discord that reigns in their thoughts.[42]

---

39 The keys to the tapestries also name a few other captains who are not identified by name in the prints. The tapestry that corresponds to figure 31, *The Battle Order at Jarnac*, identifies the presence in the Huguenot ranks of La Noue, Briquemaut, and La Louve. The tapestry corresponding to figure 32, *The Battle of Jarnac* identifies La Valette as the commander of duke of Anjou's light horse.

40 *La France Protestante* (2nd ed.), I, 415ff, s.v. "Astarac".

41 *D'Encre et de sang*, p. 37; personal communication from Thierry Crépin-Leblond.

42 Above the image of the Constable fallen from his horse one reads: "Apres avoir sept fois embrassé la victoire/Ce grand chef meurt icy avec beaucoup d'honeur./Juges si le vaincu

Here we see prints from Tortorel and Perrissin serving as a model for tapestries made in southwestern France that memorialize a Huguenot commander's military service while deploring the country's recent divisions.

Agrippa d'Aubigné's poems and historical writings offer a second illustration of Tortorel and Perrissin's influence within French Protestant circles. Certain prints from the series clearly seared themselves deeply into d'Aubigné's memory, nourishing both his poetic imagination and the vengeful anti-Catholicism that still burned so fiercely within him in 1616, when he personally financed the establishment of a printing house in Maillé to publish his verse epic, *Les Tragiques*, and his multi-volume history of the years 1550-1602, the *Histoire universelle*.[43] One scene that especially haunted him was plate 14 *The Massacre at Tours*, with its figuration of such episodes as a newborn baby reaching its arm skyward as it disappears beneath the surface of the Loire and a child held aloft as a target for shooting practice. (Recall that these details are not reported in any other early printed account of the event.) In book five of *Les Tragiques* entitled "Les Fers", a visionary evocation of the horrors of the civil war, the events in Tours represent the acme of the horrors:

> But the hideous stamp of the picture of Tours
> Eclipsed the others in which the multitude
> Impetuously ran to brute cruelties
> That would have shocked even the icy Scythians.
> There, to the eye of the almighty shone the sight
> Of the killing hand and knife. There
> He saw three hundred half dead, starved for three days
> Taken from a suburban temple and bound,
> Then delivered so to the butchering band
> To be felled coupled together on the river's bank;
> There the tragic screams pitilessly rent the air,
> There children in the water brought the price of a crown,
> Ripped from the merchants to die,
> Their names, errors, spans, marks, distinctions unknown.
> What crime could they have committed before even living?
> It sufficed to die to be able to die,
> Those who hadn't yet tasted life
> Had to be made to taste the blows of death.
> So belling, trembling, dragged to the river's port
> And end of their days, left for dead,

meritoit tant de gloire/Combien on doibt priser la gloire du vainqueur." Above the two scenes of Jarnac one reads regarding Condé: "Pour la foy, pour mon Roy, pour ma chère patrie,/ J'entre dans le combat et j'y finis ma vie." And "D'un feu saint et divin ayant son ame esprise,/ Ce grand prince eust esté des chrestiens le recours,/ Si, lorsqu'il allumait le flambeau de l'Eglise,/ Le malheur n'eust estaint le flambeau de ses jours."

43 Madeleine Lazard, *Agrippa d'Aubigné* (Paris, 1998), pp. 353-4, 397-401; André Thierry, *Agrippa d'Aubigné, auteur de l'histoire universelle* (Lille: Atelier de reproduction des thèses, 1982), pp. 31-45.

They watched their mother's breasts pierced through,
Clutched the legs of their father's killers;
Their little feet fled the blood, no longer water,
They chanted to their executioners, *nenni, never*
The ultimate rod, ordeal of those their age,
Would ennoble them in blood and carnage.
Of the mothers split open, one aborted child
Was cast on the waters and carried away
As far as eyes could track him,
Raised an arm heavenward to call down his ire.
Some moved by pity went among the bodies,
Running through once more those where heart and spirit yet clung together.
When these slashers encountered a face
Whose beauty shook their courage,
The less hard let fall first their arms, then their steel;
Others snatched this up, filled with the hell,
Overriding pity to despoil the beauty,
Stripping it naked before their plain view,
Taking pleasure in soiling its living whiteness
To darken with death its color ingenue.
Youths formerly reprimanded for their vice
Dug in the entrails of the still breathing chief justice
For the gold they believed was hidden there, like the
Romans unwinding the guts of the Jews.[44]

This poem was written between 1577 and 1589.

D'Aubigné reprised the same event in his *Histoire universelle*, written between 1593 and 1612, which he considered to be a sort of prose substantiation of, and extended commentary upon, the fevered vision poured out in his poem.[45] The massacre of Tours occupies several paragraphs in the first chapter of book three, "The events that caused the Huguenots to rise up". According to d'Aubigné, who was often extremely careless about facts and dates, the massacre of Vassy inspired further bloodbaths in Cahors, Sens, Auxerre, and Tours. Not only are three of these four instances of violence represented in Tortorel and Perrissin; the massacre of Cahors in fact took place several months before Vassy, and that of Tours several months afterward, after the civil war had begun. That d'Aubigné groups them together here suggests the influence of the prints on his historical imagination. Of these four incidents, the massacre of Tours is the only one about which he provides any details. Those he provides include all of the most pathos-laden vignettes shown in the print of the scene: the children having a price set on their heads; the newborn who raised his hand heavenward when thrown into the river; the woman stripped naked before being killed; the judge disemboweled in

---

44 Agrippa d'Aubigné, *Les Tragiques* ed. F. Lestringant (Paris, 1995), pp. 246-7.

45 Thierry, *D'Aubigné, auteur de l'histoire universelle*, p. 5.

search of the money he was thought to have swallowed. Tortorel and Perrissin was not d'Aubigné's only source for the killings in Tours. He includes a detail not found in the print, namely that the Huguenots held for three days within the church of the faubourg de La Riche were bound together two by two before being led off to their death. He places the total number of victims at 300, where the key to the print sets the number at 200.[46] The picture, and indeed the entire series, nonetheless obviously deeply influenced him. In her exhaustive study of his world-view, Marie-Madeleine Fragonard finds that at least eleven prints from the series provided sources for *Les Tragiques*.[47] For this self-described "violent partisan" of unyielding vigilance against Rome's sanguinary puppets, the most detailed and pathetic scenes of Huguenot victimization were those most vividly recalled. For d'Aubigné the print series was indeed a chronicle of the cause's suffering.

The third indication of the series' influence in shaping the historical consciousness of later generations of Huguenots is provided by the historical calendars produced by francophone Protestant printers in the late sixteenth and seventeenth century. Replacing the pre-Reformation calendars that listed the feasts, fasts, and holy days of the church, these note, alongside the weeks, months, and phases of the moon, the most noteworthy historical events that took place during each month of the year. Jean Crespin published the first Genevan calendar of this sort in 1552, adapted from a German prototype by Paul Eber. Many other printers produced variants over the subsequent decades to accompany the small format editions of the psalms or Bible purchased by so many French Protestants of all walks of life.[48]

During the first half-century of their existence, these Huguenot historical calendars focused primarily on episodes of Biblical history, especially events of the Old Testament. Buyers were reminded that on February 11 Noah first saw the mountain top after forty days in the ark, and that on February 18 the dove returned with an olive branch. A small number of recent events in international church history were also noted, such as that on February 18 "the true servant of God M. Luther died in the year 1546", or that on August 17 "the reformation according to the truth of the Gospel" began in Geneva in 1535.[49]

---

46 D'Aubigné, *Histoire universelle*, II, 7-13, esp. 12-13.

47 Fragonard, *Poésie religieuse d'Agrippa d'Aubigné*, p. 859.

48 The history of these calendars is fascinatingly sketched in Max Engammare, *L'ordre du temps. L'invention de la ponctualité au XVIe siècle* (Geneva, 2004), ch. 4. See also Gilmont, *Bibliographie des éditions de Crespin*, I, 28-9; Eugenie Droz, "Le calendrier genevois agent de la propagande" and "Le calendrier lyonnais" in *Chemins de l'hérésie* (4 vols., Geneva, 1970-76), II, 433-56, III, 1-29.

49 For this period I have looked at seven calendars: *Les pseaumes mis en rimes francoises* ([Geneva]: Antoine Vincent, 1562) [BPU, Bb 1666]; *Calendrier historial et lunaire* (Lyon: Gabriel Cotier, 1564) [BPU, Bb 2262 Rés]; *Kalendrier historial* (St Lo: Thomas Bouchard and Jacques Le Bas, 1565) [BPU Bb, 1733 Rés]; *Kalendrier ou almanach historial* (Geneva: Thomas Courteau, 1566) [BPU, Bb 670]; *Calendrier Historial* ([Geneva]: Francois Estienne,

Soon after 1600, the episodes depicted in Tortorel and Perrissin invaded these calendars en masse, part of a wholesale restructuring that focused them far more exclusively on French history, and most especially on events from the first decade of the Wars of Religion and from Henry IV's struggle against the Catholic League. The earliest calendar that I have seen with this new focus was published in French in Leiden in 1606 by Louis Elsevier. It includes twenty events from the years 1559-1570. Seventeen of these are scenes in Tortorel and Perrissin. These include not only such landmark happenings as the death of Henry II, the massacre of Vassy, or the battles of Dreux and Moncontour, but also lesser episodes such as the battle of St Gilles, the massacres of Sens, Tours, and Cahors, and the siege of St Jean-d'Angély. Often these are recorded in phrases that echo exactly titles of the prints: "le Duc de Guise blessé à mort", "St Jean d'Angély assiegée par le Roi Charles 9", "l'entreprise d'Amboise descouverte".[50] The calendar does not, however, note the events from the series that redounded to the discredit of the Protestant cause, such as the Michelade or the capture of Montbrison. The three events from 1559-1570 that are not figured in the *Wars, Massacres and Troubles* are the death of Francis II, the promulgation of the Edict of January at what is dubbed the Estates of St Germain-en-Laye, and the massacres of August 1, 1562 in several localities in Provence.

Huguenot historical calendars continued to be produced until the revocation of the Edict of Nantes.[51] As the years passed, a few major events from each successive decade found their way into them: the banishment of the Jesuits after the attempt on Henry IV's life by Jean Chastel; his assassination

1567) [BPU, Ga 135bis]; *Calendrier historial et lunaire* (Geneva: Abel Rivery, 1576) [BPU, Bb 2143]; *Calendrier historial et lunaire* ([Geneva]: Jacob Stoer, 1580) [BPU, Bb 2309]; *Calendrier historial et lunaire* (Geneva: pour Pierre Mourier, 1606) [BPF, R 9805].

50 *Les Pseaumes de David* (Leiden: Louis Elsevier, 1606) [BPF, André 169]. Engammare, *L'ordre du temps*, p. 165, first pointed out the calendars' debt to Tortorel and Perrissin.

51 I was able to locate and consult the following French-language calendars from the years 1610-1685: *Calendrier historial* (Geneva: Pierre and Jacques Chouet, 1618) [BPU, Bb 2362 Rés]; *Les pseaumes de David* (Sedan: Jean Jannon, 1620) [Musée Historique de la Réformation, Geneva, O6e (620)]; *Les Pseaumes de David* (Paris: Pierre Des-Hayes, 1641) [BPF, 13246]; *Les Pseaumes de David* (Paris: Pierre Des-Hayes, 1652) [I would like to thank Max Engammare for bringing this edition to my attention and furnishing me with a copy from a private collection]; *Les Pseaumes de David* (Paris: Antoine Cellier, 1661) [BPF, 8o 9859]; *Les Pseaumes de David* (Paris: Antoine Cellier, 1667) [BPF, André 124 (2)]; *Les Pseaumes de David* (Paris: Antoine Cellier, 1675) [BPF, 8o 18078]; *Les Pseaumes de David* (Paris: Antoine Cellier, 1680) [BPF, 8o 19192]. To judge by the BPF's excellent catalogue of its holdings of old Bibles and psalters, the frequency with which these calendars were printed declined somewhat after 1660. A diminishing percentage of the psalters in the library's collection are bound with such calendars. The only printer to produce them from 1661 onward was Antoine Cellier of Paris/Charenton. This may be linked to the proliferation after 1661 of single-sheet almanachs with calendars, which may have reducing the demand for calendars to accompany psalters. See here Maxime Préaud, *Les effets du soleil. Almanachs du règne de Louis XIV* (exhibition catalog, Paris, 1995), pp. 11-13.

by "the detestable Ravaillac"; the birthdays and coronation dates of successive kings; foreign affairs including battles and conquests of the Thirty Years War, the execution of Charles I of England, and the restoration of his son Charles II. But what is most striking is how heavily events from the years 1559-1570 and 1585-1594 continue to be represented. (By contrast, no mention is made of any episodes from the last round of religious wars between 1621 and 1629.) In a 1680 calendar printed by Antoine Cellier for sale at Charenton, no less than 25 events from the years 1559-1570 still appear, twenty of them episodes depicted in Tortorel and Perrissin.[52] More than a century after they took place, the siege of St Jean d'Angély, the battle of St Gilles, and the surprise of Nîmes were still deemed memorable. Given how widely disseminated these calendars are likely to have been, one could hardly imagine a more powerful form of influence upon the historical consciousness of later generations than this molding of the contents of these cheap and widely distributed calendars by the *Wars, Massacres and Troubles*.

The prints also contributed to fixing an image of Huguenot victimization among foreign Protestants. This is shown by a group of six paintings made in Germany and subsequently acquired by English owners that replicate scenes from the *Quarante Tableaux*. Four of these seem to have been copied directly from the prints by Tortorel and Perrissin. Two were painted after Hogenberg's reproductions, as can be inferred from the fact that the composition of the painting is reversed in the same manner as the Hogenberg copy. Each painting represents a key episode from the series' opening meta-narrative: Anne Du Bourg's good counsel ignored with tragic consequences, a brief moment when Protestant doctrines and grievances were heard out, then a spasm of Catholic violence that initiates the civil wars. The paintings known are: *The Mercuriale*, *The Death of Henry II*, *The Execution of Anne Du Bourg*, *The Colloquy of Poissy*, *The Massacre of Cahors*, *The Massacre of Vassy*. The legends painted under the scenes nearly always replicate those accompanying the Hogenberg copies, which include partisan terms such as "papist" not found in the Genevan prints, and which describe the massacre of Vassy as occurring "with frenzied rage and cruelty". The legend for the painting of *The Execution of Anne Du Bourg* goes beyond even the Hogenberg text, informing the viewer that the painting shows how the "tyrannical Guises" who ruled "like a Jezabel" put the "pious president" to death.[53]

---

52 The events from 1559-1570 in this calendar not shown in Tortorel and Perrissin are the Edict of January, the massacres of Provence in 1562, the fatal wounding of Anthony of Navarre before Rouen, the 1563 creation of the *juridiction consulaire* in Paris, and the issuing of the 1568 edict of pacification before Chartres.

53 The painting of *The Mercuriale held at the Augustins in Paris 10 June 1559*, oil on canvas, 123 × 150 cm., was acquired in 1997 by the Musée Calvin in Noyon from an English collection. It is reproduced in *D'Encre et de sang*, p. 36. The other five paintings, of identical dimensions and materials, are part of the British royal collection at Hampton Court. All six

While the baron de Fontrailles' tapestries, Agrippa's *Tragiques*, the Huguenot historical calendars, and the German paintings testify to the various ways in which the *Quarante Tableaux* shaped both French and foreign Protestant historical memory of this period in subsequent generations, at least one French Catholic historian used and appreciated the series for its informational value. This was Léon Ménard (1706-1767), author of a five-volume *Civil, Ecclesiastical and Literary History of the City of Nîmes* whose account of that city's experience during the Wars of Religion is still the most detailed and illuminating account of a French city under Huguenot domination during this era. Originally a member of the *cour présidial* of Nîmes, Menard followed the path trod by so many eighteenth-century Frenchmen with intellectual aspirations and moved to Paris in middle age to participate in the scholarly circles there. His ambitions were crowned with a seat in the Royal Academy of Inscriptions and Belle-Lettres. For his history of Nîmes, he had access to exceptionally rich documentation, some of it now lost. Being Catholic, he had no hesitations about reporting violent or illegal Huguenot actions of a sort that Protestant historians typically swept under the rug. But while partisan enough to use the label "the so-called reform" when describing Protestantism, he scrupulously respected documentary evidence and did not hesitate to dismiss as wholly fantastic elements of the account of the Michelade found in the Jesuit Maimbourg's *History of Calvinism* or the Augustinian Martin's *History of the Life of St. Augustine and of Several Saints of His Order*. In discussing the surprise Huguenot raid that retook the city in November 1569, he cites the evidence of Tortorel's print to help resolve the vexed question of just where the raiders were able to slip through the town's defenses and into the city. His judgment of the print is worth citing at length:

> This is a monument of the period undoubtedly made with the most exact fidelity. We know that it was common at that time to carve in woodcut form the chief events that took place throughout the civil wars, such as battles, the capture of cities, and massacres. These prints were made in Lyon, some by Tortorel, others by Perrissin, two engravers of that city. They may be found gathered into volumes in the cabinets of the curious. The design of this one followed by the engraver had been made on the spot by people who were well informed about both the place and the manner in which the *religionnaires* slipped into the city. The event was quite recent, and one cannot suspect the print of the slightest error.[54]

---

of these paintings are described in an excellent unpublished article by Frédéric Panni, "Un cycle de peintures allemandes de la fin du XVIe siècle d'après les gravures de Tortorel et Perrissin," copy in the possession of the Musée Calvin. I owe thanks to the museum's current director, Barbara Sibille, for bringing this to my attention and providing me a copy.

54 Ménard, *Histoire civile, ecclesiastique et littéraire de la ville de Nismes*, V, notes, p. 9; also pp. 2-3, passim. There is a brief biographical entry about Ménard in *La grande encyclopédie* (31 vols., Paris, 1885-1902), s.v. "Ménard, Léon ".

For this critical historian who knew well the relevant sources and the topography of the city, Tortorel's print had such verisimilitude that he thought it was based on a drawing made on the spot. So highly did he esteem the two prints of Nîmes in the series that he had reproductions of them engraved by the Parisian artists Anna Fonbonne and P.F. Tardieu for use as illustrations in his book, thus becoming the first of many subsequent historians to use Tortorel and Perrissin prints as book illustrations.

The Visual Reporting of Current Events After Tortorel and Perrissin

While the afterlife of the *Quarante Tableaux* reveals that the print series was widely acquired and recalled in the centuries after its first appearance, it had surprisingly little immediate impact in stimulating graphic artists to attempt similar projects in either France or Geneva in the decades after 1570. No French or Genevan entrepreneur stepped into the void left by Castellin's death to attempt a Second Volume of wars, massacres, and troubles. None attempted another pictorial account of current history for more than two decades. French production of single-sheet news prints also fell off between 1571 and 1587, after having risen notably in the 1560s. Where 17 single-sheet news prints are known from the years 1560-1570, just 9 are known from the longer period 1571-1587. Strikingly, these include depictions of the royal siege and conquest of Sommières in 1573, the long and ultimately unsuccessful siege of La Rochelle in the same year, the 1576 meeting of the Estates-General in Blois, four depictions of monstrous births or notorious brigands—but no depiction of the most notorious event of all of these years, the Saint Bartholomew's Massacre. At least five German news prints depicted this "horrible Inquisition that took place at the royal wedding in Paris", as one called it.[55] Pope Gregory XIII considered it a victory over heresy of such evident justice that he had Vasari include it in the frescoes for the Vatican Sala Regia, the audience hall where visiting dignitaries were received.[56] The Huguenot painter from Amiens François Dubois, who is thought to have taken refuge in Geneva after 1572 and certainly died there in 1584, painted a

55 *Erschreckliche Inquisition so sich auff der koniglischen Hochzeit zu Paris in Franckreich zugretagen in Monat Augusti des 72 Jars*, colored woodcut with extensive text, Nuremberg, Leonhard Blumel, 1572, Zentralbibliothek Zurich, Wickiana; BN, Estampes, Hennin 660-3; Henri Bordier, *Peinture de la Saint-Barthélemy par un artiste contemporain comparée avec les documents historiques* (Geneva, 1878), section 2 "les gravures de la Saint-Barthélemy".

56 Alexandra Herz, "Vasari's 'Massacre' Series in the Sala Regia—the Political, Juristic and Religious Background," *Zeitschrift für Kunstgeschichte* 49 (1986), 41-54; Herwarth Röttgen, "Zeitgeschichtliche Bildprogramme der katholischen Restauration unter Gregor XIII, 1572-1585," *Münchner Jahrbuch der Bildenden Kunst*, 3rd ser., 26 (1975), 89-122; Loren Partridge and Randolph Starn, "Triumphalism and the Sala Regia in the Vatican" in *Triumphal Celebrations and Rituals of Statecraft* (University Park, 1990), pp. 22-82.

view of the event at an unknown date between those years for an unknown patron and purpose.[57] Why French and Genevan graphic artists avoided this subject is hard to explain, especially since Dubois's patron clearly felt it important to record its sanguinary details with the care characteristic of Tortorel and Perrissin's massacre scenes, and since Catholic pamphlets had no hesitation about crowing about the event, which they depicted as sweet revenge for the Huguenot sedition, warfare, and iconoclasm of the preceding decade.[58] Notwithstanding, the massacre may have been too searing for graphic depictions of it to have seemed widely marketable in either France or Geneva.

Rather than in France or Geneva, it was in and around Cologne that Castellin and company's experiment lit a spark. The key figure here was Frans Hogenberg, whose copies of the *Wars, Massacres and Troubles* were soon followed by a string of other historical series. Hogenberg's historical print series had a variety of qualities lacking in the *Quarante Tableaux*. They were all etched, ensuring both speed of production and a standard look within longer suites. They employed a smaller format than Tortorel and Perrissin (roughly 20 × 28 cm, as opposed to 32 by 50), further facilitating their rapid production. Hogenberg did not share Tortorel and Perrissin's *horror vacui*. His prints concentrate more sharply on a few key moments of the events they depict, rarely employ simultaneous narration, and are devoid of the extraneous details from everyday life or nature that fill up the dead spaces of the *Wars, Massacres and Troubles*. This too would have hastened their production. Hogenberg also adopted a standard format for the accompanying text: a brief verse account of the event in question. These verse captions do not clarify details within the prints as minutely as Tortorel and Perrissin's keys, but they enable viewers looking though a suite of the prints to grasp the essential character and outcome of each event far more quickly. All of these features contributed to the success of his historical series, as did Cologne's location astride the major trade routes between the Low Countries and Italy and the city's emergence in these years as an important center of current-events printing, which meant that Hogenberg was well situated both to gather

---

57 François Dubois, *The Saint Bartholomew's Massacre*, oil on wood, 94 × 154 cm, Musée cantonal des Beaux-Arts, Lausanne; Bordier, *Peinture de la Saint-Barthélémy*; *Le monde selon François Dubois, peintre de la Saint-Barthélemy* (exhibition catalog, Lausanne, 2003). This painting displays close parallels to some of the massacre scenes from Tortorel and Perrissin in its probable reliance on a written source (Simon Goulart's *Memoires de l'Estat de France sous Charles neufiesme*) and its placement of numerous small, closely described episodes within broad open spaces in an urban landscape meant to evoke the place in which the event occurred without being topographically precise. It also rivals the best known scenes from Tortorel and Perrissin in the frequency with which it is reproduced in books about this era.

58 E.g. Beauxamis, *La marmite renversée et fondue*; de Saconay, *Genealogie et la fin des huguenaux*.

information about events elsewhere and to disseminate his prints widely.[59] As we have already seen, Hogenberg allowed more partisan party labels and emotional adjectives to slip into his captions than was true of the legends accompanying the full sets of the *Quarante Tableaux*. His depictions of Spanish cruelty in the Netherlands are at times extreme. The degree of accuracy and exactitude of his Dutch views varies considerably. Nonetheless, his suites of both Dutch and French events offer an impression of verisimilitude, a richness of information, and a sobriety of labeling that recalls Tortorel and Perrissin.[60] One can imagine them appealing to Catholics as well as Protestants. As Cologne was a predominantly Catholic city and the surrounding region a mosaic of confessions, this too should have added to their success.

Successful they were. More than any other artist-entrepreneur, Hogenberg first revealed the full commercial possibilities of current events news prints, suites, and book illustrations. The standard catalogue of the historical scenes that issued from his workshop shows that from 1570 to 1631 he and his son and successor Abraham made or published 468 etchings depicting recent events. The greatest number concerned events in the Netherlands or nearby portions of Germany. The earliest were series depicting prior events. Many of the later views were first published as single sheets shortly after the event in question, before subsequently being collected into suites. Thanks to his simplified style, Hogenberg and the artists who worked for him could turn out a print within four to six days after news of an event first reached Cologne, which would have lent such prints considerable news value.[61] Hogenberg's growing reputation also led a number of North German and Scandanavian rulers to hire him to chronicle their victories and court festivities in works that contain a larger component of panegyric. Between 1587 and 1589 he etched suites displaying the marriage of duke Johann Wilhelm of Jülich, the funeral procession of king Frederick II of Denmark, the outstanding deeds of the same ruler, and the achievements of the Swedes in their recent wars with Muscovy.[62]

Hogenberg also collaborated with Michael von Aitzing or Aitzinger after this Austrian nobleman educated in both mathematics and the law moved to

---

59 Hellwig, *Hogenberg—Geschichtsblatter*, passim; Horst, *Opstand in zwart-wit*, p. 20; Veldman, "Keulen als toevluchtsoord," p. 45.

60 The following University of Antwerp students helped me better understand Hogenberg's point of view and working methods through their excellent contributions to a discussion of this problem during a guest lecture: Nele Averens, Tim Bisschops, Yannick Bochen, Jos Crabbe, Ellen Decraene, Raoul De Kerf, Machteld De Rijck, Sonja Deschrijver, Elke Kunkels, Hugo Lambrechts, Dorien Leyers, Petra Maclot, Hans Mertens, Daneilla Meys, Karen Milants, Anke Nuytemans, Barbara Ortiz, Anneleen Perneel, Jeroen Puttevils, Peter Saenen, Aline Sax, Rafel Scmytka, Hendrik Vandenberghe, Marijke Van Eekert, Eva Van Hansewijck, Jorn Van Tillo, Sophie Willekens, Andy Wynants.

61 Hellwig, *Hogenberg—Geschicthsblatter*, p. 14.

62 *Ibid.*, p. 8.

Cologne in 1579, where he soon emerged as an important chorographer and current-events publisher. Hogenberg published a version of Aitzinger's geographic and historical account of the Low Countries, *De Leone Belgico*, in 1583 with 114 illustrations, many of them scenes from his historical suites. A subsequent edition in 1596 contained 265 prints. At some point during the 1580s, Aitzinger achieved an enduring position in the history of journalism by assembling the most important accounts and documents concerning the leading events of the preceding six months into volumes offered for sale at the Frankfurt book fair. These comprised the first "*messerelationen*", twice yearly recapitulations of recent news that are seen by historians of the press as an important step down the road toward regularly appearing periodicals. Other printers in Frankfurt and Cologne soon followed with rival compilations of their own, each accusing their competitors of being excessively partisan and gullible, while they offered the impartial truth. These pan-European *messerelationen* were not the only forms of instant history produced by Aitzinger and his rivals. They also brought out accounts covering longer spans of time devoted to a single country or area. Hogenberg's etchings were used to illustrate at least one of these volumes as well, a *History of the League in France* published in 1591 that includes eleven Hogenberg views of French events from 1587 to 1590.[63]

Just as Hogenberg had quickly pirated Tortorel and Perrissin, other printmakers tried to horn in on his business. A graphic suite of views of events in the Netherlands between 1572 and 1574 of a nearly identical format and appearance to Hogenberg's but by a different, unknown artist has been recomposed from prints scattered across a number of Dutch libraries.[64] The July 1574 banishment from Antwerp of the printmaker Arnout Nicolai for producing a set of prints with "scandalous inscriptions in honor of the rebels against His Majesty" suggests that still a third such set may also have been made—unless Nicolai was the artist responsible for the series just mentioned, but this seems improbable since its captions are still more even-handed than Hogenberg's and do not appear scandalous to the king's honor.[65] Still another suite of historical prints was made by the Wierix brothers after designs by Martin de Vos soon after troops suspected of being in communication with Don John of Austria were driven out of Antwerp in 1577 and the remaining

---

63 *Historia von der Liga in Franckreich* (n.p., 1591), copy in the Folger Shakespeare Library (Washington), Acq. 252836. The events depicted run from the battle of Coutras to the duke of Parma's relief of Paris and subsequent withdrawal from France. The work as a whole is a compilation of documents, manifestos, and accounts of events from 1585 to early 1591, perhaps a translation of one of the editions of Simon Goulard's *Memoires de la Ligue*.

64 Simon Groenveld, "Het Engelse kroniekje van Walter Morgan en een onbekende reeks historieprenten (1572-1574)," *Bijdragen en Mededelingen betreffende de Geschiedenis der Nederlanden* 98 (1983), 19-74.

65 *Ibid.*, pp. 29, 32.

troops in the citadel swore allegiance to the States of Brabant. With their frontispiece that compares the leaders of this action to the three Horatii and mannered depictions of the graceful dance of collaboration among these local heroes, these mix a heavy dose of panegyric into their reporting.[66] (See figure 37.) Yet more fully in the eulogistic tradition of the *Victories of Charles V* was the 1583 Antwerp publication etched by Jan van der Straet or Stradanus, *The Exploits of the House of Medici*.[67]

Other printmakers in and around Cologne experimented with different forms of collaboration between the visual and verbal reportage of current events. The collections of the Bibliothèque Nationale contain a number of German prints of French events from the 1590s that contain the numbers to a key within the image but no accompanying text printed outside the border, just phrases within it such as "read about this battle in the *Navarrische Zeitung*", or "this true *abcontrafactung* of the besieged city of Paris is clarified by the numbers in the *Parisische zeitung* dated August 1590".[68] To fully understand the print, a purchaser had to acquire the news report as well. From 1595 on, Frankfurt *messerelationen* began regularly to be illustrated with engravings.[69] A series of artists including Theodore de Bry (b. Liege, active in Frankfurt from 1588 to 1598), his sons Johann Israel and Johann Theodor de Bry (active in Frankfurt 1598-1609 and 1619-1624), Georg Keller (b. Frankfurt, active there 1595-1634), and Matthias Merian (b. Basel, active in Frankfurt as heir to the de Bry enterprise 1624-1650), made Frankfurt a place where

---

66 Van der Stock, *Printing Images in Antwerp*, pp. 163-7; Marie Mauquoy-Hendrickx, *Les estampes des Wierix conservées au Cabinet des Estampes de la Bibliothèque Royale Albert 1er. Catalogue raisonné* (3 vols., Brussels, 1979), II, 300; Charles Avery, "Antwerp, August 1577: The 'Spanish Fury' and the Liberation of the Citadel: A Series of Bronze Plaquettes after Martin de Vos," *The Connoisseur* (August 1977), 252-63.

67 *Mediceae familiae rerum feliciter gestarum victoriae et triumphi* (Antwerp: Philips Galle, 1583), in Manfred Sellink ed., *Philips Galle* (New Hollstein Dutch and Flemish 10, 4 vols., Rotterdam, 2001), III, 198-206. Strip-like views in the manner of Nicolaus Hogenberg and Robert Peril's depiction of Charles V's 1530 entry into Bologna were also made of the funeral processions of William of Orange (by Hendrik Goltzius, 1584) and Sir Philip Sidney (by Theodore de Bry, 1588): *Funeral Procession of William, Prince of Nassau-Orange in Delft, August 3rd 1584*, suite of etchings, title and 11 plates, each 16 × 36 cm, in Hollstein Dutch and Flemish, VIII, 97, reproduced in Walter L. Strauss, *Hendrik Goltzius 1558-1617: The Complete Engravings and Woodcuts* (2 vols., New York, 1977), I, 324-35; Riggs, *Hieronymus Cock*, p. 191.

68 *Lisz von disere Schlacht in der Navarrischen Zeitung*, etching, 18.5 × 27.5 cm, BN, Estampes, Hennin 925; *Explicatio dieser Buchstaben*, etching, 18 × 28 cm, BN, Estampes, Hennin 927 and Maz., 5921F; *Von disse ware abcontrafactung der Stadt und gewaltige belagerung Paris, Vintman durch die ziffer inder Parisische zeitung ercleret datum Austi 1590*, engraving, 22 × 28.5 cm, Boutier, *Plans de Paris*, p. 103; *Lisz hiervon inder Parisischen Zeitung 1590*, etching, 18.3 × 28 cm, BN, Estampes, Hennin 940; *Wie der Konig auss Franckrich und Navarra den Prosiand abschlege findestu Weiter durch die buchstaben in der Parisische Zeittung explicir*, etching, 18 × 28 cm, 1596, BN, Estampes, Hennin 1092.

69 Hellwig, *Hogenberg*, p. 26; Thieme-Becker, s.v. "Georg Keller".

FIGURE 37. Jan Wierix after Martin de Vos, *The Negotiation between the German Mercenaries and Roeck, Beurs and Liedekerke* from *Patria Libertati Restituta*, 1577, etching, 28 × 22 cm, Bibliothèque Royal de Belgique, Cabinet des Estampes, A 14 62.

FIGURE 38. Anonymous, *The Siege and Capture of Gournay*, c. 1589, colored woodcut, 18.5 × 27 cm, Bibliothèque Mazarine, 5921 F.

current-events printmaking was tightly linked to the production of printed news accounts.[70] Recent scholarship has indicated that the etching found in the Introduction to this book of *The Broadsheet Peddler* was probably produced in Frankfurt around 1590.[71] It illustrates well the link between the visual and the verbal reporting of current event forged there at just this moment.

In France, the downturn in the production of current-events prints of the 1570s and early 1580s gave way to a new burst of activity in this domain during Henry IV's long struggle to secure his succession to the throne against the Catholic League. The shocking news of the assassination of the duke and cardinal of Guise at Blois in 1588 was reported in a number of Parisian single-sheet

70 Thieme-Becker, s.v. "de Bry", "Georg Keller", "Matthaeus Merian"; Lucas Heinrich Wüthrich, *Das Druckgraphische Werk von Matthaeus Merian die altere* (2 vols., Basel, 1966-72), II, 12.

71 Weber ed., *Wunderzeichen und Winkeldrucker*, pp. 48-9; Seelig and Bartrum eds., *Jost Amman* (New Hollstein German 4), II, 167.

woodcuts. Several printmakers of the rue Montorgueil subsequently linked their business to the cause of the League. In addition to producing the polemical and satirical prints directed against Henry III and the laudatory depictions of Jacques Clément's subsequent assassination of the "wicked Herod" that are well known through Pierre de L'Estoile's album of *Les belles figures et droleries de la Ligue*, they chronicled several minor early battlefield victories by *ligueur* champions, such as the duke of Mayenne's capture of Gournay in September 1589 (figure 38).[72] Once Paris fell under siege in 1590, however, visual news reports chronicling victories of the League ceased to appear. They did not resume after the siege was raised, victims of the broader decline in publishing activity of all sorts due to the death or departure of so many.[73]

For his part, Henry of Navarre was a ruler who recognized the utility of works of art in building loyalty to his person almost as soon as he reached maturity. He made sure to attach a painter to his household while still governor of Guyenne and regularly rewarded loyal servants with portraits of himself that they could display in their private residences. (Some complained that they had hoped for better compensation!)[74] As soon as the struggle against the Catholic League began in 1585, he took pains to publicize his good will to the kingdom's Catholic majority through printed pamphlets that he distributed to his diplomatic agents to ensure their wide circulation. Following the assassination of Henry III, the royal printer Jamet Mettayer in Tours became the hub of an organized effort to spread what one historian has called "veritable official bulletins" about his campaigns and victories.[75] Only in the last phase of his succession struggle, however, were the graphic arts added to his propaganda arsenal. Two figures were especially important here: his topographer royal and military engineer Claude Châtillon (1559-1611), and the Paris print publisher Jean Le Clerc IV (1560-c. 1622), who is believed to have taken refuge in Tours between 1590 and 1594.[76]

---

[72] *Les Belles figures et drolleries de la Ligue*, Vol. 4 of Pierre de L'Estoile, *Mémoires-journaux* eds. Brunet, Champollion et al. (12 vols., Paris, 1875-96); Keith Cameron, *Henri III, a Maligned or Malignant King? Aspects of the Satirical Iconography of Henri de Valois* (Exeter, 1978); Benedict, "Marmites and Martyrs,", pp. 127-30; Maz., 5921 F, which contains prints of *La ville de Gournay en Normandie, nagueres assiegee & Prise par Monsieur le Duc de Mayenne*, colored woodcut, 18.5 x 27 cm, and *Surprise faicte par le Marquis de Mainelay sur le Sieur de Bornivet*, colored woodcut, 15.5 x 32 cm.

[73] Denis Pallier, *Recherches sur l'imprimerie à Paris pendant la Ligue (1585-1594)* (Geneva, 1976), passim, esp. pp. 16, 129, 137.

[74] Jacques Peret, "L'iconographie d'Henri de Navarre à l'époque de la bataille de Coutras et au début de son règne en France: le rôle de François Bunel" in *Quatrieme centenaire de la bataille de Coutras* (Pau, 1988), 175-201, esp. 178-9.

[75] Pallier, *Imprimerie à Paris pendant la Ligue*, p. 85. Henry's efforts to publicize his policies and intentions toward the kingdom's Catholics may be followed through the pamphlets in the Lb series of the BN, notably Lb 34 253, 255, 259, 262, 263, 283, 289, 290, 355, 359, 505, 684, 733, 738, 766, and Lb 35 86, 87, 92, 95, 276, 302.

[76] Préaud et al., s.v. "Leclerc Jean IV (1560-1621/1622)".

Châtillon entered Navarre's service around 1580 and was named topographer royal around 1591.[77] As was increasingly standard practice at this time, he accompanied his master's armies on campaign, drawing fortresses, sieges, and battles after life in order to assist in the planning of siege operations and to record engagements for training future generations of military men. During the last phase of Henry's combats against the League and its Spanish and Savoyard allies, four of Châtillon's views of the king's military operations were published in graphic form: the conquest of La Fère from the Archduke Albert in 1596, the siege of Amiens in 1597, the withdrawal of the Spanish from Amiens in 1598 (figure 39), and the siege of Montmélian in Savoy in 1600. The last three of these were printed and sold by Le Clerc.[78] Their publication, often accompanied by extensive text hailing the king's victories, was probably meant to counter the still more numerous images of Spanish triumphs in the fighting along France's northern border that Adriaen Huybrechts or Huberti published on the other side of the frontier in Antwerp from 1595 onward.[79] The appearance of Châtillon's views amid this propaganda battle was an early instance of a phenomenon that would become common in the next century: royal military engineers being allowed to make and sell prints after their battlefield drawings to supplement their income and spread their employer's glory. Perhaps the most famous publication to emerge

---

77 For Châtillon's career and biography: David J. Buisseret, "Les ingénieurs du roi au temps de Henri IV," *Comité des Travaux Historiques et Scientifiques: Bulletin de la Section de Géographie* 77 (1964), 40-51.

78 *La ville et chasteau de la Fére en Picardie, assiegée et prise par le Roy Henry le Grand l'an 1595*, intaglio, 38 × 51.5 cm [repositories: BN, Estampes, Hennin 1083; Chantilly, Estampes H. 66]; *Porfille Damiens 1597*, intaglio, 9.5 × 33 cm, "J De Weert fe[cit]; par Claude Chastillon topographe du roy" with accompanying text signed by Chastillon "A Paris, chez Jean Le Clerc, 1597", Maz., 5921F; *La retraicte d'Albert cardinal d'Austriche, Chef & conducteur de l'armée Espagnolle, au secours de la ville d'Amyens*, intaglio, 15.5 × 41 cm, par Claude Chastillon topographe du roy, with accompanying text "A Paris par Jehan Le Clerc 1597" [repositories: BN, Estampes, Hennin 1116; Maz., 5921F]; *Le portraict de la ville et chasteau de Mont-Mellian en Savoye assiegee par le Roy de France et de Navarre. 1600*, woodcut, 31 × 48.5 cm, "par Cl. Chastillon, Topographe du Roy" "A Paris chez Jean le Clerc" and "A Lyon Pour Leonard Odet" [repositories: Maz., 5921F; Deutsches Historisches Museum (Berlin), RB 92 2979].

79 BN, Estampes includes views by Huybrechts of the Spanish capture of Dorlans (1595), the siege of Cambrai (1595), the capture of Ardres (1596), a victory over the duke of Bouillon (July 24, 1596), the failed French attempt on Arras (1597), and the siege of Amiens in 1597. Hennin 1076, 1082, 1095, 1099, 1106, 1109. Other views by the same artist of the siege of Hulst (1596) and Rijnsberg (1598) may be found in BM Grenoble, S 66 B. Huybrechts is a fascinating figure. Early in his career as an engraver, he made several works with anti-Spanish or evangelical implications, After the Spanish reconquest of Antwerp in 1585, he turned to making Catholic devotional prints and was the publisher of Richard Verstegan's famous *Theatre of the Cruelties of the Heretics of Our Time*. His involvement with Verstegan may have moved him in the direction of making current events prints. On the earlier phases of his career, see James Clifton, "Adriaen Huybrechts, the Wierix Brothers, and Confessional Politics in the Netherlands," *NKJ* 52 (2001), 105-25.

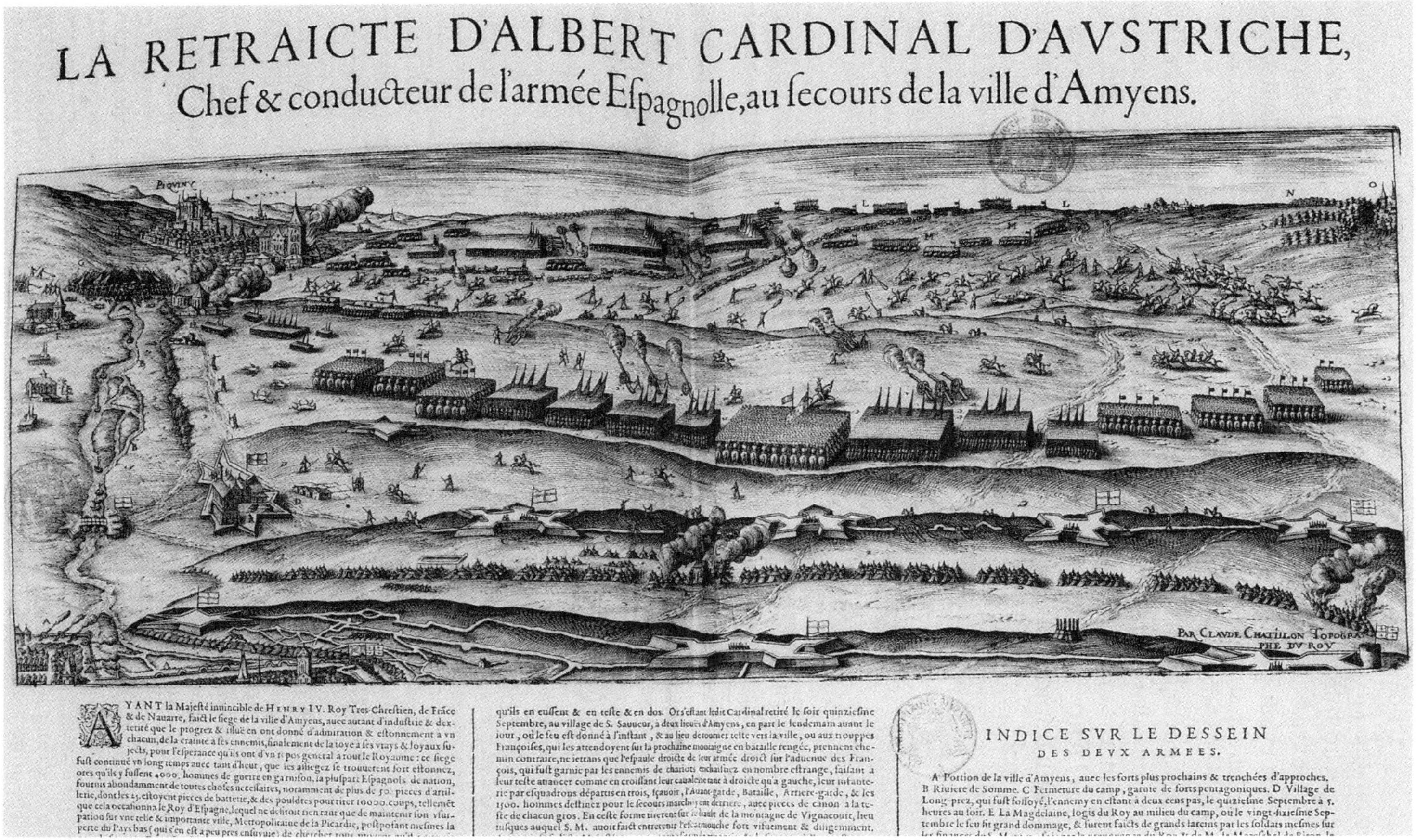

FIGURE 39. Claude Châtillon, Jean Le Clerc publisher, *The Retreat of Albert of Austria from Amiens*, 1597, intaglio, 15.5 × 41 cm, BN, Estampes, Hennin 1116, Cliché Bibliothèque nationale de France.

from this practice would be the series of views of Louis XIV's victories known as the *Large Conquests* based upon the drawings of Sebastien de Beaulieu, who followed the army so closely that he lost an arm at the siege of Phillipsburg.[80] It also became increasingly common around this time for current event printmakers to travel with armies and make their views after battlefield sketches, even when they were not employed as military engineers.[81]

Le Clerc not only published at least three of Châtillon's views of Henry IV's triumphs, but also many of the satirical woodcuts attacking the League that proliferated as cause began to crumble in 1594.[82] In 1596, to reinforce the image that Henry was eager to create for himself as a good Catholic duly reconciled with Rome, he issued a print of the column erected in the king's honor in the Eternal City by Pope Clement VIII.[83] In 1606 he etched and printed a series of three views by Nicolas Bollery of Henry entering his capital in 1594, heading to Notre Dame to offer prayers of thanks (figure 40), and then watching with satisfaction as the Spanish troops previously garrisoned in the city left through the Porte St Denis.[84] Since these were made twelve years after

---

80 As early as 1642, Beaulieu received an exclusive royal privilege to print "all of his plans of the cities and places that have been or will be taken by our armies, as well as their notable battles, combats, sieges and encampments". This touched off sharp protests by a group of Paris engravers. The crown had to retreat and specify that the ban applied only to direct copies of Beaulieu's works. Mireille Pastoureau, "Les atlas imprimés en France avant 1700," *Imago Mundi* 32 (1980), 57-60, and, more broadly, György Rósza, *Schlachtenbilder aus der Zeit der Befreiungsfeldzüg* (Budapest, 1987), p. 22; Isabelle Richefort, "L'œuvre gravé de van der Meulen" in *A la gloire du Roi. Van der Meulen, peintre des conquêtes de Louis XIV*, pp. 322-7; Brendan Dooley, "Le battaglie perse del principe Giovanni," *Quaderni Storici* 115 (2004), 83-118.

81 Klinkert, *Nassau in het nieuws*, p. 47.

82 Among Le Clerc's productions were *La pauvreté et lamentation de la Ligue*, *La delivrance de la France par le Persée François* and *Les entre paroles du Manant de-ligué, et du Maheutre.* For these prints and others of this era, see L'Estoile, *Mémoires-Journaux*, IV, 291-4, 300-04; Crouzet, *Guerriers de Dieu*, II, illustrations immediately preceding p. 385; Benedict, "Marmites and Martyrs," pp. 130-31; Denise Turrel, *Le blanc de France. La construction des signes identitaires pendant les guerres de Religion (1562-1629)* (Geneva, 2005), pp. 83-87.

83 *Colonne dressee a Rome en la place S. Antoine au nom et a la memoire de Henry IIII Treschrestien Roy de France et de Navarre a present regnant*, etching, "A Paris par Jehan Le Clerc 1596", Chantilly Fol CL 025.

84 *Reduction miraculeuse de Paris, sous l'obéissance du Roy très chrestien Henri IV, et comme Sa Majesté y entra par la Porte Neufve, le mardi 22 mars 1594*; *Comme le Roy alla incontinent a l'Eglise de ND rendre graces solenelles a Dieu*; and *Comme Sa Majeste le mesme jour estant a la porte S. Denis, veid sortir hors de Paris les garnisons estrangeres que le Roy d'Espagne y entretenoit*, etchings, 22 × 23 cm, 22 × 30 cm, 22.5 × 30 cm, N. Bollery pinxit, Jean le Clerc execudit [repositories: BN, Estampes, Hennin 1042-4; Arsenal, Estampes 213 (83-7); Chantilly, Estampes H. 25-7, Louvre, Rothschild 5274-6 LR]. The extensive text made to accompany these images is reproduced in L'Estoile, *Mémoire-Journaux*, IV, 306-28. The prints are undated, but the text states (p. 307) that twelve years have passed since

FIGURE 40. Jean Le Clerc after Nicolas Bollery, *Henry IV Heads to Notre Dame to Give Thanks for Regaining Paris*, 1606, etching, 22 × 30 cm, BN, Estampes, Hennin 1043, Cliché Bibliothèque nationale de France.

the events they depict, they can be seen as a short historical series of a kind not dissimilar to Tortorel and Perrissin or Hogenberg, although with more extensive accompanying printed text.

The wars of the last part of the sixteenth century also were recorded in a series of engravings made in Geneva in 1590-1591, the first current-event prints known to have been produced in that city after the break-up of the team responsible for the *Quarante Tableaux*. Four large engravings, all dated 1590 and signed with the interlocking initials MB/BM, depict and report events from Geneva's war of 1589-1593 against the duke of Savoy. These show (1) a series of skirmishes in the vicinity of the fort d'Arve between June 8 and July 12, 1589 (figure 41); (2) a battle of July 26, 1589 in the pays de Faucigny; (3) the Genevan conquest of the fort of Versoix on November 8, 1589; and (4)

---

the events depicted took place, enabling us to date them to 1606. One of these prints is reproduced with additional commentary in *French Renaissance in Prints*, pp. 424-5.

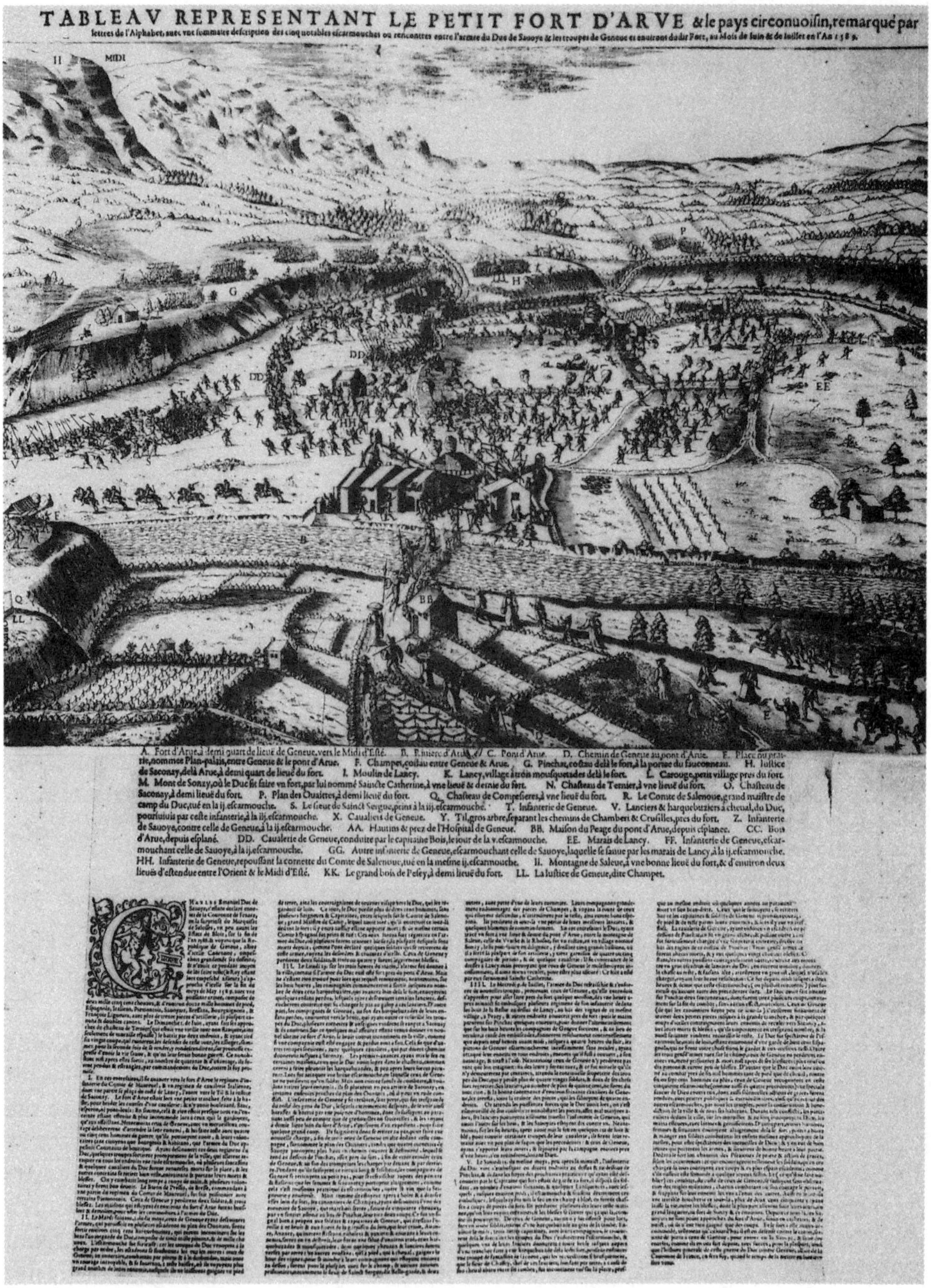

FIGURE 41. Michel Bénard, *The Small Fort of Arve*, 1590, engraving, 37.5 × 51.5 cm, BN, Estampes, Hennin 851, Cliché Bibliothèque nationale de France.

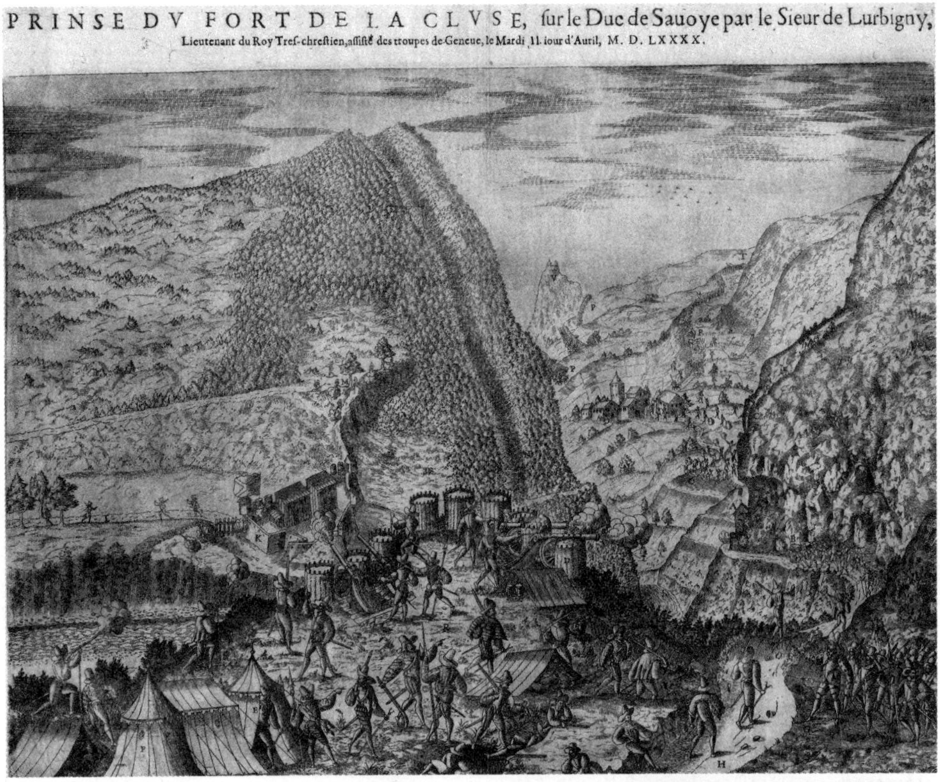

FIGURE 42. Michel Bénard, *The Capture of the Fort of La Cluse*, 1590, engraving, 28 × 37 cm, Centre d'Iconographie genevoise, coll. BPU, 46 M 1590.

the capture of the fort of La Cluse on April 11, 1590 by French troops under the sieur de Lurbigny assisted by the Genevans (figure 42).[85] A fifth engraving whose accompanying text is dated January 31, 1591 offers a general view of the region entitled "chorography or exact description... of the environs of the city of Geneva" together with a brief written "discourse of the memorable things that occurred in the war between the duke of Savoy and that city from

85 *Tableau representant le petit fort d'Arve*, engraving, 37.5 × 51.5 cm, with title, key and explanatory text on a second 39 × 54.5 cm sheet, CIG, 46 M 1589, 1-3, BN, Estampes, Hennin 851; *Pourtraict de la rencontre entre l'armée du Duc de Savoye et celle de Berne et de Geneve, au pays de Faucigni*, engraving, 20.5 × 33.5 cm image only, 31.5 × 35 cm with key and title [repositories: CIG, 46 M 1589, 4-5; BN, Estampes, Hennin 850]; *Le fort de Versoy et ses dependances, prins par les compagnies de Geneve sur le Duc de Savoye le huictiesme jour de Novemb l'An 1589*, engraving, 32 × 38 cm image only, 41 × 41 cm with title and key, explanatory text on a second 19 × 38 sheet [repositories: CIG, 46 M 1589, 6-10; BN Estampes, Hennin 915-7]; *Prinse du fort de la Cluse sur le Duc de Savoye*, engraving, 28 × 37.5 cm, key and explanatory text on a second 32 × 40 cm sheet [repositories: CIG 46 M 1590; BN Estampes, Hennin 932].

the beginning of April 1589 to the beginning of the year 1591".[86] Since these images are of different size, they do not compose a consistent suite. Each was printed with an extensive key and accompanying text. These too lack a common format, several being so long that they require a full 40 × 54 cm sheet of their own. Despite this inconsistency of size and format, the fact that the views of the first events represented in this cluster of prints were not made until a year after they occurred suggests that the quintet of images was meant to offer a visual history and commemorative record of Genevan exploits in an ongoing war that had started to go well, rather than news bulletins made in the immediate aftermath of each event. Since their titles highlight the joint action of Genevan, French, and Bernese troops, one purpose may have been to report Geneva's successful resistance against the Savoyard threat to a larger Swiss and French audience in order to encourage continued support.[87] The prints also reached a German-speaking audience through a publication that illustrates anew how current-events publishers were experimenting at this time with different combinations of print and images. Paul Brachfeld, a Frankfurt printer active in current-events printing who would be one of the first to produce illustrated *messrelationen*, acquired a number of sets of the prints, had the accompanying texts and keys translated into German, and published these as a quarto volume of 24 pages entitled *Savoyard History* (*Saphoische Historia).* This was illustrated with the engravings, folded to fit the small size of the volume.[88]

The identity of the artist responsible for these prints, long a mystery, was clarified in 1940 when Albert Choisy discovered a payment in Geneva's municipal accounts from 1601 to the goldsmith Michel Bénard "for having

---

[86] *Chorographie ou description exacte des plus remarquables lieux, tant villes, bourgades que villages, ès environs de la cité de Geneve. Avec un brief discours des choses memorables avenues en la guerre entre le Duc de Savoye et icelle cité, de puis le commencement d'Avril 1589 jusques au commencement de l'An 1591*, engraving, 28 × 37 cm, title and accompanying text on a second sheet [CIG, 46 M 1589-91, 1; BN Estampes, Hennin 974].

[87] The Savoyard war was also recounted in a "brief discours" by Simon Goulart, who accompanied the Genevan troops into the field as a chaplain. His account was vetted by a committee appointed by the Genevan authorities prior to publication. The texts accompanying these prints, while heavily dependent on Goulart's account, contain details not found in it. Paul-F. Giesendorf, *Bibliographie raisonnée de l'histoire de Genève des origines à 1798* (Geneva, 1966), pp. 544-5; L. C. Jones, *Simon Goulart 1543-1628. Etude biographique et bibliographique* (Geneva, 1917), pp. 491-501.

[88] See the copy of the *Saphoische historia. Das ist Warhaffte und ordentliche Erzehlung aller und jeder Kriegshandlungen so zwischen dem hertzogen von Saphoya und der Stadt Geneva sampt iren Bundgenossen der koniglichen Kron Franckreich und der herrschafft Bern* (n.p., 1591), BPU, Gf 1220 Rés; Jones, *Goulart*, 501-17. Brachfeld worked at different times in Frankfurt am Main and Erfurt. He published *zeitungen*, *messrelationen*, and longer "*relationes historicae*", often illustrated. *Messkataloge Willers*, V, 51, 157, 241, 309, 346-7, 383; *Verzeichnis der im deutschen Sprachbereich erscheinenen Drucke des XVI. Jahrhunderts* (25 vols. in 3 parts, Stuttgart, 1983-2000), Part 1, catalogue entries B 8229, B 8231, F 2418, N 88, N 89, R 2, R 1412, R 1413, Part 3, pp. 87, 405.

colored (*illuminé*) the portraits of the Genevan war to be given to Mr de Grandcour of Fribourg". If Bénard was not also the person who designed and engraved the plates, Choisy reasoned, why would the city council have asked him to color the prints ?[89] Not only does this document serve to identify the artist. It shows that Geneva had no specialists in hand coloring prints in 1601 and that these memorials of Genevan victories were offered by the city to important diplomatic allies a decade after the events themselves. That the artist should have been a goldsmith who only made engravings as a sideline fits with the evidence of the prints. Several display a decidedly uneasy command of perspective.

Genevan documentation indicates that Bénard probably arrived in the city from Paris not long after the July 1585 Edict of Nemours outlawed Protestant worship within France. He married in Geneva in 1586, put down roots, and was still living there in 1618.[90] Once again, an important episode in early Genevan print production turns out to have depended upon the arrival of refugee craftsmen from France.

The prints of the war between Geneva and Savoy were not Bénard's only graphic works. Ten year's later, after the duke of Savoy's surprise 1602 assault on Geneva was beaten back, Bénard engraved one of the first and most influential depictions of this "Escalade". To spread the news of Geneva's deliverance as widely as possible, at least two versions were made, one with French keys and captions and the other with accompanying text in German and Latin.[91] During the 1589-1593 war against Savoy, when Henry of Navarre was also fighting for his crown in France and Spanish troops were advancing in the Low Countries, he also engraved a throwback to the anti-papal satire of the 1560s meant to bolster Protestant morale in Geneva and beyond amid such dark days. *The Tower of Lively Faith Vainly Mined by Antichrist's Minions* (figure 43), dated 1590, shows a craggy river landscape out of which the rock of the true church arises in the foreground.[92] Atop it perches a tower with a banner, the tower of true faith, and a winged angel who leans on the cross and looks confidently upward to God, represented by the tetragrammaton. In the flatlands below, a procession of cloven-footed prelates led by the Pope in his sedan chair offer their blessings to the labors of other devils and monks who attack the hill with picks to sap it, but in vain, for those toward

89 Albert Choisy, "Identification du monogrammiste M.B.," *BSHAG* 7 (1939-42), 292.

90 *Ibid.*, p. 292.

91 *Pourtraict du costé de la ville de Geneve par ou les Savoyards entrerent le dimanche douziesme jour du mois de decembre mil six cens et deux, selon le calcul ancien, dont ils furent vertueusement repoussées*, engraving, 15 × 32 cm image only, CIG, 46 P 1602, 5-10. The engraving is unsigned but is conventionally, and convincingly, attributed to Bénard. Elizabeth Fischer, "Quelques considérations sur l'image de l'Escalade au XVIIe siècle," *Genava* 50 (2002), 66.

92 *La Tour du vive foi sappe en vain par les suppots de l'antechrist*, engraving, 29.7 × 37.5 cm [repositories: BN, Estampes, Hennin 970; Chantilly, Fol. CL 25].

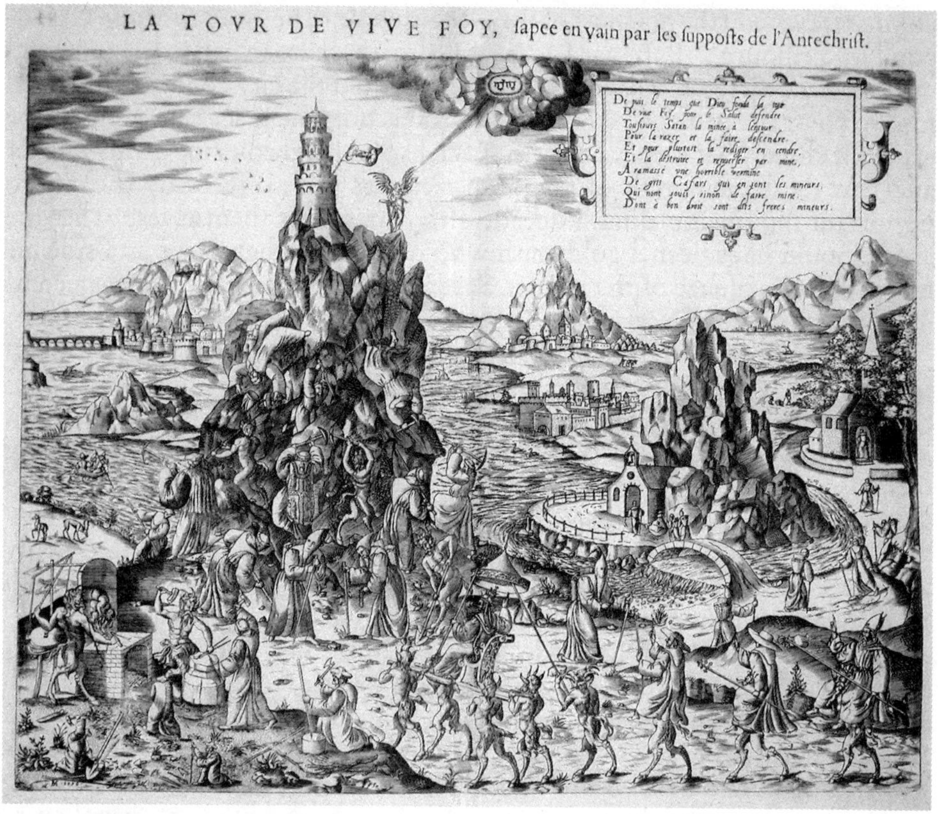

FIGURE 43. Michel Bénard, *The Tower of Lively Faith Vainly Mined by Antichrist's Minions*, 1590, engraving, Chantilly, Fol. CL 25.

the top may be seen toppling back. This, the artist explains in a printed explanation made to accompany the image, shows that the most determined enemies of truth are the first confounded. The river around the rock of faith represents the inconstancy of worldly affairs. The "synagogue" in the shadow of the rock of true faith is built from bits of stone mined from the rock but situated on the sandbar of human inventions, which is eroding. Farther to the right a second chapel represents Catholic superstitions "filled with stones taken from the rock of Scripture but completely misapplied and standing outside the foundation that is Jesus Christ." In the background are the localities where God has planted and maintained his church in this century, despite all the efforts of Satan and his adherents to destroy them. "I hope that in considering this picture you will deplore the blindness of these satellites of the Antichrist and admire the judgments that God sends daily to render their efforts vain," the artist concludes his brief address to the Christian reader.[93]

[93] A copy of this printed explanation survives in Chantilly, Fol. CL 25.

Rather than initiating a genre that stretches unbroken from the sixteenth century to modern volumes of photojournalism, graphic histories like those of Tortorel and Perrissin and Hogenberg ultimately proved to be a product of a relatively brief moment in the late sixteenth century when publishers in several parts of Europe experimented with print series of different sorts. By the end of the century, the Hogenberg publishing house had abandoned the production of self-standing pictorial histories to focus on individual current-events prints, book illustrations, or series of a more panegyrical character made on princely commission. In the first half of the seventeenth century, most sets of prints in the spirit of Tortorel and Perrissin that emphasized information over commemoration were found accompanying works of current history like the *Theatrum Europaeum*, a higher-end offshoot of the *messerelationen* elegantly produced by three generations of the Merian family and illustrated with engravings from their shop.[94] Other heavily illustrated works of this period mixed prints and extensive text.[95] Graphic histories in a spirit of *laudatio* proved more enduring, however. Virtually every major war of the seventeenth century gave rise to a suite of prints showing the battles won by the victorious side.[96]

While works like the *Wars, Massacres and Troubles* grew scarce in the seventeenth century, single-sheet graphic depictions of current events proliferated as never before. Prints depicting historical and military subjects accounted for six per cent of the total production of Paris engravers during the seventeenth century. The 1628-29 siege of La Rochelle was depicted not only in Jacques Callot's famous wall-sized view of the operation, but also in smaller prints by Melchior Tavernier, Pierre Firens, Jean Le Clerc V, and Michel de Mathonière. One Dutch printmaker active in the domain of current-events publishing during the last three decades of the century, the Amsterdam-based Romeyn de Hooghe, judged an average of more than three events per year worthy of being etched for posterity. Often his depictions

---

94 Hermann Bingel, *Das Theatrum Europaeum, ein Beitrag zur Publistik des 17. und 18. Jahrhunderts* (Wiesbaden, 1969).

95 For an example: *Description et representation de toutes les victoires tant par eau que par terre, lesquelles Dieu a octroiees Aux Nobles, Hauts et Puissants Seigneurs, Messeigneurs les Estats des Provinces Unies du Païs-bas, Souz la conduite et Gouvernement de son Excellence, le Prince Maurice de Nassau* (Leyden: J.J. Orlers, 1612) (43 illustrations within 282 printed pages).

96 For some examples: Jean-Marc Chatelain and Hermann Arnold, "War, Fame and the Classical Aesthetic: *Les Triomphes de Louis le Juste* by Jean Valdor (Paris, 1649)" in Bussmann and Schilling eds., *1648: War and Peace in Europe*, II, 95-103; Veldman, *Crispijn de Passe and His Progeny*, p. 323ff; *Teatro della guerra contro il Turco* (Rome: Giovanni Giacomo de Rossi, 1687) and *Admirables effectos de la providencia sucedidos en la vida e impero de Leopoldo Primero* (Milan, 1696), both discussed in Rósza, *Schlachtenbilder aus der Zeit der Befreiungsfeldzüge*, p. 25; *Theatrum bellicum, incipiens a Carolo II Hispaniarum Rege ad Carolum III/ Schouwburgh van den Oorlog, beginnende van Koning Karel den II Tot op Koning Karel den III* (Amsterdam: Peter Schenk, 1716).

found their way into the *Hollandsche Mercurius* as well as being sold separately. Important eighteenth century print collections abound in "*pièces historiques*" and portfolios filled with "battles, sieges, and so forth".[97]

And when truly remarkable events came along, the idea of a print series to satisfy the curiosity of those eager to visualize these events was not forgotten. Soon after the French Revolution began to shake Europe, an association of artists launched a series of *Tableaux historiques de la Révolution française* made by a group of artists and sold by subscription. Its initial prospectus promised that its chief concern was "exactitude" and "the language of truth" and that its views were based on the history of an eyewitness. Like the *Wars, Massacres, and Troubles*, it would comprise a series of prints with captions but no running text. New editions expanded the work four times over the subsequent decades, until the 1817 edition counted 145 historical scenes and 66 portraits. Publishers in Germany, Belgium and the Netherlands all rushed to copy the series. It too has recently been rediscovered by historians eager to understand and evaluate the meaning of past visual evidence as they themselves experiment with new media and incorporate images into the reconstruction and re-presentation of history.[98] The *Wars, Massacres and Troubles* of Tortorel and Perrissin clearly occupies a place of importance in the history of the use of visual media in current events publishing.

---

[97] Marianne Grivel, *Le commerce de l'estampe à Paris au XVIIe siècle* (Geneva, 1986), pp. 134-60, esp. 157-60; John Landwehr, *Romeyn de Hooghe the Etcher: Contemporary Portrayal of Europe, 1662-1707* (Leiden, 1973), passim; Jean Adhemar, "Information gravée en France au XVIIe siècle: Images sur cuivre destinées à un public bourgeois et élégant" in Jean Pierre Seguin ed., *L'Informazione in Francia nel Seicento* (Bari, 1983), pp. 11-32; *Catalogue des estampes du Duc d'Estrées* (this includes a packet of Callot's battle scenes; "le 10 nouvelles conquetes du roi par Sebastien Le Clerc"; a suite of *conquêtes* of the duke of Lorraine by Le Clerc; several sets of historical scenes by de Hooghe; van der Meulen's conquests of Louis XIV; seven lots of "pieces historiques", most by Hogenberg, including one portfolio with 380 of his historical prints; 17 packets of battle scenes by Beaulieu, Merian, "Jeremie Wolff" and others; and 8 portfolios totalling 1388 sheets of battles and sieges among the packets dedicated to "topographie et vues"); *Catalogue des estampes... d'Hermand* (this includes series of the *conquêtes du roi* by Beaulieu, van der Meulen, Le Clerc, Chatillon "et autres"; "une suite d'estampes representant les guerres des religionnaires, au nombre de 67 gravées en bois"; a portfolio of 47 prints of the siege of Malta and other historical events; "un volume des guerres civiles des religionnaires"; "deux volumes des guerres de Flandre du Duc d'Albe et autres"; "la guerre des Suisses"; and several other packets of battle scenes).

[98] *La Révolution par la gravure. Les Tableaux historiques de la Révolution française, une entreprise éditoriale d'information et sa diffusion en Europe (1791-1817)* (Vizille, 2002), passim, esp. p. 15; "Imaging the French Revolution: Depictions of the French Revolutionary Crowd", Center for History and New Media, George Mason University, and the Department of History, University of California, Los Angeles for the *American Historical Review*, http://chnm.gmu.edu/revolution/imaging/.

PART 2

THE *QUARANTE TABLEAUX*

THE PRINTS IN THE SERIES

1a. *Title Page*
1b. *To the Reader*
2. *The Mercuriale Where Anne Du Bourg Was Arrested.* Two markedly different versions of this print were made.
3. *The Tournament at Which Henry II Was Fatally Wounded.* Two markedly different versions of this print were made.
4. *The Death of Henry II*
5. *The Execution of Anne Du Bourg*
6. *The Conspiracy of Amboise*
7. *The Executions at Amboise*
8. *The Estates-General of Orléans*
9. *The Colloquy of Poissy*
10. *The Massacre of Cahors*
11. *The Massacre of Vassy*
12. *The Massacre of Sens*
13. *The Capture of Valence*
14. *The Massacre of Tours*
15. *The Capture of Montbrison*
16. *The Battle of St Gilles*
17. *The Battle Order at Dreux*
18. *The First Charge at Dreux*
19. *The Second Charge at Dreux*
20. *The Third Charge at Dreux*
21. *The Fourth Charge at Dreux*
22. *The Retreat from Dreux*
23. *The Siege of Orléans*
24. *The Fatal Wounding of the Duke of Guise*
25. *The Peace Made outside Orléans*
26. *The Execution of Poltrot de Méré*
27. *The Michelade*
28. *The Battle of St Denis*
29. *The Battle of Cognat*
30. *The Siege of Chartres*
31. *The Battle Order at Jarnac*
32. *The Battle of Jarnac*
33. *The Battle of La Roche-L'Abeille*

34. *The Siege of Poitiers*
35. *The Battle Order at Moncontour*
36. *The Rout at Moncontour*
37. *The Siege of St Jean d'Angély*
38. *The Capture of Nîmes*
39. *The Foiled Attempt on Bourges*
40. *Montbrun's Crossing of the Rhône*

Note: The prints are listed here in chronological order. The numbers correspond to those used in the standard reference work on French rare books, Jacques-Charles Brunet, *Manuel du Libraire et de l'amateur des livres* (5th ed., Berlin, 1922), V, 892-4. Some printings of the different scenes also include a number with the title. These numbers reverse the order of scenes 8 and 9, 25 and 26, and 27 and 28. Some old albums arrange these scenes in the sequence suggested by the printed numbers. Others arrange them in chronological order as is done here.

The notes facing each image provide, as appropriate for the image in question:

1. The full original title.
2. The medium or media.
3. The languages in which the accompanying text was printed.
4. A description of major changes made in the accompanying text between different printings. Not listed here are the small variants in spelling, typeface, and alignment that characterize each printing. They are described in Robert-Dumesnil, X, 258-84.
5. Basic information about the event shown.
6. A list of all known accounts of the event published prior to the prints.
7. Other known contemporary or near-contemporary visual depictions of the event.
8. A summary of the details about the event provided by the prior printed or graphic accounts that may be compared with the details in the facing image to determine how the print either agrees with or departs from these prior works.
9. Relevant bibliography. The goal here is not to provide an exhaustive bibliography of all relevant primary and secondary sources, but simply to list particularly detailed, reliable accounts of the event in question.

A number of histories of a general character dealing with events in France between 1559 and 1570 were published prior to the completion of the *Wars, Massacres, and Troubles*. These have all been examined to see if they cover the events depicted in the print series and compared with the prints where they do. They are:

[Antoine de La Roche Chandieu], *Histoire des persecutions et martyrs de l'Eglise de Paris depuis l'An 1557. jusques au tepms du Roy Charles neufviesme*. Lyon: 1563.

Loys de Perussiis, *Discours des guerres de la Comté de Venayscin et de la Provence: ensemble quelques incidentz*. Avignon: 1563.

N[icolas] R[egnault], *Discours veritable des guerres et troubles avenus au pays de Provence*. Lyon: Benoist Rigaut, 1564; Orléans: Eloi Gibier, 1564.

Loys de Perussiis, *Le second discours des guerres de la Comté de Venayscin*. Avignon, 1564.

Jean Crespin, *Actes des martyrs deduits en sept livres*. Geneva: Crespin, 1564.

Petit traitté des guerres civiles advenues en France sous les Roys François II et Charles IX. N.p., 1564; Paris, 1567.

[Pierre de La Place], *Commentaires de l'Estat de la Religion et Republique soubs les Rois Henry Francois seconds, et Charles neufieme* 1565. [Editions of this work are known to have been printed in Orléans, La Rochelle, Rouen, Paris, and Caen. A further edition appeared in 1566 under the title *Histoire de notre temps contenant les commentaires de l'estat de la religion et republique sous les rois Henri et François seconds et Charles IX*. See here Gilmont, "Premières éditions des ouvrages historiques de La Place et de la Popelinière," pp. 119-52.]

Receuil des choses memorables passees et publiees pour le faict de la religion, & estat de la France. Le Tout Depuis la publication de l'Edit du xvii de Janvier 1560. jusques à l'Edit de la pacification des troubles de ce Royaume 1562. Strasbourg: Pierre Estiard, 1565.

Histoire de nostre temps contenant le recueil des choses memorables passees & publiees pour le faict de la religion, & estat de la France. Depuis la publication de l'Edict de Janvier 1561, jusques à la Declaration faicte par le Roy de sa majorité, 1563. N.p., 1566.

Memoires de la III guerre civile et des derniers troubles de France sous Charles IX. [Geneva: Crespin], 1570.

Jean Crespin, *Histoire des vrays tesmoins de la verité de l'Evangile*. Geneva: Crespin, 1570.

[Jean de Serres], *Rerum Gallia ob religionem gestarum, libri tres*. [Geneva: Crespin], 1570.

[Christophe Landre and C. Martel], *Histoire de Nostre temps, contenant un recueil des choses memorables passees et publiees pour le faict de la Religion et estat de la France depuis l'Edict de paciffication de 23. jour de Mars, 1568 justques au jour present*. [La Rochelle: Barthélemy Berton], 1570. This work was published soon after the promulgation of the Peace of Saint-Germain in late August 1570, thus too late to have been used by the makers of the print series.

1a. ***Title Page / Premier Volume. CONTENANT QUARANTE TABLEAUX OU Histoires diverses qui sont memorables touchant les Guerres, Massacres & Troubles advenus en France en ces dernieres annees. Le tout recueilli selon le tesmoignage de ceux qui y ont esté en personne, & qui les ont veus, lesquels sont pourtrais à la verité.***

Etched border. Text in French and German.

The elements of the decorative border are similar to those found in Lyon and Antwerp pattern books and prints of the period. The emblem in the bottom roundel, a pyramid withstanding the winds with the motto "firm amid adversity (*ferme en adversité*)", is not one commonly associated with the Protestant cause. I have not been able to locate it in the standard guides to emblems and printers' marks. It may be a personal or family motto of Nicolas Castellin deployed here as a printer's mark.

1b. *To the Reader/ Au Lecteur*

Etched border. Text in French, Latin, and Italian.

2a. *The Mercuriale where Anne Du Bourg Was Arrested/ La Mercuriale tenue aux Augustins à Paris, le x. de Juin 1559. la ou le Roy Henry II fust en personne*

Etching. Title and caption known only in French.

The event. In the spring of 1559, the issue of the best course to adopt in dealing with heresy became the subject of intense debate within the special sessions of the Parlement of Paris for internal procedural and disciplinary matters known as *mercuriales*. On June 10 king Henry II attended one of the sessions at which the issue was debated. Exceptionally, since the Palais de Justice was being prepared for upcoming royal weddings, it took place in the convent of the Augustinian friars. The opinions expressed by two judges who argued for greater leniency in the handling of the offense, Anne Du Bourg and Louis Du Faur, angered the king so much that he ordered the Constable Montmorency to arrest them on the spot. Further arrest warrants were subsequently issued for six other judges who expressed similar views, three of whom fled before they could be incarcerated in the Bastille. Four of the imprisoned judges ultimately won their release with the help of their kin by showing their willingness to trim their views to the prevailing wind. Du Bourg maintained his Reformed convictions forthrightly before the special panel of judges established to hear his case and refused to recant when offered opportunities to do so. He was ultimately executed for heresy and became one of the most famous martyrs of the French Reformed cause.

Accounts of event published prior to 1570
La Vraye Histoire, Contenant l'inique Jugement et fausse procedure faite contre le fidele serviteur de Dieu Anne du Bourg (Geneva: Berthet, 1560; n.p., 1561; Lyon: J. Marceau, 1562; n.p., 1562).
[La Roche Chandieu], *Histoire des persecutions et martyrs de l'Eglise de Paris* (1563), pp. 327-31.
Crespin, *Actes des martyrs* (1564), pp. 907-30.
"Discours de la mort du Roy Henry II" in 1565 *Recueil des choses memorables.*
[La Place], *Commentaires de l'Estat de la Religion et Republique* (1565), fos. 17v-21, 29-36.
Crespin, *Histoire des vrais temoins* (1570), pp. 516, 518v-19v, 525v-36.
[de Serres], *Rerum Gallia ob religionem gestarum, libri tres* (1570), fos. 13v-14.

This representation of the scene, one of two made, probably figures the moment of Du Bourg's and Du Faur's arrest by Montmorency on the king's command, although the unusual absence of a key or explanatory legend makes it hard to be certain. The various printed accounts of the Du Bourg case focus primarily on his interrogations and statements before his judges, but they also offer details about his arrest that vary from one account to another. Uniquely, the 1564 edition of Crespin asserts that when Henry II gave the order to arrest the judges who had advocated leniency toward heretics, Du Bourg willingly followed Montmorency, raising his eyes to heaven and exclaiming "Lord, this is thy quarrel", while Du Faur threw himself at the king's knees and showed great cowardice (p. 910). This, I believe, is what is shown here.

Historical bibliography

Matthieu Lelièvre, *Anne Du Bourg, conseiller au Parlement de Paris et martyr (1520-1559)* (Toulouse, 1903).

2b. *The Mercuriale where Anne Du Bourg Was Arrested/ La Mercurialle tenue aux Augustins a Paris le 10 de Juin. 1559. ou le Roy Henry 2 y fut en personne*

Etching. Titles and captions known in French and German.

For basic information about this event, the list of accounts of it published prior to 1570, and historical bibliography, see the preceding note.

This version of the *Mercuriale* scene figures Du Bourg opining; out the window in the upper right he and an unspecified number of other judges are led away to the Bastille. The most important prior published accounts of the episode—*La Vraye Histoire*, La Roche Chandieu, the 1564 edition of Crespin, and La Place—all summarize Du Bourg's remarks and offer some details about the leading royal councillors and churchmen present. The summary of Du Bourg's remarks is particularly extensive in the 1564 *Actes des Martyrs*. This, like La Roche-Chandieu's *Histoire des persecutions*, also mentions that the king, on arriving, ordered the judges to continue their discussions (cf. key letter A). It is the only one of the prior printed histories to list all of the following as being present: Montpensier, La Roche-sur-Yon, Guise, Montmorency, St André, the privy councillors d'Avanson and Du Mortier, and the cardinals of Lorraine, Bourbon, Guise, and Châtillon (cf. key letters B and C). It specifies that, just before the king gave the order to have Montmorency arrest Du Bourg and Du Faur, the Cardinal of Lorraine drew the king aside and urged the king to do something about the opinions he had just heard. This is not figured here.

3a. *The Tournament at Which Henry II Was Fatally Wounded/ Le Tournoy ou le Roy Henri II fut blessé a mort le dernier de Juin 1559*

Woodcut. Titles and captions known in French and Latin. The great majority of surviving impressions of this version have another scene from the series printed on the back. Scenes printed on the back include numbers 11, 14, 17-24, 30, and 40. These scenes often include a number within the title, which suggests a late printing.

The event. The festivities held in Paris to celebrate the Peace of Cateau-Cambrésis and the resulting dynastic marriages between the ruling houses of France, Spain and Savoy included several days of jousting and tournaments. As the contests drew to a close on June 30, the king insisted on breaking a final lance with Gabriel de Lorges, count of Montgomery. As the two horsemen rode together, Montgomery's lance shattered as he maladroitly struck the king in the chest. A fragment of the broken lance pierced the king's visor and lodged in his eye socket. Although Henry II was badly wounded, he held onto the neck of his horse until attendants could help him down. The injury would prove fatal.

Accounts of event published prior to 1570
La publication des emprises du tournoy qui doibt estre faict à Paris (Paris: G. Corrozet and J. Dallier, 1559; Lyon: B. Rigaud, 1559).
Crespin, *Actes des martyrs* (1564), p. 927.
"Discours de la mort du Roy Henry II" in *Recueil des choses memorables* (1565).
[La Place], *Commentaires de l'Estat de la Religion et Republique* (1565), fo. 30.
Crespin, *Histoire des vrais temoins* (1570), p. 521.
[de Serres], *Rerum Gallia ob religionem gestarum, libri tres* (1570), fo. 18.

The details of the fatal tournament are best known to historians through contemporary ambassador's reports and subsequently published memoirs. The various Protestant accounts published prior to 1570 that treat the event do so briefly in the context of the Du Bourg affair and emphasize details related to the judge's arrest or the ongoing repression of heresy that suggest the working of God's admirable providences. Thus, both Crespin and the "Discours de la mort du roy" assert (with discordant details) that Montgomery had previously escorted Du Bourg to the Bastille and had just been given a commission to hunt down Protestants in Normandy. The very person whom the king had used as his agent of persecution was the unwitting instrument of his own death. La Place's *Commentaires* and the 1570 edition of Crespin note (in identical terms) that the tournament took place in the vicinity of the Bastille, where Du Bourg and his fellow judges had been imprisoned. After the king was wounded, he told those who came to his aid that he feared that he had wronged the judges. The Cardinal of Lorraine replied that such thoughts were the devil tempting him. La Place and the 1570 edition of Crespin also note that the king wobbled badly on his mount after receiving the lance in the eye. In the detail in the upper left, unidentified attendants rush to aid Henry as he clings to his mount.

Historical bibliography

John McClelland, "Le tournoi de juin 1559 et les deux François de Guise" in Yvonne Bellenger ed., *Le mécénat et l'influence des Guises* (Paris, 1997), pp. 177-85.
Philip Benedict et al., "Graphic History: What Readers Knew and Were Taught in the *Quarante Tableaux* of Perrissin and Tortorel," *French Historical Studies* 28 (2005), 206-10. The pages in question were written by Kristen Neuschel.

3b. *The Tournament at Which Henry II Was Fatally Wounded/ Le Tournoy ou le Roy Henri II fust blessé à mort le dernier de Juin 1559*

Woodcut and etching. Titles and captions known in French, Latin, Italian and German. The etched version of this print does not include the set of letters for a key found within the woodcut illustrated here. Although these letters appear within the image of the woodcut, no printing is known with a letter key beneath the image instead of the legend shown here. BN, Estampes, Ed 9 Rés contains copies of the woodcut version of this scene with scenes 11 and 14 from the series printed on the back.

For basic information about this event, the list of accounts of it published prior to 1570, and historical bibliography, see the preceding note.

Because the tournament ended in tragedy, festival books recounting the spectacle were not published, as was common for such events. I consequently have not found any detailed description of the decoration of the tournament ground, nor any source that indicates whether or not the inscription shown above the archway in this version of the scene, "HEN II GRA DEI REX GALL INVICTIS" (Henry II by the grace of God unconquered king of France), indeed adorned the square. The *Publication des emprises du tournoy* indicates that the escutcheons of all participants were to be placed on a set of columns at the end of the tiltyard.

4. *The Death of Henry II/ La mort du Roy Henry deuxieme aux tournelles a Paris le X Juillet 1559*

Woodcut. Titles and captions known in French, Latin, Italian, and German.

The event. After being helped from his mount, the king was taken to the royal chateau of the Tournelles. Initially it was hoped that he would recover from the injury, but his condition soon worsened. In response to an appeal from the duke of Savoy, Philip II sent two leading medical men from Brussels, including the celebrated Vesalius, to assist with his care. Notwithstanding their efforts, Henry II died on July 10.

Accounts of event published prior to 1570
"Discours de la mort du Roy Henry II" in *Recueil des choses memorables* (1565).

No accounts printed prior to 1570 provide details about Henry's medical care, the identity of those who gathered around him, or other details of his final days and hours. These are known to historians primarily through contemporary ambassador's reports, a manuscript relation by Vesalius, and subsequent memoirs. The very brief "Discours de la mort du roy" asserts that he died between noon and one o'clock, the same hour of the day when he ordered Du Bourg and Du Faur arrested, exactly one month after their arrest. The records of Paris's municipal government, however, give 10 a.m. as the hour of the king's death.

Historical bibliography
Alphonse de Ruble, *Antoine de Bourbon et Jeanne d'Albret* (4 vols., Paris, 1881-6), I, 319-30.
Lucien Romier, *Les origines politiques des guerres de religion* (2 vols., Paris, 1914), II, 380-9.

5. *The Execution of Anne Du Bourg/ Anne du Bourg Conseiller du Parlement de Paris bruslé a S. Jean en greve le 21 Decembre 1559*

Woodcut. Titles and captions known in French and German. BM Lyon 24601 contains a copy of this print with scene 26 *The Execution of Poltrot de Meré* printed on the back and numbered.

The event. After nearly six months of incarceration, interrogations, and appeals, Du Bourg received his final sentence on December 21. He was executed later the same day in front of the Hôtel de Ville in the Place de Grève.

Accounts of event published prior to 1570
La Vraye Histoire, Contenant l'inique Jugement et fausse procedure faite contre le fidele serviteur de Dieu Anne du Bourg (n.p., 1561 and Lyon: J. Marceau, 1562).
[La Roche Chandieu], *Histoire des persecutions et martyrs de l'Eglise de Paris* (1563), pp. 424-8.
Crespin, *Actes des martyrs* (1564), p. 930.
Petit traitté des guerres civiles, p. 4.
[La Place], *Commentaires de l'Estat de la Religion et Republique*, fos. 33-36.
Crespin, *Histoire des vrais temoins* (1570), pp. 535v-6.

The *Vraye Histoire*, La Roche Chandieu, Crespin, and La Place all provide virtually identical accounts of Du Bourg's final hours that indicate that he was conveyed to the Place St Jean en Grève in a cart, singing psalms as he went. All quote his brief final words. All state that he displayed an assured and joyful mien and had the self-possesson to take off his own outer garments. Here the identical wording of La Roche Chandieu and the 1564 edition of Crespin "luy mesme se despouilla jusques à la chemise" matches the caption of the print yet more closely than the slightly different wording found in *La Vraye Histoire*, La Place and the 1570 edition of Crespin. Likewise, in these nearly identical sources, all of which could have provided the essential information highlighted in the legend under the print, the precise description of how Du Bourg was executed found in La Roche Chandieu and the 1564 edition of Crespin is especially close to the wording of the legend here: "Et souvent reiteroit ceste priere, Seigneur mon Dieu, ne m'abandonne point jusques à ce qu'estant guindé en l'air, il fut estranglé, & puis son corps jeté au feu." La Place and the 1570 edition of Crespin relate, "il fut executé, pendu & estranglé, sans sentir le feu: ceste grace luy ayant esté faicte par ses Juges."

6. *The Conspiracy of Amboise/ L'entreprise d'Amboise descouverte les 13, 14 et 15 du Mars 1560*

Woodcut and etching. Titles and captions known in French, Latin, Italian, and German.

Important variants of accompanying text. Certain details found in the key to the woodcut reproduced here are not included in the key to the etching. These are that Pardaillan's pistol failed to fire, that this gave La Renaudie the opportunity to kill him with his sword, and that, before dying from a gunshot fired by one of Pardaillan's servants, he was able to slay that servant as well (see key letters F and G).

The event. The precise goals of the different parties involved in the event that contemporary sources variously label as the "conspiracy", "enterprise", or "tumult" of Amboise remain uncertain to this day. Foreign ambassadors present at court as the event unfolded report that the court was gripped with fear that the king's life was in danger. An account sent by the king to the Parlement of Paris two weeks after the event and subsequently published as a pamphlet asserts that the plot "aimed at the full subversion of our state". Protestant accounts of the event published in its aftermath claim that it sought only to present views to the king that the Guises, who controlled access to him, would not allow to receive a fair hearing; the Guises, these sources assert, falsely spread the notion that the conspirators threatened the king's life in order to maintain their control over him. Some who went to Amboise wanted simply to present the king with a copy of the French Reformed confession of faith. Other disgruntled aristocrats and Reformed ministers unquestionably entered into a larger conspiracy to use force if necessary to achieve their aims, whatever these may have been. Those around the king were tipped off in advance and were able arrest many of those involved on March 15 and 16 as they gathered in the woods near Amboise. At dawn on March 17, an attempt was made to seize Amboise by force but failed. On the 19th the avowed leader of the enterprise, Jean du Barry, sieur de La Renaudie, was discovered by a royal patrol in a nearby forest and shot after a confrontation with the seigneur de Pardaillan.

Accounts of event published prior to 1570

Lettres du roy, Contenans le succinct du fait de la conspriation entreprinse contre sa maiesté (Lyon: Pierre Merant, 1560; Poitiers: N. Pelletier, 1560).

L'histoire du tumulte d'Amboyse advenu au moys de Mars MDLX ([Strasbourg], 1560).

Avertissement et complainte au peuple Francoys; Ensemble l'Histoire du tumulte d'Amboise (n.p., 1560).

Brieve exposition des lettres du Cardinal de Lorraine envoyees au nom du Roy aux Cours des Parlemens de France. (n.p., n.d.).

[La Roche Chandieu], *Histoire des persecutions et martyrs de l'Eglise de Paris*, pp. 431-41.

Crespin, *Actes des martyrs* (1564), pp. 991-5.

Petit traitté des guerres civiles, pp. 7-9.

[La Place], *Commentaires de l'Estat de la Religion et Republique*, fos. 49v-58.

Crespin, *Histoire des vrais temoins* (1570), pp. 557-8.
[de Serres], *Rerum Gallia ob religionem gestarum, libri tres* (1570), fos. 29-32.

The *Histoire du tumulte d'Amboise* is the original source for many elements of what would become the standard Protestant account of the conspiracy. According to this pamphlet, when the court got wind that the leaders of the enterprise had gathered in the chateau of Noizay, the duke of Nemours was dispatched to discover what they were up to and what they wanted. They told him that they wished to present their grievances about the Guises to the king. He promised them "sur la parole d'un Prince" that he would escort them to the king if they put down their arms. They agreed, but on arriving at Amboise were immediately imprisoned, tortured, and condemned to death for *lèse majesté*. All of the details provided in the key to this print under the letters A to F may be found in this work. The *Histoire des persecutions et martyrs de l'Eglise de Paris* of La Roche Chandieu, a known participant in the planning of the conspiracy, hews closely to the same line and explicitly cites as one of its sources a "small pamphlet" that could only be the *Histoire du tumulte*. But it adds further details, notably that the day after the group at Noizay was imprisoned, "une trouppe de gens de piedz, ne sachant point ce qui estoit advenu, marchoit droit à Amboise" and were "enveloppez" by the royal cavalry who had set out from the city (cf. key letters I and K, where the wording is identical). The day after that "une autre compagnie de gens de cheval ayant cheminé toute la nuict donna sur la diane jusques aux portes du Chasteau, pensans surprendre les gardes: mais ilz furent aussi descouverts, et ne firent rien" (cf. key letter H, likewise identical). La Place follows La Roche Chandieu quite closely but does not include these last details. They are, however, to be found in the 1564 (but not the 1570) edition of Crespin's martyrology, again with wording identical to La Roche Chandieu's. None of these sources indicate the dates on which these events took place.

Historical bibliography

Henri Naef, *La Conjuration d'Amboise et Genève*. Geneva, 1922.
C. Paillard, "Additions critiques à l'histoire de la Conjuration d'Amboise," *Revue Historique* 14 (1880), 61-108, 311-55.
Jacques Poujol, "De la confession de foi de 1559 à la Conjuration d'Amboise," *BSHPF* 119 (1973), 158-76.
Lucien Romier, *La conjuration d'Amboise*. Paris, 1923.
Corrado Vivanti, "La congiura d'Amboise", Elizabeth A.R. Brown, "La Renaudie se venge: l'autre face de la conjuration d'Amboise", and Arlette Jouanna, "Le thème politique du complot contre la noblesse lors des prises d'armes nobiliaires sous les derniers Valois" in Yves-Marie Bercé and Elena Fasano Guarini eds., *Complots et conjurations dans l'Europe moderne* (Rome, 1996), pp. 439-90.

7. *The Executions at Amboise/ L'execution d'Amboise faite le 15 mars 1560*

Woodcut. Titles and captions known in French, Latin, Italian, and German.

The event. After the first groups of people arrested in the woods around Amboise were interrogated, it became clear that many were commoners with no clear idea of the goals of the enterprise who had joined it out of religious conviction, need, or loyalty to their captains. An amnesty was issued if they would return home unarmed in small groups. But after the attack on Amboise during the early hours of the 17th, royal justice against all suspected of threatening harm to the king and those around him turned harsh. The Venetian ambassador reported in a letter written that evening that nine men were hung from the battlements over the castle gate in the course of the day. He also remarked upon their constancy in meeting death. After La Renaudie was subsequently killed, his body was placed on a gibbet for several days. Between March 20 and 30, at least fifty more noblemen and soldiers were condemned to death. Many were hung or beheaded; others were reprieved at the foot of the gallows and sentenced to row in the galleys for life.

For accounts of this event published prior to 1570 and the historical bibliography, see the preceding note.

This print depicts punishments that in fact were administered over a span of nearly two weeks. The single date provided in the title, March 15, mistakenly antedates the onset of the executions by two days; in this error, it accords with the dates provided in the title to the preceding scene, which likewise err by two days. All of the most important Protestant histories of this event narrate the punishments figured in this print. All report concerning the scene at the focal point of the image (key letter C) that the conspirator who dipped his hands in the blood of his previously beheaded associates and lifted them as high as his bound arms allowed, cried out as he did so, "Lord, here is the blood of your children, avenge it." Of these histories, only La Place and the 1570 edition of Crespin identify this man as Villemongis, as does the key. (Note that the key does not quote Villemongis's words.) All also mention that after La Renaudie was killed, his corpse was brought to Amboise, hung briefly, and then quartered for public display in several places with a placard identifying him as the leader of "rebelles". Once again, only La Place and the 1570 edition of Crespin (which incorporates La Place's account of the event in toto in lieu of its prior narrative) provide the specific detail that after La Renaudie's corpse was quartered, his head was stuck on a lance and exposed on the city bridge (cf. key letter A). None of these sources specifies the precise number of bodies hung from the battlements or of heads displayed on a gibbet (cf. key letters D and E), nor do they indicate that courtiers watched the executions from the castle garden or windows. The *Petit traitté des guerres civiles* offers a much shorter account of the conspiracy and executions without many of the details found in these other sources or in this and the next print, although with a very similar overall vision of the event.

8. *The Estates-General of Orléans/ L'Assemblee des trois Estats tenus à Orleans au mois de Janvier 1561*

Etching. Titles and captions known in French and German.

The event. Called in the summer of 1560 by Francis II and those around him to deal with the fiscal crisis facing the monarchy, the Estates-General did not assemble until early in the reign of his successor, Charles IX, on December 13, 1560. Since the letters of convocation were not issued by the currently reigning king, the legitimacy of the assembly was challenged by some Protestants within the second and third estates, who hoped that they might be able to elect delegates more favorable to their cause in a second election. The assembly met until January 31, 1561. Spokesmen of each order delivered harangues summarizing the grievances and advice of each group. When no resolution to the fiscal problem could be agreed upon, the assembly was dissolved and new elections were scheduled for the spring. A second Estates-General assembled at Pontoise from August 1 to 27, 1561.

Accounts of event published prior to 1570

La description du plant du theatre faict à Orleans, pour l'assemblée des trois estatz, avec un brief discours de la seance des tenans & representans lesdictz estatz (Paris: Vincent Sertenas, Gilles Corrozet, Guillaume Niverd, 1560).

Jacques de Silly, *La Harangue de par la noblesse de toute la France, au roy très-chrestien Charles IXe, tenant ses grans Estatz en sa ville d'Orléans, le 1er jour de janvier 1560* (Paris: C. Perier, 1561; Rouen: J. de Remortier and G. Loyselet, 1561; Troyes, n.d.; Lyon, n.d.).

Jean Lange, *La Harangue du peuple et Tiers Estat de toute la France au roy très chrestien Charles IX, tenant ses Estats généraulx en sa ville d'Orléans, le 1er jour de janvier 1560* (Orléans: E. Gibier, 1560; Blois: J. Angelier, n.d.; Poitiers: N. Pelletier, 1561).

La Harangue faite par monsieur de Lospital, grand chancelier de France, en la presence du roy, ledict seigneur tenant ses grans Estatz en sa ville d'Orleans, au moys de janvier mil cinq cens soixante et ung (Blois: J. Angelier, n.d.).

Petit traitté des guerres civiles, pp. 9-10.

[La Place], *Commentaires de l'Estat de la Religion et Republique* (1565), fos. 121v-171v.

[de Serres], *Rerum Gallia ob religionem gestarum, libri tres* (1570), fos.70v-78.

Other contemporary visual representations

Pourtraict de l'assemblee des Estatz, tenuz en la ville d'Orleans, au mois de Janvier mil cinq cens soixante, woodcut, 21 × 30 cm. [repositories: Arsenal, Est 213 (37); Sächsischen Hauptstaatsarchiv Dresden, Geh Rat, 9083/1; Chantilly, Est. H 22; BN, Estampes, Hennin 466, 467].

LE VRAY POURTRAICT ET DISCOURS DE l'assemblee des trois Estats tenuz en la ville d'Orleans, woodcut, 22 × 17.5 cm. A Paris par Jehan de Gourmont et Jehan Pignot [repositories: BN, MS Fr 10193, fo 17bis; BN, Estampes, Ea.17.Rés; Brit. Mus., Foreign History, 1560].

Pourtraict du plant de la salle des estatz et de l'ordre et seance tenu en Iceulx a Orleans le XXIII decembre 1560, woodcut, 38 × 26.5 cm. [BN, Estampes, Qb.1 (1560)].

The contemporary printed depictions and descriptions of the Estates-General were very attentive to the seating arrangements of those in attendance and describe them in nearly identical fashion. *Le vray pourtraict de discours de l'assemblee des trois Estats* differs from the *Pourtraict de l'assemblee des Estatz* only in that it shows no orator speaking and depicts a room of different proportions without draperies on the tables or railings. The *Description du Plant du theatre* offers a verbal description of the seating arrangements that is identical to these two except that it lists a few more individuals and officials present. Tortorel's drawing of the assembly copies the *Pourtraict de l'assemblee des Estatz* but introduces one noteworthy change. It shows the spokesman of the clergy, Jean Quintin, addressing the assembly; the earlier print shows an unidentified speaker in a short robe. I have not been able to determine the significance of this substitution. None of the prior printed sources recounts, as does the legend, that the spokesmen of the three estates kneeled before the king, and that at the king's command the Chancellor had them rise and Quintin continue his speech.

9. *The Colloquy of Poissy/ Le Colloque tenu a Poissy, le 9 Septembre 1561*

Etching, two different versions, with only minute differences. In one, signed "TP" and probably made first, the hanging behind the central group of figures at the top of the image is decorated with curlicues. In the other, signed "I. Tortorel fecit" and shown here, the hanging is decorated with fleurs de lis and the title frequently mistakenly dates the event to December. Titles and captions known in French, Latin, Italian, and German.

The event. With the leading Catholic prelates assembled at Poissy for an assembly of the clergy, Catherine de Medici and those around her seeking to find a middle way that could end the growing religious schism invited spokesmen of the Reformed churches to address the assembly. On September 9 Theodore Beza spoke for the Protestants. His views on the eucharist angered many prelates. A few additional sessions were held, but the colloquy broke up on October 14 without advancing closer to an agreement. The fact of being allowed to address the king, leading members of the court, and the assembled Catholic prelates nonetheless seemed to the Reformed a sign of their growing legitimacy and an answer to their prior petitions to be allowed to set forth their views to the king. They hastened to publish accounts of the event and Beza's harangue.

Accounts of event published prior to 1570

La Harangue faicte par Monsieur Theodore de Besze, Ministre de la parole de Dieu, accompagné d'autres unze Ministres, et de vingt Deputés des Eglises reformees du Royaume de France, devant le Roy, la Roine sa mere, le Roy de Navarre, Princes de Condé & de la Roche-sur-Yon, Monsieur de Guise, le Connestable, & autres grans Princes et Seigneurs du Conseil du Roy, presens & oyans six Cardinaux, trente-six Archevesques ou Evesques, outre un grand nombre d'Abbez, Prieurs, Sorbonistes, & autres Docteurs scholastiques, le mardi neufieme jour de Septembre mil cinq cens soixante & un, en l'abbaye des Nonnains de Poissy (13 French language editions published 1561-2 under a variety of titles, plus translations into German [3 editions], English [3 editions] and Italian [1 edition]; see Frédéric Gardy, *Bibliographie des oeuvres théologiques, littéraires, historiques et juridiques de Théodore de Bèze* [Geneva, 1960], pp. 85-92, 98-101; John A. Tedeschi and E. David Willis, "Two Italian Translations of Beza and Calvin," *Archiv für Reformationsgeschichte*, 55 [1964], 70-72).

Ample discours des actes de Poissy (5 French language editions published 1561-2; also reproduced in *Receuil des choses memorables* 1565).

Petit traitté des guerres civiles, p. 12.

[La Place], *Commentaires de l'Estat de la Religion et Republique soubs les Rois Henry Francois seconds, et Charles neufieme* (1565), pp. 237-309.

Crespin, *Histoire des vrais temoins* (1570), fos. 580-88.

[de Serres], *Rerum Gallia ob religionem gestarum, libri tres* (1570), fos. 92-162.

Other contemporary visual representations

BN, Estampes, Hennin 474, woodcut, 12.5 × 15.5 cm, trimmed to margins eliminating accompanying text.

The BN woodcut, the *Ample discours des actes de Poissy*, La Place, and the 1570 edition of Crespin all include identical descriptions of the seating arrangements of the king, leading members of the royal family, and the six cardinals present. Tortorel's etching arranges the figures similarly. The woodcut, La Place, the 1570 edition of Crespin, and the extended title of *La Harangue faicte par Monsieur Theodore de Besze* all also indicate that Beza was accompanied by eleven other ministers, another detail that reappears in the print. The last three sources also indicate that twenty deputies of the Reformed churches attended the session. They are not figured in the image, just as they are absent from the BN woodcut, which probably furnished a direct visual source for the etching.

10. *The Massacre of Cahors/ Le Massacre faict a Cahors en Querci, le XIX Novemb. 1561*

Woodcut and etching. Titles and captions known in French, Latin, and German.

The event. Incidents of crowd violence and iconoclasm proliferated across France in the years 1560 and 1561. The massacre in Cahors was one of the deadlier Catholic attacks of the era on Protestants gathered for worship. The Protestants claimed that they had the approval of the king's lieutenant general to assemble for worship within the city. They were gathered in the house of the seigneur de Cabrères when they were attacked by a group of Catholics. Protestant sources claim that the attack was premeditated and organized by leading local churchmen and the university chancellor. Forty to fifty people were killed.

No account of this incident published prior to 1570 is known. It is known to historians through brief descriptions in several contemporary letters and memoirs, a manuscript account probably written by Corneille Bertram (BPU, MS Tronchin 8, fos. 47-8), and a narration first printed in the *Histoire ecclesiastique* and incorporated into Crespin from 1582 onward that follows this manuscript account very closely, albeit with a few significant changes of detail. The print agrees with the manuscript in identifying Cabrères as the owner of the house where the Reformed were assembled to worship and in asserting that the corpses of 25 to 30 of the victims were laid out along the street in front of the house (key letter D; this was done, according to the manuscript, "pour faire plus belle monstre de leur rage et cruauté"). The MS does not specify that the attackers set fire to three corners of the house (cf. key letter B), that the victims were led to the main gate to be killed there (cf. key letter C), or that those clergymen who had stirred up the attack did so from a nearby church (cf. key letter F).

11. *The Massacre of Vassy/ Le Massacre fait a Vassy le premier jour de Mars. 1562*

Woodcut. Titles and captions known in French, Latin, and German.

The event. On March 1, 1562, the duke of Guise and his men slew a number of Protestants worshipping within a barn in the small Champagne town of Vassy, near the Guise family seat of Joinville. Contradictory accounts of what triggered the violence subsequently circulated. The Protestants charged that the incident was an unprovoked attack. The duke and his supporters said that those within the barn drew first blood. Nothing historians have subsequently discovered allows one to give greater credit to one version or the other. The incident cost at least several dozen Protestants their lives. While other incidents of religious violence had troubled France during the preceding months and years, this would prove the most fateful and subsequently notorious. The involvement of the duke of Guise, a focus of Huguenot suspicion and hatred since 1559, triggered fear that the massacre betokened a larger scheme to slaughter the Protestants. They mobilized in the name of self-defense, precipitating the maneuvers and counter-maneuvers that eventuated in the First Civil War.

Accounts of event published prior to 1570
Discours au vray et en abbregé, de ce qui est dernierement advenu à Vassi, y passant Monseigneur le Duc de Guise (Paris: Guillaume Morel, 1562).
Histoire de la cruautee exercee par Françoys de Lorraine, Duc de Guyse, et les siens en la ville de Vassy, le premier jour de Mars 1562 (n.p., 1562, also Caen, 1562 as *Destruction du saccagement, exerce cruellement par le Duc de Guise et sa cohorte*).
Discours entier de la persecution et cruauté exercée en la ville de Vaissy, par le Duc de Guyse, le 1 de Mars 1562 (n.p., 1563, reprinted in Crespin, *Actes des martyrs* (1564), pp. 1013-23, *Receuil des choses memorables* (1565).
Petit traitté des guerres civiles, pp. 14-15.

According to the pro-Guise *Discours au vray et en abbregé, de ce qui est dernierement advenu a Vassi, y passant Monseigneur le Duc de Guise*, the duke first approached the barn where the *prêche* was being held with just two of his men, intending simply to remonstrate with the worshipers. Those inside fired shots at him, pelted him with stones, and drew blood. His detachment of 30 soldiers then invaded the church and killed 25 to 30 of those inside. Two different Protestant accounts of this event found their way into print in its wake: a short *Histoire de la cruauté exercée par Francoys de Lorraine, Duc de Guise, et les siens en la ville de Vassy*, written immediately after the event, and a longer *Discours entier de la persecution et cruauté exercée en la ville de Vassy, par le Duc de guyse, le 1 de Mars 1562*, that the internal evidence of the text suggests was written after May 1563 by the former minister of the congregation. Both depict an unprovoked attack on the congregation of 1200 assembled worshippers (cf. key letter A) by 200 cursing Guisard soldiers. Both indicate that the duke of Guise himself joined the fray (cf. key letter B). Both say that many of those inside the barn fled across the roof to save themselves, as the duke's harquebusiers shot at them (cf. key letters F and G). The latter work, however, is far more detailed. It adds that the cardinal of Guise watched the violence unfold from behind the cemetery wall outside (cf. key letter E). It maintains that attacking soldiers paused to tear the poor box from the wall and empty it of its contents (cf. key letter I). It recounts the miraculous deliverance of the congregation's minister, who escaped death when the hilt of an attacking soldier's sword broke as he raised it for the coup de grace (cf. key letter D). As this unfolded, the military trumpeters sounded their trumpets twice (cf. key letter K). Once all of the Protestants had fled from the barn, the duke found a book in it that he did not recognize—a Bible. (This detail does not find its way into the print.) The final toll of the massacre according to this pamphlet was 50-60 dead and 250 wounded. The *Histoire de la cruauté* puts the numbers at 45 dead and 80-100 wounded. Ernest Lavisse first noted the close agreement between the print of the massacre and the narrative of the *Discours entier de la persecution*.

12. *The Massacre of Sens/ Le Massacre fait a Sens en Bourgongne par la populace au mois d'Avril 1562, avant qu'on prinst les armes*

Etching. Titles and captions known in French and German.

The event. This massacre of Protestants was perhaps the deadliest of several that occurred in the anxious, rumor-filled weeks and months following the massacre of Vassy. During these same months the Huguenots seized control of roughly a third of France's largest cities and attacked many religious houses. Still other localities witnessed street fighting between partisans of the two faiths. In Sens, the night watch and guard of the city gates was reinforced to forestall trouble. The Protestants prudently ceased assembling for worship. Nevertheless, elements of the Catholic population ransacked and demolished the barn outside of town that the Huguenots had used for worship, then attacked and killed known Protestants. The violence lasted from April 12 to 14.

Accounts of event published prior to 1570
Historia wie Jemerlich und erbarmlich die armen Christen des Reformierten Evangelischen Kirchen zu Sens aus haimlichen Practicken des Cardinals und Ezbischoften daselbst umbbracht geschmecht und verhergt worden sind (n.p., 1562). A now lost French version of this pamphlet probably also circulated. The 1565 *Receuil des choses memorables* prints a letter from Condé to Catherine de Medici dated April 19, 1562 in which he asks justice for those slain in Sens and refers to an account of the massacre that he is sending along. This account is not printed in the *Receuil*, but the expanded 1570 edition of Crespin includes a "Histoire lamentable du massacre des fideles de l'Eglise reformee en la ville de Sens en Bourgogne" with contents identical to the 1562 pamphlet that is probably this account and the source for the German translation. *Petit traitté des guerres civiles*, pp. 31-2.

The 1562 pamphlet recounts this massacre in considerable detail. It contains every one of the numerous episodes of cruelty and wasteful destruction illustrated in the print and explained in the key. Still other incidents mentioned in the pamphlet did not find their way into the print. The sole feature of the print that lacks an explicit analogue in the pamphlet is the assertion in key letter K that victims of the massacre were thrown into the Yonne "estans les trois à quatre ensemble à une piece de bois par Radeaux".

13. *The Capture of Valence/ La prinse de Vallence en Dauphiné ou fut tué le S. de la Motte Gondrin le 25 avril 1562*

Etching. Titles and captions known in French, Latin, Italian, and German.

The event. Hector de Pardaillan, seigneur de La Motte-Gondrin, the king's lieutenant-general in Dauphiné and acting governor in the absence of the duke of Guise, was known for his tough implementation of the legislation restricting and punishing Protestant worship prior to the edict of January 1562. Valence was one of the towns seized by the Huguenots in the aftermath of Vassy. La Motte-Gondrin was in the city at the time but was unable to prevent the Huguenot takeover. Instead, a crowd of vengeful Protestants stormed his residence and killed him.

Accounts of event published prior to 1570
Loys de Perussiis, *Discours des guerres de la Comté de Venayscin et de la Provence* (Avignon, 1563), p. 27.
Petit traitté des guerres civiles, p. 17.
"Lettre du Seigneur Baron des Adretz a la Royne Mere touchant la Mort de la Motte-Gondrin" in *Receuil des choses memorables* (1565).

Both published Protestant accounts, the *Petit traitté* and the baron des Adrets' letter, emphasize the element of revenge in the killing but offer few details about it. The former simply notes that the *menu peuple* "l'ont fait mourir, et pendu à sa fenetre;" the latter that "ledit peuple esmeu" besieged La Motte-Gondrin's lodgings and could not be prevented from killing him. The Catholic Perussis, who dates the event to April 29, provides a fuller report. La Motte Gondrin first tried to disperse the threatening crowd that had gathered outside his house by addressing it from an upper window. When this failed, he put on his military gear and the collar of the Order of St Michael, to no avail. The attackers broke down his door, promised to do him no harm if he laid down his arms, then killed him after he did so and hung his body from the window of his house. His corpse was later taken down, dragged it through the city, and left to rot (cf. key letters C-E). The fullest report of all about the massacre by somebody who was in Valence at the time comes from the diary and chronicle of the Catholic François Joubert. (This, of course, would not have been available to those responsible for designing this image.) It dates the takeover of the city to April 25 and places the slaying of La Motte-Gondrin on the next day. According to its version, the Huguenots besieged La Motte-Gondrin's lodgings from all sides and set fire to the main door. The lieutenant general tried to flee across the rooftops but was caught on the roof of a nearby house. He put up a stout fight, then agreed to lay down his arms on a promise of safety. His Huguenot captors did not keep their word. After he was killed, his corpse was hung by the armpits from the window of the house where he was caught. (Cf. letter keys B-D, G.) The details in the print that the attackers found an artillery piece in the entryway and cut down his body "so that the people would recognize him when it fell" (letter keys E, H) do not appear in any source from this period that I have located.

Historical bibliography

Memoires de Francois Joubert et de Salomon de Merez de divers événements en Dauphiné ed. E. Maignien (Grenoble, 1886), pp. 48-50.

14. *The Massacre of Tours/ Le Massacre fait a Tours par la populace au mois de Juillet. 1562*

Woodcut and etching. Titles and captions known in French, Latin, and German.

Important variants of accompanying text. The etching and certain printings of the woodcut bear, instead of a key, the legend: "La populace de Tours s'esleve contre ceux de la Religion, & en massacre jusqu'au nombre de deux cents ou environ: les tirant premierement d'une Eglise, ou on les avoit mis prisonniers, au fauxbourg de la Riche, & fait demeurer sans boyre n'y manger deux ou trois jours: Puis les tue & noye. Mesmes ayant attaché le President Bourgeoys à un arbre, luy arrache le coeur & les entrailles."

The event. Tours was one of the first cities where the Huguenots secured political domination in the wake of the massacre of Vassy. In July, the combined royal and Catholic forces retook it after a brief siege directed by the marshal de St André. The Huguenots negotiated surrender terms according to which they were promised safe passage from the city, but the agreement was not respected and many of the city's Protestants were killed.

Accounts of event published prior to 1570
Petit traitté des guerres civiles, pp. 39-40.

The account in the *Petit traitté* is silent about the details of the massacre except for the indignant exclamation: "Quelles cruautez sont ce de lier quatre, cinq, six, maintenant sept, maintenant huit pauvres femmes, tant de basse condition, que Demoiselles à une barre, commes les boeufs au joug, puis en tel estat les precipter en la riviere?" This suggests that word of such incidents must have circulated orally. No prior printed or manuscript source is known for most of the very specific incidents of cruelty shown in the print. A detailed account of the violence subsequently appeared first in the *Histoire ecclesiastique des Eglises reformees au royaume de France* and then in editions of Crespin's martyrology from 1582 onward. Certain episodes figured in the print, notably the disembowelment of the president of the presidial court Jean Bourgeau (key letter E upper right), also appear in this account. It also notes the imprisonment of many Huguenots in a church in the faubourg La Riche. But the episodes shown in the print explained by key letters F- K do not reappear in it. It likewise contains many details not found in the print. The two accounts disagree about the length of time the Huguenots were held in the church of La Riche. The *Histoire ecclesiastique* does not specify the number of people held or say that they were deprived of food and water.

Historical bibliography
David Nicholls, "Protestants, Catholics and Magistrates in Tours, 1562-1572: The Making of a Catholic City During the Religious Wars," *French History*, 8 (1994), 14-33.

15. *The Capture of Montbrison/ La Prinse de la ville de Montbrison au pays de Forest au mois de juillet 1562*

Woodcut and etching. Titles and captions known in French, Latin, Italian, and German.

Important variants of accompanying text. The etching bears, instead of a key, the legend: "La Baron des Adrets, et monsieur de Ponsenat ayant fait bresche à la ville de Montbrison, entrerent dedans sans grande resistance, ou ledit des Adrets fait sauter plusieurs prisonniers tant Gentils-hommes que soldats, du grand Donjon en bas."

The event. While large Protestant and royal/Catholic armies massed and maneuvered between the Loire and Seine valleys during the summer and fall of 1562, encounters between smaller armies took place in the peripheral provinces. Montbrison was a Catholic bastion in the Forez that housed a small Catholic garrison. On July 15 François de Beaumont, baron des Adrets, at the head of troops of Huguenot footsoldiers raised in Dauphiné, Provence, the Lyonnais and Auvergne, took it after a brief siege. He and his men subsequently massacred many of the residents and soldiers. The Catholic commander Montcelard and a number of his soldiers were thrown to their death from the top of the citadel tower.

Accounts of event published prior to 1570
Histoire des triomphes de l'egli[se] Lyonnoise. Avec la prinse de Montbrison (Lyon, 1562).

The strongly partisan *Histoire des triomphes de l'egli[se] Lyonnoise*, which depicts the civil war as a conflict between "Christians" and "Papists" and Montcelard as a notorious blasphemer, is stingy with details about the course of the siege, saying simply that des Adrets positioned his artillery against Montbrison on July 15, made a breach in the wall that night, and took the city. It estimates that 3-400 "caffars" were subsequently killed for throwing stones at the besieging soldier. Montcelard and eleven others are said to have jumped to their death trying to escape.

16. *The Battle of St Gilles/ La deffaite de S. Gilles en Languedoc, au mois de Septembre 1562*

Etching. Titles and captions known in French, Latin, Italian, and German.

The event. This is another encounter that took place away from the main theatre of conflict. After being driven out of Provence, a body of Protestant troops seeking to aid their co-religionists in Montpellier engaged the Catholic forces of the counts of Sommerive and de Suze, who had entered Languedoc from Provence and the Comtat and laid siege to the little town of St Gilles. The Protestants built a pontoon bridge resting on boats to convey their cavalry and artillery across a branch of the Rhône on September 27 and engaged the enemy soon after. (No available source specifies the precise date.) The battle ended in one of the most decisive Protestant victories of the fighting in this region. Coming after a series of Protestant setbacks, it stopped the advance of the Catholic forces into Languedoc and buoyed Huguenot morale sufficiently to be memorialized in prose and poetry.

Accounts of event published prior to 1570
Loys de Perussiis, *Le second discours des guerres de la Comté de Venayscin* (Avignon, 1564), pp. 2-3.
Brief et veritable discours de la deffaite des Provencaux, appellée la Bataille de Sainct Gilles in *Receuil des choses memorables* (1565).
Ode Hystoriale de la bataille de Sainct Gile (Lyon, 1563).
Petit traitté des guerres civiles, pp. 54-5.

The narration by the Catholic Perussiis is the most detailed early printed account of this event and the only one to indicate that the advancing Protestants built a pontoon bridge resting on boats. Such a bridge appears in the image although it is not highlighted in the accompanying key. The *Brief et veritable discours* identifies Bouillargues as the captain who led the first Huguenot charge (key letter L). It also asserts that the Catholic troops besieging St Gilles had three pieces of artillery. (Cf. key letter C, which specifies two.) The *Ode Hystorialle* reports that the Catholic troops laying siege to St Gilles spent their nights "avecq leurs paillardes . . . Et dansant gaillardes". (Cf the scenes of banqueting and gambling highlighted by key letter B). Some specific details indicated by the key, notably that the operation involved three companies of Huguenot troops who had come from Provence, and that the defenders inside St Gilles also made sorties, are not indicated in any of these sources.

17. *The Battle Order at Dreux/ L'ordonnance des deux armees de la bataille de Dreux donnee le 19 Decemb. 1562*

Etching. Titles and captions known in French, Latin, Italian, and German.

The event. The battle of Dreux was the most important engagement of the First Civil War. The main body of the Huguenot army, with approximately 13,000 men commanded by Condé and Coligny, was moving toward Normandy to join with the English troops sent by queen Elizabeth. It was pursued by the royal and Catholic army numbering about 19,000 under Guise, Montmorency, and St André. On the night of December 18-19 the royal army crossed the Eure and forced an engagement. The two armies drew up against one another on a plain between the villages of Epinay and Blainville near Dreux.

Accounts of event published prior to 1570
Avvisi novamente venuti de le cose di Francia. Dove s'intende minutamente il principio, et il fine della giornata fatta tra Chiatres & Ordan, con il numero delle genti d'arme, e cavalli de l'uno et l'altro essercito, et anco li strattagemi usati del Duca di Ghisa et del Principe de Condè (Padua: Griffo, 1563).
Aviso de Parigi della Vitoria Anta novamente di Francia (n.p., n.d.).
Zwo warhafftige und newe zeytungen aus Franckreich . . . was sich zwischen dem Hertzogen von Guise . . . auff einer Seiten und auff der andern Seiten mit dem Hertzogen von Conde . . . begeben hat von dem 12 Tag Decemb. . . . bis auff den 10. tag Martii dieses 1563 Jars (n.p. [Strasbourg], 1563).
Petit traitté des guerres civiles, pp. 55-7.
Brief discours de ce qui est advenu en la bataille donnee pres la ville de Dreux in *Receuil des choses memorables* (1565).
Discours de la bataille de Dreux, dicté par feu monseigneur Francois de Lorraine (Paris; veuve V. Sertenas, 1576; a now lost edition of 1565 is also mentioned in Hauser).

Other contemporary visual representations
Le vray pourtraict et plante de la bataille donnee par Monsieur de Guise contre les Huguenots, intaglio, 38.5 × 33 cm, Paris: "au clos Bruneau, à l'enseigne Sainte Catherine", n.d. [BN, MS Fr 10193, fo 259 bis; reproduced in *MC*, IV, 687 a & b].
Le vray pourtraict de la bataille donne par M. de Guise devant Dreux, woodcut, 49 × 40.2 cm, Paris: Mathurin Breville, 1563 [BN, MS Fr 10193, fo 259 bis; Bodleian Gough 43 f. 167, reproduced in *MC*, IV, 178 a & b; Lestringant, "Quatre 'canards'", p. 181; Idem, *Thevet*, p. 149].

A variety of verbal and visual news accounts printed both immediately after the event and in subsequent years describe the battle. Each appears to be essentially independent of the other; there is agreement about general details, but no repetition of the same precise information from one account to another, except that the two news prints produced in Paris list the various units of troops in the same order and terms. The fullest descriptions of the disposition of the two armies prior to the battle are provided by these prints and by the *Discours de la bataille de Dreux.* The visual reports all offer the same general depiction of the Protestant army arrayed in rows advancing toward the royal troops deployed in a broad arc behind two sets of cannons, although the Paris news prints locate the viewer behind the royal lines while Tortorel and Perrissin place the viewer at an angle to the battle slightly behind the Protestant forces. The order of the various Catholic units is described with care in both Paris news prints and the *Discours*. These all describe alternating units of cavalry and infantry, with the Spanish troops who had come to aid the French crown on the far right of the Catholic line, Breton and French troops on the far left. The duke of Guise and his men are toward the right of their line; the Constable Montmorency is toward the left; St André and Damville are between them. Tortorel and Perrissin's depiction agrees. No other source, however, indicates the number of companies or *enseignes* in each unit as this print does. The Parisian visual and verbal reports offer considerably fewer details about the identity of the Huguenot commanders leading the different units. Much of the information in key letters A-I cannot be found in any source printed prior to 1570.

Historical bibliography

Raymond de Coynart, *L'Année 1562 et la bataille de Dreux. Etude historique et militaire* (Paris 1897).

James B. Wood, *The King's Army: Warfare, Soldiers and Society during the Wars of Religion in France, 1562-1576* (Cambridge, 1996), ch. 7.

18. *The First Charge at Dreux/ La premiere charge de la bataille de Dreux, la ou M. le Connestable fut prins, le 19. Decembre 1562*

Woodcut and etching. Titles and captions known in French, Latin, Italian, and German.

The event. The battle began at around noon and lasted until nightfall. In the first phase of the battle, the Protestant cavalry, French and German, attacked the crown's Swiss troops and the Constable's cavalry on the left side of the royal/Catholic arc, putting Montmorency's men to flight and capturing the Constable.

For the accounts of this event published prior to 1570 and historical bibliography, see the preceding note.

The *Avvisi novamente venuti* and the *Vray pourtraict et plante* state that the Huguenots first contemplated attacking Guise's squadrons but decided that the Swiss and the Constable's cavalry were easier targets. Condé's cavalry charged through the Constable's ranks three times. The *Avvisi* adds the detail that La Rochefoucauld captured the Constable. The *Discours de la bataille de Dreux* mentions that the Constable's horse was shot out from under him, that the regiments of d'Aumale and Damville were scattered, and that the Swiss rallied together. The Protestant *Brief Discours* says that the attackers took six pieces of enemy artillery, broke their cavalry and infantry, and killed many Swiss. The Tortorel and Perrissin print thus departs from the previously published sources in identifying the leaders of the various Huguenot charges and the number of units at their command (key letters A-K). It also offers details about the wounds received by Montmorency found in none of the prior printed sources (see key letter M).

19. *The Second Charge at Dreux/ La deuxieme charge de la Bataille de Dreux, ou M. le P. de Condé poursuit la victoire le 19 Deceb. 1562*

Etching. Titles and captions known in French, Latin, Italian, and German.

The event. The Huguenots directed the second phase of their attack against the Swiss. After weakening the Swiss with a cavalry charge, they threw their German landsknechts against them, but the stout resistance that the German footsoldiers encountered led them to retreat quickly and barricade themselves in the village of Blainville. Significant numbers of troops on both sides of the conflict had yet to enter the fray.

For the accounts of this event published prior to 1570 and historical bibliography, see the note accompanying plate 17.

Few of the early printed accounts provide many details about this phase of the battle. The Protestant *Brief discours* indicates that the Huguenot triumph at this point in the battle might have been more complete yet had their French and German infantry not performed "lachement". Cf. key letter G, which shows Condé's German landsknechts fleeing the scene of battle.

20. *The Third Charge at Dreux/ La troisieme charge de la bataille de Dreux, ou M. le Prince de Condé fut prins, le 19 Decembre 1562*

Woodcut and etching. Titles and captions known in French, Latin, Italian, and German.

The event. In the decisive third phase of the battle, the Huguenots threw their remaining cavalry against the Swiss and broke their formation. The German cavalry shouted "Victory!" Some headed off to join the looting of the royal/Catholic baggage train. Early reports on the battle that reached Paris depicted it as an alarming rout. But Condé and Coligny realized that a large fraction of the Catholic troops had yet to enter the battle and sought to regroup their scattered cavalry units. Guise and St André now led their men into the fray, directing their attack against the Huguenot infantry, which they quickly routed. Various units of Protestant cavalry withdrew into a nearby wood to try to regroup. In this withdrawal Condé was captured. Coligny took over the Huguenot command and rallied the prince's cavalry.

For the accounts of this event published prior to 1570 and historical bibliography, see the note accompanying plate 17.

The different early printed accounts of the battle agree on the broadest outline of this phase of the combat but offer different details. The *Discours de la bataille* credits Biron with holding off a Protestant attack as the Catholic army's fortunes neared its low point, claims that the Swiss were able to withstand the successive attacks against them and counter-attack, gives credit to St André and the Gascons for routing the landsknechts, and states that Condé's horse was wounded in the leg, which is what allowed him to be taken. The Protestant *Brief Discours* says that Condé also received a minor wound to the face and that Coligny rallied the French and German cavalry and attacked St. André. The two Paris news prints identify by name upward of two dozen Catholic officers, "hardis capitaines et chevalliers," who played important roles in the victorious Catholic charge. No prior published accounts indicate the details found in the facing print that batallions of Condé's landsknechts fled to Blainville without fighting or that Damville captured Condé.

21. *The Fourth Charge at Dreux/ La quatrieme charge de la Bataille de Dreux, ou M. le Mareschal S. André fut tué, le 19 Decemb. 1562*

Etching. Titles and captions known in French, Latin, Italian, and German.

The event. Having rallied about a thousand horsemen in the woods, Coligny was able to draw them up in battle formation and mount one final challenge to the royal and Catholic forces. Guise ordered a unit of veteran French infantry under the count of Martigues to advance and protect his now scattered and outnumbered cavalry. This unit was able to form itself into a square and withstand a last desperate Huguenot attack around nightfall. During this phase of the battle the marshal St André had his horse shot from beneath him. Surrounded by Protestant soldiers, he initially surrendered to an ancient rival, Jean Perdriel de Bobigny, but then gave himself over to the prince of Porcien. Bobigny, angered at losing so rich a ransom, shot St André in the head as he rode behind Porcien.

The accounts of the battle published prior to 1570 say relatively little about this phase except for some details about St André's death. Several Catholic news accounts indicate that the marshal was killed not in the heat of battle but after he was taken prisoner. Thus, the *Avvisi* narrates that St André got separated from his fellows, encountered the Huguenot cavalry regrouping in the wood, and was taken and killed. He was subsequently found "morto e spogliato" with a bullet in the head. The *Discours de la bataille* says that he was "prins et depuis tué". The Protestant *Brief Discours* simply records that he was killed and his body plundered. Poltrot de Méré, the assassin of the duke of Guise, also included a few words about St André's death, based on what he learned while in Protestant-controlled Orléans. These appear in his published deposition about his killing of the Guise discussed below in the notes to scene 24. Poltrot declared that St André surrendered first to an unidentified nobleman, then to Porcien, which provoked the first nobleman to shoot him. Brantôme's life of St André, written at the end of the century and not published until 1661, identifies Bobigny as the first nobleman and asserts that he shot St André through the head as he rode behind Porcien because he believed St André to have unfairly seized land belonging to him. Though the key to this incident (N) mentions none of these details, the portion of the image itself devoted to it shows St André shot at close quarters at close quarters while mounted behind a second knight. This print's depiction of both sides rallying their men and of Guise's French veterans arrayed in a square under attack from all sides by the Protestant cavalry has no direct basis in any of the prior published accounts. The same is true of the details indicated in letter keys A-C.

Historical bibliography concerning the death of St André

Lucien Romier, *La carrière d'un favori. Jacques d'Albon de Saint-André maréchal de France (1512-1562)* (Paris, 1909), pp. 380-81.

22. *The Retreat from Dreux/ La retraite de la bataille de Dreux, le 19. Decemb. 1562*

Etching. Titles and captions known in French, Latin, Italian, and German.

The event. In the wake of the battle, both sides claimed victory, although the prudent Huguenot captain François de La Noue wrote that those Protestants who thought that the battle was no defeat because they had withdrawn at nightfall in an orderly fashion were fooling themselves, since the Catholics slept on the battlefield and captured many enemy standards and cannon. Casualties on both sides were extensive: about 6,000 in all according to the most careful recent estimate. Many of the dead were found frozen and naked the next morning, their bodies having been stripped and looted overnight.

For the accounts of this event published prior to 1570 and historical bibliography, see the note accompanying plate 17.

The Protestant *Brief Discours* ends on the note of the Catholics being driven back in Coligny's last charge, followed by an enumeration of prominent royalist noblemen killed, wounded or taken prisoner. One Paris news print labels the battle a Catholic victory. The other simply highlights the cost of the battle to both sides and the kingdom as a whole. One Italian *avviso* claims that the Huguenots fled towards Orléans. The other more reservedly asserts that Guise won much glory; it also notes the capture of the English ambassador and the Huguenot minister François Perrussel. The *Discours de la bataille* reports that Coligny and his troops withdrew from the battlefield to a spot two leagues away. The Admiral wanted to renew the combat the next day but was talked out of it by his German cavalry commanders. In this print both sides are said to withdraw. The key also speaks of soldiers on both sides being murdered. The upper portion of the image shows bodies being stripped of their clothes and arms, dragged into piles, and buried.

23. *The Siege of Orléans/ Orleans assiegé au mois de Janvier 1563*

Etching. Titles and captions known in French, Latin, Italian, and German.

The event. After the battle of Dreux, the duke of Guise, now commanding the royal army, rebuilt his depleted ranks and moved toward Orléans, the great Huguenot rallying point and stronghold throughout the First Civil War. His men drew up before the city on February 5, 1563. On the next day they were able to take the faubourg of Portereau, which was located across the Loire from the main part of the city. Several days later they took the two towers and fort that protected the north side of the bridge across the river. But they were not able to advance across the bridge and take the islands in the Loire where the Protestants concentrated their defenses, in part because the defenders sapped one arch of the bridge to render the span impassable. The attack became an extended siege that continued until the negotiation of peace in March.

No accounts of this event published prior to 1570 are known. It is known to historians primarily through contemporary ambassadors' reports and subsequent accounts by Beza, La Noue, d'Aubigné and others.

Historical bibliography

Bernard de Lacombe, *Les débuts des guerres de religion (Orléans, 1559-1564): Catherine de Médicis entre Guise et Condé* (Paris, 1899), pp. 287-312.

24. *The Fatal Wounding of the Duke of Guise/ Le Duc de Guise est blessé a mort le 18 Fevrier 1563*

Woodcut and etching. Titles and captions known in French, Latin, Italian, and German.

Important variants of accompanying text. Some printings of the etching in both French and Latin have, instead of the key, the following legend: "Du Meray dict Poltrot, ayant l'opportunité d'executer son entreprise, prie Dieu premierement dans ung bois, ayant attaché son cheval à ung arbre: Puis s'approchant de Monsieur de Guise, qui est accompagné du capitaine Rostain, luy delasche un coup de pistolle, et le blesse de trois bales en l'espaule; dont il mourut peu de jours apres, en son logis qui estoit prochain nommé les valins. Lequel coup estant faict, ledit Du Meray s'enfuit."

The event. As the duke of Guise returned to his lodgings outside Orléans after inspecting the siege works on the evening of February 18, he was shot three times in the shoulder by Jean de Poltrot, sieur de Méré. He died of the wounds six days later. Poltrot fled, but was captured the next day. When interrogated he said that the Admiral Coligny had recruited him for the mission to kill the duke, and that he had been encouraged in the enterprise by Theodore Beza. His deposition was sent to the Admiral to give him an opportunity to respond to the accusation. It also quickly found its way into print in Paris and was spread by Catholic agents among the German troops assisting the Huguenots. Coligny and Beza denied the accusation and hastened to have their denial printed by presses in Protestant-controlled towns, including in German and Latin translation.

Accounts of event published prior to 1570

L'interrogatoire et deposition faicte a un nommé Jehan de Poltrot (Paris, 1563).

Response a l'interrogatoire nagueres faict a un nommé Jehan de Poltrot, soy disant Seigneur de Merey, touchant la mort du feu Duc de Guise (Caen, 1562; Orleans: Eloi Gibier, 1563; n.p. 1563; reprinted in *Recueil des choses memorables* 1565; also German translation n.p., 1563; Latin translation n.p., 1563).

Lettre de l'Evesque de Riez, au Roy, contenant les actions et propos de Monsieur de Guyse depuis sa blessure jusques a son trepas (Paris: Jacques Kerver, 1563).

Petit traitté des guerres civiles, pp. 59-60.

Poltrot's deposition, reprinted with Coligny's response, states that he followed the duke and shot him three times from a distance of six or seven paces as the duke approached a crossroads near his lodgings. The duke was on foot at the time and accompanied by a gentleman who walked ahead of him; a second, mounted on a mule, was speaking with him. (Cf. the details in the center of the image, which are significantly different.) This text does not identify the chateau where the duke was lodging. The account of the duke's last days by the bishop of Riez places the shooting at a crossroads between two large walnut trees and also states that Poltrot shot Guise three times from behind. His wife met him when he reached the chateau of Cornay, his lodging place according to the bishop. No account of the event published prior to 1570 that I have found states that Poltrot prayed in the woods before carrying out his enterprise, provides the detail that he waited amid five walnut trees for Guise to pass, identifies Tristan de Rostaing, a royal financial official and messenger, as one of those accompanying Guise, or indicates that he was lodging in the chateau de Vaslins (cf. key letters B-E). Independent evidence confirms the accuracy of these last two details, however, for a letter written by Catherine de Medici immediately after the event identifies the sieur du Rostaing as the only person with the duke when he was shot, while several sources indicate Vaslins as the duke's lodging place. The 1580 *Histoire ecclesiastique des Eglises reformees au royaume de France* also reports that Poltrot prayed in a wood prior to carrying out his attack, furnishing the additional details that he asked God to indicate to him if his plan did not agree with the divine will and to furnish him the strength and courage to kill the tyrant. This text does not mention the detail found in key letter D and repeated in the alternate legend that he first tied his horse to a tree.

Historical bibliography

A. de Ruble, *L'assassinat de Francois de Lorraine, duc de Guise* (Paris, 1897).

Pierre de Vaissière, "Jean Poltrot seigneur de Méré, meurtrier de M. de Guise (1563)," *Revue des Etudes historiques* 12 (1910), 1-61.

25. *The Peace Made outside Orléans/ La paix faite en l'isle aux Boeufz pres Orleans, le 13. Mars. 1563*

Etching. Titles and captions known in French, Latin, Italian, and German.

The event. Following the assassination of the duke of Guise, Catherine de Medici, who had recurrently tried to negotiate a settlement throughout the First Civil War, redoubled her efforts. The months of imprisonment that both Condé and Montmorency had endured since being captured at Dreux made them more forthcoming. On March 4 and 5 Condé was conveyed under heavy guard to Orléans from Amboise, where he had been held. On March 6 or 7 (the sources differ) he met with Montmorency, who had been held in Orléans, on a small island in the river where a boat covered with planks and surmounted with a tent had been moored to offer them shelter in which to meet. They preferred to parley while walking around the island, out of earshot of Damville, L'Aubespine and d'Oysel, who joined them on the island. The meeting was promising enough for each prisoner to be allowed temporarily to rejoin and consult with his party. When Condé outlined preliminary terms that he had discussed with Montmorency to the Huguenot ministers inside Orléans, they strenuously protested any accord other than one that renewed the terms of the Edict of January and included punishment for those guilty of the massacres of Vassy and Sens. Later that day 72 ministers in the city signed a statement to the same effect addressed to Condé. Their protests were in vain, as were the efforts of Protestant hard-liners within the city to subvert the negotiations and incite new conflict by desecrating holy objects and mocking an effigy of the Pope from the top of the ramparts to goad the assailants. On March 12 the basis for an accord was reached. The edict of pacification was promulgated in Amboise on March 19, published in the royal camp on March 22, and in Orléans on March 29.

The peace negotiations are known to historians primarily through diplomatic correspondence and the *Histoire ecclesiastique des Eglises reformees au royaume de France*, which includes the text of the ministers' protest. Several features of the print—the date given in the title, which does not correspond with any specific day of negotiation revealed by surviving sources; its relative sparsity of precise details; the depiction of two tents on the Ile aux Boeufs when contemporary sources mention a single tent on a boat alongside the island—all suggest that the makers of the series were not well informed about the parleys.

Historical bibliography

Lacombe, *Les débuts des guerres de religion (Orléans, 1559-1564)*, pp. 319-34.

26. *The Execution of Poltrot de Méré/ L'execution de Jean de Poltrot dit Merey a Paris, le 18. Mars, 1563*

Woodcut and etching. Titles and captions known in French, Latin, Italian, and German.

Important variants of accompanying text. Illustrated here because of the quality of the impression is the rare and apparently early printing of this etching with the verse legend. All other printings have as the legend: "Le S. Jean Poltrot, dict du Meray pour avoir tué Monsieur de Guise devant Orleans est tiré à quatre chevaux et desmembré, en la place sainct Jean en Greve, à Paris."

The event. After being brought to Paris, Poltrot retracted the accusations he made against Coligny and Beza under torture at Orléans. He was condemned to be branded with hot irons and then drawn and quartered by four horses in the Place de Grève in Paris, after which his head was to be displayed on a lance in front of the Hôtel de Ville and the four quarters of his body placed on gibbets at each of the chief gates of the capital. Amid his ordeal, he asked to have the punishment stopped so that he could discharge his conscience. He then retracted his retraction and accused Coligny once more. The four horses drawing him could not pull his limbs apart and the executioner had to assist them with his sword.

No account of Poltrot's final hours published prior to 1570 is known. The details of his execution are known to historians through several detailed ambassador's reports, memoirs, and a long account in the *Histoire ecclesiastique des Eglises reformees au royaume de France.*

For the historical bibliography about this event, see the note accompanying plate 24.

27. *The Michelade/ Le Massacre fait à Nismes le 1 d'Octobre en Languedoc 1567. en la nuict*

Etching. Titles and captions known in French, Latin, and German.

The event. After living under a Protestant regime during the First Civil War, Nîmes was governed by a city council dominated by its Catholic minority following the restoration of peace. On September 30, 1567, in a coup designed to coincide with the effort of the leading Protestant nobleman to capture the king at Meaux that touched off the Second Civil War, armed Huguenots rode into the city and seized control of it. After rounding up many of the city's Catholics and holding them briefly in several locations, the new Protestant masters of the town marched certain of them by torchlight into the courtyard of the bishop's palace in small groups and slew between 30 and 100 with swords and daggers out of the sight of most of the city's population. The victims included many clergymen and a number of those who had played prominent roles in city government in the preceding period. Many of the corpses were thrown down the courtyard well. A year and a half after the event, the Parlement of Toulouse condemned 104 people to death for their role in the violence. Most escaped seizure, but four were arrested and decapitated. The massacre is usually known as the Michelade since it took place on Saint Michael's night.

No account of this event was published prior to 1570. It is known to historians through subsequent Catholic histories and thanks to the surviving records of a detailed investigation carried out in 1568 by a judicial official of Beaucaire. The depositions for this investigation identify among the victims the Augustinian prior Jean Quatrebras, the first consul of the city Guy Rochette, his half-brother Robert Gregoire, the lawyer François de Gras, and the captain Vidal (cf. key letters B, D, E, and F). No records indicate a victim by the name of Gandarre (key letter C). One deponent places the number of those thrown down the well at 72. According to Ménard, a painting in the possession of the Augustinian house of Nîmes in the eighteenth century, now apparently lost, depicted the martyrdom of Quatrebras. A largely fanciful account of his martyrdom also appears in the *Histoire de la vie de S. Augustin et de plusieurs saints etc. de son ordre* (Toulouse, 1641). It will be noted that none of the perpetrators of the massacre are identified in the key. One of their leaders was the captain Bouillargues, who also commanded the Protestant forces at St Gilles and appears in the key to scene 16.

Historical Bibliography

Leon Ménard, *Histoire civile, ecclesiastique, et littéraire de la ville de Nismes* (7 vols., Paris, 1750-58), V, pp. 9-21 of text, 1-5 of notes, and 24-60 of preuves.

Joshua Millet, "A City Converted: The Protestant Reformation at Nimes, 1532-67" (Harvard University Ph.D. dissertation, 2000), ch. 4.

Allan A. Tulchin, "The Michelade in Nîmes, 1567," *French Historical Studies* 29 (2006), 1-35.

28. *The Battle of St Denis/ La bataille de Sainct Denis, donnee la veille S. Martin 1567*

Woodcut and etching. Titles and captions known in French, Latin, Italian, and German

The event. This battle, which took place on November 10, 1567, was the most important military engagement of the short Second Civil War. After the failed Protestant attempt to seize the king at Meaux that triggered the conflict, Condé and Coligny moved their troops toward Paris and took several small towns around the capital, including St Denis. On November 10 the Constable Montmorency led a large body of troops against the Reformed forces arrayed on the plain between St Denis and Paris. In the course of the battle the Constable was fatally wounded, but his troops were able to control the battlefield, retake St Denis, and drive the Protestants away from Paris.

Accounts of event published prior to 1570
Lettres du Roy envoyees a Monseigneur le president de Birague . . . contenans advis de la victoire qu'il a pleu a Dieu luy donner en quelque renconctre sur les ennemis (Lyon: Benoist Rigaud, 1567).

Other contemporary visual representations
Le portrait de la ville de Paris, cité & universite, aveq le plan du camp des deux armees, woodcut, two plates, each 33.5 × 41.2 cm depicting Paris and the battle of St Denis, accompanying text by André Thevet, Paris, Mathurin Bréville, n.d. The bottom half of this image showing the battle was subsequently reproduced and published as *[Pour]trait veritable de la Bataille, donnee entre Paris et S Denis, le 10 novembre 1567*, woodcut, 37.5 × 16.5 cm, Lyon, Jean Le Maistre, 1570 [BM St Denis, MS E 1, reproduced in Jean Boutier, *Les Plans de Paris des origines (1493) à la fin du XVIIIe siècle: étude, carto-bibliographie et catalogue collectif* (Paris, 2002), pp. 92-4; Etienne Vitelli, *Commentaires sur la guerre civil de France 1567* ed. Lombard-Jourdan; BN C & P, Res Ge D 23410].
Eyewitness sketch, probably by the son of Sir Henry Norris, [Public Record Office, MPF 313, CSPF/E dated Nov 10, 1567; reproduced in Vitelli, *Commentaires*, p. 17; Wood, *The King's Army*, p. 83.]

This event is known to historians primarily through manuscript reports and accounts in later memoirs and histories. The royal letter announcing the victory to the king's lieutenant in Lyon, published as a news pamphlet, offers only the most skeletal of accounts. Two contemporary visual reports also survive about it, one of which was published at the time in woodcut form. Perrissin's rendering of the events of the battle is impossible to reconcile with this woodcut—one, it is worth noting, that the eyewitness Etienne Vitelli judged to be highly unreliable. No prior printed source is therefore known for the depiction and details of the battle offered in this view and the accompanying key.

Historical bibliography

Anne Lombard-Jourdan, "La bataille de Saint-Denis (10 novembre 1567). Tradition, propagande et iconographie," *Memoires de la Fédération des Sociétés Historiques et Archéologiques de Paris et de l'Ile de France* 29 (1978), 7-54.

Etienne Vitelli, *Commentaires sur la guerre civile de France 1567* ed. Anne Lombard-Jourdan (Paris, 2005).

29. *The Battle of Cognat/ La rencontre des deux armees Francoises à Congnac pres de Gannat en Auvergne, le 6 Janvier. 1568.*

Woodcut and etching. Titles and captions known in French, Latin, Italian, and German.

The event. This battle involved several units of Huguenot troops raised in Auvergne and neighboring provinces who were heading toward Orléans to join with Condé's men. Catholic forces under the command of the governor of Auvergne, Gaspard de Montmorin, count of Saint-Hérem, sought to block their passage. The Huguenot armies were led by the viscounts of Mouvans and Montclar. In the encounter the Protestant troops were able to withstand the initial cavalry charges of the Catholics, counter-attack, and gain a decisive victory. One of St Hérem's lieutenant commanders, Jean Mottier de La Fayette, seigneur de Hautefeuille, was killed in the battle. The Protestant cavalry commander who led the critical charge, François de Boucé, seigneur de Poncenat, subsequently died as well—according to La Popelinière and subsequent authors, from shots fired by his own men who did not recognize him when he returned to the camp that night.

No accounts of this event published prior to 1570 are known. It is know to historians chiefly through subsequent accounts by La Popelinière, d'Aubigné, and de Thou.

30. *The Siege of Chartres/ La ville de Chartres assiegée et batue par Monsieur le Prince de Condé au mois de Mars 1568*

Etching. Titles and captions known in French and German.

The event. The prince of Condé's troops approached Chartres on February 28, 1568 after having gained ample reinforcements in Lorraine in the form of German mercenaries led by the future count Palatine John Casimir. Their siege of the Catholic-held city was relatively brief, for, despite an important assault that was repulsed on March 7, the siege had only been under way for two weeks when the attackers learned that peace negotiations to end the Second Civil War had begun. A truce was declared. The attackers had withdrawn by March 17. The Peace of Longjumeau was signed on March 23.

Other contemporary visual representations
2 copies of a contemporary painting existed in 1897, one belonging to Société Archéologique de l'Eure et Loir, the other to the Bibliothèque Municipale; the original is now in the Museum of Chartres, the copy of the BM burned in a fire in 1944, but another copy made in the 19th century is known.

No accounts of this event published prior to 1570 are known. It is known to historians through subsequent accounts by La Noue, d'Aubigné, and de Thou and thanks to good local records that have been the basis for several excellent modern studies.

Historical bibliography
Henri Lehr, "Le siège de Chartres par Condé en 1568," ch. 2 of *La Réforme et les Eglises réformées dans le département actuel d'Eure-et-Loir (1523-1911)* (Chartres, 1912), pp. 40-70.
Wood, *The King's Army*, ch. 8.

31. *The Battle Order at Jarnac/ L'ordonnance des deux armees Francoises entre Cognac et Chasteau-neuf, le 13 Mars 1569*

Etching. Titles and captions known in French, Latin, Italian, and German. Three printings (two in French and one in German) mistakenly label this scene "La rencontre des deux armees Francoises entre Cognac et Chasteau-neuf, le 13 Mars 1569".

The event. This encounter, usually known as the battle of Jarnac, is one of the most famous battles of the Third Civil War. Although it was not particularly deadly—perhaps 400 Protestant and 200 Catholic soldiers were killed—the prince of Condé was among the victims, and the event was trumpeted in numerous pamphlets and *avvisi.* The royal army of about 27,000 men, commanded by the young duke of Anjou under the guidance of Gaspard de Saulx-Tavannes, had been pursuing the Huguenots led by Condé and Coligny since both armies had left their winter quarters in late January. On the night of March 12-13, Tavannes was able to move the royal army across the Charente by rebuilding a bridge near Chateauneuf broken by the Huguenots and constructing a second pontoon span nearby. The next day he and his men moved downriver toward Cognac and engaged the rear guard of the Protestant forces in three discrete encounters near Vibrac, Bassac, and Triac. This print shows the armies drawn up for the most important of these engagements at Bassac. (The village is represented at the bottom of the print, letter key K.) The main body of the Huguenot forces did not take part in the battle and was able to take refuge behind the walls of Cognac and Saintes.

Accounts of event published prior to 1570
Discours de la bataille donnée par Monseigneur le Duc d'Anjou entre la ville d'Angoulesme et Jarnac, le XIII jour de mars (Lyon: B. Rigaud, 1569).
Le vray discours de la bataille donnée par monsieur le trezieme jour de Mars, 1569 Entre Chasteauneuf et Jarnac (Paris: Guillaume de Nyverd, 1569; reprinted Rouen: Martin le Mégisseur, Lyon: Michel Jove).
Eigendtlicher und warhaftiger bericht welcher gestalt der Durchleuchtig hochgeborn Furst von Conde in Franckreich wider alle Kriegs Recht verretterisch und erbermlich ermordet und umbbracht worden, single sheet news print illustrated with a portrait of Condé (n.p., n.d.) [BN, Estampes, Hennin VII 616].
Seguita la dichiaratione della rotta et morte del Conde & suo essercito (Padua: L. Pasquati, n.d.).
Lettera scritta dalla corte del Re Christianissimo nella quale si racconta il successo della Giornata seguita a XIII di Marzo tra i catolici & gli ugonotti (Venice: Domenico Farri, 1569).
Discours de la defaitte du Prince de Condé (n.p., n.d.) (song) Arsenal 8 H6230 (2).
Memoires de la III. guerre civile, pp. 75-80.

The French and Italian *avvisi* and pamphlets reporting this event have but scant agreement with the details found in this and the following image, except that the Italian *avvisi* also reveal that Anjou was able to rebuild the bridge across the Charente and bring his troops across it (letter key M). The *Memoires de la III. guerre civile* also mentions the bridge across the Charente. It includes several details about the disposition of the Protestant troops before the encounter that accord with this image, locating the position of Coligny's troops prior to the battle on the right side of the Huguenot forces and alongside a wood (cf. key letter A), with five *enseignes* of footsoldiers close by led by the sieur de "Puiviau" (Christophe Claveau, sieur de Puyviaud-Claveau; cf. letter key E). But the majority of the individuals and units identified in the key (d'Andelot, Soubise, Briquemault, the prince of Navarre, and Choisy on the Huguenot side; the counts Rhingrave and Bassompierre, Montpensier on the Catholic side) are not named in any of these prior printed accounts, nor is any reference made to the royal artillery on a hill guarded by Swiss troops, which appears prominently in this print (key letter T) and the next (key letter N).

Historical bibliography

S-C. Gigon, *La troisième guerre de religion: Jarnac-Moncountour* (Paris, 1909).
Anne-Marie Cocula, "Dreux, Jarnac, Coutras: le rebondissement de la vendetta des Grands" in *Quatrième centenaire de la bataille de Coutras* (Pau, 1988), pp. 17-37.

32. *The Battle of Jarnac/ La rencontre des deux armees Francoises entre Cognac et Chasteauneuf le 13 Mars 1569*

Woodcut and etching. Titles and captions known in French, Latin, Italian, and German.

The event. In the course of the day's fighting, the prince of Condé, Robert Stuart (who brought down Montmorency at the battle of St Denis), and a number of other prominent Protestant captains were killed or taken prisoner. Protestant sources soon charged that Condé had been shot from behind after surrendering on the battlefield. Subsequent accounts of the battle written by noble chroniclers and historians of both faiths likewise agree that Condé was shot from behind by François de Montesquiou after he had surrendered to Cybard Tison, sieur d'Argence. Brantôme, the Catholic chronicler of the mores of the court, adds that before the battle the young duke of Anjou gave orders to kill Condé if possible.

For the accounts of this event published prior to 1570 and historical bibliography, see the preceding note.

In focusing its depiction of the course of this battle on the sequence of events that resulted in Condé's death, this print follows the *Memoires de la III. guerre civile* both in its selection of events to highlight and in the details that it provides about them. As Condé's men charged the royal troops led by the duke of Anjou, this source recounts, a large squadron of German reiters also attacked them on their flank (cf. key letters B-D). The Protestant cavalry was put to flight and chased by the Catholics (cf. key letter P). All of the details found in letter keys G-L about how Condé was trapped beneath his mount in the melée, helped to his feet by one of his men, taken prisoner by the sieurs d'Argence and St Jean, but then shot from behind by Montesquiou likewise appear in this source, right down to the assertion that the fatal bullet passed through his skull and came out below his eye. The Catholic news accounts published just after the event, based on letters written by those at the battle or at court, say nothing about such treachery. Three of them simply report that Condé was killed in the fighting. The *Lettera scritta dalla corte* asserts that, after having previously been wounded in the arm, he was killed by two shots, one to the heart and another to the head, which passed through his eye. The German *flugblatt*, clearly aimed at a Protestant audience, announces right in its title that Condé was murdered "contrary to all of the laws of war" and also says that he was shot through the head from behind by Montesquiou while surrendering to St Jean and d'Argence.

33. *The Battle of La Roche-L'Abeille/ La rencontre des deux armees a la Roche en Lymosin, ou le S. Strossy fut prins le 25 Juing 1569*

Etching. Titles and captions known in French, Latin, Italian, and German.

The event. After scattering in the wake of the battle of Jarnac, the Huguenot troops were reassembled into a large force by Coligny and reinforced by a new contingent of John Casimir's German reiters. They were pursued by the royal troops, strengthened by Italian units sent by the Papacy and duke Cosimo de Medici. The two armies, each containing approximately 25,000 men, met on June 25 in a driving rainstorm at La Roche-L'Abeille. The Huguenots charged first, captured the colonel general of the royal infantry, Filippo Strozzi, and dealt their enemies more losses than they absorbed, slaying many of those who surrendered in retaliation for Jarnac. But with only weak local support in the Limousin, Coligny was not able to build on this victory, and quickly moved his men in the direction of Perigord.

Accounts of event published prior to 1570
Memoires de la III. guerre civile, pp. 117-21.

The *Memoires de la III. guerre civile* offers substantial details about the course of the battle that are identical to ones found in the print. However, the two do not match exactly in their depictions of the deployment of the various Protestant troop units, nor does each work identify by name exactly the same participants. Six of the ten captains or commanders identified by name in the key to the print (Briquemault, Mouy, La Loue, Rouvray, La Motte, and Brillaut) are also mentioned in the account in the *Memoires.* This likewise accords the last two of these the leading role in the attack against Strozzi's men that led to their rout and his capture, even though they were initially protected behind a palisade (cf. key letters M, T). It asserts that 5-600 Catholics were killed "et trente que capitaines en chef, Lieutenans, qu'enseignes" (cf. letter key V). Not mentioned in the *Memoires* but identified by name in the print are Autricourt, Avantigny, and Soubise.

Historical bibliography
Franck Delage, *La troisième guerre de religion en Limousin. Combat de La Roche-l'Abeille* (Limoges, n.d.).

34. *The Siege of Poitiers/ Poityers assiegé par M. les Princes le 24. de Juilet & tout Aoust jusques au 7. de Septembre 1569*

Etching. Titles and captions known in French and German.

The event. Moving northward after the victory at La Roche-L'Abeille, Coligny and his German allies directed their attention at the provincial capital of Poitiers, under Catholic control, which they besieged on July 24. The city's defence was led by the young duke Henri of Guise and the count of Lude, governor of Poitou. Over a thousand experienced cavalrymen, many Italian or German, also took part. Although the attackers made a number of breaches in the wall and attempted several assaults, they were thrown back each time. The siege lasted for more than six weeks before the attacking Huguenots finally abandoned it. Their losses due to disease, combat, and desertion numbered in the thousands.

Accounts of event published prior to 1570
Discours du succes des affaires passez au siege de Poictiers . . . Envoyé à Monseigneur de Mandelot Gouverneur de Lyon (Paris, H. de Marnef, 1569; Rouen: Martin Le Mégissier, n.d.; n.p., n.d.).
[Martin Liberge], *Ample discours de ce qui c'est faict et passé au siege de Poictiers* (Paris: Nicolas Chesneau, 1569).
Memoires de la III. guerre civile, pp. 153-85.

Other contemporary visual representations
Vero disegno della nobilissima Citta di Poitiers . . .Con il tremendo assedio di essa, etching, 33 × 40 cm [BN, C & P, Rés Ge DD 1140 (78)].
François Nautré, *Figure et plan de la ville de Poictiers assiegee 1569 par Gaspard de Coligni Admiral de France, estant lors Maire Sire Joseph Le Bascle; la dite figure levee par commandement de Sire Jan Pidoux Maire et de messieurs les Pairs et Eschevins, l'an 1619*, oil on canvas, 194 × 365 cm, Musée Sainte-Croix, Poitiers.

The Italian news print about the event includes a number of details about the batteries unleashed against the city, but none of these details match those provided in this print. The long pamphlet account based upon a letter sent to Mandelot reports the initial battery against the Anjoubert bridge (cf. key letter C) and a number of subsequent episodes, but the chronology and details it provides rarely match the print. The longer history by the Catholic eyewitness Liberge reports the episodes indicated by letters D through M. Both it and the preceding account also highlight several incidents omitted from the print, notably an unsuccessful final assault against the city launched on September 3. While there is considerable agreement between Liberge's history and the image, small differences can also be noted. Liberge indicates that 800 cannon shots were fired in the fusillade of August 24; key letter L says 700; the Paris news pamphlet offers no specifics. The details about the demolition of the tower of the St Cyprien bridge (key letter D) highlight different aspects of this operation. Liberge does not mention, as does key letter F, that those captured during the sortie of August 12 were taken into the city. The *Memoires de la III. guerre civile* mentions all of the details shown in the sections of the print corresponding to letters C through M.

It also asserts that 700 cannon shots were fired on August 24 and that the reiters captured on August 12 were taken into the city. It mentions that once the tower on the St Cyprien bridge was knocked down, the defenders who had previously stationed themselves at the top of the tower could no longer harm the attackers who had taken control of St Cyprien abbey (cf. key letter D). The *Memoires de la III. guerre civile* also recounts the assault of September 3 absent from the print. Liberge reports that the defenders lost 20 "valiant gentlemen" of whom 10-12 bore the title of captain; 60-80 soldiers; and a "large number" of the common people put to work rebuilding breaches in the ramparts and walls. He estimates 2,000 losses among the attackers, not counting the many deserters. The *Discours du succes* says that the defenders lost a third of their soldiers and about a thousand of the civilians put to work on the fortifications. It places losses among the attackers at 4-5,000 dead. The *Memoires* says nothing about casualties on either side.

35. *The Battle Order at Moncontour/ L'ordonnance des deux armees pres de Moncontour le 3 Octob. 1569*

Etching. Titles and captions known in French, Latin, Italian, and German.

The event. After rebuilding their forces, the royal commanders were able to pursue Coligny's troops, weakened after the long, unsuccessful siege of Poitiers. They caught them on October 3 near the village of Moncontour in northern Poitou and were able to engage them in battle.

Accounts of event published prior to 1570

[Nicolas de Neufville de Villeroy], *Discours de la bataille et cruelz assaultz Donnez entre Mont-contourt et Hervaulx* (Paris: G. de Nyverd, n.d.; Rouen: Martin Le Megissier, n.d.; also under the title *Discours de la bataille du lundy troisieme jour d'octobre 1569*, Paris: Jean Dallier, n.d.; n.p., n.d.; also with modifications under the title *Discours de la bataille et victoire obtenue par le Roy sur ses ennemys et rebelles*, Tours: R. Sifleau, 1569; Orléans: E. Gibier, 1569; also with additional material under the title *Discours de la bataille gaignée par Mgr le duc d'Anjou . . . Avec la missive envoyée par S.M. à M. de Mandelot*, Lyon: M. Jove, 1569).

Le cantique du roy T.C. pour son exultation de la victoire . . . Aussi la prophétie encontre Geneve (Lyon, 1569).

La complainte du regret de Gaspard de Colligny, qui fut admiral de France (Lyon, 1569).

Memoires de la III. guerre civile, pp. 199-211.

Other contemporary visual representations

Il ordene del fattodarme fano ira Catolici et Ugonotti alle 3 di ottobre 1569 nella gran campania di Marconiet vicina a Moncontour, intaglio, 33.5 × 44.5 cm [BN, Estampes, Hennin 631].

Victoria di Chatolici contra Hugonoti, intaglio, 42 × 30 cm [BN, C & P, Res Ge DD 1140 (79)].

The long roll of combatants on both sides shown here lists far more participants than any known prior account. The widely reprinted news pamphlet based on Villeroy's account identifies 17 Catholic commanders but only indicates the general disposition of the Protestant forces, without identifying the commanders of the units. The Italian news print *Il ordene del fattodarme*—which aligns the Catholic troops differently from the order described in the *Discours*—offers an overlapping but not identical list of 18 Catholic commanders and identifies Coligny, Mansfeld, and "Mr de Brigniol" on the Huguenot side. The Genevan *Memoires de la III. guerre civile* names five of the Huguenot commanders and one Catholic. Nearly all of the Catholic commanders and troop units mentioned in the *Discours de la Bataille* appear among the 28 Catholic and 26 Protestant officers mentioned in the key to this print. The overlap is less great with the *Ordene del fattodarme*. The location of the various units as shown in this print sometimes matches the indications provided in the prior accounts but at other times does not. For instance, the *Discours* places the troops of Cossé and Mansfeld on the left flank of the royal forces, where they also appear in Tortorel's rendering (units O and P). It places the reiters of the marquis of Baden on their right flank, but the print places them in the rear (unit L).

36. *The Rout at Moncontour/ La desroute du camp de M. les Princes et la desfaite des Lansquenets, à Moncontour le 3 Octob. 1569*

Etching. Titles and captions known in French, Latin, and German.

The event. The royal forces took the offensive at the battle of Moncontour, attacking the Huguenot cavalry and the allied German reiters. The Protestants fell back but were able to regroup and mount a brief counter-attack. The royal cavalry and the crown's Swiss pikemen then drove into the heart of the Protestant army, routing their cavalry and overwhelming the German landsknechts. The Swiss gave their enemies no quarter, wreaking vengeance for their losses at La Roche-L'Abeille.

For the list of accounts and images of this event published prior to 1570, see the preceding note.

Although the *Memoires de la III. guerre civile* does not describe the battle order of the rival armies in detail and cannot have served as the source for the preceding image, its brief account of this battle highlights the same details that are at the center of the narrative provided by this image. It particularly emphasizes the combined attack of the royal cavalry and Swiss, supported by artillery, against the Protestant landsknechts, who were "cut to pieces" (cf. the central portion of the image and key letters E-H), and the fact that amid the rout Mansfeld and Louis of Nassau were able to coordinate an organized retreat of 14 *cornettes* of reiters, "chose remarquable en telle desroute" (cf. key letter B). It also mentions that two prominent Huguenot captains, La Noue and d'Assier, were taken prisoner. They are also the only two prominent prisoners named in the *Discours de la Bataille*—and in the print (key letters C and D). The *Discours* reports that 10,000 Protestants in all were slain, including two commanding officers, Autricourt and La Loue. The Catholics suffered 300 casualties. The *Memoires* puts the Protestant toll at 4,000-4,200, mainly landsknechts. While giving no figure for the Catholics, it insists that their casualties came primarily from the ranks of the cavalry in "large number, including great lords". The numerous dead men and horses and abandoned standards and weapons shown in this print figure the carnage of this exceptionally bloody battle. The standards are those of both parties.

37. *The Siege of St Jean d'Angély/ Sainct Jean d'Angely assiegé par le Roy Charles 9. le 14. Octob. 1569 jusques au 2. Decembre 1569.*

Woodcut. Titles and captions known in French and German.

The event. St Jean d'Angély, under Huguenot control, became the focus of the royal army after its triumph at Moncontour. Armand de Gontaut, baron de Biron, grand master of the artillery, summoned the city to surrender on October 12 and began the siege on October 16. Despite a large siege train, the attackers required almost seven weeks to complete the task, as Armand de Clermont, seigneur de Piles, organized a determined resistance. De Piles several times refused generous capitulation terms. After exhausting his ammunition, he was still able to negotiate a surrender with a badly depleted royal army that gave a safe-conduct to all those in the city who wished to leave for Angoulême. This was negotiated on December 2. The defenders marched out of the city on December 3.

Accounts of event published prior to 1570
Discours au vray de ce qui s'est passé au siege de Sainct Jean d'Angely (Angoulesme: Jean de Minieres, 1569; reprinted in *Histoire de Nostre temps*).
Memoires de la III. guerre civile, pp. 227-38, 253-6, 260-70.

Written by several ministers who had been inside the besieged city and dedicated in gratitude to de Piles for preserving their lives, the *Discours au vray* offers certain details also found in the image but with minor variations. For instance, it reports a sortie involving 50-60 horse led by capitain La Motte and 300-400 footsoldiers led by "des Essarts and other captains" that spiked 5-6 enemy cannon, set 15-16 sacks of powder on fire, and took two standards. (Cf. key letter L, where des Essarts is not mentioned as the captain of the footsoliders and different figures are given about the results of the sortie.) While there is considerable agreement between the *Discours au vray* and this print, the accord is total between all of the details provided in letter keys K-M and the *Memoires de la III. guerre civile* with the tiny exception that the *Memoires* states that "*almost* 100" defenders died in the siege, while letter key N says "*around* 100". Concerning the sortie reported in key letter L, the *Memoires* writes, "les assiegez firent une sortie de cinquante ou soixante chevaux, et de trois à quatre cents pietons par la porte de Nyort.... La cavallerie estoit conduite par le capitaine la Motte, lequel alla donner sur deux cornettes de cavallerie qui estoyent en garnison à la justice qui est du costé de Nyort, lesquelles ayant rompu, il en tua quelques uns, print l'un des drappeaux, et amena en la ville l'un des cornettes blessé, dont il mourut tost apres. Les gens de pied estoyent conduits par plusieurs Capitaines qui donnerent dans les trenchees des Catholiques: lesquelles ils leur firent abandonner avec les colouvrines, qui furent incontinent enclouees, et le feu mis à cinq ou six cacques de poudre. Prindrent aussi un drappeau de gens de pied, et plusieurs armes des asseigeans: et le tout rapporterent en la ville, dans laquelle ils se retirerent tost apres. En ceste saillie furent tuez environ trente ou quarante des Catholiques, les assiegez n'y laissans qu'un des leurs qui fut blessé à la retraite." Concerning the death of Martigues reported in key letter K, it reports, "Le 29 Novembre Sebastien de Luxembourg conte de Martigues, chevalier de l'ordre, capitaine de cinquante hommes d'armes, et

Lieutenant general pour le Roy en la duché et pays de Bretaigne, fut atteint d'un coup de harquebuze à la teste, lu estant à la batterie: dont il mourut au grand regret des Catholiques."

38. *The Capture of Nîmes/ La surprinse de la ville de Nismes en Languedoc par ceux de la Religion le 15. de Novembre 1569. en la nuit*

Etching. Titles and captions known in French and German.

The event. Catholic worship was restored in Nîmes following the end of the Second Civil War, and the city was preserved under Catholic control at the eruption of the Third Civil War through the forceful action of Guillaume de Joyeuse, governor of Languedoc. On the night of November 15, 1569 Protestant troops coming from Privas and Aubenas were able to retake the city with the aid of allies within. In a prearranged plan, those inside the city removed grills protecting several mill races, enabling Huguenot soldiers to slip into the mills and hide. That night the soldiers launched an attack against the Porte des Prêcheurs timed to coincide with the arrival of a second group of men from Privas and Aubenas. The guards at the gate were overwhelmed. The city's governor, St André, broke his leg jumping from the chateau in an effort to save himself and died soon thereafter. Many other defenders of the city, officials, and priests were killed as well. Thousands of Huguenots who had fled the city during the period of Catholic domination now returned. Once retaken, Nîmes remained under Protestant control for the remainder of the Third Civil War.

Accounts of event published prior to 1570
Memoires de la III. guerre civile, pp. 258-9.

The *Memoires de la III. guerre civile* recounts all of the details of this episode figured in the print. Certain passages in the key are copied all but verbatim from this work. For instance, the *Memoires* assert (p.259), "Le sieur de Sainct-André gouverneur d'icelle, se voyant surprins pensa se sauver au chasteau: mais se jettant d'une fenestre en bas en la rue il se rompit une jambe, et fut prins, et mourut environ deux jours apres. En la ville furent tuez à ceste entree environ cent ou six vingts hommes, et peu de jours apres, quelques gens de justice." The text in key letters E & F can be seen to be virtually identical.

Historical bibliography
Ménard, *Histoire civile, ecclesiastique, et littéraire de Nismes*, V, pp. 50-56 of text and 6-11 of notes.

39. *The Foiled Attempt on Bourges/ L'entreprinse de Bourges en Berry descouverte sur ceux de la Religion le 21 de Decembre 1569*

Etching. Titles and captions known in French and German.

The event. Several Huguenot captains—the sources disagree about their names—hatched a plot with a soldier inside Catholic-controlled Bourges, Ursin Palus, to have him open a gate in the Grosse Tour and deliver the city to them. Palus double-crossed them and notified the city's governor, Claude de La Châtre, who laid a trap for the attackers. On the appointed night, December 21, François de Briquemault led 1200 men out from La Charité. After the first of these men were let through the appointed gate in the Grosse Tour, grills specially prepared for the trap were lowered behind them and explosives that had been set were detonated. Roughly a dozen attackers were killed and others were taken prisoner.

Accounts of event published prior to 1570
Discours de l'entreprinse et conspiration faicte par ceux de la nouvelle opinion. . . sur la ville de Bourges (Paris: Au Mont St Hilaire a l'enseigne du Pelican, 1569; reprinted Lyon: Michel Jove, 1570).
Memoires de la III. guerre civile, pp. 276-81.

The *Discours de l'entreprinse et conspiration* includes many of the details included in the print, including the identity of the captain of the guards of the Grosse Tour (key letter A), the number of those killed, the names of those taken prisoner (key letter D), the role of Ursin Palus, and the system of grills and explosives put in place to trap the attackers. It asserts that the attackers intended to kill all of the men in the city, marry their widows, seize the city's tax revenues, and establish a Parlement in Bourges. The *Memoires de la III. guerre civile* omits these last assertions and includes not only all of the details also found in the *Discours de l'entreprinse* that reappear in the print, but also all further precise details offered by the image such as the number of men accompanying the baron de Renty and the seigneur des Essarts (key letter D) and the number and identity of the additional troops sent to surprise the city (key letters G and H).

40. *Montbrun's Crossing of the Rhône/ La rencontre des 2 armees francoyse faicte au passage de la riviere du rosne en dauphine le 28 Mars 1570*

Etching. Titles and captions known in French and German.

The event. After the defeat at Moncontour, Coligny led most of what remained of the main body of the Protestant army south toward Montauban, where it wintered. Certain regional units were released. This print depicts a daring but relatively minor exploit accomplished by Charles Du Puy, seigneur de Montbrun, as he led perhaps 1-3,000 troops raised in Dauphiné back to their home province. To block their return, the Catholic governor of Dauphiné, Bertrand Raimbaud de Simiane, baron of Gordes, had outfitted several boats with men and arms to patrol the Rhône. Montbrun and his men were nonetheless able to cross the river. A small advance party slipped across the Rhône and hastily constructed an earthenwork fort on the Dauphiné side. The Protestants then held the gunboats at bay with fire from this fort and from their Vivarais citadel of Le Pouzin while ferrying the rest of their men across. On learning of their crossing, Gordes led his soldiers out against them, but the Protestants repulsed his attack, nearly killing him and imprisoning his lieutenant Rosset. They followed up by taking Loriol and Livron, assuring themselves control of an important stretch of the river, while Gordes's men fell back to Valence. Soon thereafter, a much larger body of Protestant troops associated with Coligny's army, which had moved eastward toward the Rhône, was able to cross the river without impediment and briefly threaten Montélimar.

No account of this event published prior to the completion of the print series is known. Brief narratives may be found in the subsequent national histories of de Thou, La Popelinière, d'Aubigné, and slightly fuller accounts in several local histories, notably Perussis' third volume, only published in the eighteenth century, and Louis Videl's 1638 biography of Lesdiguières. Perussis asserts that Montbrun crossed the river with 400 horse and two companies of infantry. He notes that Gordes's horse was shot beneath him and that his lieutenant Rosset was taken prisoner (cf. key letters D and F). Videl, who also records these details, places Montbrun's forces at 200 horse and 800 foot. So that his men would not think of retreating back into the Vivarais, Videl asserts, Montbrun sent all of his boats back across the river after ferrying his men over, giving them no choice but to stand and fight. Many of the details in the print and accompanying key—St Ange's hasty construction of an earthenwork fort, the size of the different troop units involved, the killing of Gordes's *enseigne* Bottière, the role of M. de Lusan in leading the Huguenot charge—are provided in no other source about this event that I have located.

Historical bibliography

Eugène Arnaud, *Histoire des Protestants du Dauphiné* (2 vols., Paris, 1875), I, 240-54.

PHOTO CREDITS FOR THE PLATES IN PART 2

Plates 1a, 8, 11, 13—Brit. Mus.; plate 1b—Arsenal; plates 2a, 25, 26—BN; plates 2b, 7, 16, 17, 18, 21, 22, 27, 33—Houghton Library, Harvard; plate 3a—Library of Congress; plates 3b, 4, 5, 6, 9, 10, 15, 19, 20, 24, 28, 29, 31, 32, 34, 35, 36, 37, 38, 39, 40—BPU; plates 12, 14, 23, 25 (title and key only), 30—BM Lyon.

APPENDICES

1. The Contracts for the Series

A. April 18, 1569 (AEG, notaire A. Santeur III, fo. 248)

Ledit jour hon Jaques Le Challeux tailleur d'hystoires de Rouan habitant à Genève et hon Jean Persin de Lyon peintre aussi habitant à Geneve, lesquels de leur vouloir faire (?) ont promis et promettent à Srs Nicolas Castellin et Pierre le Vignon presens et acceptans, ascavoir ledict Le Challeux de tailler sur tablettes de bois toute une hystoire circunstance et dispendances d'icelle que luy sera monstree et fournie par les dits Castellin et Le Vignon, jusques à ce qu'elle soit deuement faite, agencee et parfaicte comme apartient, jusques à point d'imprimer, et le dit Persin promet la bien duement et entierement pourtraire, ainsi qu'il apartient; à devoir commencer, ascavoir ledit Persin dez demain et sans cesser jusques à ce que ladite besongne soit faicte, et ledit Le Challeux à commencer dez le premier de may prochain jusques à ce qu'icelle besongne soit achevee. Laquelle besongne ilz promettent faire moyennant le prix et somme de quinze livres tournois pour chacun d'eux par mois, payables à chacun de mois en mois, en faisant ladite besongne. Et promettent faire l'un et l'autre ladite besongne en bonne et saine conscience sans qu'ilz decelent et descouvrent la dite besongne à homme que ce soit, jusques à ce qu'elle soit entierement imprimee et achevee pour les dits Castellin et le Vignon, aux fins de quoy ont presté expres serment de ne descouvrir, dire ny deceler ladite besongne, et ne entreprendront ny feront aucune besongne pour autruy que ceste-cy ne soit faite. Et clauses requises presents Vincent de Lanoy et Philippe Dorré habitans à Geneve, tesmoins."

B. July 23, 1569 (AEG, notaire A. Santeur VI, fo. 70)

"Marché. Ledict jour honn Jean Persin et Jacques Torterel de Lion ont promis et promettent au sr Nicole Castellin present, assavoir de lui tailler en cui[v]re et en eau forte comme ceux qu'il a convenu, toute l'hystoire à eux fournie et mise en avant par ledit Castellin et ladite besogne poursuyvre, jusques à ce qu'elle soit parachevee sans la delaisser, et ce moyennant la somme de quattre escus vaillans dix francs pour chacune planche, payables à mesure et portion que ladite besogne se fera. Presents Vincent de Lanoy et Francois Rivete."

2. Castellin and Le Vignon's Production Costs

In his 1969 study of the Genevan book trade between 1565 and 1580, Hans Joachim Bremme used the relatively copious surviving documentation about this project to explore profit margins within the book trade. His calculations led him to suggest that the partnership of Castellin and Le Vignon netted a profit of a hundred per cent or more on the *Quarante Tableaux*. Unfortunately, Bremme's calculations turn out to have been flawed in a number of ways. This appendix reviews the evidence used by Bremme and corrects it in light of what has been learned here. Even if no confident final estimate of the entrepreneurs' profits or losses can be made, the exercise offers insight into the costs of their venture that is worth presenting because information about production costs in the print publishing business is relatively scarce.

Using the known contracts about the project, Bremme placed the entrepeneurs' costs for cutting the wood blocks, etching the copper plates, buying paper, acquiring presses, and having the images printed by Jean de Laon at 3,243 livres. This broke down as follows:

90 livres for cutting the wood blocks.
400 livres for cutting the copper plates
150 livres for the roller presses and type
923 livres for 560 reams of paper of different qualities
1680 livres to print all of the sheets of paper purchased.

Bremme further computed that the number of reams of paper acquired by Castellin was enough to print 7,000 copies of the *Quarante Tableaux*. The February 1570 valuation of the goods and equipment in Castellin's house and shop places the value of his hundred books of histories at one livre apiece. If Castellin succeeded in selling 7,000 copies of the print series for that price, Bremme reasoned, he would have more than doubled his initial investment, even when the cost of shipping the work to distant markets is included. "The engraving collection of J. Tortorel and J. Perrissin . . . is evidence that a printing project could amass an extraordinary profit."[1]

In the absence of an entrepreneur's own account books, estimating the profitability of a sixteenth century venture such as this is fraught with difficulties, for merchants rarely used notaries to record every deal they struck, leaving critical gaps in the information about their outlays and income. Furthermore, Bremme misread certain documents pertaining to the project and misinterpreted others. Like most previous commentators on the *Quarante Tableaux*, he assumed that the notarized contracts pertaining to the project offered a full guide to its elaboration and consequently underestimated how long the artists involved in the project actually worked on it. Most seriously of all, he was unaware of the record of the sale of Castellin's and Le Vignon's

---

[1] Bremme, *Buchdrucker und Buchhändler zur Zeit der Glaubenskämpfe*, p. 31.

remaining assets after their death, which indicates actual sale prices for the suite of prints far below the 1570 estimate of one livre apiece. As is suggested in chapter 1, how profitable this project was would have depended above all on whether the entrepreneurs actually sold most copies of the series at a price close to the one livre estimate they placed on the value of each set in 1570, or whether sold them for little more than the 8-10 sols that the remaining copies brought at auction in 1572.

Reviewing Bremme's estimate of the project's costs brings to light four errors.

1.) The estimated cost of 90 livres to carve the wood blocks appears to be based on the assumption that Perrissin and Le Challeux each worked on these for the three months from the first to the second contract at the wages of 15 livres per month specified in the first contract. As chapter 1 makes clear, however, the carving of wood blocks continued well into 1570. Le Challeux probably worked on the project for more than a year, from May 1, 1569, the date the first contract specified that he was to begin carving the drawings furnished him by Perrissin, until some point in the middle of 1570. If we estimate that he worked for exactly one year, i.e. until May 1, 1570, he alone would have had to be paid 180 livres. Perrissin would have received at least three months' pay, or a further 45 livres, under the same contract. At least one block was given to Jean II de Gourmont to be carved. No contract tells us what he charged. The minimum costs for designing and carving the seventeen 32 × 50 cm wood blocks made for the series almost certainly exceeded 225 livres.

2.) The estimate of 400 livres to etch the copper plates seems to be based on the assumption that the artists made 40 copper plates for the series at a cost of 10 livres per plate. The July 1569 contract indeed specified a price of 4 écus or 10 "francs" (a Genevan synonym for livres) per plate, but Bremme does not appear to have realized that the artists never finished a complete set of either woodcuts or etchings, and that only 37 etchings in all were made for the series. Castellin would have owed Perrissin and Tortorel 370 livres for their labor on this. He would also have had to pay for the copper plates themselves. The February 1570 inventory of the possessions he offered as collateral lists 47 copper plates valued together at 200 livres. What is uncertain is whether this can be taken as an indication of the value of 47 unetched plates, or whether the valuation set on these plates also takes into account some of the surplus value added by the labor of the etchers.

3.) Bremme arrived at his estimate of 150 livres for the presses and type required for the project by doubling the valuation of 70 livres placed on these in the February 1570 list of the goods that Castellin mortgaged to obtain the extension of his loan from Gertrude Le Vignon. He did so because he mistakenly took the list of mortgaged assets be a post-mortem inventory of Pierre LeVignon's half of the partnership's goods. The partners' true costs for this equipment would in fact have been closer to 70 livres.

4.) The estimate of paper costs contains several errors in reading or calculation. The various surviving contracts show that Castellin and Le Vignon acquired 530 reams of paper, not 560 as Bremme asserts. When the payments made in different currencies are adjusted to a single currency, they work out to a total of 860 livres, or about 162 livres per 100 reams.

A more accurate calculation of the fixed costs involved in the project would thus yield the following estimates:

Purchasing 47 copper plates:	200 livres[2]
Designing and etching the copper plates	370 livres
Designing and carving the wood blocks	≥ 225 livres
Presses and type	70 livres
Total Fixed Costs	865 livres

Production costs can still be estimated at 3 livres per ream of paper for the printing of the series, the sum noted in the contract with Jean de Laon. The paper used would have cost just over 1 livre 12 sous per ream. Paper and printing of each 100 reams would thus have amounted to 460 livres. This would yield 1,200 copies of the full series of 40 prints and 1,600 of the original set of 30 prints.

[2] This is the valuation provided in the February 6, 1570 mortgage inventory and assumes no added value as a result of the fact that many of the plates would already have been etched.

SOURCES AND BIBLIOGRAPHY

Print collections and copies of Tortorel and Perrissin or other albums of historical prints

The following museums and libraries with important holdings of sixteenth-century prints and rare books were visited and searched methodically for copies of Tortorel and Perrissin or other early prints of a historical character: Albertina, Vienna; Biblioteca Marciana, Venice; Bibliothèque Nationale de France (Cabinet des Estampes, Collection des Cartes et Plans, Manuscrits, and Réserve de Livres Rares et Précieux); Bibliothèque de l'Arsenal, Paris; Bibliothèque Mazarine, Paris; Bibliothèque Municipale de Lyon; Bibliothèque Publique et Universitaire de Genève; The British Museum, London; The Free Library of Philadelphia; the John Hay Library, Brown University, Providence (especially the Anne S.K. Brown Military Collection); Kunstmuseum Basel (Kupferstichkabinett); Louvre, Collection Rothschild; Metropolitan Museum, New York; The National Gallery, Washington; the Newberry Library, Chicago; the Rijksmuseum (Prentenkabinet), Amsterdam; the Universitätsbibliothek Rostock; and the Zentralbibliothek, Zurich.

Between these museums and libraries and the growing volume of bibliographic resources now available on line as well as in print, the following bound volumes containing some or all of the *Quarante Tableaux* were located. Those followed by an "O" are ones that I have judged to be what I call throughout this study "old albums", i.e. either volumes of the prints bound prior to 1800 or volumes with more recent bindings containing prints from the series numbered in an early hand in a manner that suggests that the prints were all part of the same album since some point in the sixteenth or seventeenth century. Those followed by an asterisk are volumes that I have personally examined. For all others I obtained detailed descriptions from printed catalogues or through written and/or oral communication with curators of these collections.

Aberdeen University Library, pif9(44)2 Per. (O)
Biblioteca Nacional (Madrid), ER 2843 (O)
Biblioteca Nazionale (Florence), raccolta Lafrery 2 (O)
Bibliothèque Cantonale et Universitaire, Lausanne, 3 E 499 (*)
Bibliothèque de l'Arsenal, Estampes 212 (*); Estampes 330 (*); Estampes 331 (O*)
Bibliothèque de l'Histoire du Protestantisme Français (Paris), André 1154 (O)
Bibliothèque Mazarine, Rés 5921D (O*); Rés 5921E (O*); Rés 5921F (O*)
Bibliothèque Municipale d'Avignon, Estampes Atlas 75 (O)
Bibliothèque Municipale de Grenoble, Rés S 66 (O*)
Bibliothèque Municipale de Lyon, 22036 (O*); Rés 24014 (O*); 24601 (O*)
Bibliothèque Municipale de Rouen, Leber 5950 (O*)
Bibliothèque Municipale de Toulouse, Rés A XVI 27 (O)
Bibliothèque Municipale de Troyes, SG.1.606
Bibliothèque Municipale de Versailles, Rés in fol A 82m (O*)

Bibliothèque Nationale de France, Rés fo La 21a-7 (O*); Rés fo La 21-7 alpha (O*); Rés fo La 21-7 beta (O*)
Bibliothèque Nationale de Suisse, KCf 2 Rés
Bodleian Library, Antiq.b.U.1 (O*)
Deutsches Historisches Museum, Berlin, RB 92 2979 (O*)
Free Library of Philadelphia, Art P 769 T 63 (*)
Getty Museum and Library, Los Angeles, 85-B23898 (O)
Herzog August Bibliothek, Wolfenbüttel, 8.12 Hist 2o (O)
Houghton Library, Harvard University, Typ 565.70.681 F (*)
Library of Congress, Rosenwald 1074 (*)
Louvre, Collection Rothschild L 138 (*); L 139 LR (O*)
Médiathèque du Mans, SA F* 4405 (O)
Metropolitan Museum, Elisa Whittelsey Collection, accession no. 51.580.4 (O*)
Musée Condé, Chantilly, Fol CL025 (O*)
Newberry Library, Chicago, Wing fZp 539.T63 (O*)
New York Public Library, Spencer Collection (O*)
Real Biblioteca de Palacio (Madrid), IX/7226
Rijksmuseum Amsterdam, 329 A1 (*); 329 A2 (O*)
Stadt- und Universitätbibliothek Basel, Frey K I 19 (O)
Stadt- und Universitätbibliothek Bern, Kp II 47 (O*)
Universitätsbiblithek Rostock, Rb 4654 (O*)
Universität- und Landesbibliothek Halle, 1297 2o (O); Pon 11n 4100 2o (O)
Universiteitsbibliotheek Amsterdam, OF 79-1 (O*)
Zentralbibliothek Zürich, Graphische Sammlung R 54 (O)

Other particularly instructive volumes of maps or historical views that I consulted include Arsenal, fo H 1749; Bibliothèque Mazarine, Rés 5921A; Bibliothèque Municipale de Grenoble, S 66 B; Bibliothèque Nationale de France, Cartes et Plans Rés Ge EE 1402; British Library, Maps c7.e.2; Universitätsbibliothek Rostock, Da 3 (1-4).

Archival materials and manuscripts

Archives d'Etat, Geneva
Bourgeoisie, A 6, Livre de Bourgeois
Juridiction Civil H 1 a, 7
Notaires A. Santeur III, VI, P. Cusin II, III
Pieces Historiques, 1880
Registres du Conseil, 63, 64
Registres du Consistoire, 27
Registres des Particuliers, 16
Archives Municipales de Lyon
CC 1233
EE 24
GG 86, piece 1 (réserve)
Archives Nationales, Paris
Minutier Central XVIII/209
Bibliothèque Municipale de Lyon
MS 156 "De Tristibus Galliae"
Bibliothèque Publique et Universitaire, Geneva
MS Tronchin 8

Zentralbibliothek, Zurich
Wickiana, Frankreich, 12, 14, 15, 18

Published source collections and books published prior to 1800

Des aller Durchleuchtigisten Grossmechtigsten fursten und herrn herrn Maximilans Romischen Kaysers . . . Schlachten und Ritterliche Thaten. Vienna: Raphael Hofhalter, n.d. [1559].

Anjubault and H. Chardon eds. *Recueil de pièces inédites pour servir à l'histoire de la Réforme et de la Ligue dans le Maine.* Le Mans, 1867.

Aubigné, Agrippa d'. *Histoire universelle.* André Thierry ed. 11 vols., Geneva, 1981-2001.

–. *Les Tragiques.* Frank Lestringant ed. Paris, 1995.

Avertissement et complainte au peuple Francoys; Ensemble l'Histoire du tumulte d'Amboise. N.p., 1560.

Aviso de Parigi della Vitoria Anta novamente di Francia. N.p., n.d.

Avvisi novamente venuti de le cose di Francia. Dove s'intende minutamente il principio, et il fine della giornata fatta tra Chiatres & Ordan, con il numero delle genti d'arme, e cavalli de l'uno et l'altro essercito, et anco li strattagemi usati del Duca di Ghisa et del Principe de Condè. Padua: Griffo, 1563.

Aymon, Jean. *Tous les Synodes Nationales des Eglises Réformées de France.* 2 vols., The Hague, 1710.

Beauxamis, Thomas. *La marmite renversée et fondue, de laquelle Nostre Dieu parle par les saints Prophetes.* Paris, 1572.

Belleforest, Francois de. *La cosmographie universelle de tout le monde.* Paris: Nicolas Chesneau, 1575.

[Beza], *Correspondance de Théodore de Bèze.* Henri Meylan et al. ed. 28 vols. to date, Geneva, 1960-.

Borluyt, Guillaume. *Historiarum memorabilium ex Exodo, sequentibusque libris descriptio.* Lyon: Jean de Tournes, 1558.

–. *Ghesneden Figueren wyten nieuwen testamente.* Lyon: Jean de Tournes, 1557.

Brantôme, Pierre de Bourdeille, seigneur de. *Oeuvres complètes.* Ludovic Lalanne ed. 11 vols, Paris, 1864-82.

Brieve exposition des lettres du Cardinal de Lorraine envoyees du nom du Roy aux Cours des Parlemens de France. N.p., n.d.

[Burel, Jean]. *Memoires.* Saint-Vidal, 1983.

Calendar of State Papers and Manuscripts, Relating to English Affairs, Existing in the Archives and Collections of Venice. R. Brown et al. eds. 38 vols., London, 1864-1940.

Le cantique du roy T.C. pour son exultation de la victoire . . . Aussi la prophétie encontre Geneve. Lyon, 1569.

Catalogues de la collection d'estampes de Jean V, roi du Portugal par Pierre-Jean Mariette. Marie-Thérèse Mandroux-Franca and Maxime Préaud ed. 3 vols., Lisbon-Paris, 1996-2003.

Catalogue des estampes, cartes geographiques etc. de Monseigneur le Maréchal Duc d'Estrées. Paris: Jacques Guerin, 1741.

Catalogue des estampes et desseins du cabinet de feu M. d'Hermand. Paris: Gabriel Martin, 1739.

Chaumeau, Jean. *Histoire de Berry.* Lyon: Antoine Gryphius, 1566.

La complainte du regret de Gaspard de Colligny, qui fut admiral de France. Lyon, 1569.

Jean Crespin, *Actes des martyrs deduits en sept livres.* Geneva, 1564.

–. *Histoire des vrays tesmoins de la verité de l'Evangile* Geneva, 1570.

–. *Histoire des martyrs persecutez et mis a mort pour la verité de l'Evangile, depuis le temps des apostres jusques à present (1619).* Daniel Benoit ed. 3 vols., Toulouse, 1887.

La description du plant du theatre faict à Orleans, pour l'assemblée des trois estatz, avec un brief discours de la seance des tenans & representans lesdictz estatz. Paris: Vincent Sertenas, Gilles Corrozet, Guillaume Niverd, 1560.

Destruction du saccagement, exercee cruellement par le Duc de Guise et sa cohorte, en la ville de Vassy, le premier jour de Mars 1561. Caen, 1562.

Discours au vray de ce qui s'est passe au siege de Sainct Jean d'Angely. Angoulême: Jean de Minieres, 1569.

Discours au vray et en abbregé, de ce qui est dernierement advenu à Vassi, y passant Monseigneur le Duc de Guise. Paris: Guillaume Morel, 1562.

Discours de la bataille donnée par Monseigneur le Duc d'Anjou entre la ville d'Angoulesme et Jarnac, le XIII jour de mars. Lyon: B. Rigaud, 1569.

Discours de la bataille et cruelz assaultz Donnez entre Mont-contourt et Hervaulx. Paris: G. de Nyverd, n.d.

Discours de l'entreprinse et conspiration faicte par ceux de la nouvelle opinion. . . sur la ville de Bourges. Paris, 1569.

Discours du succes des affaires passez au siege de Poictiers. Paris: H. de Marnef, 1569.

Du Pinet, Antoine. *Plantz, pourtraitz et descriptions de plusieurs villes et forteresses tant de l'Europe, Asie et Afrique, que des Indes, et terres neuves.* Lyon: Jean d'Ogerolles, 1564.

Durme, M. van ed. *Supplément à la correspondance de Christophe Plantin.* Antwerp, 1955.

Epitome chronicorum regum galliae à Pharamundo ad Carolum euis nominis nonum. Una cum eorundum iconibus ad vivum, quantum fieri potuit, expressu. Paris: Guillaume Le Noir, 1566.

Epitome de la corographie d'Europe, illustré de pourtraitz des villes plus renommées d'icelle. Lyon: Balthazar Arnoullet, 1553.

Gelder, H.A. Enno van. *Gegevens betreffende roerend et onroerend bezit in de Nederlanden in de 16e eeuw.* The Hague, 1972.

Die Geuerlicheiten und eins Teils der Geschichten des loblichen Streitbaren und hochberumbten Helds und Ritters Tewrdannckhs. Nuremberg, 1517.

[Goulart, Simon]. *Mémoires de l'estat de France sous Charles neufiesme.* [Geneva: Vignon], 1576.

–. *Mémoires de la Ligue.* 2nd ed., 4 vols., [Geneva], 1602-1604.

Grodecki, Catherine ed. *Documents du minutier central des notaires de Paris: Histoire de l'art au XVIe siècle (1540-1600).* 2 vols., Paris, 1986.

Guigue, G., Kleinclausz, A. and Focillon, H. eds. *Les dessins d'élève et notes de comptabilité de Jérome Durand, peintre et verrier lyonnais 1555-1605.* Lyon, 1924.

Histoire de nostre temps contenant le recueil des choses memorables passees & publiees pour le faict de la religion, & estat de la France. Depuis la publication de l'Edict de Janvier 1561, jusques à la Declaration faicte par le Roy de sa majorité, 1563. N.p., 1566.

Histoire des triomphes de l'egli[se] Lyonnoise. Avec la prinse de Montbrison. Lyon, 1562.

Histoire du tumulte d'Amboise. Strasbourg, 1560.

Histoire ecclesiastique des eglises reformees au royaume de France. 2 vols, "Anvers" [Geneva], 1580.

Histoire ecclesiastique des eglises reformees au royaume de France. G. Baum and E. Cunitz ed. 3 vols, Paris, 1883-9.

Historia von der Liga in Franckreich. N.p., 1591.

Historia wie Jemerlich und erbarmlich die armen Christen des Reformierten Evangelischen Kirchen zu Sens aus haimlichen Practicken des Cardinals und Ezbischoften daselbst umbbracht geschmecht und verhergt worden sind. N.p., 1562.

[Joubert, Francois]. *Memoires de Francois Joubert et de Salomon de Merez de divers événements en Dauphiné.* E. Maignien ed. Grenoble, 1886.

La Juste et Saincte Defense de la ville de Lyon. Lyon, 1563.

Kaiser Maximilians Theuerdank. Facsimile reprint and commentary. 2 vols., Stuttgart, 1968.

Kinds, Karel ed. *Kroniek van de opstand in de Lage Landen, 1559-1609.* N.p., 1999.

La Fosse, Jehan de. *Les "Mémoires" d'un curé de Paris (1557-1590) au temps des guerres de religion.* Marc Venard ed. Geneva, 2004.

[Landre, Christophe and Martel, C.], *Histoire de Nostre temps, contenant un recueil des choses memorables passees et publiees pour le faict de la Religion et estat de la France depuis l'Edict de paciffication de 23. jour de Mars, 1568 justques au jour present.* N.p., 1570.

La Noue, François de. *Discours politiques et militaires.* Basel, 1595.

[La Place, Pierre de]. *Commentaires de l'Estat de la Religion et Republique soubs les Rois Henry Francois seconds, et Charles neufieme.* N.p., 1565.

La Popelinière, Lancelot Voisin, sieur de. *La vraye et entière histoire des ces derniers troubles, advenus tant en France qu'en Flandres et pays circonvoisins.* N.p., 1572.

–. *Histoire de France.* [La Rochelle: Pierre Haultin], 1581.

–. *Les Trois Mondes.* Anne-Marie Beaulieu ed. Geneva, 1997.

[La Roche Chandieu, Antoine de]. *Histoire des persecutions et martyrs de l'Eglise de Paris depuis l'An 1557. jusques au tepms du Roy Charles neufviesme.* Lyon, 1563.

L'Estoile, Pierre de. *Les Belles figures et drolleries de la Ligue.* Vol. 4 of *Mémoires-journaux.* G. Brunet, A. Champollion et al. ed. 12 vols., Paris, 1875-96.

Lettera scritta dalla corte del Re Christianissimo nella quale si racconta il successo della Giornata seguita a XIII di Marzo tra i catolici & gli ugonotti. Venice: Domenico Farri, 1569.

Lettres de Cathérine de Médicis. Hector de La Ferrière ed. 11 vols., Paris, 1880-1943.

Lettres du roy, Contenans le succinct du fait de la conspriation entreprinse contre sa maiesté. Lyon: Pierre Merant, 1560.

[Liberge, Martin]. *Ample discours de ce qui c'est faict et passe au siege de Poictiers.* Paris: Nicolas Chesneau, 1569.

Matthieu, Pierre. *Les deux plus grandes plus celebres et memorables resjouissances de la ville de Lyon.* Lyon, 1598.

Mémoires de Condé, servant d'éclaircissement et de preuves à l'Histoire de M. de Thou. 6 vols., London, 1743.

Memoires de la III guerre civile et des derniers troubles de France sous Charles IX. [Geneva: Jean Crespin], 1570.

Memoires de la troisieme guerre civile, et des derniers troubles de France. [Geneva: Jean Crespin], 1571.

Ménard, Leon. *Histoire civile, ecclesiastique, et littéraire de la ville de Nismes.* 7 vols., Paris, 1750-58.

Menestrier, C-F. *Bibliotheque curieuse et instructive de divers Ouvrages Anciens et Modernes, de Litterature et des Arts.* Trevoux, 1704.

Die Messkataloge Georg Willers. Bernhard Fabian ed. 5 vols., Hildesheim, 1972-2001.

Montaiglon, Anatole de ed. "Statuts de la corporation des peintres de Rouen." *Archives de l'Art Français* 6 (1858-60), 179-201.

Morice, Dom Hyacinthe ed. *Memoires pour servir de preuves à l'histoire ecclesiastique et civile de Bretagne.* 3 vols., Paris, 1713-46.

Neuwe livische Figuren. Frankfurt: Georg Raben, 1573.

Ode Hystoriale de la bataille de Sainct Gile. Lyon, 1563.

Paradin, Guillaume. *Historiarum memorabilium ex Genesio descriptio.* Lyon: Jean de Tournes, 1558.

Pericaud, Antoine. *Notes et documents pour servir à l'histoire de Lyon pendant la Ligue.* Lyon, 1844.

Perussiis, Loys de. *Discours des guerres de la Comté de Venayscin et de la Provence: ensemble quelques incidentz.* Avignon, 1563.

–. *Le second discours des guerres de la Comté de Venayscin.* Avignon: 1564.

Petit traitté des guerres civiles advenues en France sous les Roys François II et Charles IX. n.p., 1564.

Poldo d'Albenas, Jean. *Discours historial de l'antique et illustre cité de Nismes.* Lyon: Guillaume Rouille, 1560.

La publication des emprises du tournoy qui doibt estre faict à Paris. Paris: Gilles Corrozet and Jean Dallier, 1559.

Receuil des choses memorables passees et publiees pour le faict de la religion, & estat de la France. Le Tout Depuis la publication de l'Edit du xvii de Janvier 1560. jusques à l'Edit de la pacification des troubles de ce Royaume 1562. Strasbourg: Pierre Estiard, 1565.

Registres des déliberations du bureau de la ville de Paris. Vol. 5, ed. Alexandre Tuetey, Paris, 1892.

[Regnault, Nicolas]. *Discours veritable des guerres et troubles avenus au pays de Provence.* Lyon: Benoist Rigaut, 1564.

Rooses, Max ed. *Correspondance de Christophe Plantin*. 9 vols., Antwerp, 1885-1918. Reprint Liechtenstein, 1968.

[Rüxner, Georg]. *Anfang, ursprung und herkomen des Thurniers inn Teutscher Nation*. Simmern, 1532.

–. *Thurnier Buch*. Frankfurt-am-Main, 1566.

Saconay, Gabriel de. *Discours des premiers troubles advenus à Lyon*. Lyon, 1569.

–. *Genealogie et la fin des huguenaux, et descouverte du Calvinisme*. Lyon: Benoist Rigaud, 1572.

Seguita la dichiaratione della rotta et morte del Conde & suo essercito. Padua: L. Pasquati, n.d.

Senn, Matthias ed. *Die Wickiana. Johann Jakob Wicks Nachrichtensammlung aus dem 16. Jahrhundert. Texte und Bilder zu den Jahren 1560 bis 1571*. Zurich, 1975.

[Serres, Jean de]. *Rerum gallia ob religionem gestarum, libri tres*. [Geneva: Crespin], 1570.

Sleidan, Johann. *Histoire de l'estat de la religion et republique sous Charles V*. [Geneva]: Jean Crespin, 1556.

Stegmann, André ed. *Edits des guerres de religion*. Paris, 1979.

Stirling Maxwell, W. ed. *The Procession of Pope Clement VII and the Emperor Charles V after the Coronation of Bologna*. Edinburgh, 1875.

Vitelli, Etienne. *Commentaires sur la guerre civile de France. De la surprise de Meaux à la bataille de Saint-Denis (1567). Avec un plan d'André Thevet*. Anne Lombard-Jourdan ed. Paris, 2005.

Le vray discours de la bataille donnée par monsieur le trezieme jour de Mars, 1569 Entre Chasteauneuf et Jarnac. Paris: Guillaume de Nyverd, 1569.

La Vraye Histoire, Contenant l'inique Jugement et fausse procedure faite contre le fidele serviteur de Dieu Anne du Bourg. Geneva: Berthet, 1560.

Reference works and catalogs

Abraham Bosse, savant graveur. Paris-Tours, 2004.

A la gloire du Roi. Van der Meulen, peintre des conquêtes de Louis XIV. Dijon, 1998.

Allgemeines Lexikon der bildenden Künstler von der Antike bis zur Gegenwart begründet von Ulrich Thieme und Felix Becker. 37 vols., Leipzig, 1907-50.

Gli arazzi della battaglia di Pavia. Naples, 1999.

Andresen, Andreas. *Jost Amman, 1539-1591, Graphiker und Buchillustator der Renaissance*. Amsterdam, 1973.

Arrigoni, Paolo and Bertarelli, Achille. *Le stampe storiche conservate nella Raccolta del Castello Sforzesco*. Milan, 1932.

Audin, Marius and Vial, Eugène. *Dictionnaire des artistes et ouvriers d'art du Lyonnais*. 2 vols., Paris, 1919.

Bagrow, Leo. *Giovanni Andrea di Vavassore: A Venetian Cartographer of the 16th Century. A Descriptive List of His Maps*. Jenkintown, Pa., 1939.

Bartram, Giulia. *German Renaissance Prints 1490-1550*. London, 1995.

Baudrier, Jean. *Bibliographie lyonnaise*. 11 vols., Lyon, 1895-1914.

Bénézit, E. *Dictionnaire critique et documentaire des peintres sculpteurs dessinateurs et graveurs.* New ed. 14 vols., Paris, 1999.

Boutier, Jean. *Les plans de Paris des origines (1493) à la fin du XVIIIe siècle: Etude, carto-bibliographie et catalogue collectif.* Paris, 2002.

Borroni Salvadori, Fabia. *Carte, piante e stampe storiche delle raccolte lafreriane della Biblioteca Nazionale di Firenze.* Rome, 1980.

Brun, Carl ed. *Schweizerisches Künstler-Lexikon.* 4 vols., Frauenfeld, 1905-17.

Brunet, Jacques-Charles. *Manuel du Libraire et de l'amateur des livres.* 5th ed., 6 vols., Berlin, 1922.

[Burgkmair]. *Hans Burgkmair, das graphische Werk.* Stuttgart, 1973.

Bury, Michael. *The Print in Italy 1550-1620.* London, 2001.

Bussmann, K and Schilling, Heinz eds. *1648: War and Peace in Europe.* 3 vols., Münster-Osnabrück, 1998.

Cohn, Marjorie B. *A Noble Collection: The Spencer Albums of Old Master Prints.* Cambridge, Ma., 1992.

[Cranach]. *Lucas Cranach d. Ä. Das gesamte graphische Werk.* Munich, n.d.

Dackerman, Susan. *Painted Prints: The Revelation of Color.* Baltimore, 2002.

D'Encre et de sang. Les guerres de religion gravées par Tortorel et Perrissin (1570). Ecouen-Noyon, 2006.

The Dictionary of Art. 34 vols., New York, 1996.

Drugulin, W. *Historischer Bildatlas.* Leipzig, 1863.

Duplessis, G. *Inventaire de la collection d'estampes relatives à l'histoire de France, leguée en 1863 à la Bibliothèque Nationale par Michel Hennin.* 4 vols., Paris, 1877-82.

Einblattholzschnitte des XV. Jahrhunderts aus dem Kupferstichkabinett Basel. Basel, 1994.

French, Joseph ed. *Tooley's Dictionary of Mapmakers.* Revised edition. 2 vols. to date, Tring, Hertfordshire, 1999- .

The French Renaissance in Prints from the Bibliothèque Nationale de France. Los Angeles, 1994.

Ganado, Albert. *Valletta Città Nuova. A Map History (1566-1600).* Valletta, 2003.

– and Agius-Vadalà. *A Study in Depth of 143 Maps Representing the Great Siege of Malta of 1565.* Valletta, 1994.

Gardy, Frédéric. *Bibliographie des oeuvres théologiques, littéraires, historiques et juridiques de Théodore de Bèze.* Geneva, 1960.

Geisberg, Max. *The German Single-Leaf Woodcut 1500-1550.* Rev. ed., 4 vols., New York, 1974.

Giesendorf, Paul-F. *Bibliographie raisonnée de l'histoire de Genève des origines à 1798.* Geneva, 1966.

Gilmont, Jean-François. *Bibliographie des éditions de Jean Crespin, 1550-1572.* 2 vols., Verviers, 1981.

González de Zárate, Jesús María. *Real Colección de Estampas de San Lorenzo de El Escorial.* 11 vols., Vitoria, 1992.

Die Graphiksammlung des Humanisten Hartmann Schedel. Munich, 1990.

Graven Images: The Rise of Professional Printmakers in Antwerp and Haarlem, 1540-1640. Evanston, 1993.

Haag, E. and E. *La France protestante.* 2nd ed., 6 vols, Paris, 1877-88.

Hans Holbein the Younger: The Basel Years 1515-1532. Basel, 2006.

Harms, Wolfgang and others eds. *Deutsche Illustrierte Flugblätter des 16. und 17. Jahrhunderts.* 5 vols. to date, Munich and Tübingen, 1980 - .

Hauser, Henri. *Les sources de l'histoire de France. XVIe siècle (1494-1610).* 4 vols., Paris, 1906-15.

Hellwig, Fritz. *Franz Hogenberg – Abraham Hogenberg: Geschichtsblätter.* Nördlingen, 1983.

Henkel, Arthur and Schöne, Albrecht. *Emblemata: Handbuch zur Sinnbildkunst des XVI und XVII Jahrhunderts.* Stuttgart, 1967.

Hennin, Michel. *Les monuments de l'histoire de France. Catalogue des productions de la sculpture, de la peinture et de la gravure relatives à l'histoire de la France et des Français.* 10 vols., Paris, 1856-63.

Hind, A. M. *Catalogue of Early Italian Engravings preserved in the Department of Prints and Drawings in the British Museum.* 2 vols., London, 1909-10.

Hirth, Georg. *Kulturgeschichtliche Bilderbuch aus vier Jahrhunderten.* 2 vols., Munich, 1923.

Hollstein, F.W.H. et al. *Dutch and Flemish Etchings, Engravings and Woodcuts, ca. 1450-1700.* 57 vols., Amsterdam, 1949- .

–. *German, Engravings, Etchings and Woodcuts, ca. 1450-1700.* 55 vols., Amsterdam, 1954-.

Images Parisiennes du XVIe siècle rue de Montorgueil. Auction catalog, Galerie de Chartres, 2004.

Italian Etchers of the Renaissance and Baroque. Boston, 1989.

Jérome Cock, éditeur d'estampes et graveur 1507?-1570. Brussels, 1970.

Kagan, Richard ed. *Spanish Cities of the Golden Age: The Views of Anton van den Wyngaerde.* Berkeley, 1989.

Kaiser Maximilian I. Bewahrer und Reformer. Wetzlar, 2002.

Karrow, Robert W. Jr. *Mapmakers of the Sixteenth Century and Their Maps: Bio-Bibliographies of the Cartographers of Abraham Ortelius, 1570.* Chicago, 1993.

Landwehr, John. *Romeyn de Hooghe the Etcher: Contemporary Portrayal of Europe 1662-1707.* Dobbs Ferry, NY, 1973.

Lindsay, Robert O. and Neu, John. *French Political Pamphlets 1547-1648: A Catalog of Major Collections in American Libraries.* Madison, 1969.

Linzeler, André and Adhémar, Jean. *Inventaire du fonds français: Graveurs du XVIe siècle. Bibliothèque Nationale département des estampes.* 2 vols., Paris, 1932-38.

Martin-de Vesvrotte, Sylvie. *Dictionnaire des graveurs-éditeurs et marchands d'estampes à Lyon aux XVIIe et XVIIIe siècles et catalogue des pièces éditées.* Lyon, 2002.

Mauquoy-Hendrickx, Marie. *Les estampes des Wierix conservées au Cabinet des Estampes de la Bibliothèque Royale Albert 1er. Catalogue raisonné.* 3 vols., Brussels, 1979.

McDonald, Mark ed. *The Print Collection of Ferdinand Columbus (1488-1539): A Renaissance Collector in Seville*. 3 vols., London, 2004.

Le Monde selon François Dubois. Lausanne, 2003.

Parshall, Peter and Schoch, Rainer. *Origins of European Printmaking: Fifteenth-Century Woodcuts and Their Public*. Washington, 2005.

Pastoureau, Mireille. *Les Atlas français XVIe-XVIIe siècles. Répertoire bibliographique et étude*. Paris, 1984.

Préaud, Maxime. *Les effets du soleil. Almanachs du règne de Louis XIV*. Paris, 1995.

–, Cassselle, Pierre, Grivel, Marianne, and Le Bitouzé, Corinne. *Dictionnaire des éditeurs d'estampes à Paris sous l'Ancien Régime*. Paris, 1987.

Reallexikon zur deutschen Kunstgeschichte. 9 vols. to date, Stuttgart-Munich, 1937- .

La Révolution par la gravure. Les Tableaux historiques de la Révolution française, une entreprise éditoriale d'information et sa diffusion en Europe (1791-1817). Vizille, 2002.

Robert-Dumesnil, A.P.F. *Le peintre graveur français*. 11 vols., Paris, 1835-71.

Rosand, David and Muraro, Michelangelo. *Titian and the Venetian Woodcut*. Washington, 1976.

Rüge, W. "Alteres kartographische Material in deutschen Bibliotheken," *Nachrichten von der Königliche Gesellschaft der Wissenschäftlicher in Göttingen* (1904): 40-64.

Schlachten, Schlachten, Schlachten. Vienna, 1984.

Seelig, Gero and Bartrum, Giulia eds. *Jost Amman*. New Hollstein German 4, 2 vols., Rotterdam, 2001.

Sellink, Manfred ed., *Philips Galle*. New Hollstein Dutch and Flemish 10, 4 vols., Rotterdam, 2001.

Sman, Gert Jan van der. *Le siècle de Titien. Gravures vénitiennes de la Renaissance*. Zwolle, 2003.

Spike, John T. *L'incisione del corteo trionfale di Carlo V di Nicolaus Hogenberg*. Urbania, 1999.

Stadt und Hof: Schwerin als Residenzstadt im 16. Jahrhundert. Schwerin, 1995.

Strauss, Walter L. *Hendrik Goltzius 1558-1617: The Complete Engravings and Woodcuts*. 2 vols., New York, 1977.

Sylvestre, M. L.-C. *Marques typographiques*. Paris, 1853.

Tanis, James and Horst, Daniel. *Images of Discord: A Graphic Interpretation of the Opening Decades of the Eighty Years' War*. Bryn Mawr, 1993.

Tooley, Ronald Vere. *Tooley's Dictionary of Mapmakers*. New York, 1979.

Waals, Jan van der. *Prenten in de Gouden Eeuw van kunst tot kastpapier*. Rotterdam, 2006.

Weber, Bruno ed. *Wunderzeichen und Winkeldrucker 1543-1586: Einblattdrucke aus der Sammlung Wickiana in der Zentralbibliothek Zürich*. Zurich, 1972.

Wien 1529. Die erste Turkenbelagerung. Vienna, 1979.

Wüthrich, Lucas Heinrich. *Das druckgraphsiche Werk von Matthaeus Merian d.a.* Basel, 1966.

Books and articles published since 1800

Adamson, John ed. *The Princely Courts of Europe 1500-1750.* London, 1999.

Adhémar, Jean. "La Rue Montorgueil et la formation d'un groupe d'imagiers parisiens au XVIe siècle," *Le Vieux Papier* 21 (1954): 25-34.

–. "Information gravée en France au XVIIe siècle: Images sur cuivre destinées à un public bourgeois et élégant" in Jean Pierre Seguin ed. *L'Informazione in Francia nel Seicento.* Bari, 1983.

Alpers, Svetlana. *The Art of Describing: Dutch Art in the Seventeenth Century.* Chicago, 1983.

Arblaster, Paul. "Current-affairs Publishing in the Habsburg Netherlands, 1620-1660, in Comparative European Perspective" Oxford University D. Phil. thesis, 1999.

Arnaud, Eugène. *Histoire des Protestants du Dauphiné.* 2 vols., Paris, 1875.

–. *Histoire des Protestants de Provence, du Comtat Venaissin et de la Principauté d'Orange.* Paris, 1884.

–, *Histoire des Protestants du Vivarais et du Velay.* 2 vols., Paris, 1888.

Aspects de la propagande religieuse. Geneva, 1957.

Avery, Charles. "Antwerp, August 1577: The 'Spanish Fury' and the Liberation of the Citadel: A Series of Bronze Plaquettes after Martin de Vos," *The Connoisseur* (August 1977): 252-63.

Baker, Christopher, Elam, Caroline and Warwick, Genevieve eds. *Collecting Prints and Drawings in Europe, c. 1500-1750.* Aldershot, 2003.

Baldass, Ludwig. *Der Kunstlerkreis Kaiser Maximilians.* Vienna, 1923.

Barbier, Frédéric et al eds. *Le livre et l'historien.* Geneva, 1997.

Becker, C. *Jobst Amman, Zeichner und Formschneider, Kupferätzer und Stecker.* Nieuwkerk, 1961.

Beijerman-Schols, J. et al. *Geschiedenis in Beeld.* Zwolle, 2000.

Benedict, Philip. "Of Marmites and Martyrs: Images and Polemics in the French Wars of Religion" in *The French Renaissance in Prints.* Los Angeles, 1994.

–, Bryant, Lawrence and Neuschel, Kristen. "Graphic History: What Readers Knew and Were Taught in the *Quarante Tableaux* of Perrissin and Tortorel," *French Historical Studies* 28 (2005): 175-230.

Bercé, Yves-Marie and Fasano Guarini, Elena eds. *Complots et conjurations dans l'Europe moderne.* Rome, 1996.

Bingel, Hermann. *Das Theatrum Europaeum, ein Beitrag zur Publistik des 17. und 18. Jahrhunderts.* Wiesbaden, 1969.

Blanc, Nathalie. "Imprimeurs et imprimés à Lyon pendant le consulat protestant 1562-1563". Mémoire de maitrise, Université de Lyon II, 1999.

Bonnaure, Pierre. "Des images à relire et à réhabiliter. L'oeuvre gravé de Tortorel et Perrissin," *BSHPF* 138 (1992): 475-514.

Boorsch, Suzanne. "*The Massacre of the Innocents* after Francesco Salviati by Giovanni Battista Cavalieri," *PQ* 16 (1999): 266-73.

Bordier, Henri. *Peinture de la Saint-Barthélemy par un artiste contemporain comparée avec les documents historiques.* Geneva, 1878.

Borea, Evelina. "Stampa figurativa e pubblico dalle origini all'affermazione nel Cinquecento." *Storia dell'arte italiana.* Part 1 *Materiali e problemi.* Vol. 2 *L'artista et il pubblico.* Turin, 1979.

Borgeaud, Charles. *Histoire de l'Université de Genève. L'Académie de Calvin 1559-1798.* Geneva, 1900.

Bourne, Molly. "Francesco II Gonzaga and Maps as Palace Decoration in Renaissance Mantua," *Imago Mundi* 51 (1999): 51-82.

Bouza, Fernando. *Communication, Knowledge, and Memory in Early Modern Spain.* Philadelphia, 1999.

Bowen, Karen L. "Illustrating Books with Engravings: Plantin's Working Practices Revealed," *PQ* 20 (2003): 3-33.

– and Imhof, Dirk. "18,257 Impressions from a Plate," *PQ* 22 (2005): 265-78.

– and Imhof, Dirk. *Plantin and the European Book Market: Introducing Engraved Illustrations in the Sixteenth Century.* forthcoming Cambridge, 2007.

Boyer, Jean-Claude. "Les représentations guerrières et l'évolution des arts plastiques en France au XVIIe siècle." *XVIIe Siècle* 148 (1985): 291-307.

Brassart, Wolfgang. *Das Historienbild im Zeitalter der Eloquenz von Raffael bis Le Brun.* Berlin, 2003.

Bremme, Hans Joachim. *Buchdrucker und Buchhändler zur Zeit der Glaubenskämpfe. Studien zur Genfer Druckgeschichte 1565-1580.* Geneva, 1969.

Brown, John L. *The Methodus ad Facilem Historiarum Cognitionem of Jean Bodin: A Critical Study.* Washington, 1939.

Brun, Robert. *Le livre français illustré de la Renaissance.* Paris, 1969.

Buisseret, David "Les ingénieurs du roi au temps de Henri IV," *Comité des Travaux Historiques et Scientifiques: Bulletin de la Section de Géographie* 77 (1964): 13-84.

– ed. *Monarchs, Ministers and Maps: The Emergence of Cartography as a Tool of Government in Early Modern Europe.* Chicago, 1992.

Bulgarelli, Tullio. *Gli Avvisi a stampa in Roma nel Cinquecento.* Rome, 1967.

Burke, Peter. "Early Modern Venice as a Center of Information and Communication" in John Martin and Dennis Romano eds. *Venice Reconsidered: The History and Civilization of an Italian City-State 1297-1797.* Baltimore, 2000.

–. *Eyewitnessing. The Uses of Images as Historical Evidence.* Ithaca, 2001.

–. "Rome as a Center of Information and Communication for the Catholic World, 1550-1650" in Pamela M. Jones and Thomas Worcester eds. *From Rome to Eternity: Catholicism and the Arts in Italy, ca. 1550-1650.* Leiden, 2002.

Cameron, Keith. *Henri III, a Maligned or Malignant King? Aspects of the Satirical Iconography of Henri de Valois.* Exeter, 1978.

Campbell, Tony. *The Earliest Printed Maps 1472-1500.* London, 1987.

Caprariis, Vittorio de. *Propaganda e pensiero politico in Francia durante le guerre de religione I (1559-1572).* Naples, 1959.

Carlino, Andrea. "Fatti contraffatti tra curiosità e scienza. Note su Konrad Gesner e la collezione di fogli volanti di Johann Jacob Wick," *Art + Architecture en Suisse* 57 (2006): 37-44.

Cederlöf, Olle. "The Battle Painting as a Historical Source: An Inquiry into the Principles." *Revue Internationale d'Histoire Militaire* 26 (1967): 119-44.

Censer, Jack et al. "Imaging the French Revolution: Depictions of the French Revolutionary Crowd: An On-Line Collaboration". *Http://chnm.gmu.edu/revolution/imaging.*

Chaix, Paul. *Recherches sur l'imprimerie à Genève de 1550 à 1564.* Geneva, 1954.

–. "Un pamphlet genevois du XVIe siècle: *l'Antithèse* de S. Du Rosier. Recherche iconographique" in *Mélanges offerts à M. Paul-E. Martin.* Mémoires et Documents publiés par la Société d'Histoire et d'Archéologie de Genève 40. Geneva, 1961.

Chareyre, Philippe. "Le Consistoire de Nîmes 1561-1685". Thèse de doctorat, Université Paul Valéry Montpellier, 1987.

Chartier, Roger and Martin, Henri-Jean eds. *Histoire de l'édition française.* 4 vols., Paris, 1982-6.

Chatelain, Jean-Marc. *La bibliothèque de l'honnête homme. Livres, lecture et collections en France à l'âge classique.* Paris, 2003.

Chazalon, Christophe. "Les *Icones* de Théodore de Bèze (1580) entre mémoire et propagande," *BHR* 66 (2004): 359-76.

–. "Histoire du livre illustré à Genève (1478-1600)," *Art + Architecture en Suisse* 57 (2006): 24-31.

Checa Cremades, Fernando. *Carlos V. La Imagen del poder en el Renacimento.* Madrid, 1999.

Choisy, Albert. "Identification du monogrammiste M.B.," *BSHAG* 7 (1939-42): 292-3.

Clifton, James. "Adriaen Huybrechts, the Wierix Brothers, and Confessional Politics in the Netherlands," *NKJ* 52 (2001): 105-25.

Cocula, Anne-Marie. "Dreux, Jarnac, Coutras: le rebondissement de la vendetta des grands". *Quatrième centenaire de la bataille de Coutras.* Avènement d'Henri IV, Quatrième
Cententaire, I, Coutras. Pau, 1988.

Courboin, François. *Histoire illustrée de la gravure en France.* Part 1, *Des origines à 1660.* Paris, 1923.

Courteault, Paul. *Blaise de Monluc historien. Etude critique sur le texte et la valeur historique des* Commentaires. Paris, 1908.

Coynart, Raymond de. *L'année 1562 et la bataille de Dreux.* Paris, 1894.

Crouzet, Denis. *Les guerriers de dieu. La violence au temps des troubles de religion (vers 1525-vers 1610).* 2 vols., Seyssel, 1990.

Cuneo, Pia. *Art and Politics in Early Modern Germany: Jörg Breu the Elder and the Fashioning of Political Identity ca. 1475-1536.* Leiden, 1998.

– ed. *Artful Armies, Beautiful Battles: Art and Warfare in Early Modern Europe.* Leiden, 2002.

Cust, Richard. "News and Politics in Early Stuart England," *Past and Present* 112 (1986): 60-90.

Dahl, Folke, Petibon, Fanny and Boulet, Marguerite. *Les débuts de la presse française. Nouveaux aperçus.* Göteborg, 1951.

Dardier, Charles. "Jean de Serres historiographe du roi. Sa vie et ses écrits d'après des documents inédits 1540-1598," *Revue Historique* 22 (1883): 291-328.

Davis, Natalie Zemon. "On the Protestantism of Benoît Rigaud," *BHR* 17 (1955): 246-51.

– "Le milieu social de Corneille de La Haye (Lyon, 1533-1575)," *Revue de l'Art* 47 (1980): 21-8.

Debal, Jacques. "Les plans et perspectives d'Orléans de Gilles Hotot à Charles Pensée," *Bulletin de la Société d'Archéologie et d'histoire de l'Orléanais* 13 (1994): 102-27.

–. *Orléans, une ville, une histoire*. Orléans, 1998.

Decrue, Francis. *Anne duc de Montmorency connétable et pair de France sous les rois Henri II, François II et Charles IX*. Paris, 1889.

Delage, Franck. *La troisième guerre de religion en Limousin. Combat de La Roche-L'Abeille*. Limoges, n.d.

Delen, A.J.J. *Histoire de la gravure dans les anciens Pays-Bas et dans les provinces belges des origines à la fin du XVIII*e *siècle* Part 2 *Le XVI*e *siècle – les graveurs illustrateurs*. Paris, 1934.

Denucé, Jan. *Oud-Nederlandsche Kaartmakers in Betrekking met Plantijn*. 2 vols, Antwerp, 1912.

Deonna, Waldemar. *Les arts à Genève des origines à la fin du XVIII*e *siècle*. Geneva, 1942.

–. "Un bois gravé de J. Perrissin (XVIe siècle) au Musée de Genève" in *Mélanges Louis Bosset*. Lausanne, 1950.

Desgraves, Louis. *Eloi Gibier imprimeur à Orléans (1536-1588)*. Geneva, 1966.

Dickens, A.G. and Tonkin, John M. *The Reformation in Historical Thought*. Oxford, 1985.

Dietz, Alexander. *Frankfurter Handelsgeschichte*. Frankfurt, 1910; repr. Glashütten im Taunus, 1970.

Dooley, Brendan and Brown, Sabrina A. eds. *The Politics of Information in Early Modern Europe*. London, 2001.

–. "The Wages of War: Battles, Prints and Entrepreneurs in Late Seventeenth-Century Venice," *Word and Image* 17 (2001): 7-24.

–. "Le battaglie perse del principe Giovanni," *Quaderni Storici* 115 (2004): 83-118.

Droz, Eugénie. *L'imprimerie à La Rochelle I: Barthélemy Berton 1563-1573*. Geneva, 1960.

–. *Chemins de l'hérésie*. 4 vols., Geneva, 1970-76.

Dubois, Claude-Gilbert. *La conception de l'histoire en France au XVI*e *siècle (1560-1610)*. Paris, 1977.

Dufour, Alain. *Théodore de Bèze*. Paris, 2002.

Duportal, Jeanne. *Contribution au catalogue général des livres à figures du XVII*e *siècle (1601-1633)*. Paris, 1914.

Ecker, Gisela. *Einblattdrucke von den Anfängen bis 1555*. Göppingen, 1981.

Ehrle, Francesco. *Roma prima di Sisto V*. Rome, 1908.

Ehrmann, Jean. "Massacre and Persecution Pictures in Sixteenth Century France," *JWCI* 8 (1945): 195-99.

–. *Antoine Caron: peintre des fêtes et des massacres*. Paris, 1986.

Eisler, William. "The 'Wunderkammer' of Charles V: The Emperor, Science, Technology and the Expanding World," *Annali dell'Istituto storico italo-germanico in Trento* 19 (1993): 11-52.

El Kenz, David. *Les bûchers du roi. La culture protestante des martyrs (1523-1572)*. Seyssel, 1997.

–. "La sacralisation par l'image au temps des guerres de religion. (Etude comparée des massacres d'un livret calviniste et d'un livret catholique)" in Michèle Ménard and Annie Duprat eds. *Histoire, images, imaginaires (fin XVe siècle-début XXe siècle)*. Le Mans, 1998.

Engammare, Isabelle and Gilmont, Jean-François. "La gravure réformée. De la méfiance à l'usage raisonnable et raisonné" in J.-L. Sadoulle ed., *L'histoire au prisme de l'image*. Louvain-la-Neuve, 2003.

Engammare, Max. "Les figures de la Bible. Le destin oublié d'un genre littéraire en image (XVIe-XVIIe s.)," *Mélanges de l'Ecole française de Rome: Italie et Méditeranée* 106 (1994): 549-91.

–. *L'ordre du temps. L'invention de la ponctualité au XVIe siècle*. Geneva, 2004.

Fehl, Philipp. "Vasari e Stradano come panegiristi dei Medici: Osservazioni sul rapporto tra verità storica e verità poetica nella pittura di fatti storici" in *Il Vasari storiografo e artista: Atti del Congresso internazionale nel IV Centenario della morte*. Florence, 1974.

–. "Vasari's Extirpation of the Huguenots: The Challenge of Pity and Fear," *Gazette des Beaux-Arts* 84 (1974): 257-84.

Fischer, Elizabeth. "Quelques considérations sur l'image de l'Escalade au XVIIe siècle," *Genava* 50 (2002): 65-72.

Fox, Adam. *Oral and Literate Culture in England 1500-1700*. Oxford, 2000.

Fragonard, Marie-Madeleine. *La poésie religieuse d'Agrippa d'Aubigné et son expression*. Paris, 2004.

Franklin, Alfred ed. *Les grandes scènes historiques du seizième siècle*. Paris, 1886.

Galinier, Cécile. "Le receuil de Tortorel et Perrissin". Mémoire de maitrise, Université de Paris IV-Sorbonne, 1996.

Garnier, Armand. *Agrippa d'Aubigné et le parti protestant. Contribution à l'histoire de la Réforme en France*. 3 vols., Paris, 1928.

Gigon, S-C. *La troisième guerre de religion: Jarnac-Moncontour*. Paris, 1909.

Gilmont, Jean François. *Jean Crespin, un éditeur réformé du XVIe siècle*. Geneva, 1981.

–. "Les premières éditions des ouvrages historiques de La Place et de La Popelinière" in R. Peter and B. Roussel eds., *Le livre et la Réforme*, special issue of the *Revue Française de l'Histoire du Livre* (1987), 119-52.

–. "La première diffusion des 'Mémoires de Condé' par Eloi Gibier en 1562-1563" in P. Aquilon and Henri-Jean Martin eds. *Le livre dans l'Europe de la Renaissance*. Paris, 1988.

Glorieux, Guillaume. *A l'enseigne de Gersaint. Edme-François Gersaint, marchand d'art sur le pont Notre-Dame (1694-1750)*. Seyssel, 2002.

Gombrich, E. H. *Art and Illusion: A Study in the Psychology of Pictorial Representation*. New York, 1961.

Grafton, Anthony and Jardine, Lisa. "'Studied for Action': How Gabriel Harvey Read His Livy," *Past & Present* 129 (1990): 30-78.

Graves, Amy. "La méthode pragmatique: la pratique de l'histoire dans les *Mémoires de Condé* et leurs prolongations," in D. Bohler and C. Maignien Simonin eds., *Ecritures de l'histoire (XIVe-XVIe siècles).* Geneva, 2005.

–. "Memory, Tragedy and History: The Poetics of Agrippa d'Aubigné's Account of the Saint Bartholomew's Day Massacre," *Renaissance Journal* 2 (2005): 30-48.

Greffe, Florence and Lothé, José. *La vie, les livres et les lectures de Pierre de l'Estoile.* Paris, 2004.

Grivel, Marianne. *Le commerce de l'estampe à Paris au XVIIe siècle.* Geneva, 1986.

Groebner, Valentin. *Defaced: The Visual Culture of Violence in the Late Middle Ages.* New York, 2004.

Groenveld, Simon. "Het Engelse kroniekje van Walter Morgan en een onbekende reeks historieprenten (1572-1574)," *Bijdragen en Mededelingen betreffende de Geschiedenis der Nederlanden* 98 (1983): 19-74.

Guigue, Georges. "Jean Perrissin peintre lyonnais (1564-1608)," *Réunion des Sociétés des Beaux-Arts des départements* (1891): 429-60.

Guilleminot, Geneviève. "Religion et politique à la veille des guerres civiles. Recherches sur les impressions françaises de l'année 1561." Thèse de l'Ecole des Chartes, Paris, 1977.

Hajós, Elizabeth M. "The Concept of an Engravings Collection in the Year 1565: Quicchelberg, *Inscriptiones vel Tituli Theatri Amplissimi,*" *Art Bulletin* 40 (1958): 151-5.

Hale, J.R. *Artists and Warfare in the Renaissance.* New Haven, 1990.

Haskell, Francis. *History and Its Images: Art and the Interpretation of the Past.* New Haven, 1993.

Hepp, Frieder. *Religion und Herrschaft in der Kurpfalz um 1600 Aus der Sicht des Heidelberger Kirchenrats Dr. Marcus zum Lamm (1544-1606).* Heidelberg, 1993.

Herz, Alexandra. "Vasari's Massacre Series in the Sala Regia–the Political, Juristic, and Religious Background." *Zeitschrift für Kunstgeschichte* 49 (1986): 41-54.

Highley, Christopher and King, John N. eds. *John Foxe and His World.* Aldershot, 2002.

Higman, Francis M. "Le domaine français, 1520-1562" in Jean-François Gilmont, *La Réforme et le livre. L'Europe de l'imprimé (1517-v. 1570).* Paris, 1990.

Histoire générale de la presse française. Vol. 1, *Des origines à 1814.* Paris, 1969.

Horn, Hendrik J. *Jan Cornelisz Vermeyen: Painter of Charles V and His Conquest of Tunis.* 2 vols., Doornspijk, 1989.

Horst, Daniel R. *De Opstand in zwart-wit: Propaganda-prenten uit de Nederlandse Opstand (1566-1584).* Zutphen, 2003.

Infelise, Mario. *Prima dei giornale. Alle origine della publica informazione.* Rome, 2002.

Jones, Leonard Chester. *Simon Goulart, sa vie et son oeuvre 1545-1628.* Geneva, 1916.

Jouan, Andrée. "Thomas de Leu et le portrait français de la fin du XVIe siècle," *Gazette des Beaux-Arts* 6th ser. 58 (1961): 203-22.

Jouanna, Arlette et al. *Histoire et dictionnaire des guerres de religion*. Paris, 1998.

Kelley, Donald R. *Foundations of Modern Historical Scholarship: Language, Law and History in the French Renaissance*. New York, 1970.

–. *François Hotman: A Revolutionary's Ordeal*. Princeton, 1973.

–. "Johann Sleidan and the Origins of History as a Profession," *Journal of Modern History* 52 (1980): 573-98.

–. *Faces of History from Herodotus to Herder*. New Haven, 1998.

Kingdon, Robert M. *Myths about the St. Bartholomew's Day Massacres 1572-1576*. Cambridge, Ma., 1988.

Klinkert, Christi M. *Nassau in het Nieuws. Nieuwsprenten van Maurits van Nassaus militaire ondernemingen uit de periode 1590-1600*. Zutphen, 2005.

Knapp, James A. *Illustrating the Past in Early Modern England: The Representation of History in Printed Books*. Aldershot, 2003.

Knecht, Robert J. *The French Civil Wars, 1562-1598*. Harlow, 2000.

Koerner, Joseph Leo. *The Reformation of the Image*. Chicago, 2004.

Kohlndorfer, Ruth. "Jacques Bongars (1554-1612): Lebenswelt und Informationsnetzwerke eines frühneuzeitlichen Gesandten," *Francia* 28/2 (2001): 1-16.

Kunzle, David. *The Early Comic Strip: Narrative Strips and Picture Stories in the European Broadsheet from c. 1450 to 1825*. Berkeley, 1973.

–. *From Criminal to Courtier: The Soldier in Netherlandish Art 1550-1672*. Leiden, 2002.

Lacombe, Bernard de. *Les débuts des guerres de religion (Orléans, 1559-1564): Catherine de Médicis entre Guise et Condé*. Paris, 1899.

Landau, David and Parshall, Peter. *The Renaissance Print 1470-1550*. New Haven, 1994.

Lazard, Madeleine. *Agrippa d'Aubigné*. Paris, 1998.

Lehr, Henri. *La Réforme et les Eglises réformées dans le département actuel d'Eure-et-Loir (1523-1911)*. Chartres, 1912.

Lelièvre, Matthieu. *Anne Du Bourg, conseiller au Parlement de Paris et martyr (1520-1559)*. Toulouse, 1903.

Lepreux, Guy-Michel. *La peinture à Paris sous le règne de François 1er*. Paris, 2001.

Lestringant, Frank. "Quatre 'canards' topographiques d'André Thevet au début des guerres de religion – 1562-1563," *Le livre et l'estampe* 32 (1986): 157-196.

–. "Une cartographie iconoclaste: 'La Mappe-Monde Nouvelle Papistique' de Pierre Eskrich et Jean-Baptiste Trento (1566-1567)" in *Géographie du monde au Moyen Age et à la Renaissance*. Paris, 1989.

–. *André Thevet. Cosmographe des derniers Valois*. Geneva, 1991.

–. *Une sainte horreur, ou le voyage en Eucharistie XVIe-XVIIIe siècle*. Paris, 1996.

Leuschner, Eckhard and Rouillard, Philippe. "Metamorphoses of a Plate: *The Battle of Las Navas de Tolosa* by Villamena after Tempesta," *PQ* 19 (2002): 235-53.

Lever, Maurice. *Canards sanglants. Naissance du fait divers*. Paris, 1993.

Lignereux, Yann. *Lyon et le roi. De la "bonne ville" à l'absolutisme municipal (1594-1654)*. Seyssel, 2003.

Lincoln, Evelyn. *The Invention of the Italian Renaissance Printmaker.* New Haven, 2000.

Lombard-Jourdan, Anne. "La bataille de Saint-Denis (10 novembre 1567). Tradition, propagande et iconographie," *Memoires de la Fédération des Sociétés Historiques et Archéologiques de Paris et de l'Ile de France* 29 (1978): 7-54.

Manuth, Volker. "Denomination and Iconography: The Choice of Subject Matter in the Biblical Paintings of the Rembrandt Circle," *Simiolus* 22 (1993-94): 235-52.

Mariéjol, Jean H. *La Réforme et la Ligue – L'Edit de Nantes (1559-1598).* Vol. 6, part 1 of Ernest Lavisse, *Histoire de France depuis les origines jusqu'à la Révolution.* Paris, 1904.

Marnef, Guido. *Antwerp in the Age of Reformation: Underground Protestantism in a Commercial Metropolis, 1550-1577.* Baltimore, 1996.

McClelland, John. "Le tournoi de juin 1559 et les deux François de Guise" in Yvonne Bellenger ed. *Le mécénat et l'influence des Guises.* Paris, 1997.

McDonald, Mark P. "The Print Collection of Philip II at the Escorial," *PQ* 15 (1998): 15-35.

McKitterick, David. *Print, Manuscript and the Search for Order 1450-1830.* Cambridge, 2003.

Meserve, Margaret. "News from Negroponte: Politics, Popular Opinion, and Information Exchange in the First Decade of the Italian Press," *Renaissance Quarterly*: 59 (2006), 440-80.

Millet, Joshua. "A City Converted: The Protestant Reformation at Nimes, 1532-67". Harvard University Ph.D. dissertation, 2000.

Minerbi Belgrado, Anna. *L'avènement du passé. La Réforme et l'histoire.* Paris, 2004.

Monter, E. William. *Calvin's Geneva.* New York, 1967.

–. "Historical Demography and Religious History in Sixteenth-Century Geneva," *Journal of Interdisciplinary History* 9 (1979): 399-417.

Moreno Garbayo, Justa. "Grabados de la Batalla de San Quintin," *Revista de Archivos, Bibliotecas y Museos* 71 (1963): 359-70.

Morrall, Andrew. *Jörg Breu the Elder: Art, Culture and Belief in Reformation Augsburg.* Aldershot, 2001.

Mottu-Weber, Liliane. *Genève au siècle de la Réforme. Economie et Refuge.* Geneva, 1987.

Mulcahy, Rosemary. "Enea Vico's Proposed Triumphs of Charles V," *PQ* 19 (2002): 331-40.

Mulryne, J.R. and Goldring, Elizabeth eds. *Court Festivals of the European Renaissance: Art, Politics and Performance.* Aldershot, 2002.

– et al. eds. *Europa Triumphans. Court and Civil Festivities in Early Modern Europe.* Aldershot, 2004.

Naef, Henri. *La Conjuration d'Amboise et Genève.* Geneva, 1922.

–. "Justice pour La Renaudie," *BSHPF* 117 (1971): 296-316.

Nicholls, David. "Protestants, Catholics and Magistrates in Tours, 1562-1572: The Making of a Catholic City During the Religious Wars," *French History* 8 (1994): 14-33.

Nicollier-De Weck, Béatrice. *Hubert Languet (1518-1581). Un reseau politique international de Melanchthon à Guillaume d'Orange*. Geneva, 1995.

Nuti, Lucia. "The Perspective Plan in the Sixteenth Century: The Invention of a Representational Language," *Art Bulletin* 76 (1994): 105-28.

O'Connell, Sheila and Paisey, David. "*This Horryble Monster*: An Anglo-German Broadside of 1531," *PQ* 16 (1999): 57-63.

Oelke, Harry. *Die Konfessionsbildung des 16. Jahrhunderts im Spiegel illustrierter Flugblätter*. Berlin, 1992.

Orenstein, Nadine et al. "Print Publishers in the Netherlands, 1580-1620" in *Dawn of the Golden Age: Northern Netherlandish Art 1580-1620*. Amsterdam, 1993.

Paas, John Roger ed. *Augsburg, die Bilderfabrik Europas. Essays zur Augsburger Druckgraphik der Frühen Neuzeit*. Augsburg, 2001.

Pallier, Denis. *Recherches sur l'imprimerie à Paris pendant la Ligue (1585-1594)*. Geneva, 1976.

Panni, Frédéric. "Un cycle de peintures allemandes de la fin du XVIe siècle d'après les gravures de Tortorel et Perrissin". Unpublished article.

Parent, Annie. *Les métiers du livre à Paris au XVIe siècle (1535-1560)*. Geneva, 1974.

Parshall, Peter. "The Print Collection of Ferdinand, Archduke of Tyrol," *Jahrbuch der Kunsthistorischen Sammlungen in Wien* 78 (1982): 139-84.

–. "Imago Contrafacta: Images and Facts in the Northern Renaissance," *Art History* 16 (1993): 544-79.

Partridge, Loren and Starn, Randolph. "Triumphalism and the Sala Regia in the Vatican" in *Triumphal Celebrations and Rituals of Statecraft*. University Park, 1990.

Pastoureau, Mireille. "Les atlas imprimés en France avant 1700," *Imago Mundi* 32 (1980): 45-72.

Peret, Jacques. "Iconographie d'un futur roi de France: Henri de Navarre (1553-1584) in *Henri de Navarre et le royaume de France 1572-1589*. Special number of *Revue de Pau et du Béarn* (1984).

–. "L'iconographie d'Henri de Navarre à l'époque de la bataille de Coutras et au début de son règne en France: le rôle de François Bunel". *Quatrième centenaire de la bataille de Coutras*. Avènement d'Henri IV, Quatrième Cententaire, I, Coutras. Pau, 1988.

Petitfrère, Claude. "Une ville mise en scène: Tours d'après l'iconographie générale des XVIe-XVIIIe siècle" in Petitfrère ed. *Images et imaginaires de la ville à l'époque moderne*. Tours, 1998.

Pettegree, Andrew. "Protestantism, Publication and the French Wars of Religion. The Case of Caen" in Robert J. Bast and Andrew C. Gow eds. *Continuity and Change. The Harvest of Late Medieval and Reformation History*. Leiden, 2000.

–. "Protestant Printing during the French Wars of Religion. The Lyon Press of Jean Saugrain" in Thomas A. Brady et al eds. *The Work of Heiko A. Oberman*. Leiden, 2003.

–. *Reformation and the Culture of Persuasion*. Cambridge, 2005.

Piaget, Arthur and Berthoud, Gabrielle. *Notes sur le livre des martyrs de Jean Crespin*. Neuchâtel, 1930.

Pognon, E. "Les plus anciens plans de villes gravés et les événements militaires," *Imago Mundi* 22 (1968): 13-19.

Pomian, Krzysztof. *Des saintes reliques à l'art moderne: Venise-Chicago XIIIe-XXe siècle*. Paris, 2003.

Popelka, Liselotte. "Schlachtenbilder–Bemerkungen zu einer verachteten Bildgattung" in *Schlachten, Schlachten, Schlachten*. Vienna, 1984.

Poujol, Jacques. "De la confession de foi de 1559 à la Conjuration d'Amboise," *BSHPF* 119 (1973): 158-76.

Preda, Alessandra. "L'*Histoire de la Mappe-Monde Papistique* de Jean-Baptiste Trento et ses sources italiennes," *BSHPF* 145 (1999): 245-61.

Prestwich, Menna. "Patronage and the Protestants in France, 1598-1661: Architects and Painters" in Roland Mousnier and Jean Mesnard eds., *L'Age d'or du mécénat (1598-1661)*. Paris, 1985.

Racaut, Luc. *Hatred in Print: Catholic Propaganda and Protestant Identity during the French Wars of Religion*. Aldershot, 2002.

Riggs, Timothy A. *Hieronymus Cock: Printmaker and Publisher*. New York, 1977.

Robbins, Kevin C. "Rewriting Protestant History: Printing, Censorship by Pastors, and the Dimensions of Dissent among the Huguenots–the La Popelinière Case at La Rochelle, 1581-85" in Andrew Pettegree et al. eds., *The Sixteenth-Century French Religious Book*. Aldershot, 2001.

Romier, Lucien. *La carrière d'un favori. Jacques d'Albon de Saint-André maréchal de France (1512-1562)*. Paris, 1909.

–. *Les origines politiques des guerres de religion*. 2 vols., Paris, 1914.

–. *La conjuration d'Amboise*. Paris, 1923.

Rondot, Natalis. *Les Protestants à Lyon au dix-septième siècle*. Lyon, 1891.

–. *Graveurs sur bois à Lyon au seizième siècle*. Paris, 1898.

–. "Pierre Eskrich, peintre et tailleur d'histoires à Lyon au XVIe siècle," *Revue du Lyonnais* 5th ser., 31 (1901): 241-61, 321-54.

Rooses, Max. *Christophe Plantin, imprimeur anversois*. Antwerp, 1882.

Rosier, Bart. "The Victories of Charles V: A Series of Prints by Maarten van Heemskerck, 1555-56," *Simiolus* 20 (1990-91): 24-38.

Rósza, György. *Schlachtenbilder aus der Zeit der Befreiungsfeldzüge*. Budapest, 1987.

Röttgen, Herwarth. "Zeitgeschichtliche Bildprogramme der katholischen Restauration unter Gregor XIII, 1572-1585," *Münchner Jahrbuch der Bildenden Kunst* 3rd ser. 26 (1976): 89-122.

Rouillard, Philippe. "Marc-Antoine Raimondi. Les Massacres des Innocents," *Nouvelles de l'Estampe* no.179-180 (2001-2002): 13-32.

Ruble, Alphonse de. *Antoine de Bourbon et Jeanne d'Albret*. 4 vols., Paris, 1881-6.

–. *L'assassinat de François de Lorraine duc de Guise 18 février 1563*. Paris, 1897.

–. *Jeanne d'Albret et la guerre civile*. 2 vols., Paris, 1897.

Saxl, Fritz. "The Battle Scene without a Hero," *JWCI* 3 (1939-40): 70-87.

Schilling, Michael. *Bildpublizistik der frühen Neuzeit. Aufgaben und Leistungen des illustrierten Flugblatts in Deutschland bis um 1700*. Tubingen, 1990.

Schimmelpfennig, Bernhard. "The Two Coronations of Charles V at Bologna, 1530" in J.R. Mulryne and Elizabeth Goldring eds. *Court Festivals of the European Renaissance: Art, Politics and Performance*. Aldershot, 2002.

Schmidt, Peter. *Die Grosse Schlacht. Ein Historienbild aus der Frühzeit des Kupferstichs*. Wiesbaden, 1992.

Schottenloher, Karl. *Flugblatt und Zeitung: Ein Wegweiser durch das gedruckte Tagesschrifttum*. Berlin, 1922.

Schrader, Stephanie. "'Greater than Ever He Was': Ritual and Power in Charles V's 1558 Funeral Procession," *NKJ* 49 (1998): 68-93.

Scribner, R.W. *For the Sake of Simple Folk: Popular Propaganda for the German Reformation*. Cambridge, 1981.

Schumann, Jutta. "Das politisch-militärische Flugblatt in der zweiten Hälfte des 17. Jahrhunderts als Nachrichtenmedium und Propagandamittel" in Wolfgang Harms and Michael Schilling eds. *Das illustrierte Flugblatt in der Kultur der Frühen Neuzeit*. Frankfurt, 1998.

Seguin, Jean Pierre. "L'illustration des feuilles d'actualité non périodiques en France aux XVe et XVIe siècles," *Gazette des Beaux-Arts* 6th ser. 52 (1958): 35-50.

–, "La découverte de l'Italie par les soldats de Charles VIII 1494-1495 d'après les journaux occasionnels du temps," *Gazette des Beaux-Arts* 6th ser. 58 (1961): 127-34.

–. *L'information en France de Louis XII à Henri II*. Geneva, 1961.

–. *L'information en France avant la périodique: 517 canards imprimés entre 1529 et 1631*. Paris, 1964.

Senn, Matthias. *Johann Jakob Wick (1522-1588) und seine Sammlung von Nachrichten zur Zeitgeschichte*. Zurich, 1974.

Serebrennikov, Nina Eugenia. "Plotting Imperial Campaigns: Hieronymus Cock's Abortive Foray into Chorography," *NKJ* 52 (2001): 186-215.

Shapiro, Barbara J. *A Culture of Fact: England, 1550-1720*. Ithaca, 2000.

Sharratt, Peter. *Bernard Salomon illustrateur lyonnais*. Geneva, 2005.

Sman, Gert Jan van der. "Print Publishing in Venice in the Second Half of the Sixteenth Century," *PQ* 17 (2000): 235-47.

Smith, David R. "Willem Buytewech as a Journalist: Perspectives on Description and Narration," *Konsthistorisk Tidskrift* 60 (1991): 169-94.

Stock, Jan van der. *Printing Images in Antwerp: The Introduction of Printmaking in a City, Fifteenth Century to 1585*. Rotterdam, 1998.

Sutherland, N. M. *The Massacre of St Bartholomew and the European Conflict 1559-1572*. London, 1973.

Sypher, George Wylie. "La Popelinière's *Histoire de France*: A Case of Historical Objectivity and Religious Censorship," *Journal of the History of Ideas* 24 (1963): 41-54.

Tallon, Alain. *La France et le Concile de Trente (1518-1563)*. Rome, 1997.

Tedeschi, Martha. "Publish and Perish: The Career of Lienhart Holle in Ulm" in Sandra Hindman ed. *Printing the Written Word: The Social History of Books, c. 1450-1520*. Ithaca, 1991.

Terlinden, Charles. *Kaiser Karl V. Vorläufer der europäischen Idee.* Zurich, 1978.

Thierry, André. *Agrippa d'Aubigné. Auteur de l'Histoire universelle.* Lille, 1982.

Thomson, David. *Renaissance Paris: Architecture and Growth, 1475-1600.* Berkeley, 1984.

Tinsley, Barbara Sher. *History and Polemics in the French Reformation: Florimond de Raemond: Defender of the Church.* Selingsgrove, Pa., 1992.

Tulchin, Allan A. "The Michelade in Nîmes, 1567", *French Historical Studies* 29 (2006): 1-35.

Tümpel, Christian. "Jordaens, a Protestant Artist in a Catholic Stronghold: Notes on Protestant Artists in Catholic Centres" in *Jacob Jordaens (1593-1678).* Antwerp, 1993.

–. "Die Reformation und die Kunst der Niederlande" in Werner Hoffmann ed. *Luther und die Folgen für die Kunst.* Munich, 1983.

Turrel, Denise. *Le blanc de France. La construction des signes identitaires pendant les guerres de Religion (1562-1629).* Geneva, 2005.

Vaissière, Pierre de. "Jean Poltrot seigneur de Méré, meurtrier de M. de Guise (1563)," *Revue des Etudes historiques* 12 (1910): 1-61.

Veldman, Ilja M. "Keulen als toevluchtsoord voor Nederlandse kunstenaars (1567-1612)," *Oud Holland* 107 (1993): 34-57.

–. *Crispijn de Passe and His Progeny (1564-1670): A Century of Print Production.* Rotterdam, 2001.

Verbiest, Frans. "De Lierse Furie, Anno 1595 in Beeld, Boek en Blad," *Noordgouw,* I (1961): 119-43, II, 13-42.

Vermaseren, B. A. "La première édition des *Commentaires* de Jean de Serres," *BHR* 23 (1961): 118-20.

Veyrin-Forrer, Jeanne. "Un collectionneur engagé, François Rasse Des Neux, chirurgien parisien" in *La lettre et le texte. Trente années de recherches sur l'histoire du livre.* Paris, 1987.

Voet, Leon. *The Golden Compasses: A History and Evaluation of the Printing and Publishing Activities of the Officina Plantiniana at Antwerp.* 2 vols., Amsterdam, 1972.

Waal, Henri van de. *Drie Eeuwen vaderlandsche Geschied-Uitbeelding 1500-1800. Een iconologische Studie.* The Hague, 1952.

Wahrman, Dror. "From Imaginary Drama to Dramatized Imagery: The *Mappe-Monde Nouvelle Papistique,* 1566-67." *JWCI* 54 (1991): 186-205.

Watanabe-O'Kelly, Helen. *Court Culture in Dresden: From Renaissance to Baroque.* Basingstoke, 2002.

–. "Festival Books in Europe from Renaissance to Rococo." *The Seventeenth Century* 3 (1988): 181-201.

Watt, Tessa. *Cheap Print and Popular Piety, 1550-1640.* Cambridge, 1991.

Weisflecker, Hermann. *Kaiser Maximilian I. Das Reich, Osterreich und Europa an der Wende zur Neuzeit.* 5 vols., Munich, 1971-86.

Wildenstein, Georges. "Le goût pour la peinture dans la bourgeoisie parisienne entre 1550 et 1610," *Gazette des Beaux-Arts* 38 bis (1951).

–. "L'imprimeur-libraire Richard Breton et son inventaire après décès, 1571," *BHR* 21 (1959): 364-79.

Wiltenburg, Joy. "True Crime: The Origin of Modern Sensationalism," *American Historical Review* 109 (2004): 1377-1404.

Wood, James B. *The King's Army: Warfare, Soldiers, and Society during the Wars of Religion in France, 1562-1576*. Cambridge, 1996.

Woodward, David. *Maps as Prints in the Italian Renaissance: Makers, Distributors and Consumers*. London, 1996.

Zerner, Henri. *L'art de la Renaissance en France. L'invention du classicisme*. Paris, 2002.

INDEX

D

E

F

G

Mise en pages :
Nadine Casentieri, Genève

IMPRIMERIE MEDECINE HYGIENE GENEVE SUISSE

juin-2007

Imprimé à Genève - Suisse